THE GUINNESS BOOK OF
THEATRE FACTS AND FEATS

Mr PHELPS AS MACBETH.

I go, and it is done; the bell invites me.
Hear it not, Duncan; for it is a knell
That summons thee to heaven, or to hell.

ACT 2, SCENE 1.

THE GUINNESS
BOOK OF
Theatre
FACTS & FEATS

Michael Billington

With Research by
TONI HUBERMAN

The Performing Arts Lodge
110 The Esplanade
Toronto, Ontario

GUINNESS SUPERLATIVES LIMITED
2 Cecil Court, London Road, Enfield, Middlesex

Editors: Anne Marshall and Josie Holtom

Designer: Jean Whitcombe
Layout: David Roberts

© Michael Billington and Guinness Superlatives Limited, 1982

Published in Great Britain by Guinness Superlatives Limited
2 Cecil Court, London Road, Enfield, Middlesex.

ISBN 0-85112-239-6

British Library Cataloguing in Publication Data

Billington, Michael
The Guinness Book of Theatre Facts and Feats
I. Theater
I Title
792 PN 2037

Photoset in Mallard by Sprint. Printed and bound in Great Britain
by Butler and Tanner Ltd, Frome, Somerset.

Frontispiece
**Actor-manager Samuel Phelps, who ran Sadlers Wells as a
Shakespeare house, seen here in his famous 1847 Macbeth.**

CONTENTS

ACKNOWLEDGEMENTS

It would be impossible to acknowledge every library ransacked, every source raided, every book plundered. But I must, above all, thank my researcher Toni Huberman both for the work she undertook and the inspiration she provided; my editors at Guinness Books, Anne Marshall and Josie Holtom, for spotting errors and omissions and for kindly keeping me on the rails whenever I was likely to veer off them; my wife, Jeanine, for undertaking some valuable re-typing and tolerating my involvement with the book over a long period.

I must also pay tribute to a few invaluable reference books: *Who's Who in the Theatre* (16th edition) edited by Ian Herbert; *The Oxford Companion to the Theatre* edited by Phyllis Hartnoll; *World Theatre* by Bamber Gascoigne; *Golden Ages of the Theatre* by Kenneth Macgowan, William Melnitz and Gordon Armstrong; *The Theatres of London* by Raymond Mander and Joe Mitchenson; *Theatre London* published by the British Centre of the International Theatre Institute; The Mitchell Beazley pocket companion to *Shakespeare's Plays* by J C Trewin; *Everyman's Companion to Shakespeare* by Gareth and Barbara Lloyd Evans; *The Reader's Encyclopedia of World Drama* edited by John Gassner and Edward Quinn.

I should also like to thank John Goodwin, Head of Publicity/Publications at the National Theatre, Peter Harlock, Publicity Controller at the Royal Shakespeare Company and his assistant Diana for their invaluable assistance in compiling lists of productions.

For their help in supplying photographs I should also like to thank: Mary Evans Picture Library, Frontispiece, p.10, 12, 18, 22, 29, 31, 32, 33, 39, 40, 41, 45, 46, 47, 48, 49, 50, 56, 63, 65, 67, 68, 75, 76, 77, 89, 90, 91, 119, 121, 126, 151, 152, 153, 160, 165, 190, 192, 193, 198, Japan Information Centre, p.15, 64, Victoria and Albert Museum, p.20, 24, 35, 48, 49, 50, 77, 90, 172, 175, 181, 189, Italian State Tourist Office p.20, Chichester Festival Theatre, p.25, Peter Bloomfield p.26, Dewynters p.30, 129, Mick Little p.36, 37, Illustrated London News p.38, Popperfoto, p.51, 55, 61, 66, 70, 81, 82, 85, 87, 93, 95, 97, 101, 104, 119, 122, 125, 132, 137, 140, 144, 145, 146, 149, 154, 156, 157, 158, 162, 163, 164, 166, 170, 185, 195, 201, BBC Hulton Picture Library, p.53, 69, 74, 88, 92, 94, 95, 96, 98, 113, 114, 120, 127, 131, 133, 134, 142, 143, 171, 187, The Museum of the City of New York, p.57, 58, 59, 106, 107, 108, 109, 116, 139, 177, 179, 185, Peter Saunders, p.72, 73, Torrington Douglas, p.73, Holte Photographics for Royal Shakespeare Company photographs, p.79, 81, 82, 83, 86, 206, 211, Nobby Clarke p.99, 104, 204, Zoe Dominic p.100, 112, Chris Davies p.102, 214, John Haynes p.117, 120, 214, Donald Cooper p.118, 202, John Donat Photography p.175, Punch p.101, 168, 199, Genista Streeten p.103, 137, 146, 203, 205, Doug McKenzie p.111, Sotheby Parke Bernet p.135, Sadlers Wells Theatre p.141, Mander and Mitchenson p.154, 157.

But in acknowledging all this assistance, I should like to make it clear that I personally am responsible for any flaws in the crystal.

Michael Billington

PREFACE

'Good wine,' according to Shakespeare, 'needs no bush.' But *The Guinness Book of Theatre Facts and Feats* does perhaps need a word or two of prefatory explanation.

The first thing to say is that writing and compiling it has been an enjoyable but roughish task; and the reason is that the theatre, glorying in its ephemerality, has never been very good at keeping records. In many other areas of human activity — such as cricket, soccer, athletics, cinema even — there is an honourable statistical tradition. But the theatre has for centuries operated on the razed-ground principle, often destroying the territory it has lately occupied. If you want to find out who won the FA Cup in 1932, it is not too difficult to find out. But if you want to discover what was playing at the Old Vic or the Comédie Française that season, you have to do a lot more digging.

Fortunately, various institutions and individuals have sought to combat the theatre's built-in transience. Volumes like *Who's Who In The Theatre* and *The Oxford Companion to the Theatre*, individuals like Raymond Mander and Joe Mitchenson, assemblages of programmes, photos and cuttings like the Enthoven Collection at the Victoria and Albert Museum have constantly tried to keep the record straight. But, in writing this book, I found there are often considerable variations in relatively simple things like dates of birth or of first productions; and the further back you go in time, the cloudier the records become.

I offer this as a statement of fact rather than apology: naturally, I have sought to vouch for the factual accuracy of everything in the book. But I would like to put in a plea for the theatre to do rather more to ensure that its activities are preserved. I know that even the most lavishly-subsidised organisation cannot run to a house-archivist; but it helps if someone is there keeping production lists up-to-date. I also wish the commercial theatre (in Britain especially) would make public both attendance figures and profit-and-loss accounts so that we had some statistical proof of the relative popularity of specific productions. We know how long productions run.

We rarely, if ever, know if they ended up in the black or the red.

The second thing to say about this book of *Facts and Feats* is that value-judgements have inevitably crept in. You can't, for instance, compile a list of internationally-known playwrights and actors without (on grounds of space alone) excluding some famous names: reviewers (and readers) should have great fun telling me who I have omitted. But, on top of that, a book about the theatre would be very dry if it didn't include some opinions. I have, to take a tiny example, included my own list of the best American plays since 1940. I did that partly to complement a list of pre-1940 plays once compiled by George Jean Nathan. But I also did it partly to stimulate readers to challenge me with lists of their own. I believe a book like this should not only be accurate. It should also offer some intellectual fun.

One other point. I have tried to make this book as wide-ranging and international as possible: you can't tackle the theatre's origins without looking both East and West. But if the book does have a slight Anglo-American bias, it is partly for reasons of language and partly because it is written by someone familiar with the theatre of those two countries. I have no doubt that a similar volume written in Moscow or Tokyo would regard theatre in the USSR or Japan as the starting-point.

But I hope the book gives the non-specialist reader a clear picture of the theatre's history and of its present-day practice. The problem with a book like this is that you have to stop somewhere. I could have spent the rest of my working life adding, subtracting, discovering new data; and still never published. But, for practical purposes, I have had to take late 1981 – early 1982 as a cut-off point. Obviously new records will be made, new information will come in; and I hope that in subsequent editions it will be possible to keep the book continuously fresh and up-to-date. For the moment I trust it will give readers information, pleasure and even something to challenge and argue with.

Michael Billington
London, April 1982

CHAPTER 1

Origins

The oldest extant drama dates from 3200 BC. It springs from an Egyptian legend acted out at religious ceremonies. Osiris, god of good and life, is murdered by Set, god of evil and nothingness. Isis and Horus, Osiris's wife and son, gather the flesh of the dead god until he is resurrected and life and good are brought back to the world. The play ends with the coronation of Horus as king of Egypt. It thus contains the dramatic elements of conflict between good and evil and the fertility pattern of a fight, a death and a rebirth. It exists in a papyrus discovered at Thebes in 1895.

The Greeks

The beginnings of Western drama, however, are to be found in ancient Greece. Drama evolved from the dithyramb: a choral song chanted in honour of Dionysus, nature god of fertility. The figure of Dionysus was carried in procession, his altar was erected in the centre of a playing floor and he was accompanied by a chorus of 50 men dressed as satyrs: half-human, half-animal figures in a shaggy goat's skin adorned with a protruding phallus.

The first formal lyrics to replace the improvised words of the dithyramb date from around 600 BC. They are credited to a poet and musician, Arion of Mehtymna. Thespis, who lived in Attica in the 6th century BC, took the next innovatory step by introducing an actor to talk to the chorus, provide narration and act out dramatic episodes. Then the Athenian tyrant, Pisistratus, reorganised the Dionysian festivals and started a system of annual competitions in the writing and presentation of dithyrambs and tragedies (derived from the Greek words *tragos* or goat and *ode* or song).

Thespis was the winner of **the first-ever dramatic competition** in 534 BC. Since he toured his actors around in a cart which they used as a stage or performing platform, Thespis was also **the first theatrical trouper**: hence the use of the word Thespian today as a synonym for actor.

For three centuries after Thespis, Athens was the theatrical capital of the Grecian world. Two great festivals provided a showcase for drama: the City Dionysia, devoted mainly to tragedy, in late March and early April and the Lenaea, devoted to comedy, held in January. For the City Dionysia a poet provided three tragedies and one satyr-play, an obscene burlesque of heroic legends, to make a single day's entertainment.

These festivals provided the first examples of private patronage and public subsidy in drama. The *archon*, a city official, chose the poets to be allowed to compete and assigned to each of them a *choregos*, a rich patron who would organise the production and pay all expenses: **the first example of a theatrical 'angel' or backer**. But since the *choregos* underwrote all expenses in return for paying no taxes that year, Athens itself provided the first instance of enlightened civic subsidy.

Performances took place in the theatre of Dionysus at the foot of the Acropolis and in the 5th century BC wooden seats or stands were erected for spectators on the hillside: the word theatre in fact derives from the Greek *theatron* which denoted a hillside hollow full of seats. All

Theatre of Dionysus at Athens where Western drama began in the 5th century BC.

the complete Greek plays to have survived date from 490 to 390 BC but the existing Theatre of Dionysus in Athens dates from a later period. The auditorium was built under Lycurgus in 330 BC and the stage area in AD 61 under Nero. But five stones survive from the wall that supported the original dancing-floor or *orchestra* and the hillside site remains the same.

The first great dramatist whose work still survives is Aeschylus (525-456 BC). Only seven of his 90 plays exist today but they are enough to make him the founding father of western drama. By reducing the size of the chorus from 50 to 12, by introducing a second actor to the cast and by including simple properties and painted backdrops, he transformed something resembling oratorio into drama. He was also a thematic writer, making the three plays he entered for the Dionysia a connected trilogy in which sin provokes sin until justice reasserts itself.

Aeschylus's oldest surviving play (and **the first extant western drama**) is *The Persians* dating from 472 BC. It centres on the triumph of the Athenian fleet over the Persian invaders at Salamis in 480 BC. But the emphasis is not on Greek victory but Persian disaster with the universe seen as a great mantrap that has an empire caught in its jaws.

The only trilogy of Aeschylus to survive complete is *The Oresteia*. It was written in 458 BC and consists of *Agamemnon*, the *Choephori* and the *Eumenides*. The first play opens in Argos a few hours after the capture of Troy. Its climax is the murder of Agamemnon on his return by Clytemnestra. In the second play Agamemnon's son, Orestes, returns from exile to avenge his father's death and departs pursued by the Furies. In the final play he stands trial before the

Athenian court of Areopagus. The votes are evenly divided but the goddess Athene gives her casting vote for Orestes's acquittal. This great trilogy inspired many subsequent writers including Sophocles, Euripides, Seneca, Voltaire, Eugene O'Neill and Jean-Paul Sartre. In this century *The Oresteia* has been presented three times in London: in 1905 by F.R. Benson's company at the Coronet Theatre, in 1961 at the Old Vic by the Oxford Playhouse Company, and in 1981 at the Olivier Theatre.

Little is known of Aeschylus's personal qualities, though his plays have a hallucinatory quality which may have inspired the story that 'he composed his tragedies while drunk'. Legend also has it that an eagle mistook his bald head for a rock and dropped a tortoise on his pate in order to break the shell.

Sophocles (496-406 BC) was the first great rival to Aeschylus. In 468 BC at the age of 27 he won a victory over him at the Dionysia and, all told, he gained more first prizes than any other Greek dramatist: 18 in less than 30 years. His plays were more intricate in plot than those of Aeschylus: more concerned with the interplay of character than divine justice. Only seven of his 100 plays survive of which the most famous is *Oedipus Rex* (429 BC). It is the story of the King of Thebes who, in fulfilment of a pronouncement of the oracle at Delphi, unwittingly murdered his father, Laius, and married his mother, Jocasta. Sophocles wrote a sequel, *Oedipus at Colonus*, produced after his death in 401 BC by his grandson, in which the old, blind, exiled hero is redeemed through suffering. The legend of Oedipus has inspired many other dramatists including Seneca, Corneille, Dryden, Gide, Cocteau and T.S. Eliot. The 'Oedipus complex' has also become a standard term of Freudian psychoanalysis describing the sexual impulses of a boy towards his mother and jealousy of his father. *Oedipus Rex* has been performed many times in this century, most notably by Laurence Olivier at the New Theatre, London in 1945 when he produced a searing, unforgettable cry of pain: a sound, he has revealed, based on a cry he heard in the Canadian forests where skunks are trapped by making their tongues adhere to a layer of salt.

Euripides (484-406 BC) was the most revolutionary of the Greek tragic poets. He changed tragedy from a conflict between man and the divine laws into a battle in man's own soul between his good and evil impulses. Though he dealt with mythological characters he presented them realistically: as a result, he won fewer first prizes at the Dionysia (only five) than Aeschylus or Sophocles. What is remarkable is the anti-war nature of much of his work (particularly *The Trojan Women*) even though he was writing at the time of the war between the Athenians and the Spartans which began in 431 BC and ended in 404 BC with the total defeat of Athens. But his most revived play is *The Bacchae*, posthumously produced in 405 BC, which shows the conflict between Dionysus, god of ecstasy and fertility, and the arrogant and straitlaced Pentheus: a classic, pre-Freudian study of the dangers of repression which at one point shows Pentheus, disguised as a woman, voyeuristically observing the fervent rites of the Bacchantes. Today, Euripides is the most popular of the Greek dramatists: when the Royal Shakespeare Company in January 1980 mounted a ten-play cycle, *The Greeks*, seven of the works chosen came from this dramatist.

Aristophanes (448-380 BC) was **drama's first satirist**: the supreme exponent of Greek Old Comedy which derived, like tragedy, from the dithyrambs and satyr plays. It achieved respectability in 486 BC when it was officially admitted by the City Dionysia. Aristophanes's main theme was the desire for freedom and his weapons included surrealist fantasy, political propaganda, personal lampoon and lyric poetry. Of his 40 works eleven still survive. The most famous are *Peace* (421 BC) in which an Attic farmer ascends to Heaven on the back of a dung-beetle and finds that Zeus and the other gods have abandoned mankind, buried Peace and left the Greeks to the tender mercies of war and turmoil; *The Birds* (414 BC) in which two average Athenians decide to opt out of Athenian life and form a Utopia midway between earth and heaven; and *Lysistrata* (411 BC) in which the women of Athens attempt to end the long-drawn out war between Athens and Sparta by refusing to sleep with their men until peace has been declared. Claimed alike by conservatives and radicals, Aristophanes created a popular theatre not unlike music-hall or vaudeville in its mixture of styles. The Old Comedy of Aristophanes was eventually replaced by the New Comedy of Menander (343-292 BC) in which comic plots from private life took the place of political and aesthetic satire.

The oldest surviving Greek playhouse is at Epidaurus. It consists of a semi-amphitheatre built by the architect Polycleitus in 340 BC and has seats for 1200 spectators. From this one can make certain deductions. Between the banked spectators and the raised stage there was a circular space (the orchestra or dancing-place) where the chorus performed. Behind the orchestra there was a long, shallow acting area known as the *proskenion*. The *proskenion* (from which we get our word 'proscenium') was in front of the *skene* or scene-building. This provided a dressing-room for the actors and possibly a place for a quick change of mask or costume when an actor was playing two or three parts. The *skene* had short wings at each end and was eventually pierced with three doors. From the 5th century BC the roof of the *skene* was used as a place on which a god could appear or from which he could be lowered to resolve the difficulties of the plot (hence the term *deus ex machina*). At either side of the orchestra and near the stage was a *parados* or entranceway.

The plan of a Greek theatre: a semi-circular shape that still serves as a model for modern architects.

All performances in Greek theatre were given out of doors in broad daylight. But this does not mean the Greeks forswore spectacle and scenic device. In 458 BC Aeschylus's hero, Agamemnon, entered in a chariot. *Periaktoi*, painted revolving prisms, were placed at the side of the skene to indicate changes of locale.

The first known examples of theatrical machinery were introduced in the 5th century BC. The eccyclema was a platform on wheels that could be moved through a doorway to reveal an interior scene or even a person. In a comedy by Aristophanes, *The Archarnians* (425 BC), someone knocks on Euripides's door and demands that the dramatist come out. 'But I'm not at leisure', says Euripides. 'At least be wheeled out', comes the reply. The mechane was a crane-device used to hoist mortals up to Heaven (as with Trygaeus in *Peace*) or gods down to earth. It could also be used to remove a dead body.

Greek drama was rooted in ritual and made heavy use of masks and costumes. Masks indicated the age, sex, mood and station of a character. They also enabled the actor to play a variety of roles and, with their exaggerated

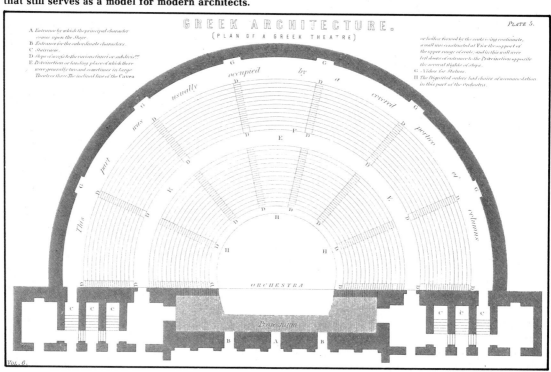

GREEK ARCHITECTURE.
(PLAN OF A GREEK THEATRE)

PLATE 5.

A *Entrance by which the principal character comes upon the Stage*
B *Entrance for the subordinate characters*.
C *Staircase.*
D *Steps or sweeps to the various tiinoi or subdivia*
E *Proscinction or landing places of which there were generally two and sometimes in large Theatres three The inclined line of the Cavea*

or hollow formed by the seats swing continuate, a wall was constructed at F for the support of the upper range of seats, and in this wall were left doors of entrance to the Praecinction opposite the several tlights of Steps.
G *Vidoes for Statues.*
H *The Dignified orders had chairs of accommodation in this part of the Orchestra.*

ORCHESTRA

Proscenium

Vol. 6.

features and megaphone-like mouthpiece, to communicate across the vast distances of Greek theatres. In Thespis's time they were made out of stiffened linen but later it was found that cork or wood had better acoustical properties. Masks could also be frightening: those of the Furies in Aeschylus's tragedy, *The Eumenides*, created a panic at its première in 458 BC.

Actors wore a *chiton*, a long, vividly-coloured garment reaching from neck to ankles, and sometimes a shorter mantle. To set the principals off from the chorus the tragic actor wore an elaborate head-dress, the *onkos*, and a thick-soled shoe, the *cothurnus*, while the chorus wore low shoes. A soft-soled shoe, the *soccus*, was always worn in comedy.

Greek drama, as it developed, used three male actors playing a variety of parts, male and female. Actors enjoyed an honourable place in Greek society, comparable to that of priests. But **the first theatrical union** was formed in the middle of the 4th century BC. It was known as the Artists of Dionysus and was intended to preserve the privileges of professional actors. These included travel through foreign and hostile states to give performances, and exemption from military service. The guild also included full-time poets, chorus-members, trainers and musicians.

Greek drama developed in a territory, Attica, slightly smaller than Gloucestershire: in its heyday, its inhabitants were as numerous as those of present-day Bristol. But it left its mark on world drama in many ways. It gave us the basic forms of tragedy and comedy. By dividing the action of a play up with choric odes, it gave us the five-act pattern. It also supplied us with the terminology of theatre and established the open stage, amphitheatrical shape to which we have circuitously returned: the links between Epidaurus and the Olivier Theatre in the National complex are not hard to see and many of Sir Peter Hall's opening productions there marked out the stage in the shape of the Greek orchestra.

The Romans

Entertainment, in the crudest sense, dominated straight drama under the Romans. Under the Tarquins in the 6th century BC the *ludi Romani* (Roman games) were held each September complete with chariot racing and boxing matches. From 300 BC Atellan farces, dialect plays from the Campania district full of obscene allusions and stock characters, became part of the games. In 264 BC, the first year of the Punic War, gladiatorial combats were added to the games with prisoners being allowed to hack each other to death for the amusement of the crowd.

The first literary plays to be part of the games date from 240 BC, the first year of the peace. They were translations by Livius Andronicus (284-204 BC) of a Greek tragedy and comedy. This set the pattern for the future: no single play survives with a plot invented by a Roman, and actors playing the comedies of Plautus and Terence wore Greek rather than Roman costume. Even after the arrival of written drama the delight in circus and spectacles continued: under the Emperor Nero a play was given called *House on Fire* in which a house was burnt and the actors were allowed to keep whichever of the rich furnishings they dare retrieve.

Temporary wooden stages were built for each performance in Rome. The stage was long and narrow (sometimes as much as 180ft (55m) long) and represented a city street usually in Athens. The wooden background consisted of doors providing an entrance to one, two or three houses.

The first permanent stone theatre was built by Pompey in the Campus Martius in 55 BC: he circumvented the moral qualms of the Romans about theatre by placing a temple to Venus Victrix above the last row of the auditorium. But scores of Graeco-Roman theatres were built around the Mediterranean just before the birth of Christ and these had a definite pattern to them. The Greek orchestra was shrunk to a semi-circle. The skene occupied the entire diameter of the stage. On occasions there were roofs jutting out over the stage and awnings spread over the audience.

Though based on Greek New Comedy, Roman Comedy still has its own robust farcical quality and has had considerable influence on other writers. Only 21 of the 130 plays ascribed to Titus Maccius Plautus (251-184 BC) have survived but they show a deft manipulation of such stock characters as intriguing slaves, braggart warriors, old men in love and lubricious courtesans. They have also been an invaluable comic source for subsequent dramatists.

Plautus's *Menaechmi*, about the presence in

one city of long-separated twins and the identity-confusions that result, was utilised by Hans Sachs, Carlo Goldoni, and Shakespeare in *The Comedy of Errors*. His *Amphitruo* (186 BC) is not only the sole Roman specimen of mythological parody in its depiction of Jupiter taking the place of a mortal husband in bed but was also a source for Molière, Dryden and Giraudoux. Moreover, two Broadway musicals, Rodgers and Hart's *The Boys from Syracuse* (1938) and Stephen Sondheim's *A Funny Thing Happened on the Way to the Forum* (1962), have both been derived from Plautus. The latter was drawn from a number of the plays but in the end retained only one Plautine line: Miles Gloriosus's 'I am a parade'. The other notable Roman comic dramatist was Terence (195-159 BC) but though his plays were more respectful of structure and logic than those of Plautus they were less theatrically effective: Julius Caesar criticised them for lacking the necessary comic spirit.

The first dramatist to bring violence and death onto the stage was the Roman tragedian, Seneca (4BC - AD65). He wrote ten tragedies which concentrate on the battle between the Stoic absolutes of passion and reason. Both his Stoic philosophy and his dramatic technique also had enormous influence on English Elizabethan dramatists. The pie of human flesh baked for the hero of his *Thyestes* turns up again in Shakespeare's *Titus Andronicus*. A single line of his *Agamemnon* ('The only path that's safe for crime is crime') can be traced through Kyd, Shakespeare, Jonson and Webster. The five-act structure, the use of ghosts and supernatural machinery, the coining of didactic tags were all passed on by Seneca to the Elizabethans. When Peter Brook directed his *Oedipus* at the National Theatre in 1968 one critic said it proved Seneca to be as actable as Euripides or Sophocles.

From Seneca's suicide in AD 65 to the invasion of Italy by the barbarians in 568 almost nothing of dramatic interest was produced. Roman amphitheatres featured gladiatorial contests, animal baiting and sea-battles. In AD 200 the Roman theologian, Tertullian, called theatre 'the shrine of Venus' and the 'Church of the Devil'. In the 5th century actors were forbidden by church law from practising their professions. Only the mimes, descendants of the Greek *phlyakes* who presented a burlesque knockabout comedy, kept the notion of theatre alive. They

lived on into the Dark Ages. But the decline from the great days of Aeschylus was total.

The East

INDIA

Drama languished in the West from shortly after the birth of Christ to the 10th century AD: at precisely that time it flourished in the East.

In India the ground rules for drama were laid out in a treatise, *Natyashastra*, by the sage Bharata: it was written around 100 BC and constantly revised. It demands that art should give pleasure as a step towards the ultimate peace of the mystic's meditation. It also precisely defines the conventions of the stage including gesture (24 finger gestures, 36 eye movements, 16 positions of the feet on the earth and in the air), dance, decor, rules on playwriting, theatre architecture.

Classical Indian drama, dating from the first century AD, is written in the Sanskrit language and falls into two categories: plays of mythological or historical content (*nataka*) and plays with invented stories and less exalted characters (*prakarana*).

The earliest plays were written by Bhasa, numbered 13 in total, and were found in Trivandrum, a city in Southern India. Apart from legendary tales of gods and princesses deriving from the great Sanskrit epic, the *Mahabharata*, they also include the truncated *Charudatta in Poverty*, the story of a rich merchant who became poor through his generosity and who was saved by a virtuous courtesan. This story was elaborated in the most famous of the prakarana, *The Little Clay Cart*. It is of unknown authorship, has been dated around AD 150 and, with its well-meaning clown, pompous judge and half-wit prince, is close in spirit to the world of Plautus.

The most highly-praised Indian playwright was Kalidasa (c. 373-415) whose best-known work was *Shakuntla*, a courtly love-story revolving round a secret marriage and a magic spell embodied in a ring: a story duplicated in the Norse sagas used by Richard Wagner in *Der Ring des Nibelungen* (1876). The golden age of Sanskrit drama lasted until the 8th century. It

The traditional Noh Theatre stage with the cedarwood floor and the temple-roof above: clearly a modern audience still believes there is no business like Noh business.

then lost its creative energy and from the 11th to the 18th centuries the various forms of classical dance dominated Indian theatre.

CHINA

From the 8th century BC there are records of entertainments at religious festivals combining pantomime, singing, dancing and acrobatics.

The world's first known formal drama school dates from the 8th century AD when the T'ang emperor, Ming Huang (713-756) set up an academy for actors in the pear garden of his court at Chang-an. Chinese actors are still often called 'children of the pear garden' and Ming Huang is regarded as the patron of their craft.

Chinese drama did not, however, really flourish until the Yüan dynasty (1271-1368).

Denied a career in the old civil service, abolished by the Mongols, the intelligentsia found themselves reduced in status to somewhere between prostitutes and beggars and so devoted their energies to theatre. Plays were performed in palaces, temples and in the open air: surviving illustrations of outdoor performances show a roofed-in acting area, a small thrust stage and an audience milling about on three sides in a manner that prefigures the Elizabethans.

JAPAN

This country has produced and absorbed a remarkable variety of theatrical forms. They can be categorised as follows:

Kagura

A masked dance on mythological themes imported from China around AD 540.

Bugaku

A mask-play, with dance and music, based on

religious beliefs originating in China in the 7th and 8th centuries and enacted on a square podium.

Noh

A play originally for the nobility and warrior classes based on the ritualistic code of honour of the Samurai and the contemplation of Zen Buddhism. In 1375 one of the wandering *sarugaku-no-no* companies led by an actor called Kanami and including his 12-year-old son, Zeami, was taken into the service of the shogun Yoshimitsu. At court, father and son developed the Noh play as still practised by Japanese companies. The stage is a square podium open on three sides, made of polished cedar wood with a temple roof above and a back wall decorated with a painted pine tree. The play is acted by the protagonist (*Shite*), the supporting character (*Waki*), the followers (*Tsure*) and the chorus. The female roles are played by men. Poet and playwright, W.B. Yeats, director Jacques Copeau and composer Benjamin Britten are amongst many western artists influenced by Noh.

Later Japanese theatrical forms include *Kabuki*, a popular offshoot of Noh, originating in 1600; *Joruri*, a puppet-theatre founded in the 17th century; and *Bunraku*, which uses life-sized puppets manipulated by several handlers and dates from 1871.

The Middle Ages

Meanwhile in the West, theatre went underground during the Dark Ages. The tradition was kept alive only by wandering minstrels, jugglers and *jongleurs*, remnants of the Roman mimes and Greek *phlyakes*. It re-emerged through the medieval church and the Roman Catholic liturgy. Choral processions, the singing of the Mass, the consecration of bread and wine as the body and blood of Christ had kept alive the notion of ritual. But one can pinpoint the stages by which ritual evolved into drama:

923-934

The first recorded trope (a phrase, sentence or verse introduced by the choir as an embellishment of part of the Mass) in the Easter service of the Monastery of St. Martial at Limoges.

950

The Easter trope from the monastery at St. Gall was the simplest and most explicit. It consisted of four lines in Latin and told the story of the three Maries and their visit to the sepulchre.

970

St. Ethelwold, bishop of Winchester, writes that his order have decided to follow the French practice of using tropes to 'fortify the faith of the ignorant populace'. But four brethren acted out the trope turning it into a mini-drama. On Good Friday the entombment of Christ was symbolised by laying out a crucifix, wrapped in cloths, in a special recess in the high altar — which stood for the holy sepulchre. On Easter morning a monk was to go and sit by the sepulchre. Three more monks, 'stepping delicately as those who seek something', then approached the sepulchre in imitation of the women with spices coming to anoint the body of Jesus. The following dialogue then ensued in Latin:

The Angel: Whom seek ye?
The Maries: Jesus of Nazareth.
The Angel: He is not here, he is risen as he foretold. Go, announce that he is risen from the dead.
The Maries: Alleluia. The Lord is risen.

The Angel then took the three Maries to the sepulchre to show them the empty cloths in which the crucifix had been wrapped and buried on the Friday. This led into the exultation of the *Te Deum.*

From this simple scene developed numerous Christmas ceremonials, liturgical plays and the use of scenic properties inside the church to indicate different settings.

1170

The first extant, non-liturgical play, *Jeu d'Adam* (*Play of Adam*), presented on the steps of a French cathedral. Written almost entirely in French, it is **the first example of an acted play in the vernacular.** It is also **the first outdoor play of the Christian era:** it relates the story of Adam and Eve, Cain and Abel and the Prophets foretelling the coming of Christ. Settings are precise. Paradise is represented by a platform 'with curtains and cloths of silk hung around it at such a height that persons there may be visible from the shoulders upwards'. There are also directorial pointers and ambitious stage effects: at one point three or four devils tie Adam and Eve with chains and pull them off to Hell from which smoke belches out and a great clatter of pots and kettles can be heard.

1311

Pope Clement V formally decrees the Feast of Corpus Christi, specifically set aside for the performance of religious works. From this spring the English and French mystery plays (from the Latin word *ministerium* meaning 'an event of mystical significance'), the Italian *sacre rappresentazioni*, the Spanish *autos sacramentales*, the German *Geistliche Spiele*. Staging practices varied from country to country. The French sometimes used ancient amphitheatres, the Italians the Roman Coliseum, the Spaniards courtyard theatres, the Germans market-place trestle-tables.

1375

The oldest extant English mystery cycle: the Chester cycle comprising 24 plays of unknown authorship covering the scriptural story from the fall of Lucifer to the Last Judgement. Presented by trades guilds, the cycle was produced during three successive days on pageant wagons proceeding from stop to stop throughout the city. According to a later Chester historian: 'This pageant or carriage wagon was a high place made like a house with two rooms, being open on the top; in the lower room they apparelled and dressed themselves and in the higher room they played; and they stood upon six wheels'. Guilds were also assigned plays relevant to their craft. At Chester the water-leaders and drawers in Dee acted *Noah's Flood* and the cooks *The Harrowing of Hell*.

Other English towns that produced their own cycles were York (48 plays first presented in 1376), Wakefield (32 plays dating from the early 15th century and generally thought to be the best of the cycles) and Lincoln (thought to be the source of the N-Town cycle dating from 1468). The cycles were performed in England until 1580 when they were suppressed by a hostile Protestant government. As production of mystery plays became more common, so also methods of staging became more sophisticated. At Coventry, where two nativity plays are still extant, the records of the Drapers' Company list the following props: 'Hell-mouth — a fire kept at it; windlass and three fathoms of cord; earthquake, barrel for the same ... three worlds painted ... a link to set the world on fire'. Symbolism also entered into the costuming: the Coventry torturers in the Passion wore 'jackets of black buckram ... with nails and dice upon

them'. The actors were paid for their work. In one town a man received three shillings and four pence for 'pleaying God' and another man four pence 'for hangying Judas'.

1402

The first company of European actors to occupy a permanent playhouse was the Confrérie de la Passion: a group of amateur actors granted by Charles VI the exclusive right to present holy drama in Paris. They gave performances in a hall at the Hôpital de la Trinité. They continued to perform there until 1548 when the mysteries were banned because earlier productions indulged in farce and innuendo.

1425

The first complete English Morality Play: *The Castle of Perseverance*. The Morality was an allegorical piece in which personified virtues and vices struggled for the soul of man. This play covers the birth, maturity, death and salvation of mankind.

It also contains the first person in English drama introduced purely to hasten the action and make it more vigorous in the character of Backbiter, a malicious comic intermediary.

1470

The most popular and successful early French farce, *Maître Pierre Pathelin*. A story of dupers being duped, it went through 30 editions by 1600. Farce derived from the practice of enlivening medieval passion plays with purely comic sequences: hence its origin from the French verb 'farcir' meaning 'to stuff'. **The most famous early English farce** (early 15th century) was *The Second Shepherd's Play* in the Wakefield Mystery Cycle in which Mak the sheep-stealer hides a stolen lamb in swaddling clothes and is rumbled by the shepherds.

1493

The first professional actors in England: Henry VII employs four or five men at the English court as Players of the King's Interludes (passages in the evening's entertainment at a banquet).

1500

Everyman, **the most famous medieval Morality play,** based on a Dutch original. The hero, having received his death summons, watches as Kindred, Goods, Fellowship, Strength and Beauty depart until only Good Deeds goes with him to the grave.

1520

The most popular Interlude was John Heywood's *The Play Called the Four P's*, a lying contest beween a palmer, a pardoner, an apothecary and a pedlar. Such plays as this acted as a bridge between medieval religious drama and Elizabethan comedy.

1533

The first completely secular English farce, John Heywood's *Johan Johan*, in which a wife humiliates her peasant husband while engaged in amorous dalliance with her priestly lover. Such anti-clerical mockery was a sign that the

iternational theatre of the church was yielding ground (in 1547 Catholic Italy banned all religious plays as did France the following year) and that medieval drama, having passed through the stages of liturgical ritual and allegorical conflict, was about to become more earthly. Man in the Renaissance was about to become the measure of all things. Over two millennia the foundations of drama had been laid, the basic forms of tragedy, comedy and farce established and various methods of staging been experimented with. The exciting question was what would happen next and what form would the new playhouses take.

Elizabethan Theatre in an Inn Yard.

CHAPTER 2

Theatres

Ideas about staging plays have developed in many different ways in different countries from the Renaissance to the present day: the progress has been a complex one from the first attempts at scenic illusion to the multifarious forms of the modern playhouse. Each century has, in fact, produced its own innovations, its own method of giving form and substance to drama.

Fifteenth century

1454

In Spain, town records show that dancers and jugglers were hired to appear in *autos sacramentales*, portable religious plays enacting stories from the Bible or lives of the saints. The plays were staged on pageant wagons (like modern carnival floats) called *carros*. Outdoor performances became *La Fiesta de los carros*: the festival of the carts. At each stop the wagons were backed up against a platform on which the actors played important scenes. The Spanish also developed another kind of stage called *la roca*: a platform carried by twelve men on which stood Jesus, Mary and various evangelists and saints.

1486

First documented accounts of elaborate scenic illusion. Ercole d'Este, duke of Ferrara, produced Plautus's *Menaechmi* in a courtyard. It was presented upon 'a wooden stage with five battlemented houses. There was a window and a door in each. Then a ship came in . . . and crossed the courtyard. It had ten persons in it and was fitted with oars and a sail in a most realistic manner'.

1489

Development of Italian spectacle. For *Il Paradiso*, a mythological episode staged in the ducal palace at Milan, Leonardo da Vinci designed a mountain-top, the two halves of which split at the front and swung back to reveal a glittering heaven.

1491

Scenic illusion went indoors when Ercole revived *Menaechmi* in a palace and had Nicollo del Cogo paint 'a prospect of four castles'.

Sixteenth century

1520

First recognisable public theatre created in Malaga, Spain. It was created by placing a stage platform against the inner end of a patio in an inn-yard. The patio was open to the sky. Two or three galleries looked down on it from all four sides. There was a covered entryway from the street.

1545

The first person to elaborate the principles of scenery and set design was Sebastiano Serlio in Book 2 of his *Architettura* (it appeared in Paris under the title *Le second livre de la perspective*). It contained drawings of three types of classic scenery: the tragic set with its lofty palaces, the comic set with its city houses, the satyr play with its landscape of trees, hills and cottages. It also

The Hôtel de Bourgogne: the first public playhouse in France. Turlupin and Robert Guerin are seen on stage with the King's Players.

described the techniques of false perspective, of the stage rake, of how to create thunder and lightning and coloured light by placing a bottle of red wine in front of a torch.

1550

Opening of Hôtel de Bourgogne: **the first public playhouse in France** and the first formal one to be built anywhere since the fall of Rome.

1554

Northern Spain's first public theatre at Valladolid. Created out of a courtyard formed by the backs of several houses. These courtyards — usually filled with refuse — were known as *corrales*. A typical *corral* had a broad stage with a

front curtain stretching from one side of the courtyard to the other. Rooms and windows of the surrounding houses served as boxes for the more privileged spectators.

1576

England's first public playhouse, the Theatre, designed and built by James Burbage opened in the Middlesex parish of St. Leonard's Shoreditch. It lay half a mile outside the Bishopgate entrance to the city because London's city fathers had forbidden the performance of plays within their boundaries. The Theatre cost £600, was built of wood and circular in shape.

1577

James Burbage built a second theatre, the Curtain, in Shoreditch. It was so called because it was built on a piece of land variously known as Curten Close or Courtein.

1584

Opening of Italy's first permanent playhouse since the fall of Rome, the Teatro Olimpico at Vicenza. Today it is **Europe's oldest surviving theatre.** It was designed by Palladio for the Academia Olimpica and his purpose was 'to construct a theatre according to the ancient use of the Greeks and Romans'. Thirteen rows of auditorium seats followed the shape of an

The Teatro Olimpico at Vicenza designed by Palladio and used by Joseph Losey in his film of 'Don Giovanni'.

The Swan Theatre, London from a drawing of 1596 by Johannes de Witt. The only known picture of an Elizabethan playhouse stage.

ellipse. There was a flat orchestra floor for the chorus, a raked stage, a long back wall including a triumphal arch and five doorways all with short vistas of streets in steep perspective.

1585

Teatro Olimpico opened with *Oedipus Rex*. A contemporary spectator described the occasion: 'When the time had come to lower the curtain, a very sweet smell of perfume made itself felt to indicate that in the city of Thebes, according to ancient legend, incense was burned to placate the wrath of the gods. Then there was a sound of trumpets and drums and four squibs exploded. In the twinkle of an eye the curtain fell before the stage . . .'

1587

Philip Henslowe built the Rose Theatre in London where it was sited at the corner of Rose Alley and Maiden Lane.

1594

The only London Elizabethan theatre of which we possess a drawing and precise description, the Swan, opened. According to a visiting Dutchman, John de Witt, it was one of 'four theatres of noteworthy beauty', could accommodate 3000 spectators and was built 'of concrete and flint stones and supported by wooden columns painted in such excellent imitation of marble that it might deceive even the most cunning'.

1599

Globe Theatre opened on London's Bankside. It was built out of the timber used to erect the original theatre and was the venue for Shakespeare's plays. Thomas Platter of Basle described a visit made there on 21 September: 'After dinner at about two o'clock, I went with my party across the water; in the straw-thatched house we saw the tragedy of the first Emperor Julius Caesar very pleasantly performed, with approximately fifteen characters; at the end of the play they danced together admirably and exceedingly gracefully, according to their custom, two in each group dressed in men's and two in women's apparel'. This is the first recorded performance at the Globe.

Seventeenth century

Below top: The Globe Theatre as it might have been with 'A Midsummer Night's Dream' in full swing. Below bottom: Victorian melodrama, complete with rapacious villain, at a "penny-gaff" theatre.

1600
The Fortune Theatre, the only Elizabethan playhouse for which we have authentic specifications, built in Finsbury. It occupied a square site 80 by 80ft (24.4 × 24.4m) on the outside and 55ft (16.8m) each way within. The stage itself was 43ft (13m) wide (as compared with the present-day Mermaid which is 39ft (11.9m) wide and Chichester 32ft (9.7m) wide).

1618
The first theatre to be equipped with a permanent proscenium arch: the Teatro Farnese in Parma designed by Giambattista Aleotti. The auditorium was a horseshoe of raised seats holding 3500 spectators and between it and the stage was an orchestra floor that was used for spectacle and even flooded for one production. There was a wide proscenium and a deep stage behind.

1634
Paris acquired a second theatre for the paying public, the Théâtre du Marais. A forerunner of the Comédie Française, it opened on 31 December in a converted tennis court in the rue Vieille-du-Temple.

1641
Venice's Teatro Novissimo introduced an important scenic innovation. For *La festa teatrale della finta pazzia* Giacomo Torelli, a great scenic magician, invented a device by which eight pairs of wings were all linked to a counterweight system and could be changed instantaneously when one person, even 'a single boy of 15 years', released the weights. Torelli's invention swept through Europe and a complete example of his machinery can still be seen under the stage of the Court Theatre at Drottningholm, Sweden.

1641
Opening of the Théâtre du Palais Royal, Paris. Long and narrow, it held about 600 people and its stage was equipped with all the latest Italian perspective scenery.

1642
Theatres in England closed by Act of Parliament under Cromwell.

1656
Perspective scenery introduced onto the London stage at Rutland House by Sir William Davenant in an operatic entertainment, *The Siege of Rhodes*: 'a representation of the art of prospec-

tive in scenes and the story sung in recitative musick'.

1663

The first theatre on the site of Drury Lane built by Thomas Killigrew under a charter granted by Charles II. It opened as the Theatre Royal, Bridges Street, Drury Lane on 7 May with *The Humorous Lieutenant* by Beaumont and Fletcher.

1680

The foundation of **the world's first national theatre:** the Comédie Française. It was founded by Louis XIV with the merging of the company of the Théâtre du Marais and the Hôtel de Bourgogne with which Molière's troupe was amalgamated in 1673. It underwent many changes (during the Revolution it was split into the radical Théâtre de la Republique and the conservative Théâtre de la Nation) but it was reformed in 1803 and remains **the oldest national theatre** with **the longest continuous acting tradition.**

1689

The Comédie Française moved to a new house in St. Germain des Près: the first in France to be built with a horseshoe-shaped auditorium.

Eighteenth century

1720

Opening of the first theatre, the Little Theatre, in the Haymarket. It began with *La Fille à la Mode, ou le Badaud de Paris* performed by the French Comedians of His Grace, the Duke of Montague. It became the Theatre Royal, Haymarket in 1766.

1722

First Danish language theatre, the Theater on Lille Gronnegade, opened in Copenhagen with a royal licence: founded by a Frenchman, it began with a Molière.

1732

Theatre Royal, Covent Garden, opened with a revival of *The Way of the World* by William Congreve, under the management of John Rich.

1741

First Austrian National Theatre in Vienna founded by Empress Maria Theresa in the Hofbauhaus near the Hofburg as a Court Theatre. In 1776 the Burgtheater was proclaimed Deutches National-theater under the administration of the Court.

1765

First Polish National Theatre founded in Warsaw.

1766

Court Theatre founded at Drottningholm near Stockholm. Both the stage machinery by Donato Stopani and the original decor have survived.

1767

First public theatre in New York opened: the John Street Theater.

1788

Royal Dramatic Theatre founded in Stockholm: it has remained the leading Swedish Theatre with the status of a National Theatre.

1794

Theatre Royal, Drury Lane reopened (the third to be built on that site) under the management of Richard Brinsley Sheridan. The dramatic season began with *Macbeth* starring Kemble and Mrs Siddons.

Nineteenth century

1804

Tanks of water installed at Theatre Royal, Drury Lane for aquadramas (spectacles in which the stage was flooded for representation of the battle of Trafalgar and other sea-fights).

1817

Passion for scenic accuracy developed fast. The architect Karl Friedrich Schinkel designed a set in Berlin for *Die Jungfrau von Orleans* that gave spectators a vista of the city and cathedral at Rheims.

1821

Opening of the large Chestnut Theater in New York. It had four tiers and a capacity of nearly 2500. At the same time the Theatre Royal, Drury Lane (the fourth) seated 3060 and Covent Garden 3000.

1856

Charles Kean, actor and manager of the Princess Theatre, took his passion for realism to absurd lengths. One scene in his production of *A Midsummer Night's Dream* took place in the workshop of Quince the Carpenter and 'guaranteed the furniture and tools introduced

Her Majesty's Theatre, London re-designed in 1897 by C.J. Phipps for Herbert Beerbohm Tree.

in this scene are copied from discoveries at Herculaneum'.

1863
Charles Fechter, French actor, became manager of the Lyceum London and introduced radical changes in scene shifting and lighting. He divided the Lyceum stage into a jigsaw puzzle of sections that could be lowered to a depth of 7ft (2.1m) for scene changes.

1881
First use of curtains to denote the ends of scenes in a production by Irving at the Lyceum.

1886
E.W. Godwin, himself a dedicated archaeological realist, gave a great boost to the opposite movement by staging Todhunter's *Helena in Troas* at Hengler's Circus. He constructed a Greek stage without a proscenium arch. Actors were on a platform in close touch with the audience: not behind a picture-frame.

1887
Founding of the Théâtre Libre in Paris by André Antoine: a small private theatre club for the production of plays by the new naturalistic playwrights. It closed in 1897.

1888
Present Royal Court Theatre in Sloane Square opened. Designed by Walter Emden and W.R. Crewe, it seated 642 people and had a stone and red-brick facade in Italian Renaissance style. It opened with *Mamma,* a farcical comedy adapted from the French by Sydney Grundy.

1897
Opening of Her Majesty's Theatre in the Haymarket (the fourth on that site) under the management of Herbert Beerbohm Tree. Tree's emphasis on spectacular realism reached its height in his 1900 production of *A Midsummer Night's Dream* which had a carpet of real grass, real rabbits, thickets of blossom, a splendid palace, lights and airy shapes: given that his wife also acted in the plays, it was said that you couldn't see the wood for the Trees. Oscar Wilde protested that the scene-painter was being replaced by the carpenter.

1898
Foundation of Moscow Art Theatre by Stanislavsky and Nemirovich-Danchenko. The theatre opened with A.K. Tolstoy's *Tsar Fyodor Ivanovich.*

1899
Adolphe Appia, a French-Swiss, published *Die Musik und die Inscenierung* which had great influence on stage design and lighting. He rejected flat, painted scenery and employed light as the visual counterpart of music, enhancing the mood of the play and linking the actor to the setting.

Twentieth century

1903
Max Reinhardt in Berlin begins his own revolu-

The interior of the Chichester Festival Theatre, Sussex which opened in 1962.

tion against the prevailing Naturalism by founding the Neues Theater, Berlin, where he produced plays by Gorky, Wilde and Schiller.

1904
Abbey Theatre opened in Dublin by Lady Gregory and W.B. Yeats to house the company of the Irish National Dramatic Society. In 1924 it became **the first state-subsidised theatre** in the English-speaking world.

1913
Jacques Copeau opens the Théâtre du Vieux Colombier in Paris in an effort to 'bring back true beauty and poetry' to the French stage and to create a new kind of ensemble style.

1923
V.E. Meyerhold, Russian actor and director, opens the Meyerhold Theatre in Moscow to develop his own kind of theatre based on music, mime, silent film, circus and the Chinese style of acting. In 1937 the theatre was closed because it did not conform to the Stalinist doctrine of Socialist Realism.

1923
Provincetown Players, an experimental group of American actors and directors, open the Provincetown Playhouse in New York under the management of Kenneth Macgowan, Robert Edmond Jones and Eugene O'Neill. This is the recognised beginning of the off-Broadway movement.

1932
Shakespeare Memorial Theatre in Stratford-upon-Avon opens with the two parts of *Henry IV* played over an afternoon and evening.

1949
First production of the Berliner Ensemble, founded by Bertolt Brecht, at the Deutsches Theater, East Berlin: the play was *Herr Puntila und sein Knecht Matti*. In 1954 the company moved into their own permanent home, the Theater am Schiffbauerdamm.

1956
In April the English Stage Company, under the direction of George Devine, took over the management of the Royal Court Theatre, Sloane Square beginning their tenancy with Angus Wilson's *The Mulberry Bush*.

1958
Belgrade Theatre, Coventry opens: the first new playhouse to be built in Britain after the Second World War.

1962
Reopening of Victoria Theatre, Stoke-on-Trent: **Britain's first permanent theatre-in-the-round.**

1962
Chichester Festival Theatre opens: **the first large-scale, open-stage theatre to be built in Britain.**

1965
Opening of Vivien Beaumont Theater, part of New York's Lincoln Center for the Performing Arts. Designed by Eero Saarinen with the collaboration of the stage designer Jo Mielziner.

1976
Opening of Britain's National Theatre on the South Bank after 148 years of committed steadfast campaigning.

1982
Opening of the Barbican Centre in the City of London, the largest centre for arts and conferences in Western Europe.

The Barbican Centre nestling between twin towers of residential flats, includes a concert hall, two theatres, three cinemas, a library, and art gallery. The Barbican Theatre is now the London home of The Royal Shakespeare Company.

London Theatres

There are 51 functioning mainstream theatres in central London: more within the space of two square miles than in any other capital city. In addition there is a large and proliferating number of 'fringe' venues, both in the inner city and the suburbs.

These are the mainstream theatres:

ADELPHI THEATRE
Strand, WC2E 7NH
Seating: 1500
History: There have been four theatres on this site — The Sans Pareil (1806), the Theatre Royal, Adelphi (1858), The Century Theatre (1901) and the current Adelphi (1930). In 1834 **the first mechanical 'Sinking Stage' in Britain** was installed. In its time the theatre has been the home of Dickensian adaptations, popular melodrama and George Edwardes musical comedy. Since 1930 the theatre has housed Coward and Cochran revues, opera and ballet and has recently been associated with a string of musical revivals (*Show Boat* 1971, *The King and I* 1973, *My Fair Lady* 1979).
Longest run: *Charlie Girl* (1965), 2202 performances.

ALBERY THEATRE
St Martin's Lane, WC2 4AH
Seating: 879
History: Opened in 1903 as the New Theatre under Charles Wyndham (changed its name to the Albery in 1973 in memory of Sir Bronson Albery). Saw the first London production of Shaw's *Saint Joan* (1924), of the longest-recorded run (186 performances) of *Romeo and Juliet* with Olivier, Gielgud, Ashcroft, Evans (1935), and of famous Old Vic seasons from 1944 to 1950 when it became the company's official home. Olivier in *Richard III* (1944). *Oedipus* and *The Critic* (1945) and Richardson in *Henry IV, Parts I and II* (1945) became part of theatrical legend. Olivier returned in 1971 playing *Long Day's Journey Into Night* with the National Theatre.
Longest run: *Oliver* (1960), 2618 performances.

ALDWYCH THEATRE
Aldwych, WC2B 4DF
Seating: 1004
History: Opened in 1905. Has enjoyed two famous periods. From 1925 to 1933 it was the home of Ben Travers's Aldwych farces including *A Cuckoo in the Nest* (1925), *Rookery Nook* (1926), *Thark* (1927), *Plunder* (1928). From December 1960 to March 1982 it was also the London home of the Royal

Shakespeare Company (including Peter Daubeny's World Theatre Seasons from 1964 to 1973). Many famous productions include *The Wars of the Roses* (1964), Brook's *Midsummer Night's Dream* (1971), *Travesties* (1974). Last RSC performance: *Richard II* with Alan Howard on 13 March 1982.

Longest run: *It Pays To Advertise* (1924), 598 performances.

AMBASSADORS THEATRE
West Street, WC2H 9ND
Seating: 460
History: Opened in 1913. Home of hugely popular intimate revue, many with Hermione Gingold and Henry Kendall, from 1939 to 1947. On 25 November 1952 Agatha Christie's *The Mousetrap* was sprung on an unsuspecting public. It stayed there until March 1974.

Longest run: *The Mousetrap* (1952), 8862 performances before transferring to St. Martin's in 1974.

APOLLO THEATRE
Shaftesbury Avenue, W1V 7HD
Seating: 792
History: Built in 1901, the fourth theatre in the new roadway (1887) running through the centre of Soho. Home of the Pelissier Follies from 1908 to 1912, of *Abie's Irish Rose* (1927), Sherwood's *Idiot's Delight* (1938), Rattigan's *Flare Path* (1942), Gielgud played there in *40 Years On* (1968) and, with Ralph Richardson, in *Home* (1970).

Longest run: *Boeing, Boeing* (1962). 2035 performances (including three other theatres).

ARTS THEATRE CLUB
6/7 Great Newport Street, WC2H 7JA
Seating: 337
History: Opened in 1927 as a club outside censorship restrictions. Run by Alec Clunes from 1942 to 1953 as a pocket National Theatre. British premières of *Waiting For Godot* (1955) and *Waltz of the Toreadors* (1956) directed by Peter Hall. RSC staged experimental season in 1962. Caryl Jenner's Unicorn Theatre for Children took over in 1967.

Longest run: *Dirty Linen* (1976), 1667 performances.

ASTORIA THEATRE
157 Charing Cross Road, WC2H OEN
Seating: 1141
History: Built as 'London's Supreme Cinema' on the site of a jam factory in 1927. Translated into a theatre in 1977 with *Elvis*, a multi-media tribute to the King.

BARBICAN THEATRE
Barbican Centre, EC2Y 8DO
Seating: Main theatre 1166 Studio theatre 200
History: Part of the Barbican Centre for Arts and Conferences first mooted in 1955. Opening: June 1982 with RSC in Shakespeare's *Henry IV Parts One and*

Two. Future home in London of the RSC and a vital element of the largest centre of its kind in Europe.

CAMBRIDGE THEATRE
Earlham Street, WC2 9HU
Seating: 1280
History: Opened in 1930 with Bea Lillie in *Charlot's Masquerade*. Has staged musicals (*Half a Sixpence, Chicago*), opera (home of Jay Pomeroy's New London Opera Company from 1946 to 1948), ballet, revue and legitimate drama (including Ingmar Bergman's National Theatre production of *Hedda Gabler* in 1970).

Longest run: *The Reluctant Debutante* (1955), 752 performances.

COLISEUM
St Martin's Lane, WC2N 4ES
Seating: 2358
History: Opened in 1904 by Sir Oswald Stoll as a variety house with a number of startling innovations: a mobile lounge to take royal parties to their boxes, post office facilities in the foyers, boxes at rear stalls level, **first revolving stage in Britain** with three revolves that moved separately. 1930: **first stage demonstration of television.** Famous for presentation of American musicals: *Kiss Me Kate* (1951), *Guys and Dolls* (1953), *Pajama Game* (1955). Sadler's Wells Opera Company took over in August 1968 becoming English National Opera in 1974.

Longest run: *Annie Get Your Gun* (1947), 1304 performances.

COMEDY THEATRE
Panton Street, SW1 4DN
Seating: 820
History: Opened in 1881. 1905: John Barrymore made his first London appearance here in *The Dictator*. 1956: New Watergate Theatre Club was formed to present unlicensed plays including *A View From the Bridge* (1956), *Tea and Sympathy* (1957), *Cat on a Hot Tin Roof* (1957). Male nudity was seen in *Fortune and Men's Eyes* (1968) and female nudity in *Steaming* (1981).

Longest run: *There's a Girl in My Soup* (1969), 2547 performances (having started at the Globe).

CRITERION THEATRE
Piccadilly Circus, W1V 9LB
Seating: 592
History: Opened in March 1874 with H.J. Byron's *An American Lady*. Marie Tempest appeared in five plays between 1926 and 1929. Terence Rattigan's *French Without Tears* opened in 1936 and ran for 1039 performances. An adaptation of Irish Murdoch's *A Severed Head* opened in 1963 and ran for 1043 performances.

Longest run: *A Little Bit of Fluff* (1915), 1241 performances.

THEATRE ROYAL, Drury Lane
Catherine Street, WC2B 5JF
Seating: 2245
History: Four theatres on or near this site. The first, opened by Thomas Killigrew with a patent from Charles II, was built in 1663. Sir Christopher Wren built a second theatre (after a fire had burned down the first) which opened in 1674. The theatre was rebuilt again in 1794, under Sheridan's management, and destroyed by fire in 1809. A fourth theatre opened in 1812 and has since been much renovated and remodelled.

The four Drury Lanes are full of legend. Nell Gwynne made her debut there in 1665. God Save the King was first sung there in 1741 and Rule Britannia in 1750. Sheridan's *School For Scandal* was given its first performance in May 1777. A chariot-race was staged in *Ben-Hur* (1902), a horse-race in *The Whip* (1909), an earthquake in *The Hope* (1911). In recent years it has become a home for American musicals.
Longest run: *My Fair Lady* (1958), 2281 performances.

DUCHESS THEATRE
Catherine Street, WC2B 5LA
Seating: 477
History: Opened in 1929. Associated in the thirties with the plays of J.B. Priestley including *Laburnum Grove* (1933), *Eden End* (1934), *Cornelius* (1935), *Time and the Conways* (1937). More recently has staged *The Dirtiest Show in Town* (1971) and *Oh Calcutta* (1974). Very popular with Japanese businessmen.
Longest run: *Oh Calcutta* (1974), 2434 performances (including Royalty Theatre).

DUKE OF YORK'S THEATRE
St Martin's Lane, WC2N 4BG
Seating: 641
History: Opened as the Trafalgar Square Theatre in 1892. First production here of Barrie's *The Admirable Crichton* (1902), *Peter Pan* (1904), *What Every Woman Knows* (1908). Charlie Chaplin played here in Gillette's *Sherlock Holmes* (1905). Nancy Price's People's National Theatre took over between 1933 and 1936. Alan Ayckbourn's first London hit, *Relatively Speaking* (1967), enjoyed a good run. In 1980 it became **the first London theatre to be owned by a commercial radio station,** Capital Radio.
Longest run: *Is Your Honeymoon Really Necessary* (1944), 980 performances.

FORTUNE THEATRE
Russell Street, WC2B 5HA
Seating: 432
History: First theatre to be built in London after the First World War: opened in 1924. O'Casey, Galsworthy, Lonsdale were played here in the twenties. More recently, it has provided a home for revue and the ultimate anti-revue: *Joyce Grenfell Requests The*

Pleasure (1954), *At The Drop of a Hat* (1957), *Beyond The Fringe* (1961). At present, it is a home for outstanding Fringe productions beginning with *Brothers Karamazov* (1981).
Longest run: *Beyond The Fringe* (1961), 1184 performances.

GARRICK THEATRE
Charing Cross Road, WC2H OHH
Seating: 700
History: Opened in 1889 with Pinero's *The Profligate* 1903: actor-manager, Arthur Bourchier, became **the first person in Britain to ban a critic,** A.B. Walkley of *The Times.* The theatre survived. Walter Greenwood's *Love on the Dole* (1935) ran for 391 performances. Robert Dhéry's revue, *La Plume de Ma Tante* (1955) for 700 performances. Ira Levin's *Deathtrap* (1979) scared the pants off plenty of customers by resurrecting an assumed corpse.
Longest run: *Fings Ain't Wot They Used T' Be* (1960), 897 performances (including a run at Stratford East).

GLOBE THEATRE
Shaftesbury Avenue, W1V 8AR
Seating: 907
History: Opened in 1906 as the Hicks Theatre (it became the Globe in 1909). Riot in 1917 when some of the audience protested at the French music-hall artiste, Gaby Deslys. Notable foreign visitors in 1930 included the Pitoëffs in *Saint Joan,* the German actor Moissi as Hamlet, and a Japanese company. But very much a home of quilted successes by Fry, Rattigan, Coward and, latterly, Nichols and Ayckbourn.
Longest run: *While the Sun Shines* (1943), 1154 performances.

THEATRE ROYAL, Haymarket
Haymarket, SW1 4HT
Seating: 909
History: First theatre on this site: 1720. Second: 1821 with interior reconstructed in 1880 and 1905. John Nash's Corinthian portico survives from 1821. First performances here of Wilde's *A Woman of No Importance* (1893) and *An Ideal Husband* (1895). First licensed performance of Ibsen's *Ghosts* (1914). Famous Gielgud Repertory Season (1944-45) which pre-empted the role of a National Theatre. Since then many hit plays by Rattigan, N.C. Hunter, Enid Bagnold. But nothing as bizarre as Julia Glover's performance as Falstaff in *The Merry Wives of Windsor* (1833).
Longest run: *Ross* (1960), 763 performances.

HER MAJESTY'S THEATRE
Haymarket, SW1Y 4QR
Seating: 1263
History: Four theatres on this site: 1705, 1791, 1868 and 1897. Most famous association is with actor-

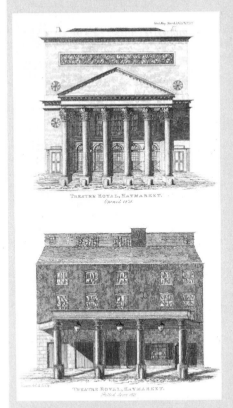

Left top: Exterior of the Theatre Royal Haymarket in 1821 with its Corinthian portico designed by John Nash. It cost £20000 and opened with 'The Rivals'. **Left bottom:** before renovation and redesign. **Above:** Interior of the same theatre in July, 1821. It was variously described as "rude", "naked", "chilling" and even "petrifying".

manager Beerbohm Tree who offered spectacular Shakespeare revivals from 1897 to 1907. In later years looked East with popular productions of *Chu Chin Chow* (1916), *Cairo* (1921), *East of Suez* (1922) and *Hassan* (1923). Latterly home of popular musicals, including *West Side Story* (1958) and *Fiddler on the Roof* (1967), and opulent plays such as *Amadeus* (1981).
Longest run: *Chu Chin Chow* (1916), 2238 performances.

LONDON PALLADIUM
Argyll Street, W1A 3AB
Seating: 2306
History: Built in 1910 as a variety house by touring circus manager, Charles Hengler. Since then has played host to the Crazy Gang, *Peter Pan* (1930-38), revue and every variety topliner including Judy Garland, Danny Kaye, Bob Hope, Jack Benny and Ken Dodd. Once described by critic Alan Brien as the only London theatre Brecht would really have enjoyed.

Longest run: *The Whirl of the World* (1924), 627 performances.

LYRIC THEATRE
Shaftesbury Avenue, W1V 8ES
Seating: 948
History: Opened in 1888 as the second building in the new Shaftesbury Avenue (the first, the Shaftesbury, has been demolished). Eleonora Duse made her first London appearance here in 1893 in *Camille*. Other star performers who appeared here include Lewis Waller, Matheson Lang, Tallulah Bankhead (*Let Us Be Gay*, 1929) and Robert Morley in *The Little Hut* (1950), directed by Peter Brook, *Hippo Dancing* (1954) and *How The Other Half Loves* (1970).
Longest run: *The Little Hut* (1950), 1261 performances.

LYRIC THEATRE, Hammersmith
King Street, W6 OQL
Seating: 534 and 128 (Studio theatre)
History: First theatre on this site: 1888. Destroyed in 1965 and rebuilt (with old Victorian plasterwork in-

tact) in 1979. Old theatre famous for seasons run by Nigel Playfair, H.M. Tennent (who in the 1940s imported stars like Ashcroft, Burton and Guinness) and the 59 Theatre Company (who in 1959 did a legendary *Brand*).

Longest run: *The Beggar's Opera* (1920), 1463 performances.

MAYFAIR THEATRE

Stratton Street, W1A 2AN

Seating: 310

History: Opened in 1963, as part of the plush Mayfair hotel, with *Six Characters In Search of an Author* starring Ralph Richardson. Has largely been used for transfers from other theatres (including *Beyond the Fringe* (1964-66) but has also included notably way-out plays by Peter Handke, Stephen Spears and Simone Benmussa.

Longest run: *The Philanthropist* (1970), 1114 performances (including Royal Court première run).

THE MERMAID

Puddle Dock, Blackfriars, EC4 4DB

Seating: 614

History: Opened in 1959 with *Lock Up Your Daughters*. Closed in 1978 and reopened in 1981 (none too happily) as part of an office-block complex. But in its heyday, under Bernard Miles's often eccentric tutelage, it craftily balanced rare Elizabeth-Jacobean plays with little-known foreign work and

A feline dancer from Andrew Lloyd Webber's musical, 'Cats' at the New London Theatre.

commercial hits. *Side by Side by Sondheim* (1978) was a particularly brilliant anthology.

Longest run: *Hadrian the Seventh* (1968), 988 performances (including transfer to Haymarket).

NATIONAL THEATRE

Upper Ground, South Bank, SE1 9PX

Seating: (Olivier) 1160, (Lyttelton) 890, (Cottesloe) 350-400

History: Project first mooted in 1848. Actual building started in 1969. The three-in-one complex began operation in 1976. It was a phased operation. The Lyttelton proscenium theatre opened first (March 1976) with Albert Finney in *Hamlet*. Next came the Olivier (October 1976) with Albert Finney in *Tamburlaine the Great*. Finally in March 1977 came the smaller Cottesloe with Ken Campbell's *Illuminatus*. Each building has had its particular successes. The Lyttelton has looked happiest with revivals of modern classics (*Death of a Salesman* (1979). The Olivier with rare, little-known work (*Tales from the Vienna Woods* (1977), *Undiscovered Country* (1979), *Galileo* (1980). The Cottesloe with promenade productions and American imports (*The Long Voyage Home* (1979), *American Buffalo* (1979)). Initially somewhat vilified, latterly calmly accepted, it is simply the best National Theatre we have.

NEW LONDON THEATRE

Parker Street, WC2B 5PW

Seating: 907

History: Built on the site of the old Winter Garden Theatre (closed 1959), it opened in 1973 with Peter Ustinov's *The Unknown Soldier and His Wife*. Described as 'a theatre of the future' it had a chequered history and was converted into a Thames television studio. But its glorious feline renaissance in 1981 with Andrew Lloyd Webber's musical, *Cats*. gave those who had abandoned hope of the New London paws for thought.

Longest run: *Cats* (1981).

THE OLD VIC

The Cut, Waterloo Road, SE1 8NB

Seating: 878

History: Opened (as the Royal Coburg Theatre) in 1818. 1880: taken over by social reformer Emma Cons who tried to redeem its low reputation as a theatrical blood-tub. 1912: Lilian Baylis, niece of Emma Cons, took over to promote good theatre at cheap prices. 1914-23: Old Vic became **first theatre in the world to produce all the Shakespeare plays contained in the First Folio.** 1931: first performance given by the Vic-Wells Ballet (which later became the Royal Ballet). 1963: Old Vic company wound up, National Theatre company moved in. 1976: Prospect Company took over from National Theatre and later revived the name of the Old Vic Company but the

The Palace Theatre, London: it opened in 1891 with 'Ivanhoe' and later became famous for the long run of 'Jesus Christ Superstar'.

enterprise foundered, helped on its way by a disastrous *Macbeth* (1980) with Peter O'Toole.

OPEN AIR THEATRE
Regent's Park, NW1 4NU
Seating: 1187
History: Opened in 1933 with *Twelfth Night*. New amphitheatre constructed in 1974. Has survived English weather, aeroplanes, gnats, rising damp to become a popular venue for summer Shakespeare and Shaw.

PALACE THEATRE
Shaftesbury Avenue, W1A 4AF
Seating: 1450
History: Opened in 1891 as The Royal English Opera House (it only became the Palace in 1911) with Sullivan's *Ivanhoe*. Here Bernhardt acted (1891), Maud Allan disrobed (in *Vision of Salome*, 1908) and Pavlova pirouetted (1910). From the success of *No, No, Nanette* (1925) musicals have ruled the Palace including *Song of Norway* (1946), *King's Rhapsody* (1949) during the run of which Ivor Novello died, and *The Sound of Music* (1961).

Longest run: *Jesus Christ Superstar* (1972), 3357 performances.

PHOENIX THEATRE
Charing Cross Road, WC2H OJP
Seating: 1012
History: Opened in 1930 with Coward's *Private Lives* and in 1936 housed the same author's *Tonight at 8.30*. Has had an up-and-down history including everything from Gielgud in *Love for Love* (1943) to Cicely Courtneidge in *Under The Counter* (1945). Coward's work claimed the stage again with *Design for Living* (1973) and Stoppard's *Night and Day* (1979) had a good run for its money.
Longest run: *The Canterbury Tales* (1968), 2082 performances.

PICCADILLY THEATRE
Denman Street, W1V 8DY
Seating: 792
History: Opened in 1928 with *Blue Eyes* starring Evelyn Laye. A year later became a cinema showing Al Jolson in *The Singing Fool*. In 1937 presented a new form of entertainment called *Choose Your Time* comprising newsreel, swingaphonic orchestra, variety turns and a short comedy. Reverted to plays in 1938, was handsomely redecorated in 1960 and has since housed musicals, classic transfers and a steady suc-

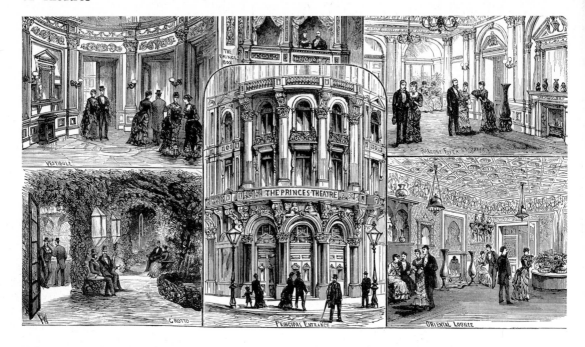

The Prince's Theatre (now the Prince of Wales), London in 1884: note the Moorish style of the Oriental Lounge and the Grotto constructed under the street-level.

cession of RSC imports including *Wild Oats* (1977), *Privates on Parade* (1978), *Piaf* (1980), *Once in a Lifetime* (1980) and *Educating Rita* (1980).
Longest run: *Educating Rita* (1980).

PRINCE EDWARD THEATRE
Old Compton Street, W1V 6HS
Seating: 1666
History: Opened as the Prince Edward in 1930 with *Rio Rita*. Unsuccessful and reopened as the London Casino in 1936 with *Folies Parisiènnes*. Rechristened Prince Edward in 1978 for *Evita*. Kept busy in the intervening years with revue, ballet, pantomime (including Twiggy in *Cinderella* (1974) and Cinerama.
Longest run: *Evita* (1978).

PRINCE OF WALES THEATRE
Coventry Street, W1V 8AS
Seating: 1088
History: Opened as the Prince's Theatre in 1884 with W.S. Gilbert's *The Palace of Truth*. Rebuilt and reopened in 1937 with *Les Folies de Paris et Londres*. Sid Field, Mae West, Frankie Howerd, Barbra Streisand and Danny La Rue have all starred in a wide-spaced theatre ideally suited to musical and revue.
Longest run: *The World of Suzie Wong* (1959), 824 performances.

THE QUEEN'S THEATRE
Shaftesbury Avenue, W1V 8BA
Seating: 989
History: Opened in 1907 with *The Sugar Bowl*. Enjoyed periods of great distinction under Sir Barry Jackson (1929-33) and under John Gielgud (1937-39) whose famous seasons included *Richard II, The School for Scandal, The Three Sisters* and *The Merchant of Venice*. The theatre was hit by a bomb in 1940 but reopened in 1959 with Gielgud in *The Ages of Man* and has since been graced by Neil Simon's *The Odd Couple* (1966) and Simon Gray's *Otherwise Engaged* (1975) and *Quartermaine's Terms* (1981).
Longest run: *Potash and Perlmutter* (1914), 665 performances.

ROYAL COURT THEATRE
Sloane Square, SW1W 8AS
Seating: 401
History: Opened in 1888 with a farcical comedy, *Mamma*, adapted from the French. It has enjoyed two great periods. Between 1903 and 1907 J.E. Vedrenne and Harley Granville-Barker staged 32 plays by 17 authors of whom Shaw was the most notable. Then in 1956 the English Stage Company took over the theatre and devoted themselves principally to the discovery of new writers: Osborne, Wesker, Bond, Storey, Hampton, were some of their major discoveries. They also had a profound effect on English direction and design and unearthed forgotten dramatists like D.H. Lawrence.
Longest run: *The Farmer's Wife* (1914), 1329 performances.

A variety of masks worn by actors in Greek classical theatre. (Mary Evans Picture Library).

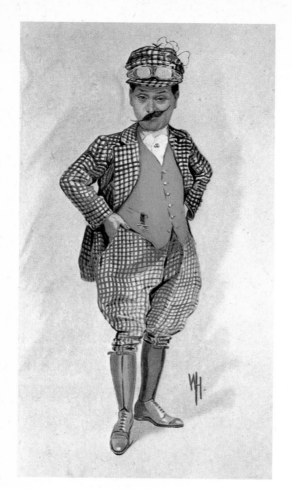

Above: Herbert Beerbohm Tree as Cardinal Wolsey in 'Henry VIII' at Her Majesty's in 1910. (Victoria and Albert Museum).

Left: Harry Tate (1872-1940), English music-hall artist famed for his motoring sketch. (Victoria and Albert Museum).

Théâtre des Variétés, Paris, which opened in 1807. (Victoria and Albert Museum).

ROYAL OPERA HOUSE, Covent Garden
Covent Garden, WC2E 7QA
Seating: 2141
History: First theatre on this site: 1732. Second: 1809. Third: 1858. Though associated with drama, pantomime, opera, ballet and civil disturbance during the first century of its existence (an attempt to raise prices in 1809 led to the Old Price riots which caused the Riot Act to be read from the stage), it has since its reopening in 1858 been synonymous with opera in Britain. It became a dance-hall during the Second World War but is now the home of both the Royal Opera and the Royal Ballet.

ROYALTY THEATRE
Portugal Street, WC2A 2HT
Seating: 1016
History: Opened in 1960 with Durrenmatt's *The Visit*. Turned into a cinema shortly afterwards and has since functioned spasmodically as a theatre with *Oh, Calcutta* (1970) and *Bubbling Brown Sugar* (1980).

SADLER'S WELLS THEATRE
Rosebery Avenue, EC1R 4TN
Seating: 1500
History: Present building opened in 1931 with *Twelfth Night* presented in conjunction with the Old Vic (though Sadler's Wells Musick House was set up in

The Opera House, Covent Garden goes up in flames following a Bal Masque in March 1856.

1683). Since then it has largely been a house of opera and ballet though *Joseph and the Amazing Technicolour Dreamcoat* played there during the Christmas of 1981.

Sadler's Wells, London in 1756: the wooden Musick House built around the well which once belonged to a local Priory and which in the Middle Ages was thought to have miraculous powers.

ST MARTIN'S THEATRE
West Street, WC2H 9NH
Seating: 560
History: Built in 1916 as a companion to the neighbour-
ing Ambassadors. Many hit shows including
Galsworthy's *Loyalties* (1922), Arnold Ridley's *The
Ghost Train* (1925), *The Shop at Sly Corner* (1945),
Sleuth (1970) and *The Mousetrap* which transferred
here in 1974 and which seems set for eternity.
Longest run: *Sleuth* (1970), 2359 performances
(including Garrick and Fortune).

SAVOY THEATRE
Savoy Court, Strand, WC2R OET
Seating: 1213
History: First theatre: 1881. Second theatre: 1929.
Built as a permanent home for Gilbert and Sullivan
operas and the D'Oyly Carte Opera Company who
have romped through many a season here. But the
Savoy has housed many other popular shows in-
cluding *Journey's End* (1929), *The Man Who Came to
Dinner* (1941), *Sail Away* (1962) and *Lloyd George
Knew My Father* (1972).
Longest run: *The Secretary Bird* (1968), 1463 perfor-
mances.

SHAFTESBURY THEATRE
Princes Circus, WC2H 8DP
Seating: 1300
History: Opened as The Princes in 1911 with *The Three
Musketeers*, (renamed the Shaftesbury in 1963).
Chequered fortunes since then mixing melodrama,
musicals, Gilbert and Sullivan, ballet. The Astaires
played here in *Funny Face* (1928) despite a run interrupted by a gas explosion. Ashcroft and Redgrave
were seen in a famous Stratford *Antony and
Cleopatra* (1953). *Hair* (1968), with its nudity and
four-letter words, made history by opening the day
after censorship by the Lord Chamberlain was
abolished. Sadly, it was robbed of its 2000th performance by the roof collapsing and the Shaftesbury
was suddenly *Hair*-less.
Longest run: *Hair* (1968), 1997 performances.

STRAND THEATRE
Aldwych, WC2B 4DF
Seating: 1076
History: Opened as the Waldorf in 1905 with a season
of Italian opera alternating with Duse in dramatic
performances (it finally became the Strand Theatre
in 1913). Its first success was Matheson Lang in *The
Barrier* followed by *Mr Wu* (1913). Since then its
many hits include *It's a Boy* (1930), *Arsenic and Old
Lace* (1942), *Sailor Beware* (1955), *A Funny Thing
Happened on the Way to the Forum* (1964) and the
evergreen farce *No Sex Please — We're British*.
Longest run: *No Sex Please — We're British* (1971),
4419 performances before transferring to the Garrick in 1982.

VAUDEVILLE THEATRE
Strand, WC2R ON4
Seating: 659
History: First theatre: 1870. Second reconstructed
theatre: 1891. Third reconstructed theatre: 1926.
The big hit of the early years was H.J. Byron's com-
edy, *Our Boys* (1875) which ran for 1362 perfor-
mances until 1879. Ibsen's *Rosmersholm* and *Hedda
Gabler* had their first English performances at
matinées in 1891. Later successes include Esther
McCracken's *No Medals* (1944). *The Chiltern Hun-
dreds* (1947), *Chips with Everything* (1962).
Longest run: *Salad Days* (1954), 2283 performances.

VICTORIA PALACE THEATRE
Victoria Street, SW1 5EA
Seating: 1565
History: Opened in 1911 as a music-hall. Venue for the
much-guyed patriotic melodrama, *Young England*
(1934): though it was mercilessly sent up, one
playgoer boasted of 150 visits and three others
claimed to have spent £150 on seats. Epic hits since
then include *Me and My Girl* (1937), a series of six
Crazy Gang revues from 1947 to 1962, *The Black and
White Minstrels* (1962) and *Annie* (1978).
Longest run: *The Black and White Minstrel Show*
(1962), 4344 performances.

THE WAREHOUSE
41 Earlham Street, WC2H 9LD
Seating: 200
History: Built in the 1870s as a vat room for a brewery,
subsequently used as a banana warehouse and
ballet studio, it was converted into a small-scale
theatre by the RSC in 1977. Vacated in 1982 because
of their move to the Barbican.

WESTMINSTER THEATRE
Palace Street, SW1E 5JB
Seating: 588
History: Opened in 1931 with Bridie's *The Anatomist*.
Initially known for its production of distinguished
plays by Ibsen, Shaw, Pirandello, O'Neill, it was
bought in 1946 by the Oxford Group (later known as
Moral Rearmament) who frequently leased it to com-
mercial managements.
Longest run: *Dial M For Murder* (1952), 425 perfor-
mances.

WHITEHALL THEATRE
14 Whitehall, SW1A 2DY
Seating: 662
History: Opened in 1930 and has forever been
associated with light popular entertainment: stripper Phyllis Dixey (1943); a long string of Brian Rix
farces beginning with *Reluctant Heroes* (1950), Paul
Raymond sex-shows starting with *Pyjama Tops*
(1969) and latterly John Wells's gamey political
spoof, *Anyone For Denis?* (1981).
Longest run: *Pyjama Tops* (1969), 2498 performances.

'GAD SIR, FIRST THE EMPIRE, NOW THIS, BLAST IT, IS NOTHING SACRED?'

Cartoon by Emmwood when 'Revuedeville' closed on 31 October, 1964.

WINDMILL THEATRE

Great Windmill St, W1V 7HE

Seating: 312

History: Opened in 1931. In 1932 *Revuedeville* initiated a policy of non-stop variety including statuesque nudity and comedy. The Windmill continued with this policy until 1964 and became **the only theatre that never closed (except for 12 compulsory days in 1939) throughout the whole of the war.** In 1974 Paul Raymond bought the theatre and restored it to something of its tawdry glory with a twice-nightly sex-show called *Rip-Off* (1976).

WYNDHAM'S THEATRE

Charing Cross Road, WC2H ODA

Seating: 759

History: Opened in 1899 with *David Garrick* by T.W. Robertson. Tallulah Bankhead made her London debut here in *To Have the Honour* (1924). A string of Edgar Wallace thrillers occupied the stage from 1926 to 1932. *George and Margaret* (1937) ran for an impressive 799 performances. In recent years many of its hits have been transfers including *A Taste of Honey* (1959), *Inadmissible Evidence* (1965) and the very popular Belt and Braces production of *Accidental Death of an Anarchist* (1979).

Longest run: *The Boy Friend* (1954), 2084 performances.

YOUNG VIC

66 The Cut, SE1 8LP

Seating: 456 and 100 (studio)

History: Opened in 1970 to present classic plays and modern works to young audiences at cheap prices. Has done some notable work including *Scapino* (1970) with Jim Dale and much-revived productions of *Rosencrantz and Guildenstern Are Dead* and *Waiting For Godot*.

Principal New York Theatres

As at 1 July 1982

	Opening Date	Capacity
Alvin	1927	1344
Ambassador	1921	1121
Anta	1925	1214
Belasco	1907	1008
Biltmore	1925	994
Booth	1913	766
Broadhurst	1917	1185
Broadway	1927	1788
Brooks Atkinson	1926	1088
Cort	1912	1088
Ethel Barrymore	1928	1099
Eugene O'Neill	1925	1075
Forty-Sixth Street	1925	1338
Harkness	1974	1022
Imperial	1923	1452
John Golden	1927	799
Longacre	1913	1115
Lunt-Fontanne	1910	1478
Lyceum	1903	995
Majestic	1927	1655
Mark Hellinger	1930	1581
Martin Beck	1924	1280
Minskoff	1973	1521
Music Box	1921	1010
New York City Center	1934	2935
New York State	1964	2279
Palace	1966	1358
Playhouse	1911	994
Plymouth	1917	1063
Royale	1927	1059
St James	1927	1583
Shubert	1913	1469
Uris	1972	1903
Vivian Beaumont	1965	1140
Winter Garden	1911	1479

Fringe theatres

The word 'Fringe' to denote small-scale theatre offering a radical alternative to the fare available in the West End was borrowed from the Edinburgh Festival and first came into use in 1968. The whole movement has grown astonishingly both in London and nationwide. The Alternative Theatre Directory (1981) lists 53 London Fringe Theatres, 119 alternative theatre companies, 51 young people's theatre companies, 66 puppet companies, 373 playwrights and 230 directors.

Principal London Fringe venues with their date of opening:

Albany Empire (Opened 1973. Burned down 1978. Reopened 1981.)

Bush Theatre (Opened 1972 above a Shepherd's Bush pub.)

Cockpit Theatre (Opened 1967)

Gate Theatre (Opened 1979. Reopened in new premises 1982.)

Half-Moon Theatre (Opened in a former synagogue 1972. Closed 1982.)

New Half Moon (Opened 1979)

Hampstead Theatre (Opened 1959)

ICA Theatre (Opened 1973)

King's Head Theatre (Opened 1970 behind an Islington pub.)

Orange Tree Theatre (Opened 1971 above a Richmond pub.)

Riverside Studios (Opened 1977)

Soho Poly (Opened 1968)

Theatre Upstairs (Opened 1969 above the Royal Court)

Tricycle Theatre (Opened 1980)

Upstream Theatre Club (Opened 1977 in a converted church hall.)

Many so-called Fringe productions have in recent years moved into the West End.

Accidental Death of an Anarchist (1979 — Belt and Braces to Wyndhams)

Educating Rita (1980 — Warehouse to Piccadilly)

Duet For One (1980 — Bush to Duke of York's)

Pal Joey (1980 — New Half Moon to Albery)

Dirty Linen (1976 — Almost Free to Arts)

The first-ever collective fringe ticket-agency was set up in the foyer of The Criterion Theatre, London 1982

Children's theatre

In Great Britain there are 21 companies regularly performing work for children. The longest-established is the Unicorn Theatre for Children founded in 1948 by Caryl Jenner as a touring group. The company became resident at the Arts Theatre, London in 1967.

Other major children's groups:

Caricature Theatre Ltd: founded in Cardiff in 1965 to promote the art of puppetry.

Mermaid Theatre's Molecule Club: founded by Lord and Lady Miles in 1967 to make the world of science theatrically exciting.

Polka: founded in 1967 to make the best work available to children.

Prof Dogg's Troupe: founded in 1968 by Ed Berman (as part of Inter-Action) to tour work to non-theatrical venues.

The largest number of specialised children's theatres is to be found in the USSR. The whole movement was systematically developed after the October Revolution and by 1935 there were 57 youth theatres. By 1965 out of some 470 professional theatres, 36 were youth and children's theatres, 73 puppet theatres. Today the Central Moscow Children's Theatre, directed by Maria Knebel, produces children's theatre on the same level as adult work. Stanislavsky, founder of the Moscow Art Theatre, when asked the difference between theatre for adults and children said simply: 'Children's theatre must be better'.

In New York there are some 26 specialised children's entertainments including Bill Baird's Marionette Theater, Theater in a Trunk and the Paper Bag Players. Well-known children's companies outside New York include Long Wharf's Access Theatre Company and the Dallas Theater Center's Magic Turtle which offers five plays a year on Saturday mornings.

An oriental shadow-play in progress at the Polka Children's Theatre, Wimbledon, London.

Right: Outside Pantaloon's House in a scene from the Polka Children's Theatre's 'Christmas Crackers'. Left: A trunk call: 'My Friends the Monkeys' at the Polka Children's Theatre.

Features of theatres

The largest building used for theatre is the National People's Congress Building (*Ren min da hui tang*) on the west side of Tian an men Square, Peking, China. The theatre seats 10 000, was completed in 1959, and is occasionally used as such as in 1964 for the play *The East Is Red*.

The largest purpose-built theatre is the Perth Entertainment Centre, Western Australia. It seats 8003, was completed in November 1976 at a cost of 8.3 million Australian dollars and has a stage area of 12 000 ft, (3660m).

The largest theatre stage in Britain is the Blackpool Opera House. It was rebuilt in July 1939 and has seats for 2975 people. Behind the 45ft (14m) wide proscenium arch the stage is 110ft (33m) high, 60ft (18m) deep and 100ft (30m) wide. There is dressing accommodation for 200 artistes.

Gas lighting was first introduced into the British theatre in the early 1800s. The Lyceum Theatre was **the first to light the stage by gas:** its bill for 6 August 1817 is headed 'The Gas Lights will this evening be introduced over the whole Stage'. **The first British theatre to be entirely lighted by gas** was Drury Lane from 6 September 1817. In the provinces, Liverpool led the way in the adoption of gas lighting in May 1818.

The first public building in London to be illuminated throughout by electricity was the Savoy Theatre from October 1881 ('About 1200 lights are used', wrote *The Times*, 'and the power to generate a sufficient current for these is obtained from large steam engines, giving about 120 horse power, placed on some open land near the theatre'). But electricity was only first used on the Savoy stage itself on 28 December 1881. *The Times* carried a special notice saying: 'Electric Light on the Stage.

Britain's first revolving stage, built in three sections,
at the Coliseum in 1904.

Horses on the treadmill: below-stage machinery showing how a horse-race was simulated at the Paris Port de Mer in 1890s. Such machinery was common at a time when the hunger for theatrical spectacle was enormous.

Special Matinée this day at two o'clock.' **The first American theatre to use electricity** was the California in San Francisco from 21-28 Feb 1879.

The first theatre to be lit by electricity on the outside was the Gaiety Theatre, London in August 1878. Neon lighting outside theatres is, of course, highly fallible. For some time *Charlot's Revue of 1924* was billed outside the Selwyn Theatre, New York as *Harlot's Revue of 1924*. Tickets became notoriously hard to obtain.

The trapdoor was an invention of the 19th century theatre. The floor of the stage often had a series of traps in it. These included the Footlights Trap enabling the footlights to be lowered below the stage for effects of darkness; the Corner Traps which enabled people to rise rapidly through the stage floor; the Grave Trap (for *Hamlet*) and the Cauldron Trap (for *Macbeth*); the Corsican Trap or Ghost Glide by which a rising figure appears to drift across the stage; and the Vamp Trap by which an actor appears to pass through solid scenery, first used in the melodrama *The Vampire* in 1820.

The smallest permanent professional theatres in Britain are Mull Little Theatre, near Dervaig, Isle of Mull, Scotland and the Community Theatre, Luton, Bedfordshire, each with a maximum capacity of 36 seats.

The first revolving stage was introduced at Kado-za doll theatre, Osaka, Japan by Namiki Shozo in 1758.

The first revolving stage in Britain was introduced at the London Coliseum in 1904. It was made up of three concentric rings capable of moving in either direction. This innovation cost the theatre's founder, Sir Oswald Stoll, £70 000.

The first curtain arrived with the proscenium arch of the Restoration Theatre of the 1660s. At first it was used only at the beginning, when raised after the prologue, and at the end. It was not until the 1750s that it was used to mark the end of an act and hide the stage during an interval.

The first person to use a curtain to hide the actual scene changes was Henry Irving in a revival of *The Corsican Brothers* in 1880: a crimson velvet curtain was set in the proscenium and lowered between scenes. But the stage-manager saw to it that the heaviest change was so well organised as to be performed in only 38 seconds.

The first Safety or Fireproof Curtain, sometimes known as the Iron, was used at Drury Lane in 1800.

Tricks and special effects were an integral part of Victorian theatre. Before that the earliest reference to theatrical trick is in the Covent Garden Inventory of 1743 which lists a 'front of garden that changes into house'. But the Victorians perfected such sound effects as the Glass Crash where broken glass and china is flung from one bucket into another; the Thunder Sheet where a suspended iron sheet is vigorously

Elaborate stage machinery operated on a pulley system at the Madison Square Theater, New York which opened in 1879 under the command of the inventive genius, Steel Mackaye.

shaken to produce the sound of the rolling of a storm; the Wind Machine where a ribbed drum is revolved against a sheet of silk.

The Victorians also loved spectacle. The most famous example was the chariot-race in *Ben Hur* (1902) which worked thus: 'The scene consists of four great cradles, 20ft in length and 14ft wide, which are moveable back and fro on railways supported by a bridge structure capable of supporting twenty tons. Each cradle bears four horses and a chariot. On each are four treadmills covered with rubber 12ft long and 2½ft wide and on these the horses are secured by invisible steel cable traces, which serve to hold the animals in their places. As the horse gallops the treadmill revolves under his feet, thereby eliminating the forward pressure created by the impact of his hoofs. An impression of great speed is created by the presence of a panoramic background, 35ft high, representing the walls of

the arena, with numbers of spectators seated in their places. This is made to revolve rapidly in a direction opposite to that in which the chariots are going.'

The orchestra pit, seating the musicians below the stage, is a Georgian innovation. In the Elizabethan theatre the musicians sat aloft in a small gallery and in the Restoration theatre they were housed in a box over the proscenium opening.

The first full-time stage designers (as opposed to architects or painters who worked in drama) appeared in the 17th century with the development of opera. The most famous and influential was Giacomo Torelli (1608-78). He was responsible for the complete set of wings at the Teatro Farnese at Parma. He was designer for the Teatro Novissimo in Venice from 1641 to 1645. After that he worked in Paris and reconstructed the backstage area of Molière's theatre, the Petit-Bourbon, so that it could encompass the latest innovations in spectacular staging.

In England the greatest innovator was Philippe Jacques de Loutherbourg (1735-1810), a French landscape artist imported by Garrick. He

"What time is the next swan?" as the opera singer asked in 'Lohengrin' when the bird failed to appear.

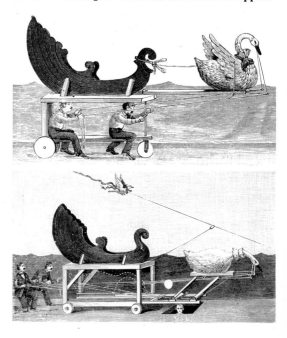

introduced head lights — or border patterns — behind the proscenium which discouraged actors from stepping outside the stage picture. He brought a touch of naturalism into the artificial scenic conventions of the time. He introduced the idea of gauze to represent fog, innovated (1773) with small models or cut-outs which passed across the stage and were moved mechanically, and for *The Wonders of Derbyshire* (1779) he made sketches in the county itself to ensure topographical accuracy.

The Victorian scenic-designers prided themselves on their total realism. Percy Fitzgerald wrote in 1870: 'The most complicated and familiar objects about us are fearlessly laid hold of by the property man and dragged upon the stage. Thus, when we take our dramatic pleasure, we have the satisfaction of not being separated from the objects of our daily life and within the walls of the theatre we meet again the engine and train that set us down almost at the door; the interior of hotels, counting-houses, shops, factories, the steam-boats, waterfalls, bridges and even fire-engines.'

Thus for Boucicault's *Janet Pride* (Adelphi 1855) the Central Criminal Court of the Old Bailey was reproduced for the last act. For the third act of Sardou's *Divorçons, Today* (1892) the designer borrowed from the Savoy hotel management napery, cutlery, glass and a group of waiters who served on the stage of the comedy every night during the run. Animals were also often brought on stage to add authenticity. For W.T. Moncrieff's *The Cataract of the Ganges* (Drury Lane 1823) horses were part of an Oriental spectacle that included a procession of Brahmin priests and a grand procession of the Rajah's army. And in J.H. Amherst's *The Invasion of Russia* (1825) Moscow burned amidst clouds of smoke and the stench of gunpowder and the remnants of the French army were ridden down by Cossacks.

The word **auditorium** — denoting the area where the audience sits — dates from 1727. The Restoration theatres from 1661 established the basic division between the Pit — the floor of the house usually sunk below gound level and filled with benches, the Boxes which stood on the same level as the stage and sometimes ran round all three sides of the Pit, and the Gallery, a second

The New Aquatic Theatre, Paris, 1895: eat your heart out, Esther Williams.

tier situated above the Boxes, often containing only two rows and designed for the less well-off spectators. **The Pay-Box,** a small cubicle where the money was taken, first appeared in the 18th century: a medium-sized theatre might have three, one each for pit, boxes and gallery. The term, the 'gods' referring to the upper gallery and its occupants, was first used in 1752. The auditorium design most familiar to modern playgoers — Stalls, Dress Circle projecting like a half-open drawer from a chest, Gallery and side Boxes — dates from the mid-Victorian era when there was a spate of theatre building lasting well into the present century: between 1866 and 1936 no fewer than 80 new theatres opened in London without counting music-halls.

The first theatre to introduce the system of queuing for pit and gallery was the Savoy in 1881. Until then it had been everyone for himself but, from its opening-date, the Savoy instituted the first come, first served principle.

The use of **incidental music** (as opposed to interpolated songs) dates back as far as Shakespeare in England and as far as Lope de Vega and Calderon in Spain. Shakespeare's comedies, in particular, often call for music as part of the opening or the climax: *Twelfth Night* 1601-2 with Orsino's opening lines 'If music be the food of love, play on'; *A Midsummer Night's Dream* (1595-56) with its Bergomask for the Mechanicals; *Much Ado About Nothing* (1598-99) where Benedick at the end cries 'Strike up, pipers'.

The practice of allowing members of the audience to sit on stage was a common feature of Elizabethan and continental theatre in the 16th and 17th centuries. It was first noticed in England in 1596 and in France in 1649. Indeed a whole play, *The Knight of the Burning Pestle* (1607) by Beaumont and Fletcher, was built around the participation in the action of a member of the audience, a grocer's apprentice. The development of more technically complex machinery finally made the visibly present audience insufferable. Voltaire banished audience-members from the stage of the Comédie Française in 1759. David Garrick achieved the same effect at Drury Lane in 1762. He also sealed off the backstage area to the public at Drury Lane in 1747. In that year Lord Hubbard's party noisily damned Garrick's production of *The Foundling,* 'the main cause of their anger, in spite of their excuses, was their being refused admittance behind the scenes'.

The catwalk is a narrow iron bridge running across the top of the stage (out of sight of the audience) and enabling the fly-men to reach any portion of the hung scenery.

The stage-door is at the back or side of the theatre and affords the link between stage and street. It is jealously guarded by a stage-door keeper. The most famous was Harry Loman, a former music-hall artist who worked with Chaplin. He became stage-door keeper of the Criterion Theatre, London in August 1955 at the age of 74 and retired in July 1977.

The playbill, the earliest form of theatre programme, **first appeared in England** in 1737 issued by the managements of Covent Garden and Drury Lane. It consisted of a small quarto sheet and was stuck up on the wall outside the theatre and distributed to coffee-houses. **The first playbills issued to the audience,** at least to occupants of the more expensive seats, free of charge, were issued by the Olympia Theatre, London in 1850.

The first magazine programme, called *Bill of the Play,* was issued by the St James's Theatre, London in 1869 and consisted of notes on the play, transport information and advertising. With the shortage of paper during the Second World War programmes became rather sparse, confining themselves to cast-lists and exiguous details about the players. But the art of good programming was restored by the National Theatre in 1963 which provided miniature booklets containing a wealth of background information. In America the admirable *Playbill* programme is distributed free of charge to all Broadway playgoers. In France the programme is also regarded as an art-form: the Renaud-Barrault Company have long distributed miniature books, often complete with play-texts.

The first theatre magazine was *The Muses Mercury* published by Andrew Bell, London in January 1707.

The first theatre matinée was given at Mitchell's Olympic Theatre, New York on 25 December 1843.

The largest number of theatres under one roof is at the New York Public Theater (opened 1967) which contains seven separate auditoria. Housed in the former Astor Library, it is under the direction of Joseph Papp. The musicals *Hair* (1967) and *A Chorus Line* (1975) both started their lives there.

The largest open-air theatre in Europe is at Scarborough, North Yorkshire. It opened in 1932 with a seating capacity of 7000 plus standing room for 9000 and a 182ft (55m) long stage. Productions continued there annually until 1968 and resumed, after a 14-year lapse, in 1982 with *Magical Musical Time Machine*.

NUMBER OF THEATRES IN UK

The British Theatre Directory (1981) lists the following numbers of theatres:

London: (including the boroughs): 93
London: (smaller club and lunchtime theatres): 45
Provinces: (including cinemas presenting live shows): 363
Amateur theatres: 36
Arts Centres (including drama in their programme): 170

PRINCIPAL THEATRE MUSEUMS AND RESEARCH CENTRES

UK

British Drama League, London, W1: Large theatrical library containing over 70 000 volumes, including many play-sets.

London Theatre Museum: Due to open in Covent Garden Flower Market in 1983. Collection housed meanwhile in Victoria and Albert Museum.

Mander and Mitchenson Theatre Collection, London, SE26: Vast private collection open to inspection by bona fide researchers.

Public Library Reference Dept, Birmingham: One of the most important Shakespeare collections anywhere including five first folios and nine quartos.

Shakespeare Institute, Stratford-upon-Avon: Memorial Theatre archives from 1874, and over 7000 volumes of Shakespeareana.

Society for Theatre Research, London, NW8: Specialist organisation publishing its own journal and pamphlets.

Victoria and Albert Museum, London, SW7: Large collection of playbills, programmes, engravings, cuttings, etc.

Westminster Central Reference Library, London, WC2: Comprehensive collection of theatre books.

USA

Folger Shakespeare Library, Washington: Includes 75 copies of the first folios of Shakespeare's plays.

Harvard College Library Theater Collection, Cambridge, Mass: More than a million playbills and programmes.

Lincoln Center Library of the Performing Arts, New York: Books, programmes, etc.

University of Texas Theater Library Collection, Austin, Texas.

FRANCE

Archives et Musée de la Comédie Française, Paris.
Bibliothèque Nationale, Paris.

GERMANY

Preussische Staatsbibliothek, Berlin.
The Theatre Museum, Munich.

USSR

Leningrad State Theatre Museum and Theatrical Library, Moscow.
Museum of the Moscow Arts Theatre, Moscow.
Museum of the Moscow State Kamerny Theatre Leningrad, Moscow.

CHAPTER 3

Actors and Actresses

The first known actor is Thespis, poet, playwright and chorus leader who won the first Athenian drama competition in 534 BC.

The most famous actor in Ancient Rome was Quintus Roscius (d.62 BC). He specialised in comic roles (Cicero delivered on his behalf a speech, *Pro Roscio Comedo*) and was renowned for his care in rehearsing every gesture before he used it on stage. He was highly paid and at his peak was said to command an annual income equalling half a million pounds sterling. His name became the symbol of acting perfection so that later generations produced the African Roscius, the Ohio Roscius, the Scottish Roscius and the Young Roscius.

The most famous of the minstrels, who kept the European acting tradition alive in the Middle Ages, was Rahare (d.1144). He was chief minstrel to Henry I of England and when he retired had enough money to found the great priory of St. Bartholomew of which he became the first head.

The full-time professional actor re-emerged in Europe in the 16th century with the rise of vernacular drama. In Spain, Lope de Rueda (1505-65) became **the first popular actor** being especially admired for his interpretation of pimps, fools and black women. In Italy, Francesco Andreini (1548-1624) and his wife, Isabella, became **the world's first married acting duo** as leaders of the Gelosi, a touring **commedia dell'Arte** company. In England, Richard Burbage (1567-1619) became **Elizabethan theatre's first star**. In France, Montdory (1594-1651) was **the first name actor**, playing Rodrigue in Corneille's *Le Cid*. He suffered paralysis of the tongue while performing before Cardinal Richelieu and spent the next 14 years in silence. During the Renaissance the actor became an identifiable figure. Since then each country has produced its own continuous list of star performers.

UK and Ireland

EDWARD ALLEYN (1566-1626) Burbage's chief rival, the creator of Christopher Marlowe's *Tamburlaine* (1587) and *Dr Faustus* (1589), manager of the Rose Theatre, son-in-law of theatrical manager, Philip Henslowe, and the founder of Dulwich College.

RICHARD BURBAGE (1567-1619) **The first great English actor**. The first to play Hamlet, Lear, Othello, Richard III. His father, James, built the first permanent playhouse in London, the Theatre. Richard started his acting career in 1584 with the Admiral's Men and appeared at the Globe Theatre under the management of his elder brother, Cuthbert. On his death, Richard Flecknoe wrote some lines of verse that ran: "No more young Hamlet, old Hieronymo; King Lear, the grieved Moor, and more beside, that lived in him, have now for ever died."

WILLIAM KEMPE (d.1608) The principal clown in Shakespeare's early plays, playing Dogberry, Peter in *Romeo and Juliet*, Shallow in *Henry IV*. He became celebrated for a long-distance Morris dance from London to Norwich

The loneliness of the long-distance Morris dancer: William Kempe, Elizabethan clown, doing his famous dance from London to Norwich.

in 1599 spending nine days dancing and 14 days resting. The feat was celebrated in a book, *Kemp's Nine Daies Wonder*, which gave a new phrase to the English language.

THOMAS BETTERTON (1635-1710) The most famous actor and theatrical manager of Restoration times. Appeared in a play by Sir Thomas Davenant, *Love and Honour*, in 1661, 'the King giving Mr Betterton his Coronation Suit in which he acted the part of Prince Alvaro'. In December 1661, he played Hamlet for the first time. Barton Booth, playing the Ghost, declared that 'instead of my awing him, he terrified me'. Samuel Pepys

Richard Burbage: the first great English actor. As someone says in Jonson's 'Bartholomew Fair': "Which is your Burbage now? . . . your best actor?"

wrote that 'he did the Prince's part beyond imagination'. He continued to play Hamlet until he was 70, making him **the oldest of all time.** Because of his dignity and fame he was **the first actor to be buried inside Westminster Abbey.**

EDWARD KYNASTON (1640-1706) The best-known female impersonator of the Restoration stage. Since not enough women could be found and trained for the stage immediately, men continued for a time to play female roles. Kynaston so fascinated the ladies of quality that he used to be collected by them after a performance and, still in costume, driven through Hyde Park for all to see. His greatest triumph was in Ben Jonson's *Epicoene* where Pepys found him 'clearly the prettiest woman in the whole house'.

MARGARET HUGHES (1643-1719) **The first professional actress on the English stage.** On 3 December 1660 at a converted tennis court called the Vere Street Theatre she appeared as Desdemona in *The Moor of Venice*, Thomas Killigrew's version of *Othello*. The audience was told during a prologue that she would appear and during an epilogue was asked: 'And how do you like her?' The applause that followed guaranteed the place of actresses on the English stage.

Thomas Betterton: the leading figure of the Restoration stage, equally admired as Hamlet and Sir Toby Belch.

James Quin: a declamatory actor and shining star ultimately eclipsed by Garrick.

JAMES QUIN (1693-1766) A fat, quarrelsome actor (said to have the deaths of two colleagues to his credit) who embodied the declamatory style of acting. A portrait of him as Coriolanus in James Thomson's tragedy displays him in plumed helmet, full periwig and wide skirt.

DAVID GARRICK (1717-79) **The first great English naturalistic actor** and a pioneering manager of Drury Lane from 1747 to 1776. He made a sensational acting debut at Goodman's Fields Theatre in London's East End on 19 October 1741 as Richard III. A week later Alexander Pope drove up from Twickenham to see the new sensation and found 'the coaches of the nobility filled up the space between Temple Bar and Whitechapel'. Garrick achieved success in both comedy (as Benedick and Abel Drugger in *The Alchemist*) and tragedy (as Hamlet, Lear, Macbeth). When Boswell asked Dr Johnson if he would not start like Garrick if he saw a ghost, Dr Johnson replied: 'I hope not — if I did, I should frighten the Ghost'. When, in the role of Macbeth, Garrick told the actor playing First Murderer, 'There's blood upon thy face' the observation had such urgency, the actor in question replied, 'Is there, by God?'.

As manager of Drury Lane Theatre Garrick introduced many technical innovations. He reduced the scale of the apron stage to accommodate more spectators. He illuminated the darker recesses of the stage by removing hoop-shaped, candle-filled chandeliers from the front to the back. He banished the snobs of high society from their privileged seats on stage. (One actress, Mrs Cibber, had been forced to play the death scene in *Romeo and Juliet* with 100 or so people with her in the tomb.) But Garrick still had to cope with disturbances. In 1755 there was a riot in the theatre when French dancers appeared in a ballet, *The Chinese Festival* just as war between England and France was about to break out. He remained a great actor, pioneering manager and competent author of some 40 plays. Dr Johnson's epitaph on Garrick: 'I am disappointed by that stroke of death which has eclipsed the gaiety of nations and impoverished the public stock of harmless pleasure'.

SARAH SIDDONS (1755-1831) **The most famous English tragic actress** and a great innovator. Born into a theatrical family (her brother was John Philip Kemble) she conquered Drury Lane at her second attempt in 1782 and stayed there for the next 27 years. Her most famous role was Lady Macbeth and her greatest innovation was to depart with tradition by laying down the candle and washing her hands with water from an imaginary ewer. Asked to describe the effect of her playing, dramatist Sheridan Knowles replied, 'Well, sir, I smelt blood. I swear that I smelt blood'. As Katherine in *Henry VIII* she so terrified the actor playing the Duke of Buckingham's surveyor that he declared he would not for the world face her again before the footlights. But she also used her power constructively. She was the first woman to discard the powdered hair and hooped skirts of the time as well as the beplumed headdresses that were the mark of the tragic actress: she favoured costumes of simple shape and cleanly draped headdresses. She made her farewell appearance on 29 June 1812 playing Lady Macbeth.

EDMUND KEAN (1787-1833) Prototype of the self-destructive, romantic actor. Illegitimate, abandoned by his mother, found and cared for by stage people, he lived the life of a strolling player till his sensational London debut on 26 January 1814 at Drury Lane as Shylock. Tradition dictated the character be played in a comedian's red beard and wig: Kean's Shylock was a

Above: David Garrick as Richard III: the role in which he caused a sensation at Goodman's Fields on 19 October 1741.

Right: Sarah Siddons, the great English actress, as Lady Macbeth in 1784. "She was tragedy personified", wrote William Hazlitt. "To have seen Mrs Siddons was an event in everyone's life."

swarthy figure in a black beard and 'the look of a man who asserts his claim to suffer as one of a race of sufferers'. He went on to triumph as Richard III, Othello, Lear and Sir Giles Over-reach in *A New Way To Pay Old Debts*. His career was interrupted by scandal when in March 1824 his affair with Alderman Cox's wife became known. *The Times* thundered calling him 'this obscene little personage'. Kean departed for America for a year but when he reappeared

Edmund Kean as the frenzied miser, Sir Giles Over-reach, in 'A New Way To Pay Old Debts', 1818.

at Drury Lane in 1827 his power and memory had gone. He collapsed on stage while playing Othello to his son, Charles Kean's, Iago, and he died shortly after. 'If he was irregular and unartist-like in his performance', said Fanny Kemble, 'so is Niagara compared with the waterworks of Versailles'.

WILLIAM BETTY (1791-1874) Known as Master Betty or the Young Roscius, he was a child prodigy who took London by storm from 1804 to 1805. On the night he played Hamlet (14 March 1805), William Pitt, First Minister adjourned the House of Commons so that its members could attend the performance: the only time the House has adjourned to watch other people act. 'The town is mad', wrote William Blake the following month, and within the year

the tide turned to such an extent that Master Betty was hissed off the stage during a performance of *Richard III*. He soon vanished but he bred a rash of imitators including the Infant Billington (a precocious girl singer) and Miss Mudie, an 8-year-old whose appearance in adult roles, as mistress and wife, in the words of James Roose-Evans, **'set an all-time record for absurdity in the annals of theatre history'**.

WILLIAM CHARLES MACREADY (1792-1873) Famous tragic actor (he was known as 'the eminent tragedian') who tried to combine the classic art of John Philip Kemble with the impulsive intensity of Kean. A notable Hamlet, Lear, Macbeth. Less successful as Othello when he was compared to 'an elderly negress of evil

William Henry West Betty ("Master Betty"): a child actor who had a brief meteoric success from 1804 to 1805. One of a rash of infant prodigies and prodigious infants.

William Macready delivering his farewell address at the Drury Lane Theatre on 26 February 1851, after his final appearance, playing Macbeth.

November 1871 as a guilt-stricken Alsatian burgomaster in *The Bells:* a role he was to perform over 800 times. He took over management of the Lyceum in December 1878 and reigned supreme there until 1899, playing in Shakespeare, melodramas and historical plays by Tennyson, Boucicault and Bulwer-Lytton. As a manager, he **introduced the blackout during which scenery could be changed unseen by the audience;** commissioned many of the leading painters of the day, such as Burne-Jones and Alma Tadema, and scenic designers; and employed a larger team than the modern National Theatre. There were 600 people working at the Lyceum, including 40 musicians, 60 gas and limelight men, 60 carpenters, 250 extras and supers, 40 artists in the property room. Irving died at Bradford on 13 October 1905 during a tour of Tennyson's *Becket*. His last words on the stage were 'Into thy hands, oh Lord, into thy hands'. He died penniless having earned over 2 million pounds during his career.

ELLEN TERRY (1847-1928) Distinguished English actress famed for her partnership, on and off stage, with Irving. First played opposite him in 1878: highly successful as Ophelia, Portia,

"Take the rope from my neck": Henry Irving in one of his greatest roles, Mathias in 'The Bells', first seen in November 1871.

repute, going to a fancy-dress ball'. As manager of both Drury Lane and Covent Garden, he restored many of Shakespeare's original texts, insisted that rehearsals be thorough, all parts equally well-played and that the production aim at a unified effect. After a final appearance as Macbeth at Drury Lane in 1851, this most reluctant actor retired to Cheltenham.

SAMUEL PHELPS (1804-78) The most ardent 19th-century champion of Shakespeare. While actor-manager-boss of Sadler's Wells (1843-62) he presented 34 of Shakespeare's plays over an 18-year span giving 4000 separate performances: the most comprehensive Shakespearean repertoire until the Old Vic in 1923 presented the complete cycle. He was also adept at stagecraft. In *Henry V* he had a march-past with 40 supers filing behind a chest-high rock. Each soldier had strapped to his body two wickerwork dummies in armour, the heads modelled by Madame Tussauds, so that the soldiers appeared to be marching three abreast.

HENRY IRVING (1838-1905) **First English actor to be knighted** (May 1895): dominant figure of the last 30 years of the century. Made his London debut in 1866 in *The Belle's Stratagem* but scored his great triumph at the Lyceum in

Mrs Patrick Campbell in Pinero's 'The Notorious Mrs Ebbsmith' at the Garrick in 1895.

Night Malvolio was followed by four miniature Malvolios; and in *Richard II* the king was accompanied by a dog who, during the deposition scene, turned from Richard to lick the hand of Bolingbroke. Presented 18 of Shakespeare's plays at Her Majesty's between 1881 and 1914 as well as the first production of *Pygmalion* in 1913. Was knighted by Edward VII in 1909 for significant accomplishments in the theatre.

MRS PATRICK CAMPBELL (1865-1940) Famous actress and caustic wit. Created the roles of Paula in *The Second Mrs Tanqueray* (1893) and Agnes in *The Notorious Mrs Ebbsmith* (1895), both by Pinero, and of Eliza Doolittle in Shaw's *Pygmalion* (1914). Went to live in America in her later, declining years but her tongue lost none of its sharpness. She said of one American actress: 'She has a Siamese forehead and a mouth like a golosh'. Critic Alexander Woollcott dubbed her 'A sinking ship firing upon her rescuers'.

SYBIL THORNDIKE (1882-1976) Fine tragic actress involved in many of the key movements of 20th-century theatre. Joined the first English repertory company under Miss Horniman at the

Sybil Thorndike as Volumnia with Laurence Olivier as Coriolanus in 'Coriolanus' at the Old Vic in 1938.

Beatrice, Olivia. Also made an impact in less taxing roles: when she played Henrietta Maria to Irving's Charles I, Oscar Wilde described her as 'like some wan lily overdrenched with rain'. Left Irving's company in 1902, managed the Imperial Theatre for some time, in 1906 created the part of Lady Cicely Waynflete in Shaw's *Captain Brassbound's Conversion*, in 1908 wrote an excellent autobiography, *The Story of My Life*.

HERBERT BEERBOHM TREE (1853-1917) Actor-manager, half brother of Max Beerbohm, founder of the Royal Academy of Dramatic Art, lecturer and author. In 1897 opened his own theatre, Her Majesty's, where he carried on the Irving tradition of lavish productions of Shakespeare. In *A Midsummer Night's Dream* live rabbits ran across the stage; in *Twelfth*

Gaiety Theatre, Manchester in 1908. Member of the Old Vic company under Lilian Baylis from 1914 to 1918. Created the role of Shaw's *Saint Joan* on 26 March 1924: her Joan was, in James Agate's words, 'boyish, brusque, inspired, exalted, mannerless, tactless and obviously, once she had served her turn, a nuisance to everybody'. She played Saint Joan for 244 performances at the New Theatre and for another 321 at the Regent's Theatre King's Cross: **the longest run ever enjoyed by any Shaw play.** She toured mining towns with the Old Vic company during the Second World War, appeared in the first season at the Chichester Festival Theatre in 1962, had a theatre named after her (the Thorndike, Leatherhead) in 1969 and made her last stage appearance at Covent Garden in 1973 in *A Fanfare for Europe*. Her ashes were buried in Westminster Abbey — the first English player to be so honoured since Irving.

EDITH EVANS (1888-1976) Famously stylish English actress. Made her debut in 1912 as Cressida, achieved fame in 1924 with her performance as Millamant in Congreve's *The Way of the World* at the Lyric, Hammersmith. For Shaw she created the parts of The Serpent and the She-Ancient in *Back to Methuselah* (1924) and Orinthia in *The Apple Cart* (1929). Was most identified in the public mind with Lady Bracknell which she played in 1939 at the Globe, in 1942 at the Phoenix and again in 1951 on film. Her most famous Shakespearean role was as the Nurse in the Olivier/Gielgud *Romeo and Juliet* at the New Theatre in 1935. W.A. Darlington described her thus: 'As earthy as a potato, as slow as a carthorse, and as cunning as a badger'.

RALPH RICHARDSON (1902-) Robust eccentric with a particular talent for jaunty sadness and ebullient despair. Stage debut in Brighton in 1921 as Lorenzo in *The Merchant of Venice*. At the reopening of Sadler's Wells in 1931 played Sir Toby Belch and subsequently Faulconbridge, Petruchio and Bottom ('a Bottom who had spent a night in Mahomet's paradise and would not forget it' wrote Robert Speaight). But Richardson's greatest successes have been in plays by living writers: notably Priestley's *Johnson Over Jordan* (1939), Bolt's *Flowering Cherry* (1957), Greene's *The Complaisant Lover* (1959), Storey's *Home* (1970) and Pinter's *No Man's Land* (1975). Famed private habits include arriving at the

Edith Evans as Josephine 'Napoleon's Josephine' at the Fortune Theatre, 1928.

stage-door on a motor-bike well into his late 70s, at one time accompanied by a parrot on his left shoulder.

JOHN GIELGUD (1904-) Classic actor with distinguished theatrical lineage: grand-nephew of Ellen Terry. First appeared on stage at the Old Vic in 1921 as the Herald in *Henry V*. Joined the Old Vic again in 1929 playing Romeo, Richard II, Mark Antony, Macbeth and Hamlet. Played Hamlet again at the Queen's in 1930, at the New in 1934, at the Empire, New York in 1936, at the Lyceum and at Elsinore in 1939, at the Haymarket in 1944. His 1934 production ran for 155 consecutive performances beating all the records for a Hamlet run since Henry Irving; his 1936 Hamlet broke both John E. Kellard's and Barrymore's record for continuous performances in New York with a total of 101. ('Hamlet', he has since said, 'is not a role that an actor should ever be asked to portray for a hundred performances on end'). Gielgud's greatest achievements have been in Shakespeare (not least as Lear, Cassius and Prospero) as well as in Wilde, Congreve and Chekhov and in recent years he has appeared with Richardson, to great acclaim, in Storey's *Home* and Pinter's *No Man's Land*. He was knighted in 1953.

LAURENCE OLIVIER (1907-) Most famous English actor of his time. Knighted in 1947. Created Baron in 1970 making him **the first theatrical lord.** The son of a clergyman, his talent was first spotted when he was a schoolboy. Ellen Terry saw him at All Saints School, Marylebone in 1917 and noted in her diary: 'The small boy who played Brutus is already a great actor'. Made his professional debut as Lennox in Macbeth in 1924, joined the Birmingham Repertory Company in 1926 and from the late 1920s became a West End leading man creating the roles of Stanhope in *Journey's End* (1928) and the hero of *Beau Geste* (1929). He alternated Romeo and Mercutio with Gielgud at the New Theatre in 1935 and played Hamlet for the first time at the Old Vic in 1937 ('the best performance of Hotspur the present generation has seen', wrote Agate). In May 1937 the Old Vic *Hamlet* was invited to play at Kronborg Castle in Elsinore: the first time an English company had played there since 1585. Rain bucketed down on the opening night and the production was transferred to a local hotel ballroom on a hastily improvised stage.

In 1944 Olivier was appointed co-director of the Old Vic with Ralph Richardson and John Burrell. Their seasons at the New Theatre from 1944 to 1946 are part of theatrical legend with Olivier playing Richard III, Astrov in *Uncle Vanya*, Hotspur and Justice Shallow and a double-bill of *Oedipus Rex* and *The Critic*. In 1955 Olivier returned to Stratford-upon-Avon for the first time since his schooldays and triumphed as Macbeth, Titus Andronicus and Malvolio. In 1961 he was appointed director of the Chichester Festival Theatre in Sussex (the first large, open-stage theatre to be built in Britain) and in 1962 became director of the National Theatre Company at the Old Vic. He directed the company's first production in October 1963, *Hamlet* with Peter O'Toole. His major roles with the company were Othello, Solness in *The Master Builder*, Captain Edgar in *The Dance of Death*, Shylock and James Tyrone in *Long Day's Journey Into Night*. He relinquished his post as director in 1973 making his last appearance with the company in Trevor Griffiths's *The Party*. He has combined non-stop stage activity with a flourishing career as a film actor and director and has also produced plays for both stage and television. In the theatre, he has conquered all the major tragic roles (Hamlet, Lear, Macbeth, Othello), has created many new characters (most famously, Archie Rice in John Osborne's *The Entertainer* in 1957) and has repeatedly shown himself to be a great comic actor. No actor before him has ever triumphed in such a wide diversity of roles or created so much history.

PEGGY ASHCROFT (1907-) Created Dame in 1956 for services to theatre and in 1962 had a theatre named after her in Croydon where she was born. Has played every major Shakespearean heroine (Cleopatra, Juliet, Viola, Imogen, Beatrice, Rosalind, Ophelia, Desdemona) with the striking exception of Lady Macbeth. Has also played with every major permanent company in England over the last half-century: with Gielgud in his seasons at the Queen's in 1937-38, with the Shakespeare Memorial Theatre at Stratford in 1953 and 1957, with the Old Vic at its reopening in 1950, with the Royal Court in 1956, with the newly-formed Royal Shakespeare Company (she played the title-role in *The Duchess at Malfi* at the Aldwych in 1960) and with the National Theatre where she became the first player to appear in the new building at a matinée performance of Beckett's *Happy Days* at the Lyttelton in March 1976.

Laurence Olivier as Richard III in the Old Vic season at the New Theatre, 1944. "In this Richard", wrote Kenneth Tynan, "was enshrined Blake's conception of active, energetic evil in all its wicked richness".

MICHAEL REDGRAVE (1908-) A star actor, knighted in 1959, whose career has been plagued by ill-health in later years. Made his first London appearance at the Old Vic in 1936 as Ferdinand in *The Tempest* and immediately became a lead actor playing Orlando in *As You Like It* and Laertes to Olivier's Hamlet. He himself played Hamlet with the Old Vic Company in 1950 and again at Stratford in 1958 making him, as Kenneth Tynan observed, 'the oldest Hamlet seen in England since 1938 when Esmé Beringer struck a glancing blow for feminism by playing the part in her 64th summer'. He appeared in the National Theatre's opening season at the Old Vic and in 1965 became director of the Yvonne Arnaud Theatre, Guildford's initial festival. His wife, Rachel Kempson, and their three children, Vanessa, Corin and Lynn, are all distinctive performers.

CYRIL CUSACK (1910-) Most famous living Irish actor. Made debut at age of 7 as Willie Carlyle in a touring production of *East Lynne*. Joined the Abbey Theatre, Dublin in 1932 and appeared in 65 of its productions. First appeared in London in 1936 as Richard in *Ah Wilderness* at the Westminster Theatre. Appeared in the first International Drama Festival at the Sarah Bernhardt Theatre, Paris, 1954 in *The Playboy of the Western World*. Worked with the RSC in London and Stratford 1963-64 and with the National Theatre in London 1974-77 where his Fluther Good in *The Plough and the Stars* (1977) was a miracle of priestly gentleness and charm.

PAUL SCOFIELD (1922-) Memorably haggard and distinctive actor who progressed from Birmingham Repertory Theatre to the Shakespeare Memorial Theatre in the mid 1940s often directed by Peter Brook. In 1955, as Hamlet, **he headed the first English company to tour post-revolutionary Russia.** Also played the title role in *King Lear* for Brook at Stratford in 1962 and subsequently in London and throughout Eastern Europe. Joined the National Theatre for the first time in 1971 to play in *The Captain of Kopenick* and since then has played Volpone, Othello, Salieri in *Amadeus* and Don Quixote.

DOROTHY TUTIN (1930-) Diminutive, fetching, emotionally powerful English actress who has played most of Shakespeare's main heroines. Made her debut in 1949; joined the Old Vic in 1950; played the affected Sally Bowles in *I Am a Camera* (1954). Founder-member of the RSC for whom she played Portia, Viola, Cressida (all 1960), Juliet (1961), Rosalind (1967). Also played Cleopatra for Prospect (1977) and Lady Macbeth for National Theatre (1978).

JUDI DENCH (1934-) Husky-voiced actress who brings heartbreak to comedy and a sense of lightness to tragedy. Made her debut as Ophelia in *Hamlet* with Old Vic (1957). A famous Old Vic Juliet in 1960 bursting with adolescent passion. Joined the RSC in 1961 to play in *The Cherry Orchard* and has also appeared with them as Viola and Hermione/Perdita in *The Winter's Tale* (the first actress to double these mother/daughter roles since Mary Anderson in 1887) in 1969 and as Beatrice and Lady Macbeth in 1976. Has also appeared in musicals: played Sally Bowles in *Cabaret* (with a voice like fractured glass) in 1968 and Miss Trant in *The Good Companions* (1975).

MAGGIE SMITH (1934-) Graduate from comedy and revue to major tragic roles: as sensitive as a thoroughbred. Made her professional debut in New York in 1956 in the New Faces '56 Revue. Joined the Old Vic in 1959, the National Theatre in 1963 for whom she played Hilde Wangel (1964), Beatrice and Miss Julie (1965), Hedda Gabler (1970). In the West End was Amanda in *Private Lives* (1972). Joined the Stratford Ontario company in 1976 to play Cleopatra, Millamant and Masha and stayed for several seasons adding to her roles Titania (1977), Lady Macbeth (1978) Rosalind, and Virginia Woolf in Edna O'Brien's *Virginia* (1980).

ALBERT FINNEY (1936-) Muscular, virile, stage-dominating actor who has lately divided his time between theatre and cinema. Made his debut in 1956 at Birmingham Rep. First appeared in London with Charles Laughton in 1958 in *The Party*. Created the title-role in *Billy Liar* (1960) and in Osborne's *Luther* (1961). Joined the National Theatre in 1965 playing the leads in Armstrong's *Last Goodnight, Miss Julie* and *Black Comedy*. Appeared at Royal Court (where he was associate artistic director 1972-75) in *Alpha Beta* (1972), *Krapp's Last Tape* (1973), *Cromwell* (1973). Rejoined the National Theatre in 1975 and officially christened the new South Bank complex in May 1976 in *Hamlet* in the Lyttelton Theatre. Played title-role in Marlowe's

Tamburlaine the Great in the opening production of the Olivier Theatre (October 1976).

ALAN HOWARD (1937-) The first actor to play the protagonist in each part of Shakespeare's seven-play history cycle. For the Royal Shakespeare Company he has played Richard II (1980), Prince Hal (1975), Henry V (1975), Henry VI (1977) and Richard III (1980). Also enjoyed great success as the actor, Rover, in the RSC production of John O'Keefe's *Wild Oats* (1976) a part that his great-grandfather, Edward Compton, played in Stratford-upon-Avon in 1882.

IAN McKELLEN (1938-) Star-player of his generation: also dedicated company-man. Made his professional debut in Coventry in 1961.

Above: Albert Finney as Luther (with Julian Glover as the Knight) in a scene from John Osborne's 'Luther' at the Royal Court, 1961.

Right: Maggie Smith (with Patricia Conolly) as Virginia Woolf in Edna O'Brien's 'Virginia' at the Haymarket, London 1981: a glittering performance that won her 'The Standard's' Award as Best Actress.

Played Aufidius in opening production of *Coriolanus* at Nottingham Playhouse (1963). Lead roles in London in *A Lily In Little India* (1965), *Their Very Own and Golden City* (1966), *The Promise* (1967). Did a famous double of Shakespeare's *Richard II* and Marlowe's *Edward II* (Edinburgh 1969. London 1969-70). Founder-member of the Actors Company (1972). Joined the Royal Shakespeare Company (1974) and played Dr Faustus (1974), Romeo, Leontes and Macbeth (1976), Face in *The Alchemist* (1977). Led a small-scale RSC touring company round the UK in *Twelfth Night* and *Three Sisters* in 1978. Played Salieri in *Amadeus* in New York (1980) for which he won a Tony Award.

America

LOUISA LANE DREW (1820-97) Actress-manager and **the first woman to run an important theater in America** (the Arch Street Theatre, Philadelphia which she took over in 1861). Started out as a child actress playing adult roles like Dr Pangloss in Voltaire's *Candide*. Married actor John Drew in 1850 and became mother of two fine actors as well as grandmother of Lionel, Ethel and John Barrymore. Ran her own theatre from 1861, appeared with many of the leading actors of the day (including Edwin Booth and the Irish comedian, Tyrone Power) and was expert in all branches of the business: said to be as good a carpenter as any who worked for her.

Edwin Booth, one of the first great American actors and the first to win a European reputation. His brother, John Wilkes Booth, assassinated President Lincoln.

EDWIN BOOTH (1833-93) Refined American tragic actor. Son of Junius Brutus Booth and brother of John Wilkes Booth who in 1865 assassinated President Lincoln in Washington DC during a performance of *Our American Cousin*. In 1869 Edwin opened the Booth Theater in New York at a cost of a million dollars and used it as a showcase for his Othello, Hamlet, Macbeth and Romeo. Was bankrupted in 1873 by the theatre's failure, took to the road again as a touring actor and in 1880 on his third visit to England alternated the roles of Othello and Iago with Irving at the Lyceum. Lewis Strang called him 'the foremost poet of his profession'.

WILLIAM GILLETTE (1855-1937) Actor-playwright whose two most popular plays were *Secret Service* (1896), a civil war melodrama, and *Sherlock Holmes* (1899), adapted with the blessing of Conan Doyle. He played Sherlock Holmes over a period of 36 years from its opening in New York to a radio broadcast in 1935 when he was 80. The play's success enabled him to build the million-dollar Gillette Castle in Hadlyme, Connecticut complete with its own miniature railway.

RICHARD MANSFIELD (1857-1907) German-born American actor who made his name in romantic works such as *Cyrano de Bergerac* (1898), and *Beau Brummell* (1890). Presented **the first Shaw production in America,** *Arms and the Man*, which ran for 16 performances, and played Dick Dudgeon in *The Devil's Disciple* (1896). Famous for his violent temper (he kicked an actor savagely when playing *Dr Jekyll and Mr Hyde*) and his melodramatic power. It was said 'there are good actors, bad actors and there is Richard Mansfield'.

JOHN BARRYMORE (1882-1942) The most gifted and least disciplined of the three Barrymores. Made his debut with sister Ethel in *Captain Jinks of the Horse Marines* (1901) when a member of the cast had to leave at short notice. Established a reputation as a serious actor as the cockney bank clerk in Galsworthy's *Justice* (1916), in *Peter Ibbetson* (1917) and *The Jest* (1919) in which he played an effeminate young poet — a role usually played by a woman. *Richard III* (1920) and *Hamlet* (1922), in which introduced the Oedipus complex between Hamlet and Gertrude, established him as the greatest living American actor. He than abandoned the stage for Hollywood returning only in 1939 in the travesty, *My Dear Children*, which burlesqued his own career as a legendary toper and womaniser. It was, according to Lloyd Lewis, 'a spiritual striptease with Barrymore himself as a sort of Gypsy Rose John'.

THE LUNTS Alfred Lunt (1893-1977) and Lynn Fontanne (1887-) were **the American theatre's most famous married couple.** They first appeared on stage together at the National Theater, Washington DC in *Made For Money* (1919). They were married in 1924 and their appearance that year in Molnar's *The Guardsman* marks the beginning of a stage partnership that involved them in some 30 productions: these included Sherwood's *Reunion in Vienna* (1931), Coward's *Design For Living* (1933), *The Taming of the Shrew* (1935), *Amphitryon 38* adapted by S.N. Behrman (1938) and Durrenmatt's savage parable, *The Visit* (1958) which opened the newly-renamed Lunt-Fontanne Theater in New York. Robert Sherwood, who provided three of their hit plays, once wrote: 'With their vanity which is blatantly, defiantly phony, the Lunts combine a humility which is real. They consider themselves always on trial.'

KATHARINE CORNELL (1898-1974) Legendary actress who, along with Helen Hayes, dominated American stage between the two world wars. Her most famous roles were in *The Green Hat* (1925), *The Barretts of Wimpole*

Lynn Fontanne, Noel Coward and Alfred Lunt in the 1933 New York production of Coward's 'Design for Living'.

Street (1931), *Romeo and Juliet* (1934), *The Doctor's Dilemma* (1941): all directed by her husband, Guthrie McClintic. She had an insatiable appetite for touring: in the 1933-34 season she went on a three-play tour of Shaw, Shakespeare and *The Barretts of Wimpole Street* that covered 74 cities and that played to half-a-million people.

Katharine Cornell as the bedridden Elizabeth Barrett in the 1931 New York production of 'The Barretts of Wimpole Street'.

Helen Hayes as Queen Victoria in Laurence Houseman's 'Victoria Regina' at the Broadhurst Theater New York 1935. Because of censorship problems the play was not given its first British public performance until 21 June 1937, the 100th anniversary of the Queen's Coronation.

PAUL ROBESON (1898-1976) Black actor of great vocal power: led the way for many others by playing major roles. Born in Princeton, NJ, the son of a former slave, he made his debut in a Harlem YWCA production of *Simon the Cyrenian* (1920). Appeared in New York in *Taboo* (1922) directed by Augustin Duncan, brother of Isadora. Later that year made his London debut in the same play, now retitled *Voodoo*, with Mrs Patrick Campbell. Appeared in 1924 in New York in O'Neill's play about miscegenation, *All God's Chillun Got Wings*: members of the cast were threatened by the Ku-Klux-Klan. Appeared in London in *The Emperor Jones* (1925), *Show Boat* (1928), in which he sang 'Ol Man River' and *Othello* (1930) with Peggy Ashcroft. Played Othello in a New York Theater Guild production (1943) which ran for a record 295 performances

and again at Stratford-upon-Avon (1959). In his latter years he was, because of his unspoken Communist sympathies, virtually a prisoner in his own country unable to work and forbidden to seek work abroad.

HELEN HAYES (1900-) The second actress, after Ethel Barrymore, to give her name to a Broadway theatre: in 1955 the Fulton Theater was renamed the Helen Hayes to commemorate her 50th year on the stage. Made her stage debut at 5, her Broadway debut at 9 in the musical, *Old Dutch*, and scored great successes in *What Every Woman Knows* (1926), *Mary of Scotland* (1933) and *Victoria Regina* (1935) which ran for 969 performances.

TALLULAH BANKHEAD (1902-68) Flamboyant actress and personality who made her New York debut in 1918 but whose greatest successes came in later years: in *The Little Foxes* (1939), *The Skin of Our Teeth* (1942) and *Private Lives* (1948). Of her Cleopatra, John Mason Brown wrote: 'Miss Bankhead barged down the

Katharine Hepburn (centre stage) as Tracy Lord in Philip Barry's 'The Philadelphia Story' which gave her her first great New York stage success in 1939. She later played the role in a memorable George Cukor film.

Nile last night as Cleopatra — and sank'. Her extravagant unreliability provoked Mrs Patrick Campbell to remark: 'Tallulah is always skating on thin ice. Everyone wants to be there when it breaks.'

JESSICA TANDY (1909-) and HUME CRONYN (1911-) were married in 1942 and have the distinction of having spent more time in bed together than any other stage couple. In October 1951 they opened at the Ethel Barrymore Theater in Jan de Hartog's *The Fourposter* and played the bed-bound characters on Broadway and on tour for the next two years. In 1978 they opened in *The Gin Game* and proceeded to play countless games of gin rummy in New York, London, on tour and in Moscow.

KATHARINE HEPBURN (1909-) Durable American actress ('an anatomical honeysuckle', said George Jean Nathan) whose early Broadway performances drew critical sneers. Made her debut in *The Czarina* (1928) 'I wanted no part of her but it wasn't easy to get rid of Hepburn', said producer Edwin H. Knopf. She later appeared in *The Warrior's Husband* (1932) and *The Lake* (1933) which inspired Dorothy Parker's famous remark that 'she registered the gamut of emotions from A to B'. Her faltering career was revived by Philip Barry's *The Philadelphia Story* (1939). Other stage successes (between films) included *Without Love* (1942), *As You Like It* (1950), *The Millionairess* (1952) which marked her London debut, the musical *Coco* (1969) which played to full houses for 9 months until she left the cast, and *The West Side Waltz* (1981). 'She is that yell', a critic once wrote, 'that shriek that is simultaneous with the bell ringing at school, the bell that signifies books clapped together, pencils thrown down, and the rush into the playground for the break .

JASON ROBARDS Jr. (1922-) Has played more

Eugene O'Neill heroes than any other living actor: Hickey in *The Iceman Cometh* (1956), Jamie in *Long Day's Journey Into Night* (1956), Erie Smith in *Hughie* (1964), James Tyrone Jr. in *A Moon for the Misbegotten* (1973) James Tyrone in *Long Day's Journey Into Night* (1976), Con Melody in *A Touch of the Poet* (1977).

MARLON BRANDO (1924-) Most influential modern American actor. Made his New York debut as the 15-year-old Nels in *I Remember Mama* (1944). In 1946 appeared in *Truckline Café* by Maxwell Anderson and Shaw's *Candida* with Katharine Cornell. But his reputation rests on *A Streetcar Named Desire* (1947) which established him as a star, Tennessee Williams as a major playwright and won the Pulitzer Prize. John Mason Brown wrote: 'Surely his voice and diction in any other actor would count as liabilities. But he converts them into assets. His slurred speech and frequently their tones convey his feelings with overwhelming clarity.' He has never appeared on stage since, partially because of a flourishing movie career.

JULIE HARRIS (1925-) Winner of the most Tony (Antoinette Perry) awards as Best Actress: for her Sally Bowles in *I Am a Camera* (1952), Joan of Arc in *The Lark* (1955) *40 Carats* (1968), her Mary Todd Lincoln in *The Last of Mrs Lincoln* (1972), her solo performance as Emily Dickinson in *The Bell of Amherst* (1976).

GEORGE C. SCOTT (1927-) Played more than 150 parts in stock companies before making New York debut in 1957 in *Richard III* at the New York Shakespeare Festival. Rex Reed described him as 'the meanest Richard III ever seen by human eyes'. Other outstanding performances in *As You Like It* (1957), *The Andersonville Trial* (1959: 'His eyes rove in a manner that recalls the German silent screen and his profile has the steely prehensile outline of an invariably victorious bottle-opener' wrote Kenneth Tynan), *The Three Sisters* (1965) which received a standing boo when it played in London as part of the World Theatre Season, *Plaza Suite* (1968), *Uncle Vanya* (1973), and *Death of a Salesman* (1975).

JAMES EARL JONES (1931-) Leading black actor. Made his New York debut in *Wedding in Japan* (1957). Won 1962 Obie Award for Best Actor in an off-Broadway production for his performance in *Moon on a Rainbow Shawl* (in which he appeared with his father, Robert Earl Jones). Won Tony Award in 1968 for *The Great White Hope* in which he played the first black heavyweight, Jack Johnson. Many Shakespeare roles include Oberon in *A Midsummer Night's Dream* (1961), title-role in *Othello* (1964 and again in 1981), Claudius in *Hamlet* (1972), *King Lear* (1973).

STACY KEACH (1941-) 'The finest American Hamlet since John Barrymore' according to New York critic Clive Barnes. Also the first imported American actor to appear with National Theatre in London in O'Neill's *Hughie* (1980). Made his New York debut in a minor part in New York Shakespeare Festival production of *Hamlet* (1964) in Central Park. Big success in off-Broadway production of *MacBird* (1967) which applied the *Macbeth* story to the death of Kennedy. Played Buffalo Bill in *Indians* (1969), Jamie in *Long Day's Journey Into Night* (1970), *Hamlet* (1972), Barnum in the American tour of *Barnum* (1981).

France

MADELEINE BÉJART (1618-72) **The first famous French actress** and founder with Molière of the Illustre Théâtre in Paris in 1643. Was the company's leading-lady, administrator, accountant and wardrobe mistress and, after the company found fame in Paris in 1658, played the part of the witty, down-to-earth servant girl in Molière's comedies. Was the sister (scandal and rumour suggested the mother) of Armande Béjart whom Molière unhappily married.

ARMANDE BÉJART (1642-1700) Molière's wife and creator of the *ingénue* role in all his major plays: Elmire in *Tartuffe*, Elise in *L'Avare*, Célimène in *Le Misanthrope*, Angélique in *Le Malade Imaginaire*. After her husband's death in 1673 she presided over his company with considerable ability. Joined the Comédie Française in 1680, retired from the stage in 1694.

JEAN-BAPTISTE DEBURAU (1796-1846) The first actor to embody the lonely, tortured, white-faced clown in the black skull-cap of Pierrot that is part of any mime's repertoire. Arrived in Paris in 1812, joined the Théâtre des Funambules in 1816 which was the home of acrobats and tightrope-walkers, became the star attraction at the rumbustious Boulevard du Crime which was the centre of popular entertainment in Paris. Features in several novels, plays and the film *Les Enfants du Paradis*, where he is played by Jean-Louis Barrault. His huge funeral was said to have been attended by every beggar, whore, thief and seamstress in Paris.

FRÉDÉRICK LEMAÎTRE (1800-76) Celebrated romantic actor who became famous overnight in 1823 when he parodied the role of Robert Macaire in a dull melodrama, *L'Auberge des Adrets*. Flaubert considered Macaire, who in 1834 became the hero of a new play, to be the greatest dramatic figure since Don Juan. Dumas père created for Lemaître the title role in *Kean*, a dramatic biography of the English actor.

RACHEL (1821-58) Leading tragédienne of her day. She had small features, a thin body, an overhanging brow. But, as Agate said, 'centuries of persistence were in her blood'. Through sheer will she conquered physical inadequacies to triumph as Racine's *Phèdre* (1843) and in Scribe and Legouvé's *Adrienne Lecouvreur* (1849). She toured to London in 1841 and the USA in 1855, was the model for the actress, Vashti, in Charlotte Brontë's *Villette* and was poetically praised by Matthew Arnold: 'The strife, the mixture in her soul, are ours; Her genius and her glory are her own.'

SARAH BERNHARDT (1844-1923) 'The most remarkable phenomenon of the 19th century', said Edmond de Goncourt. Made her first appearance at the Comédie Française in 1862, first appeared in London in 1879 in *Phèdre*, in 1893 took over the Théâtre de la Renaissance and renamed it the Théâtre Sarah Bernhardt. Her most famous appearances were in *La Dame aux Camélias*, *L'Aiglon*, *Lorenzaccio* and *Hamlet* as the Prince. Off-stage she was a notable painter and sculptress, in 1878 ascended in a hot-air balloon and died while making a film at the age of 79.

MADELEINE RENAUD (1903-) Leading French actress of her day. Made her debut in 1925 at the Comédie Française and played classic roles by Molière, Marivaux and Musset. Married Jean-Louis Barrault in 1940 and in 1946 founded with him the Compagnie Renaud-Barrault playing leading roles in plays by Camus, Montherlant, Beckett, Billetdoux and

Madeleine Renaud, with Jean-Louis Barrault, showing off the gown she wore in Sardou's 'Madame Sans-Gene' at the Theatre Sarah Bernhardt in 1957. It was the 50th production to be staged by the Compagnie Renaud-Barrault.

Duras. 'She is', said Tynan, 'one of the fine high comedy players of her day, an amused and witty creature whose sophistication, supple and mature, is excitingly spiced with ginger'. But she has also proved she can encompass pain and tragedy.

JEAN-LOUIS BARRAULT (1910-) A walking anthology of 20th-century theatre. Trained with Charles Dullin and the great mime, Étienne Decroux; assisted the innovatory Antonin Artaud; acted and directed at the Comédie Française from 1940 to 1946; left there to form his own company; became director of the Théâtre de l'Odéon in 1959; was sacked in May 1968 because of his sympathy with the rebellious students; and then opened the Théâtre d'Orsay in a famous, disused railway station.

GÉRARD PHILIPPE (1922-59) Romantic actor who achieved success in 1945 in the title role of Camus's *Caligula*, became a movie star and returned to the stage in 1951 to work with Jean Vilar's Théâtre National Populaire. He played leading roles in *Le Cid*, *The Prince of Homburg*, *Ruy Blas*, *Richard II* and *Lorenzaccio*. He died in his prime while preparing an eagerly anticipated Hamlet and was buried in the costume of *Le Cid*.

Germany

ALBERT BASSERMAN (1867-1952) One of the greatest actors of naturalistic theatre. Made his debut at Mannheim at age of 19. Joined Otto Brahm at the Deutsches Theater Berlin in 1899 and became outstanding German interpreter of Ibsen. Later worked under director Max Reinhardt, also in Berlin. Appeared in Shakespeare, Schiller, Goethe and famous productions of Sternheim's *Die Kassette* (1911), Sternheim's *Der Snob* (1914), and Schiller's *Wilhelm Tell* (1919). Left Germany after Hitler came to power and later went to USA where he appeared in films. Returned to Europe in 1946.

WERNER KRAUSS (1884-1959) Famous German actor with capacity to transform himself into whatever character he was playing. Made his name in a series of Wedekind plays at the Deutsches Theater, Berlin: *Der Kammersanger*, *Der Marquis von Keith*, *Lulu* (1914). Achieved international fame in 1919 in film of *Das Kabinett des Dr Caligari*. At Berlin State Theatre and Vienna Burgtheater played many Shakespeare roles in inter-war years. Was so brilliant in the title role of the Nazi version of Lion Feuchtwanger's *Jew Suss* that he was later prosecuted by an Allied tribunal. But he was always a great actor. Of his performance in Reinhard Goering's *Seeschlacht* (1918) critic Herbert Ihering wrote: 'The word was not accompanied by gesture, not amplified by movement: the word was gesture, the word became flesh. Krauss's acting was so intense that it was as though he had exchanged his senses: he saw the sound and heard the movement.'

GUSTAF GRUNDGENS (1899-1963) Great German actor and director. Achieved a dubious fame as the main source of Klaus Mann's novel, *Mephisto* (1936) later turned into a play and film, about an actor who reluctantly collaborates with the Nazi regime. Most famous role was Mephistopheles in Goethe's *Faust* which he

played from 1932 on. Appointed Intendant of Berlin National Theatre in 1934 where he acted in and directed plays by Shakespeare, Schiller, Goethe, Hebbel, etc. From 1958 to 1962 was Intendant of Deutches Schauspielhaus, Hamburg where he produced a number of important modern plays including Osborne's *The Entertainer* (1957) and Lawrence Durrell's *Sappho* (1959).

LOTTE LENYA (1900-81) Foremost interpreter of the works of Bertolt Brecht and Kurt Weill (who was also her first husband). Created the roles of the tart Jenny Smith in *Mahagonny* (1927) and Jenny in *Die Dreigroschenoper* (1928). Left Germany after Hitler's rise to power. Continued to act in New York where she played in *Barefoot in Athens* (1951), *Brecht on Brecht* (1962), *Cabaret* (1966). Also acted in films (including *From Russia With Love*, 1963) and left behind many recordings in her incomparably astringent voice.

HELENE WEIGEL (1900-71) Famous German actress and wife of Bertolt Brecht from 1928 to his death in 1956. Left Germany with her husband in 1933, returned from USA in 1948, became head of the Berliner Ensemble in 1949 where her roles included *Mutter Courage*: (1949), *Die Mutter* (1951), Volumnia in Brecht's *Coriolan* (1964). Said Tynan of her performance in *Mutter Courage*: 'She is never allowed to become a bawdy and flamboyant old darling: her performance is casual and ascetic: we are to observe her but not to embrace her.'

MARTIN HELD (1908-) Doyen of modern German actors. First success came in Berlin in Hauptmann's *Der Biberpelz* (1951) and Schiller's *Maria Stuart* (1952). Played in Beckett's own production of *Krapp's Last Tape* (1969) at the Berlin Schillertheater and on tour throughout Europe.

EKKEHARD SCHALL (1930-) Short, bullet-headed German actor with a remarkable quality of manic fury. Joined the Berliner Ensemble in 1952 where he became one of that company's leading actors. His many creations for them include the leads in Brecht's *Arturo Ui* (1959), *Die Tage der Kommune* (1962), *Coriolan* (1964), and *Galileo* (1979). Paradoxically, he is a great star in a famous ensemble.

Cross-dressing

Cross-dressing (or transvestism) has a notable place in acting going back to the Shakespearean heroines played by Elizabethan boys. Famous examples include:

Edward Kynaston (1640-1706) his success in Jonson and Restoration Comedy led critics to ask 'whether any woman that succeeded him so sensibly touched the audience as he'.

Mrs Verbruggen (1667-1703) popular in male roles though she had 'thick legs and thighs, corpulent and large Posteriours'.

Peg Woffington (1714-60) lover simultaneously of David Garrick and Charles Macklin but also a great success as the dashing Sir Harry Wildair in Farquhar's The Constant Couple.

Edward Kynaston, one of the last boy-players of feminine roles. Charles II once had to wait for the curtain to rise at the theatre because Kynaston, the tragedy queen, was being shaved.

Julia Glover (1781-1850) played Falstaff and Hamlet. Her Dane was much admired by Edmund Kean who in 1821 went backstage to tell her so. 'Away you flatterer', she cried, 'you come in mockery to scorn and scoff at our solemnity'.

Sarah Bernhardt (1844-1923) played the heroes in Lorenzaccio, L'Aiglon and Hamlet. 'Très grande dame', said Max Beerbohm of her Danish prince.

Laurence Olivier (1907-) played Kate in The Taming of the Shrew at the Shakespeare Memorial Theatre, Stratford-upon-Avon in 1922. 'I cannot remember any actress in the part who looked better', wrote W.A. Darlington in The Daily Telegraph.

Alec Guinness (1914-) played Mrs Artminster in Simon Gray's Wise Child at Wyndham's in 1967.

Ronald Pickup, Charles Kay, Richard Kaye and Anthony Hopkins played Rosalind, Celia, Phoebe and Audrey in As You Like It at the National Theatre in 1967. 'Shouldn't the women be wearing breasts?' was Olivier's comment after a dress-rehearsal.

John Wood played Sir John Brute, forced at one point to disguise himself as a bonneted lady of fashion, in The Provok'd Wife at the National Theatre in 1980: a role made popular by David Garrick.

Notable female Hamlets include Sarah Siddons, Julia Glover, Charlotte Cushman, Sarah Bernhardt, Eva le Gallienne, Esmé Beringer and Frances de la Tour who scored a great success in the role at the Half Moon Theatre, London in 1979.

Drag parts, in which female roles are played by men, were so called because the costumes dragged on the ground.

In China and Japan the actress is a comparatively recent innovation. In Japan the great Kabuki player, Baigyoku (who died in 1948) made his last appearance at the age of 73 in the role of a 19-year-old girl. In the late 1970s the Kabuki-trained Tamasaburo Rondo translated his skills as an onnagata (a male actor of women's roles) into Tokyo commercial theatre playing Lady Macbeth and Camille in La Dame aux Camélias.

In China the most popular stars are still male players of female roles. The greatest in living memory was Mei Lan-Fang (1894-1961) who com-

The Bunraku theatre of Japan: a popular modern puppet theatre using life-sized puppets manipulated by
black-masked handlers. It is named after Bunrakuen
who opened the first Japanese puppet-theatre in 1871
in Osaka.

bined great scholarship with a perfect physique
and a matchless falsetto voice. Between 1919
and 1935 he visited Japan, America, Europe and
the Soviet Union including Stanislavsky and
Nemorovich-Danchenko among his disciples.

Historical figures

Until the abolition of the Lord Chamberlain's
powers as theatrical censor in 1968, it was
always difficult to represent royalty, political
figures or religious leaders on the British stage
(such difficulties rarely applied outside). But
many noted historical figures have been portrayed on stage.

Jesus Christ: **The first actor to appear on the
London stage as Jesus Christ** was Vittorio
Gassmann who in 1948 played in Gian Paolo
Callegari's The Man Who Murdered Pilate.
**The show to feature most actors as Jesus
Christ** was Jesus Christ Superstar which open-
ed at the Palace Theatre, London in 1972. Five
different actors all played the hero at dif-
ferent times: Paul Nicholas, Steve Alder, Chris
Neil, Richard Barnes and Robert Farrant.
Other notable Christs: Frank Finlay who ap-
peared in Dennis Potter's Son of Man at the
Round House, London in 1969; Mark
McManus who played Christ in the National
Theatre production of The Passion in 1978.

William Shakespeare: Otto Kruger was **the first
actor to play Shakespeare** in Clemence Dane's
Will Shakespeare in 1921. John Wood was
Shakespeare in No Bed for Bacon by Caryl
Brahms and Ned Sherrin (Croydon 1964). Bob
Peck (Exeter 1973), John Gielgud (Royal Court

Right: A sinister mask from the Noh Drama of Japan. (Japan Information Centre London).

A ghostly tale from the Noh Drama. (Japan Information Centre London).

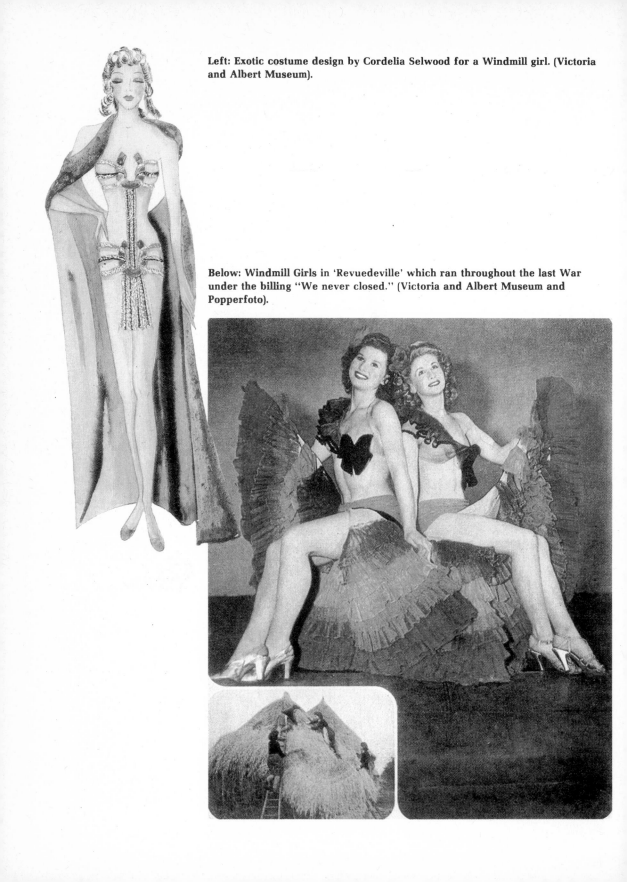

Left: Exotic costume design by Cordelia Selwood for a Windmill girl. (Victoria and Albert Museum).

Below: Windmill Girls in 'Revuedeville' which ran throughout the last War under the billing "We never closed." (Victoria and Albert Museum and Popperfoto).

1974), and Patrick Stewart (Warehouse 1976) have all played Shakespeare in Edward Bond's *Bingo*.

Queen Elizabeth I: Sarah Bernhardt in *La Reine Elizabeth* (1912); Sybil Thorndike in *The Making of an Immortal* (1928). Lynn Fontanne in *Elizabeth the Queen* (1930) subsequently filmed as *The Private Lives of Elizabeth and Essex* (1939). Flora Robson in an American summer tour of *Elizabeth the Queen* (1942) and again in *Elizabeth Tudor, Queen of England* (1970) at The Edinburgh Festival. Catherine Lacey (1958) and Valerie Taylor (1960) in Schiller's *Maria Stuart* at the Old Vic. Eileen Atkins in *Vivat, Vivat Regina* (1970) at Chichester and in London.

Queen Victoria: For a long time she could not be represented on the London stage. She was **first played in London** by Pamela Stanley in Laurence Housman's *Victoria Regina* (1937) and has since been embodied by Anna Neagle in *The Glorious Days* (1951) singing 'Drink To

Valerie Taylor wielding the whip as Elizabeth I with Gwen Watford as Mary Stuart in Schiller's 'Maria Stuart' at the Old Vic, 1960.

Henry Irving as a scarlet-ermined Cardinal Wolsey in Shakespeare's 'Henry VIII' at the Lyceum Theatre, 1893.

Me Only With Thine Eyes'; by Dorothy Tutin in *Portrait of a Queen* (1965); and by Polly James in the musical *I and Albert* (1972). In New York she was played by Beryl Mercer in *Queen Victoria* (1923) and by Helen Hayes in *Victoria Regina* (1935).

Napoleon Bonaparte: Henry Irving in *Madame Sans-Gêne* (1897); Harley Granville-Barker in *Man of Destiny* (1901); Kenneth Kent in *St. Helena* (1936); Robin Chapman in *Man of Destiny* (1958); Ewan Hooper in *War and Peace* (1962); Ian McKellen in *Man of Destiny* (1966); and Herbert Lom in *Betzi* (1975).

Cardinal Richelieu: Henry Irving (1873), Lawrence Barrett (1880), Edwin Booth (1889), Robert B. Mantell (1907), Walter Hampden (1929) all played the part in Bulwer Lytton's *Richelieu*. Also played by Jean Bouise in Roger Planchon's *Les Trois Mousquetaires* (1960); Aubrey Woods in *The Four Musketeers* (1967); and Valentine Dyall in *The Three Musketeers* (1969).

Abraham Lincoln: Frank McGlynn in *Abraham Lincoln* (1919), Raymond Massey in *Abe Lincoln in Illinois* (1938), Roy Dotrice in *Abraham Lincoln* (1979).

Thomas à Becket: Henry Irving in Tennyson's *Becket* (1893); Robert Donat in T.S. Eliot's *Murder in the Cathedral* (1937); Bruno Cremer (Paris, 1959), Eric Porter (London, 1961), Laurence Olivier (New York, 1960) and Daniel Massey (Guildford, 1972) in Anouilh's *Becket*; Richard Pasco in *Murder in the Cathedral* (1972).

The actor to have played most leading historical figures on the British stage is Henry Irving. His creations include: Louis XI, Charles I, Robespierre, Thomas à Becket, Dante, Cardinal Richelieu, Napoleon, Peter the Great, King James V, as well as Prince Hal, Richard III, Cardinal Wolsey, the Duke of Buckingham, and the King of France in plays by Shakespeare.

The first actor to play the Prime Minister of the day on stage was Bill Wallis in *Mrs Wilson's Diary* at the Theatre Royal, Stratford East in 1967. The play also portrayed the Prime Minister's wife, the Governor of the Bank of England and the Foreign Secretary. Since then Gwen Taylor has played Mrs Thatcher in *A Short Sharp Shock* at the Theatre Royal, Stratford East in 1980 and Angela Thorne played her in *Anyone For Denis* at the Whitehall Theatre in 1981.

The actor who has played most writers on the British stage is Daniel Massey. He played Tom Wrench (based on the dramatist Tom Robertson) in *Trelawny of the Wells* (1971), Lytton Strachey in *Bloomsbury* (1974), the autobiographical Leonard Charteris in Shaw's *The Philanderer* (1979), Henry James in *Appearances* (1980) and John Tanner, based on H.M. Hyndman, in Shaw's *Man and Superman* (1981).

Bernard Shaw: He was played by Richard Harris in *Love and Lectures* (1958), Jerome Kilty in *Dear Liar* (1959), John Neville in *The Bashful Genius* (1964) and *Boots With Strawberry Jam* (1967), Max Adrian in the one-man show *An Evening with GBS* (1966), Rex Harrison in *Our Theatre in the Nineties* (1977) and Robert Hardy in *Dear Liar* (1982).

Robert Browning: Brian Aherne in *The Barretts of Wimpole Street* (1930), Keith Michell in *Robert and Elizabeth* (1964), and *Dear Love* (1973).

Virginia Woolf: Yvonne Mitchell in *Bloomsbury* (1974) and Maggie Smith in *Virginia* (1980).

Ben Jonson: Arthur Lowe (1974) and David Waller (1976) in Edward Bond's *Bingo*.

Dr Johnson: Timothy West in *Boswell's Life of Johnson* (1970) and Jonathan Adams in *Heaven and Hell* (1981).

Oscar Wilde: Robert Morley in *Oscar Wilde* (1936), Tom Baker in *Feasting With Panthers* (1981).

Jonathan Swift: Alec Guinness in *Yahoo* (1976).

Mark Twain: Hal Holbrook in *Mark Twain Tonight* (1959).

Harriet Beecher Stowe: Helen Hayes in *Harriet* (1943).

Stevie Smith: Glenda Jackson in *Stevie* (1978).

Theatrical families

The largest theatrical family ever to have appeared on stage was at Ellen Terry's Jubilee Matinée at Drury Lane on 12 June 1906. In all, 22 members of the Terry family (including John Gielgud's mother, Kate) appeared in a Masked Dance from *Much Ado About Nothing* arranged by Ellen Terry's illegitimate son, Gordon Craig.

The American Barrymore family appeared together on stage only once in a double-bill by J.M. Barrie in New York in 1905. Lionel and John appeared together in *Pantaloon*, Ethel and John in *Alice-Sit-By-The-Fire*.

The only son ever to have witnessed his father's final performance at close quarters was Charles Kean. During a performance of *Othello* at Covent Garden in 1833 his father, Edmund, collapsed into his arms (he himself was playing Iago) on the lines: 'Villain, be sure thou prove my love a whore'. Edmund Kean was carried off-stage and never came back.

ACTORS DEPICTED ON STAGE
Richard Burbage: Played by Ian Hunter in Emlyn
William's *Spring 1600* (1934).

Edmund Kean: Alfred Drake in *Kean* (New York,
1961), Alan Badel in *Kean* (London, 1970).

Peg Woffington: Sybil Thorndike in *Masks and
Faces* (1915).

Mrs Siddons: Sybil Thorndike in *Mrs Siddons*
(1933).

Edwin Booth: Jose Ferrer in *Edwin Booth* (1958).

The Barrymores: Ann Andrews (Ethel) and Otto
Kruger (John) in Ferber and Kaufman's *The
Royal Family* (1927). The play was staged in
London in 1934 under the title *Theatre Royal*
with Marie Tempest, Madge Titheradge, and
Laurence Olivier. Though the family in the
play were called the Davenports, they were
quite clearly the Barrymores.

ACTORS WHO HAVE GIVEN THEIR NAME TO THEATRES
Edwin Booth: Booth Theater, New York, opened
1869.

Ethel Barrymore: Ethel Barrymore Theater, New
York, opened 1928, **the first to be named after
an American actress.**

Helen Hayes: Helen Hayes, New York, opened
1955.

Alfred Lunt and Lynn Fontanne: Lunt-Fontanne,
New York, opened 1958.

David Garrick: The Garrick Theatre, London,
opened 1889, **the first British theatre to be
named after an actor.**

Peggy Ashcroft: Ashcroft Theatre, Croydon,
opened 1962.

**Ethel Barrymore, one of the most famous members of
a great American theatrical dynasty. Her first notable
success was in 1901 in 'Captain Jinks of the Horse
Marines'.**

Yvonne Arnaud: Yvonne Arnaud Theatre,
Guildford, opened 1965.

Sybil Thorndike: Thorndike Theatre,
Leatherhead, opened 1969.

Michael Redgrave: Redgrave Theatre, Farnham,
opened 1974.

Laurence Olivier: Olivier Theatre, London, opened 1976.

Kenneth More: Kenneth More Theatre, Ilford,
opened 1974.

**The actor who put most of his own sons onto the
stage** was the American Joseph J. Jefferson
(1774-1832). Seven of his eight children became
actors. His own father, Thomas J. Jefferson
(1732-97) appeared at Drury Lane with Garrick.
Of his seven Thespian sons, the most famous was
also called Joseph J. (1829-1905). He made his
debut on the American stage at the age of 4 and
became famous for his own adaptation of the Rip
Van Winkle legend in which he appeared between 1865 and 1880.

Actors names often run in threes. There were
three Joseph Jeffersons. There were also three
Tyrone Powers. The first (1795-1841) was an
Irish-born comic actor who was very popular in

America and who was drowned in 1840 during a
transatlantic crossing on the S.S. *President*. The
second (1869-1931) was a prominent member of
Augustin Daly's company in America from 1890
to 1898. The third (1914-58) was a popular
screen actor but also appeared on stage both in
New York and London where he played in *Mister
Roberts* (1950) and *The Devil's Disciple* (1956).

The one member of a theatrical family whose
career was almost terminated before it had
begun is Vanessa Redgrave. In January 1937 her
mother, Rachel Kempson, (then eight months
pregnant), went to the Old Vic to see her husband, Michael Redgrave, playing Laertes to
Olivier's Hamlet. In a particularly violent duel

scene Michael Redgrave's sword flew out of his hand and came spinning towards the box where his wife was sitting. Lilian Baylis, the Old Vic director, flung herself in front of Rachel Kempson crying, 'Oh God, not the dear child'.

The one actress to have saved her father from bankruptcy was Fanny Kemble (1809-93). Her performance as Juliet at Covent Garden (then managed by her father, Charles) in 1829 won ecstatic reviews and brought prosperity to an ailing theatre. In that production her father played Mercutio ('My father not acting Romeo: there were many objections to that', Fanny wrote in her diary) and her mother Lady Capulet. The only recorded instance of father and daughter playing Romeo and Juliet was that of Alan and Sarah Badel in a BBC Radio production.

Acting and violence

The only actor to have killed someone in a theatre is John Wilkes Booth (1839-65) who, as a fanatical southern sympathiser, assassinated President Lincoln in Ford's Theater, Washington during a performance of Tom Taylor's *Our American Cousin* in 1865. But even before that he enjoyed a reputation for violence on and off stage. When a sword wound caused blood to run down his face during a performance of *Richard II* he cried, 'That's all right, old man. Never mind me — only come on hard for God's sake and save the fight.'

The only actor to have been killed just outside a theatre was William Terriss who on 16 December 1897 was murdered outside the stage door of the Adelphi Theatre in Maiden Lane. He was stabbed by a crazy, small-part actor with an imagined grievance against him when entering the theatre for the evening performance. Henry Irving, whose company Terriss had long been a member of, bitterly predicted: 'Terriss was an actor — his murderer will not be executed'. His forecast proved right.

Actresses in earlier ages occasionally engaged in unscripted violence. Elizabeth Barry (1658-1713) stabbed and wounded a rival actress on stage in a production of Nathaniel Lee's *The Rival Queens*. Peg Woffington (1714-60) stabbed another actress, Mrs Bellamy, who had declared war on her off-stage.

On and off the boards

Actors and actresses are famous for their eccentricities.

□ Réjane (1856-1920) drove around Paris in a carriage drawn by two mules.

□ Sarah Bernhardt (1844-1923) kept a tiger as a pet and used to relax by lying in a coffin.

□ John Barrymore (1882-1942) kept a pet vulture called Maloney who would sit on his knee and hiss contentedly ('He doesn't understand the theatrical implications of a hiss', said Barrymore. 'Means nothing personal'.

□ Bernard Miles (1907-) used to hail Thames watermen from the bridge of the Mermaid Theatre and, on one occasion, carried off a table from the headquarters of the Arts Council until he got the subvention for his theatre that he requested.

□ Ralph Richardson (1902-) has a pistol in his desk-drawer whether for ornament or emergency he has never revealed.

William Terriss, affectionately known as Breezy Bill, who was a hero of Adelphi melodramas and who ended up starring in a real-life drama when he was stabbed outside the Adelphi stage door in 1897.

"But how did you enjoy the play, Mrs Lincoln?" President Lincoln about to be shot by John Wilkes Booth during a performance of 'Our American Cousin' in 1865.

The first performer to appear totally naked on the legitimate stage in Britain was Maggie Wright playing Helen of Troy in a Royal Shakespeare Company production of *Dr Faustus* that opened on 27 June 1968.

The first example of collective nudity was in *Hair* which opened at the Shaftesbury Theatre, London on 27 September 1968. **The first American performer to appear naked** was Adah Isaacs Menken in 1863 in the title role of *Mazeppa*.

The longest consecutive performance in a single role was given by James O'Neill (1848-1920), father of dramatist Eugene, who played The Count of Monte Cristo over 6000 times from 1883 to 1891. He returned to the role again in later years.

In Britain **the actor most identified with one particular role** was Richard Goolden (1891-1981) whose performance as Mole in A. A. Milne's *Toad of Toad Hall* spanned a period of 49 years. He first played the part at the Lyric Theatre in December 1930. Originally he was asked to audition for Badger but as he left the stage A. A. Milne called him back and said 'Why not try reading Mole?'. His last appearance in the part was at the Old Vic in December 1979.

The first actress to be portrayed on a British postage stamp was Dame Sybil Thorndike. In 1982 she appeared on a series of British Post Office stamps celebrating the British theatre. Other stamps depicted the 250th anniversary of the Royal Opera House, Covent Garden, the 150th anniversary of the Strand Theatre and the 50th anniversary of the Shakespeare Memorial Theatre (now the Royal Shakespeare Theatre) at Stratford-upon-Avon.

The first actress to play a spoken dramatic role on the stage of the Royal Opera House, Covent

Ian Holm as Admiral Lord Nelson in 'A Bequest to the Nation' by Terence Rattigan, at the Haymarket Theatre, London, September 1970.

Garden was Mary Miller who acted the role of Isadora Duncan in Kenneth McMillan's ballet, *Isadora*, which had its première on 3 April 1981.

The first confederation of actors in Britain, the Actors' Association, (President: Henry Irving) was founded in 1891. In 1905 it was superseded by the Actors' Union, in 1929 by British Equity which now represents all members of the entertainment profession. American Equity was founded in May 1913. It called its first strike in 1919 and was successful in gaining better conditions. **The first actors' strike in Britain** took place in 1920.

The first known native American actor (professional) was Samuel Greville who made his debut in *Hamlet* in January 1767. According to a contemporary account: 'A young gentleman by name Mr Gravel (sic) has commenced an Actor on Account of his debts, for He is accounted an Extravagant Young Fellow ... The People in general here rather pity than condemn him: this is the consequence of loose Morals and may serve him as a Lesson to others.'

The first American-born actress to become a star was Charlotte Cushman (1816-76). She played many men's parts including Hamlet, Romeo, and Cardinal Wolsey. She was also a notable Lady Macbeth and played Lady Gay Spanker in the first American production of Boucicault's *London Assurance* in 1841. In 1907 a Charlotte Cushman club was founded in Philadelphia and still flourishes.

The first great black actor was Ira Aldridge (1804-67). Born in New York, he left there when he was 17 and came to London where he initially played slaves aspiring to freedom. Billed as the 'African Roscius' he first appeared in 1826 as Othello at the Royalty Theatre scoring a great triumph. He made five successful European tours and was especially popular in Germany and in Russia. He played Lear (for the first time) in St. Petersburg, making up a pale and ancient face but leaving his hands black. He died on tour at Lodz in Poland.

Bon Mots about Actors and Acting

Michael Wilding:
'You can pick out actors by the glazed look that comes into their eyes when the conversation wanders away from themselves'.

EVENING STANDARD (*The Standard* from 1981) award for Best Performance by an Actor and an Actress

1955 Richard Burton	Siobhan McKenna	1969 Nicol Williamson	Rosemary Harris
1956 Paul Scofield	Peggy Ashcroft	1970 John Gielgud and	Maggie Smith
1957 Laurence Olivier	Brenda De Banzie	Ralph Richardson	
1958 Michael Redgrave	Gwen Ffrancgon-Davies	1971 Alan Bates	Peggy Ashcroft
		1972 Laurence Olivier	Rachel Roberts
1959 Eric Porter	Flora Robson	1973 Alec McCowen	Janet Suzman
1960 Alec Guinness and	Dorothy Tutin	1974 John Wood	Claire Bloom
Rex Harrison		1975 John Gielgud	Dorothy Tutin
1961 Christopher Plummer	Vanessa Redgrave	1976 Albert Finney	Janet Suzman
1962 Paul Scofield	Maggie Smith	1977 Donald Sinden	Alison Steadman
1963 Michael Redgrave	Joan Plowright	1978 Alan Howard	Kate Nelligan
1964 Nicol Williamson	Peggy Ashcroft	1979 Warren Mitchell	Vanessa Redgrave
1965 Ian Holm	Eileen Atkins	1980 Tom Courtenay	Judi Dench and
1966 Albert Finney	Irene Worth		Frances de la Tour
1967 Laurence Olivier	Lila Kedrova	1981 Alan Howard	Maggie Smith
1968 Alec McCowen	Jill Bennett		

Orson Welles:
'Italy is full of actors and it's the bad ones who go on the stage'.

George Jean Nathan:
'Actors and boarding school misses keep scrapbooks'.

Bernard Shaw:
'The trouble with him is that he is in love with his wife and an actor can only afford to be in love with himself'.

Oscar Wilde:
'English actors act quite well but they act between the lines'.

Arnold Bennett:
'A good French actor is merely a French barrister who has missed his vocation'.

Michael Green:
'It seems there is a Coarse Acting streak in most amateurs including the one who during *Henry V* found himself in the wrong army and spent Agincourt fighting against his own side'.

Ralph Richardson:
'Actors cannot see the audience so develop sense for the slightest sound. They are familiar with every croup, cough, gasp and sneeze, whoopsnort and snizzle and all the drips and wheezes that flesh is heir to.'

Tyrone Guthrie:
'Audiences look at actors who have some kind of magnetism. This is largely a matter of self-confidence on the actor's part, the belief that he is, in fact, worth looking at.'

Oliver Goldsmith about David Garrick:
'On the stage he was natural, simple, affecting. 'Twas only that when he was off he was acting.'

Terry Hands:
'Actors are like racehorses. You just rein them in or whip them on and make sure you give them a lump of sugar if they do well.'

CHAPTER 4

Plays and Playwrights

Agatha Christie's *The Mousetrap* is **the world's longest-running play**. It opened at the Ambassadors Theatre, London on 25 November 1952 with Richard Attenborough and Sheila Sim in the leading roles. On 23 December 1970 it created a world record for **the greatest number of performances during a continuous run of a play at one theatre** with a total of 7511 perfor-

mances. It thereby beat the record of *The Drunkard* by W. H. Smith and a Gentleman which ran at the Theater Mart, Los Angeles from 6 July 1933 to 3 September 1953 for a total of 7510 performances. On Saturday, 23 March 1974 *The Mousetrap* finished a 21-year-run at the Ambassadors and transferred the following Monday to the larger St. Martin's Theatre without a break in the continuity of the run.

The Mousetrap is **the most widely seen modern play.** It has been presented in 41 countries and translated into 22 languages. In London (by the end of 1981) 174 actors and actresses have appeared in the play. There have been 88 understudies, 51 miles of shirts have been ironed during the run, over 212 tons of ice cream and approximately 36 000 gallons of squash and minerals have been consumed by patrons. Furnishings and curtains on the set have all been replaced during the run but two things remain constant: a leather armchair which is occupied by one of the characters, Mrs Boyle, and a clock on the mantelpiece which has a design that prevents the hands being seen from the auditorium. In March 1956 Peter Saunders, the play's presenter, sold the film rights of *The Mousetrap* to Romulus Films with the proviso that the film could not be released until six months after the end of the London stage run. The film has yet to be made.

The first play to be called *The Mousetrap* was the one presented by the travelling players to Claudius and the court at Elsinore (*Hamlet*: Act 3, scene 2, line 247). The title seems to derive from Hamlet's belief that with it he could catch the king's conscience.

AMBASSADORS THEATRE
WEST STREET, CAMBRIDGE CIRCUS, W.C.2
PROPRIETORS: AMBASSADORS THEATRE LTD.   LESSEE: J. W. PEMBERTON & CO. LTD.
JOINT MANAGING DIRECTORS: W. G. CURTIS   H. J. MALDEN
LICENSEE: J. F. H. JAY

By arrangement with
J. W. PEMBERTON & CO. LTD.

PETER SAUNDERS

presents

THE NEW PLAY BY
AGATHA CHRISTIE

Directed by PETER COTES

A youthful Richard Attenborough with Sheila Sim who were part of the original 1952 cast of Agatha Christie's 'The Mousetrap' (the world's longest running play) at the Ambassadors Theatre, London.

Below from left to right: Johnathan Darvill, Jacki Piper, Giles Cole and Helen Christie in 'No Sex Please We're British'.

Robert Dorning, with Moira Downie and Sonia Smyles, looking suitably pleased with life in the world's longest-running comedy, 'No Sex Please We're British' which moved from the Strand to the Garrick Theatre in January, 1982.

The longest-running comedy in the history of theatre is *No Sex Please We're British* which opened at the Strand Theatre, London on 3 June 1971. It has taken over £4 million at the box-office, spawned cartoons and a national catch-phrase, been produced in over 30 countries and become a national institution. It began ominously. One of its co-authors, Alistair Foot, died on its first night in Edinburgh. It got bad reviews in Edinburgh and Manchester. When it arrived at the Strand its producer, John Gale, was told it would run no more than three weeks. But it has beaten all previous contenders for the title of

Lilian Braithwaite and Mary Jarrold as the poisonous heroines of 'Arsenic and Old Lace' which opened in London in 1941 and ran for 1337 performances.

longest-running comedy: the 1939 Broadway production of *Life With Father* ran for 3214 performances, the London productions of *Arsenic and Old Lace* in 1941 and *Sailor Beware* in 1955 for 1337 and 1231 performances, respectively. One wonders what would have happened if the authors (Anthony Marriott and Alistair Foot) had retained their original title: *The Secret Life of a Sub-Branch Bank Manager.*

The longest play ever is *The Non-Stop Connolly Show* (1975) by John Arden and Margaretta Darcy which, continuously shown over the course of 26½ hours with intervals, told the story of the life of the Irish patriot, James Connolly. When presented in Dublin, the play was described by one critic as 'the cheapest doss in Dublin'.

The shortest play on record is *Breath* by Samuel Beckett. It has no dialogue, no actors and lasts for 35 seconds. It consists purely of recorded human sounds (cries and breaths) with changing lights paralleling the expanding and contracting diaphragm. It was written (rumour has it on the back of a postcard) for Kenneth Tynan's revue, *Oh Calcutta*, but was withdrawn by the author when he realised there would be naked bodies on stage giving a different significance to the 'breath'.

The world's most prolific playwright was the Spaniard, Lope de Vega Carpio (1562-1635). He wrote nearly 2000 plays as well as 1500 lyric poems. His daily output was an average of 20 pages and he claimed to have written 100 of his plays in less than a day each. Nearly 500 of his

plays survive: pastorals, histories, romances, lives of saints, legends, biblical stories. The only one to have been seen on the London stage in recent times was *La Fienza Satisfecha* (given in a John Osborne adaptation as *A Bond Honoured*) which was not a resounding success.

The longest play-title ever is *The Persecution and Assassination of Marat as Performed by the Inmates of the Asylum of Charenton under the Direction of the Marquis de Sade.* Critic Alan Brien claimed to have asked someone if he had seen the play and received the response: 'No, but I've read the title'. The *Marat-Sade,* as it came to be known, was given by the Royal Shakespeare Company at the Aldwych in 1964. In the same year they also presented a play with one of the shortest titles ever, *Eh?* by Henry Livings.

The second-longest play title is *Oh Dad, Poor Dad, Mama's Hung You In The Closet and I'm Feeling So Sad.* by Arthur Kopit (1960).

The first woman playwright was Hrotswitha, the 10th-century nun from Gandersheim, in Saxony who wrote religious playlets using the form of the Roman comedy-writer Terence. She wrote: 'I, the strong voice of Gandersheim, have not hesitated to imitate in my writing, a poet whose works are so widely read, my object being to glorify, within the limits of my poor talent, the laudable chastity of Christian virgins in that self-same form of composition which has been used to describe the shameless acts of licentious women'.

The most subversive play ever is Beaumarchais's *The Marriage of Figaro.* Professor John Plamenatz: 'No public performance of a play has ever had quite the political impact of the opening night in Paris on 27 April 1784 of Beaumarchais' *The Marriage of Figaro.* It was the occasion when the educated classes, and not least the privileged, discovered how widespread was the contempt among them for the social order to which they belonged.'

Eleven dramatists have received **Nobel Prizes** for literature: Jacinto Benavente (1922) William Butler Yeats (1923), George Bernard Shaw (1925), John Galsworthy (1932), Luigi Pirandello (1934), Eugene O'Neill (1936), Pär Lagerkvist (1951), François Mauriac (1952), Albert Camus (1957), Jean-Paul Sartre (1964), Samuel Beckett (1969).

The frontispiece from the works of Hrotswitha, a
10th century Saxon nun who was the world's first
woman playwright.

Edward Alleyn: Burbage's chief rival and the founder of Dulwich College.

John Bale, a writer of the first English history play, 'Kynge Johan'.

Possibly the wisest remark on playwriting (from Somerset Maughan to Noel Coward): 'Good dialogue is like the most charming interior decoration of a house but it is of little use if the foundations are insecure and the drains don't work'.

UK and Ireland

JOHN BALE (1495-1563) Wrote **the first history play in the English language**, *Kynge Johan* (1538), mixing the abstractions of the Morality plays with real figures from King John's reign. Bale violently rejected the Catholic faith while at Cambridge and was twice exiled when his views clashed with the government's.

THOMAS SACKVILLE (1536-1608) Author of **the first English tragedy**, *Gorboduc* or *Ferrex and Porrex*, played on New Year's Day, 1562 before Elizabeth 1. The plot was borrowed from Geoffrey of Monmouth, the revenge theme from Seneca, the pantomime and dumb-shows from Italian pageants. But what gave the work its importance was the substitution of blank verse (unrhymed iambic pentameter) for the doggerel of previous native drama. Within a quarter of a century, blank verse became the standard form used by Marlowe and Shakespeare.

THOMAS KYD (1558-94) Notable purveyor of blood and revenge in his most popular play, *The Spanish Tragedy* (1588). Is also thought to be the author of a missing *Hamlet*, the source and inspiration for Shakespeare's play.

CHRISTOPHER MARLOWE (1564-93) **First great English playwright**. Educated at the King's School, Canterbury and Cambridge, he had his first play, *Tamburlaine the Great, Part One*, produced in 1587 with Edward Alleyn in the title role. His tragedies, including *Dr Faustus* (1590), *The Jew of Malta* (1590), and *Edward II* (1592), all deal with the fate of over-reachers, assertive, god-defying individuals who become symbols of danger and excitement. *Edward II* is also **the first English play to deal openly with the subject of homosexuality**. Often thought to have been a member of the secret service, Marlowe is known to have died in a tavern at Deptford where one of his companions 'stabyd this Marlowe into the eye in such sort that, his braynes coming out at the dagger point, he shortly after dyed'.

WILLIAM SHAKESPEARE (1564-1616) **The most popular and widely-performed dramatist in world history.** His plays have been constantly produced, endlessly analysed, translated into every language, filmed, televised, turned into opera and ballet and been used as a springboard for other people's imagination.

Shakespeare was born in Stratford-upon-Avon, Warwickshire, the son of a tanner, glover and dealer in wool and hides. He married Anne Hathaway at the age of 18: she bore him a daughter, Susannah, and twins, Judith and Hamnet. Shakespeare came to London in 1592, became a member of the Lord Chamberlain's Men and enjoyed a 20 year career as actor and playwright. In all, he wrote 37 plays in a variety of forms: comedy, tragedy and history.

He wrote over 100 000 dramatic lines. The lengths of his plays, however, vary enormously: *The Comedy of Errors* (1777 lines) is the shortest, *Hamlet* (3776 lines) the longest. The average Shakespearean play is about 2700 lines long and would have been performed originally in about 2½ hours with intervals. **The longest part in Shakespeare** is that of Hamlet with 1530 lines.

Thomas Sackville, Earl of Dorset and author of 'Gorboduc', the first English tragedy.

William Shakespeare in the famous engraving by Martin Droeshout.

The proportions of verse and prose vary greatly in the plays. *Julius Caesar* is composed of 93 per cent blank verse and 7 per cent prose compared with *The Merry Wives of Windsor* with 87 per cent prose and only 13 per cent blank verse. The structure of each play is determined by the nature of the action. *Antony and Cleopatra* has the greatest number of separate locations (37) and *A Midsummer Night's Dream* (7) the fewest. The number of listed characters also varies greatly from 14 each in *Twelfth Night* and *All's Well That Ends Well* to 47 in *Henry VI, Part 2*. Shakespeare could, in fact, call upon an acting company of about 10 principal players with six each of hired players, boy learners and available extras.

Shakespeare's first plays were *Henry VI: Parts One, Two and Three* (1589-91). The three plays were based partly on Holinshed's *Histories* and partly on Foxe's *Book of Martyrs*. Long neglected or played in cut and rewritten versions, the three plays have been given in their entirety in productions by Douglas Seale (Old Vic 1953 and 1957) and Terry Hands (Stratford 1977, Aldwych 1978).

Shakespeare's plays have often been rewritten to suit contemporary taste. Restoration England, in particular, admired his genius but deplored his faults of construction, language and taste. Hence *The Law Against Lovers* (1661) blends the main plot of *Measure for Measure* with the characters of Benedick and Beatrice from *Much Ado*; Dryden's *Truth Found Too Late* (1679) was a version of *Troilus and Cressida* in which Cressida was faithful; and Nahum Tate's notorious version of *King Lear* (1681) eliminated the Fool, made Edgar and Cordelia lovers and supplied a happy ending ('Old Kent throws in his hearty wishes too'). This version was played in various forms until 1838 when William Charles Macready brought back an abridged Shakespearean text.

The play most attended by disaster and misfortune is *Macbeth*. Indeed such a curse is supposed to attend it in the theatre that if any actor so much as mentions it by name in a dressing-room, he is supposed to go outside, turn round three times, fart (or make a similar noise), knock on the door and beg to be readmitted.

The *Macbeth* curse is supposed to date from the first performance (7 August 1606) when the boy actor who was to play Lady Macbeth, Hal Berridge, was taken ill with a mysterious fever only an hour before the performance was due to begin and died in the tiring-room in the middle of the play.

Macbeth stories in our own century

1926 At the Princes Theatre, Sybil Thorndike and Lewis Casson sought to exorcise the spirits of evil by reading together the 90th Psalm: 'Thou shalt not be afraid for any terror by night'.

1934 Four actors played Macbeth in a single week at the Old Vic because of various misfortunes. Malcolm Keen (lost his voice), Alastair Sim (bad chill), Marius Goring (sacked by Lilian Baylis), and John Laurie.

1937 Laurence Olivier's first Macbeth at Old Vic darkened by three-day postponement because of change of director and death of Lilian Baylis before first night.

1954 Paul Rogers and Ann Todd played it at Old Vic. Portrait of Lilian Baylis crashed down on bar on first night. On tour in Dublin, there was an attempted suicide, company manager broke both legs, electrician electrocuted himself. In Capetown a coloured stage hand mentioned the name of the play to a passing stranger onto whose head a spear, poised high in the air on a crane fell killing him instantly.

1980: Peter O'Toole played Macbeth at Old Vic. Artistic disaster but at least no one died.

Shakespeare's plays in order of composition.

HENRY VI Parts One, Two and Three (1589-91)

Main sources: Holinshed *Histories* and Edward Halle's *The Union of Two Noble and Illustre Families of Lancastre and York*.

Key revivals: Old Vic 1953 and 1957; Stratford 1963 where the text was cut, adapted and rewritten by John Barton to form *The Wars of the Roses*; Stratford 1977 where Alan Howard played the young King Henry.

RICHARD III (1592-93)

Main sources: Holinshed and Edward Halle.

Key revivals: Goodman's Fields in 1741 with David Garrick making his London debut; Drury Lane in 1814 where Edmund Kean, according to Hazlitt, had 'a preternatural and terrific grandeur'; the New Theatre in 1944 with Laurence Olivier playing Richard as a satanic joker; Aldwych 1973 with Robert Hirsch heading the Comédie Française; 1979 Edinburgh Festival with Ramaz Chkhikvadze leading the Rustaveli Company from Georgia; 1980 at the National Theatre with John Wood as a scarlet-gowned, Irvingesque Richard.

Other versions: Filmed by Laurence Olivier in 1955: picturesque and sardonic.

Unusual facts: After *Hamlet*, Richard III (1164 lines) is the longest part in Shakespeare.

TITUS ANDRONICUS (1593-94)

Main sources: Uncertain.

Key revivals: Stratford in 1955 when, with Peter Brook directing and Laurence Olivier as Titus, it became the last of Shakespeare's plays to reach the Stratford stage; Stratford in 1972 with John Wood's Saturninus biting the ankles of his courtiers; Stratford, Ontario in 1980 in a dignified revival by Brian Bedford.

Top right: Alan Howard plays the king in the Royal Shakespeare Company's 1977 production of the 'Henry VI' trilogy. Below: Vanessa Redgrave as Kate and Derek Godfrey as Petruchio in the RSC's 1962 production of 'The Taming of The Shrew'.

THE COMEDY OF ERRORS (c.1594)

Main source: Plautus's *Menaechmi*.

Key revivals: Stratford in 1938 in a modern-dress Komisarjevsky production; Stratford 1962 in a hugely popular Clifford Williams production rushed on in an emergency; Stratford 1976 when Trevor Nunn and Guy Woolfenden turned it into a modern Aegean musical.

Other versions: The *Boys from Syracuse*, a 1938 Rodgers and Hart Broadway musical including such songs as 'This Can't Be Love' and 'Falling in Love with Love'.

THE TAMING OF THE SHREW (1593-94)

Main sources: George Gascoigne's *Supposes*, another play called *The Taming of a Shrew*.

Key Revivals: David Garrick in 1754 staged a popular rewrite called *Catherine and Petruchio*; at London's Gaiety in 1888 with the American actress Ada Rehan; at Stratford in 1922 with a 14-year-old Laurence Olivier as a schoolboy Kate; at Stratford in 1962 with Vanessa Redgrave as a loving, readily-tamed Kate; at Stratford in 1978 with Jonathan Pryce as a Christopher Sly who brawled in the stalls and tore down the stage scenery (to the amazement of many patrons who went to get the police) before turning into Petruchio.

Other versions: The Cole Porter 1948 musical *Kiss Me Kate*. Three films: a D. W. Griffith version (1908); a Fairbanks__Pickford movie (1929) with the immortal credit 'additional dialogue by Sam Taylor'; and the Burton__Taylor version (1966) that credits three writers — none of whom is Shakespeare.

TWO GENTLEMEN OF VERONA (1594)

Main source: Jorge de Montemayor's *Diana Enamorada*.

Key revivals: First recorded revival at Covent Garden 1784; Royal Court in 1904 directed by Granville-Barker; Old Vic 1957 in a Regency version; Stratford 1960 where an elaborate Peter Hall production (with everyone looking as if on their way to, or from, the Field of the Cloth of Gold) initiated the work of the Royal Shakespeare Company; Stratford in 1975 in a modern-dress version with bikinis, shades and a swimming-pool.

Other versions: Joe Papp New York musical, *Two Gentlemen of Verona* (1971).

Unusual facts: The only Shakespeare play to feature a dog, Crab.

LOVE'S LABOUR'S LOST (1594-95)

Main source: None definite.

Key revivals: Unrevived until the 19th century at Covent Garden (1839) and Sadler's Wells (1857). Plentifully revived in this century particularly at Stratford by Peter Brook (1946), David Jones (1973), and John Barton (1978) in a moving and comic version that had Rosaline and the Princess of France angrily chastising the menfolk for their frivolity in the final play-scene.

KING JOHN (1591-96)

Main source: The anonymous *The Troublesome Raigne of John, King of England* (1591).

Key revivals: Drury Lane in 1783 with Sarah Siddons as Constance; the New Theatre 1941 with Ernest Milton and Sybil Thorndike; Stratford in 1957 with Robert Harris as a haunted, grave and moving John; Stratford in 1974 in a totally rewritten John Barton version that was vehemently attacked for being misleading under the Trade Descriptions Act, since it appeared under Shakespeare's name.

RICHARD II (1595)

Main source: Holinshed's *Chronicles*.

Key revivals: Globe Theatre, 1601, when supporters of the Earl of Essex paid forty shillings for a special performance that was to precede an uprising against Queen Elizabeth by Essex — the plot was foiled and Essex executed; in Manchester, 1899, Frank Benson was a famous Richard described by C. E. Montague as 'the artist-king, tipsy with grief'. Other famous Richards include John Gielgud (Old Vic 1929), Maurice Evans (Old Vic 1934), Michael Redgrave (Stratford 1951) and Ian Richardson and Richard Pasco who alternated the parts of Richard and Bolingbroke (Stratford 1973) in a production highlighting the mirror-image similarities of the two men.

Unusual facts: Three actors played Richard during the run of a Stratford, Ontario production in 1979: an embarrassment of Richards.

ROMEO AND JULIET (1595-96)

Main source: Arthur Brooke's *The Tragicall Historye of Romeus and Juliet* (1562).

Key revivals: At the Haymarket, 1845, Charlotte Cushman played Romeo to her sister, Susan. At the New Theatre, 1935 Olivier and Gielgud alternated Romeo and Mercutio to Peggy Ashcroft's Juliet. At the Old Vic, Franco Zeffirelli directed a tumbling, noisy, realistic production with John Stride and Judi Dench. At Stratford, 1980, Anton Lesser's leather-jacketed Romeo looked as if he'd parked his motor-bike in the hall.

Other versions: Three films in 1936, 1954 and 1968. Two operas: Bellini's (1830), Gounoud's (1867). A symphony by Berlioz (1839). A Kenneth Macmillan ballet to music by Tchaikovsky (1880). A Broadway musical, *West Side Story* (1957) later filmed. A Terence Rattigan play, *Harlequinade* (1948) based on an Arts Council touring production.

A MIDSUMMER NIGHT'S DREAM (1595-96)

Main sources: Chaucer, Plutarch, Ovid.

Key revivals: At Her Majesty's (1900) Beerbohm Tree used real rabbits running about a real wood. At Old Vic, 1937, Tyrone Guthrie gave the play the full, Vic-

Above: A mirror image: Richard Pasco as the King and Ian Richardson as Bolingbroke in John Barton's RSC production of 'Richard II' in 1973. The two actors alternated the two principal roles on successive nights. Right: Alan Badel as Romeo and Claire Bloom as Juliet in the Old Vic's 1952 production of 'Romeo and Juliet'.

torian, Mendelssohn treatment complete with flying fairies. At Stratford, 1970, Peter Brook, revolutionised the play producing it in a white gymnasium set with Oberon and Puck on trapezes and Bottom and Titania's union being celebrated with flying plates. At Stratford, Ontario, 1977, Maggie Smith played Hippolyta as the Virgin Queen and Titania as a very vulnerable fairy.

Other versions: Filmed by Max Reinhardt (1935) and Peter Hall (1969). Source of Weber's opera, *Oberon* (1826) and Britten's *A Midsummer Night's Dream* (1960). The Pyramus-Thisbe episode was also played by the Crazy Gang.

Above: A floating dream. Alan Howard, Sara Kestel-man and John Kane in Peter Brook's legendary 1970 production of 'A Midsummer Night's Dream'.
Right: Robert Hardy as Hal and Eric Porter as the King in 'Henry IV Part One' at the Old Vic in 1955.

THE MERCHANT OF VENICE (1596-97)

Main sources: Giovanni Fiorentino's *Il Pecorone* (1558) and Christopher Marlowe's *The Jew of Malta* (1589).

Key revivals: At Drury Lane, 1814, Edmund Kean transformed Shylock from the usual red-wigged villain into a figure of pride and dignity. Since then notable Shylock-Portia pairings have been Henry Irving – Ellen Terry (Lyceum 1879). Michael Redgrave – Peggy Ashcroft (Stratford 1953). Laurence Olivier – Joan Plowright (Old Vic 1970). The tendency to give Shylock a touch of ill-used, heroic grandeur was interestingly reversed by Patrick Stewart (Stratford 1978) who made him a backstreet usurer in dirty gaberdine.

Other versions: Opera: *Merchant of Venice* (1922) by Adrian Welles Beecham. Musical: *Fire Angel* (1977) set in New York's Little Italy with Shylock

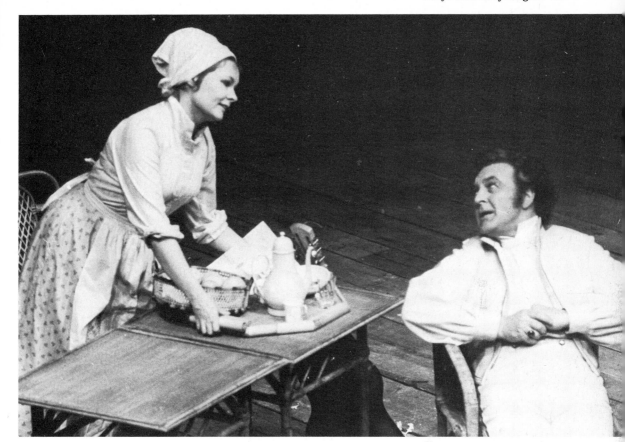

Judi Dench and Donald Sinden in John Barton's British Raj version of 'Much Ado About Nothing' at Stratford in 1976.

transformed into a loan shark and the Christians into Mafia mobsters. Plays: St John Ervine's sequel, *The Lady of Belmont* (1923), Arnold Wesker's *The Merchant* (1977) which told 'the pound of flesh' story from Shylock's point of view.

Unusual facts: A number of infant prodigies attempted parts of the play in the mid 19th century: the youngest were Ellen and Kate Bateman, respectively four and six years old, who played Shylock and Portia around American variety and lecture halls. Female Shylocks include Charlotte Cushman (1860s), Mrs Catherine Macready (1870s) and Lucille La Verne (1929) of whom *The Times* wrote: 'This Shylock occasionally left the Rialto, never the Contralto'.

HENRY IV Part One (1596-7) and Part Two (1598)

Main sources: Holinshed and Edward Halle.

Key revivals: Only in this century has the practice developed of presenting the two plays consecutively. Notable versions have been Barry Jackson's at Birmingham Repertory (1922), John Burrell's at the New Theatre (1945) with Ralph Richardson and Laurence Olivier, a quartercentenary production at Stratford (1964) directed by Peter Hall, John Barton and Clifford Williams with Hugh Griffith as a wheezing, rubicund Falstaff. In France in 1959 Roger Planchon presented a heavily-cut Brechtian version of the plays in which Prince Hal became a cunning killer. The two plays in tandem opened at the Shakespeare Memorial Theatre in 1932 and at the Barbican Theatre, London in 1982.

Other versions: Movie: Orson Welles's masterly, compressed, under-financed *Chimes at Midnight* (1966).

THE MERRY WIVES OF WINDSOR (1597-98)

Main source: None known. Legend has it that Queen Elizabeth wanted to see Falstaff in love and that the play was run up in a hurry.

Key revivals: Oscar Asche, better known for *Chu Chin Chow*, presented the play at the Garrick in 1911 in an unusually wintry setting; Glen Byam Shaw directed a notable Stratford production in 1955, and Terry Hands came up with a classic production at Stratford in 1969 (revived there in 1975) with Brewster Mason as a dignified Falstaff and Ian Richardson as a whirlwind Ford.

Other versions: Opera: Nicolai's *The Merry Wives of Windsor* (1849), Verdi's *Falstaff* (1893).

Unusual facts: Karl Marx once wrote: 'In the first act alone of *The Merry Wives of Windsor* there is more life and movement than in all German literature'.

MUCH ADO ABOUT NOTHING (1598-99)

Main sources: Ariosto's *Orlando Furioso* (1516), Spenser's *Fairie Queene* (1590).

Key revivals: At Drury Lane in 1748 Garrick played Benedick and went on playing it until his retirement in 1776; At the Lyceum in 1882 Henry Irving and Ellen Terry were a famous Benedick and Beatrice ('Beatrice's wit came jetting from her lips as if every word had just occurred to her on the spur of the moment'); at Stratford in 1949 John Gielgud's oft-revived, high Renaissance production was first seen; at Stratford in 1976 Donald Sinden and Judi Dench played the leads in an Anglo-Indian, Raj revival.

Other versions: Opera: *Beatrice and Benedict* by Berlioz (1862).

AS YOU LIKE IT (1599)

Main source: Thomas Lodge's *Rosalynde* (1590).

Key revivals: At the Old Vic, 1936, with Edith Evans; at Stratford, 1961, with Vanessa Redgrave ('her voice' said Bernard Levin, 'is a golden gate opening on lapis lazuli hinges, her body a slender, supple reed rippling in the breeze of her love'); at the Old Vic, 1967, in an all-male production; at Stratford in 1980 with Susan Fleetwood.

Other versions: Film (1936) with Elizabeth Bergner as a Germanic Rosalind and Laurence Olivier as Orlando.

Unusual facts: Rosalind is one of five Shakespearean heroines (the others are Julia, Portia, Viola and Imogen) who adopt male disguise.

HENRY V (1599)

Main source: Holinshed.

Key revivals: At the Lyceum, 1900, with Lewis Waller; at the Old Vic, 1937, with Laurence Olivier; at Stratford, 1975, with Alan Howard as a sensitive, guilt-ridden, often tearstained Henry.

Other versions: film (1944) starring and directed by Olivier: the first of his three Shakespeare films. The play was also turned into a musical for an Edinburgh Festival fringe production in the 1970s. Cut and rewritten, it was given in modern battledress at the Mermaid in 1961.

JULIUS CAESAR (1599)

Main source: Plutarch.

Key revivals: Possibly the first play that Shakespeare's company, the Lord Chamberlain's Men, presented at their new Globe Theatre in 1599. In New York, 1864, the brothers Edwin Booth, Junius Brutus Booth and John Wilkes Booth played Brutus, Cassius and Antony: the only time members of the same family have played the three parts. (Six months later John Wilkes Booth assassinated Lincoln.) In New York, 1937, Orson Welles's Mercury Theater presented a modern-dress, Fascist-set version. At Stratford, 1972, John Wood played Brutus as a bungling idealistic intellectual.

Other versions: Films: with Brando and Gielgud (1953) as Antony and Cassius and with Charlton Heston and Gielgud (1969) as Antony and Caesar.

Unusual facts: the first joint production of all four Roman plays (*Coriolanus, Julius Caesar, Antony and Cleopatra, Titus Andronicus*) was at Stratford in 1972.

TWELFTH NIGHT (1601-2)

Main source: An Italian play, *Gl'Ingannati* (1531).

Key revivals: At the Savoy, 1912, directed by Granville Barker in a black-and-silver setting; at Stratford, 1958, in a Charles II period setting with Dorothy Tutin as an exquisite page-boy Viola; at Stratford, 1969, in a Chekhovian John Barton production with Judi Dench as a broken-voiced Viola and Donald Sinden as a frontal, vaudevillian Malvolio.

Other versions: An opera (1881) by Smetana; various Broadway musicals including *Your Own Thing* (1969); A Russian film (1955) directed by Jakow Frid.

HAMLET (1601-2)

Main source: An earlier version of the story, *Ur-Hamlet*, now lost, acted 1594.

Key revivals: Max Beerbohm described the part as 'a hoop through which every eminent actor must, sooner or later, jump'. Thomas Betterton played it from 1661 to 1709 and even when over 70 'acted a young man of great expectation, vivacity and enterprise'. Johnston Forbes-Robertson (Lyceum 1897) was the archetypal 'sweet prince'. John Gielgud (first at the Old Vic in 1930) was described as 'a Stradivarius controlled by a master'. Michael Redgrave (first at the Old Vic in 1950) was agonised, athletic, princely. Albert Finney (Old Vic 1975) made you believe he might kill Claudius.

Other versions: Films: directed by Olivier (1948), Grigori Kozintsev (1964), Tony Richardson (1969). Operas: by Scarlatti (1715), Ambroise Thomas (1868), Humphrey Searle (1968). Ballet: by Robert Helpmann (1942).

Unusual facts: The longest of Shakespeare's plays; the most frequently performed; the first British play to be taken to post-revolutionary Russia in a Peter Brook — Paul Scofield version (1956); the springboard for one of the most popular modern plays, Tom Stoppard's *Rosencrantz and Guildenstern Are Dead* (1967). Stoppard has also concocted a speeded-up, three-minute version of the original, retaining all the vital features of the plot.

TROILUS AND CRESSIDA (1601-2)

Main source: George Chapman's translation of *The Iliad* (1598).

Key revivals: At the King's Hall, Covent Garden, 1912,

directed by William Poel; at the Old Vic, 1956, directed by Tyrone Guthrie in Ruritanian style; at Stratford, 1960, directed by Peter Hall and John Barton in an octagonal sandpit. In 1949 Luchino Visconti directed the play in Florence's Boboli Gardens with half the characters on horseback.

Other versions: Opera: Sir William Walton's *Troilus and Cressida* (1954).

ALL'S WELL THAT ENDS WELL (1602-3)

Main source: Boccaccio's *Decameron.*

Key revivals: At Drury Lane, 1742, with Peg Woffington as Helena; at the Vaudeville, 1940, directed by Robert Atkins for three weeks of wartime matinées; at Stratford, 1959, with a Franz Lehar court and military scenes straight out of *The Army Game;* at Stratford, 1967, directed by John Barton; at Stratford 1981, directed by Trevor Nunn in pre First World War setting.

MEASURE FOR MEASURE (1604)

Main source: George Whetstone's *Promos and Cassandra,* 1578.

Key revivals: At the Old Vic, 1933, with Charles Laughton as Angelo and Flora Robson as Isabella; at Stratford-upon-Avon, 1950, in a Peter Brook production that extended the pause where Isabella pleads for Angelo's life sometimes for as long as two minutes; at Greenwich Theatre, 1975, in a Jonathan Miller modern-dress version set in a Freudian Vienna; at the Lyttelton Theatre, 1981, in a production that set the action on a mythical Caribbean island with the Duke a sybaritic governor and Angelo as a rigid black bishop.

OTHELLO (1604)

Main source: Cinthio's Italian tale *Hecatommithi,* 1595.

Key revivals: With Edmund Kean at Drury Lane, 1814; with Tommaso Salvini, 1875, whose performance, said Henry James, was 'magnificently quiet and from beginning to end had not a touch of rant or crudity'; with Paul Robeson who played the Moor in London in 1930, in New York in 1943-44 (295 performances — a record for an American Shakespeare revival) and in Stratford in 1959; with Laurence Olivier at the Old Vic, 1964, described thus by Ronald Bryden: 'He came on smelling a rose, laughing softly, with a private delight; barefooted, ankleted, black'.

Other versions: Films: directed by Orson Welles (1955), Sergei Yutkevitch (1955), Stuart Burge (1965). Operas: Rossini's *Otello* (1816), Verdi's *Otello* (1887).

Unusual facts: Iago (1070 lines) is the third longest part in Shakespeare.

KING LEAR (1605)

Main sources: Holinshed, Spenser's *Faerie Queene,* *The True Chronicle History of King Leir,* 1594.

Key revivals: Great Lears have included Macready

Paul Robeson's last Othello (with Mary Ure as Desdemona) at Stratford-upon-Avon in 1959.

(1838), Irving (1892), Gielgud (1931, 1940, 1950, 1955), Olivier (1946), Paul Scofield (1962).

Other versions: Films: directed by Kozintsev (1970) and ending with the common people picking up the pieces after the climactic battle; directed by Peter Brook (1971) in a frozen northern Denmark.

MACBETH (1606)

Main sources: Holinshed, King James I's *Daemonologie,* 1597.

Michael Redgrave, with bandaged thumb, dies at Macduff's hands in his 1947 Aldwych 'Macbeth'.

Key revivals: With Sarah Siddons (1785-1812) whose sleepwalking scene led dramatist Sheridan Knowles to proclaim 'Well, sir, I smelt blood. I swear that I smelt blood'; with Michael Redgrave at the Aldwych (1947); with Olivier at Stratford-upon-Avon (1955) in a performance that Harold Hobson described as 'the best Macbeth since Macbeth'; and at Stratford's Other Place (1976) with Ian McKellen and Judi Dench in a chamber-production that conjured up evil.

Other versions: Films: directed by Orson Welles (1948); by Akira Kurosawa as *Throne of Blood* (1957); by George Schaefer (1960) with a Macbeth whom Penelope Gilliatt compared to 'Charlie Drake in a mohair rug'; and by Roman Polanski (1971). There was also an updated version, *Joe Macbeth*, transplanting the action to a gangster-filled Soho. Opera: Verdi's *Macbetto* (1847).

ANTONY AND CLEOPATRA (1606-7)

Main source: Plutarch's *Lives*.

Key revivals: Rarely seen in its original form until this century when it has been played by Godfrey Tearle and Edith Evans (Piccadilly 1946), Laurence Olivier and Vivien Leigh (St James's 1951), Michael Redgrave and Peggy Ashcroft (Stratford-upon-Avon 1953), John Turner and Barbara Jefford (Old Vic 1978), Alan Howard and Glenda Jackson (Stratford 1978). At the Old Vic, Turner and Jefford became the first couple in theatrical history to combine playing Shakespeare's hero and heroine with Antony and Cleopatra in Dryden's *All For Love.*

Other versions: Film: directed by Charlton Heston (1971) summarily dismissed by *The Guardian* as 'the biggest asp disaster in the world'.

TIMON OF ATHENS (1607-8)

Main sources: Plutarch's *Lives*, Lucian's *Timon Misanthropus.*

Key revivals: Shakespeare's full version was not revived in London until Samuel Phelps presented it at Sadler's Wells in 1851. Since then notable interpreters have been Robert Atkins (Old Vic 1922), André Morell (Old Vic 1952), Paul Scofield (Stratford 1965) and Richard Pasco (Stratford — Other Place 1980). In Paris (1974) Peter Brook directed it as the first full-scale production of his International Centre for Theatre Research.

CORIOLANUS (1607-8)

Main sources: Plutarch's *Lives*, Livy's *Annales*, Book 32.

Key revivals: John Philip Kemble (Covent Garden 1816) with Eliza O'Neill as Volumnia ('There is a fleshiness, if we may so say, about her whole manner, voice and person which does not suit the character of the Roman matron': (Hazlitt); Frank Benson (Comedy 1901); Laurence Olivier (Stratford 1959) of which Laurence Kitchin wrote: 'There was the bizarre impression of one man lynching a

Alan Howard's Antony expires in Glenda Jackson's arms in Peter Brook's 1978 'Antony and Cleopatra' at Stratford-upon-Avon.

crowd'; Alan Howard (Stratford 1978). John Neville also played it in December 1963 in the first production of the new Nottingham Playhouse.

Other versions: Bertolt Brecht translated and adapted the play as *Coriolan,* first produced at Frankfurt Schauspielhaus, 1962. John Osborne also updated and reworked the play in *A Place Calling Itself Rome,* published in 1973.

PERICLES (1607-8)

Main source: Gower's *Confessio Amantis.* 1390.

Key revivals: Rarely seen. But staged with Robert Eddison (Open-Air Theatre 1939); Richard Johnson (Stratford 1958) in a gaudy, kaleidoscopic version; Ian Richardson (Stratford 1969); and Derek Jacobi (Her Majesty's 1973) in a production presented as a bordello fantasy. This last version was played with great success Off-Broadway in New York, 1980.

CYMBELINE (1609)

Main sources: Holinshed, *Decameron. Book 2.*

Key revivals: At the Lyceum (1896) with Ellen Terry as Imogen and Henry Irving as Iachimo. At Stratford with a long line of remarkable actresses as Imogen: Peggy Ashcroft (1957), Vanessa Redgrave (1962), Susan Fleetwood (1974), Judi Dench (1979).

Other versions: Bernard Shaw described the play as 'for the most part stagey trash of the lowest melodramatic order'. He rewrote the last act himself as *Cymbeline Refinished* (1936).

THE WINTER'S TALE (1611)

Main source: Robert Greene's *Pandosto or The Triumph of Time* (1598).

Key revivals: At Drury Lane (1802) when John Philip Kemble and Sarah Siddons as Leontes and Hermione restored the original text. At the Lyceum (1887) when Mary Anderson doubled Hermione and her daughter, Perdita. At Stratford-upon-Avon (1969) when Judi Dench repeated the same feat.

Other versions: Film: directed by Frank Dunlop (1966) with Laurence Harvey as Leontes and Jim Dale as Autolycus.

THE TEMPEST (1611)

Main source: Montaigne's *Essays,* translated into English, 1603.

Key revivals: The play has always been a director's dream being treated as a scenic island fling (Beerbohm Tree, 1904), a study of a grizzled tyrant (Peter Brook, 1957), an essay in colonialism (Jonathan Miller, 1970), a Jacobean masque (Peter Hall, 1974). The greatest modern Prospero has undoubtedly been John Gielgud who has played the part more than any other living actor: at the Old Vic (1940), at Stratford and Drury Lane (1957) and for the National Theatre at the Old Vic (1974).

Other versions: Opera: *Der Sturm* (1956) by Frank Martin. Poetry: W. H. Auden's *The Sea and the Mirror.* Film made in 1980 and directed by Derek Jarman, set on a punkish island.

Michael Hordern's benign Prospero with Claire Bloom's Miranda in the Old Vic's 1954 'Tempest'.

HENRY VIII (1612-13)

Main sources: Holinshed, Foxe's *Book of Martyrs* (1563).

Key revivals: Fire destroyed the first Globe Theatre on Bankside during a performance on 29 June 1613. Since then the play has had spectacular revivals at the Lyceum (1892), His Majesty's (1910), Sadler's Wells (1933) with Charles Laughton as Henry, at the Old Vic (1958) with John Gielgud and Edith Evans, and at Stratford (1969) with Donald Sinden and Peggy Ashcroft.

Other versions: Outstanding BBC TV revival (1979) with Timothy West as Wolsey and Claire Bloom as Queen Katharine.

BEN JONSON (1572-1637) Poet, scholar, playwright; after Shakespeare, the greatest and most revived dramatist of the Elizabethan — Jacobean period; also, by receiving a royal pension of 100 marks, **the first (unofficial) Poet Laureate.** A bricklayer, soldier and actor before becoming a playwright, he was constantly in trouble with the law. In 1597 he was imprisoned in the Marshalsea for helping to write 'a lewd plaie ... contayninge seditious and slanderous

Alec Guinness as Abel Drugger in 'The Alchemist' at the New Theatre in 1947: "I was overjoyed", wrote Kenneth Tynan, "to watch his wistful, happy eyes moving in dumb wonder from Face to Subtle".

matter' (*The Isle of Dogs* with Thomas Nashe). In 1598 he narrowly escaped the gallows after killing fellow-actor, Gabriel Spencer, in a duel. He was imprisoned in 1604 for caricaturing King James in *Eastward Ho*. He was also involved in bitter quarrels (1599-1601) with fellow-dramatists over stylistic matters that were argued out play for play. *The Poetaster* (1601) shows Jonson taking revenge on the two rivals, John Marston and Thomas Dekker, who tried to defame him. Today best remembered for his classic satires on human greed, *Volpone or The Fox* (1606) and *The Alchemist* (1610), and for his championship of his friend and rival, Shakespeare ('He was not of an age but for all time'). Jonson's own epitaph in Westminster Abbey reads simply: 'O rare Ben Jonson'.

JOHN WEBSTER (1580-1634) Powerful tragic dramatist best known for *The White Devil* (1612) and *The Duchess of Malfi* (1613-14): both stories of love and intrigue set in Renaissance Italy, both preoccupied with violent and bizarre death, both containing great parts for actresses. Shaw dismissed Webster as the 'Tussaud laureate' while Rupert Brooke saw his characters as 'writhing grubs in an immense night. And that night is without stars or moon.'

FRANCIS BEAUMONT (1584-1616) Sole author of *The Woman-Hater* (1606), a Jonsonian satire, and *The Knight of the Burning Pestle* (1607), a parody of chivalrous romances and gullible audiences that was successfully updated by the RSC in 1981. Between 1608 and 1613 he and his partner, John Fletcher (1579-1625) worked together on some 52 plays of which the most durable is *The Maid's Tragedy* (1611), a story of carnal lust and exotic violence at the court of Rhodes. Beaumont married in 1613 and retired to Kent where he lived the life of a country gentleman.

JOHN FORD (1586-1639) One of the so-called decadent playwrights of the Jacobean era. Practised law before turning to writing in his mid-thirties. Collaborated with Dekker and Rowley on *The Witch of Edmonton* (1621). The best-known of his works are *The Broken Heart* (1625-33), *Perkin Warbeck* (1629-34) which T.S. Eliot called 'one of the very best historical plays in the whole of Elizabethan and Jacobean drama' and *Tis Pity She's a Whore* (1629-33) which is **the first English play to deal with incest** and which ends with the hero entering with his sister's heart impaled on a dagger's point.

GEORGE ETHEREGE (1634-91) **The first ma-**

jor Restoration dramatist. His play, *The Comical Revenge; or Love in a Tub* (1664) is a Molière-influenced tragi-comedy largely written in rhymed couplets. It was followed by the vastly superior *She Would If She Could* (1668) and *The Man of Mode or Sir Fopling Flutter* (1676) which set the Restoration on its course of satirising contemporary follies. 'Easy Etherege' married a rich wife, wrote little else but established a style that others were to follow.

APHRA BEHN (1640-89) **The first English woman dramatist.** Brought up in Guiana where her father was lieutenant-governor, she married a wealthy Dutch merchant in 1666, was reduced to penniless widowhood, worked for a time as a Government spy in the Low Countries, turned to writing to support herself and from 1671 to her death produced 15 plays as well as novels and poetry. Her most popular play was *The Rover* (1677), a dashing account of hot-blooded Cavaliers on the sexual rampage in Europe. It was frequently revived during the following century and last seen at Colchester in 1979 with Lynn Dearth.

WILLIAM WYCHERLEY (1640-1716) 'As King Charles was extremely fond of him upon account of his wit, some of the Royal Mistresses set no less value upon Those Parts in him, of which they were more proper judges', wrote Major Pack in 1728. But four plays between 1671 and 1676 (*Love in a Wood, The Gentleman Dancing-Master, The Country Wife, The Plain Dealer*) also established him as a first-rate observer of sexual mores. *The Country Wife* (1675), in which Mr Horner feigns impotence in order to seduce women who flock to admire his 'china', is also one of the lewdest plays in the language. Popular in its day, it was replaced in 1776 by Garrick's bowdlerised version, *The Country Girl,* and it was not until 1924 that the Phoenix Society, a Sunday night club, dared to stage the original: the cast included Isabel Jeans and Athene Seyler. Like many other British dramatists (Marlowe, Jonson, Vanbrugh, Wilde, William Douglas-Home, Robert Bolt, Joe Orton) Wycherley also saw the inside of a prison: in his case, the offence was debt.

JOHN VANBRUGH (1664-1726) The only English dramatist to also be a major architect. He started his career as an army officer with the

Mrs Aphra Behn: England's first woman dramatist and a one time Government spy.

Earl of Huntingdon's regiment and in 1690 was imprisoned in the Bastille as a spy for 18 months (though he was allowed four-course dinners and three bottles of wine a day). After such notable

William Wycherley author of one of the filthiest plays in the language, 'The Country Wife', and known to contemporaries as "rude, manly Wycherley".

William Congreve: a great Restoration stylist reduced to silence by Puritan attacks.

plays as *The Relapse* (1696) and *The Provok'd Wife* (1697) he took up architecture, designing Blenheim Palace and Castle Howard in Yorkshire: both controversial in their day. *The Provok'd Wife* also provoked the Puritans. The errant hero, Sir John Brute, at one point disguised himself as a clergyman. In 1706 this part was re-written so that Brute disguised himself as something considered less offensive—a woman.

WILLIAM CONGREVE (1670-1729) A master stylist. Wrote five plays before he was 30: *The Old Bachelor* (1693), *The Double Dealer* (1694), *Love for Love* (1695), *The Way of The World* (1700) and his sole tragedy, *The Mourning Bride* (1697). After that, apart from a collaboration with Vanbrugh and a failed opera, he wrote no more plays. He gave up partly because of the attacks of Jeremy Collier in his *A Short View of the Profaneness and Immorality of the English Stage* (1698), a Puritan pamphlet of enormous impact. When Congreve died in 1729 he left virtually the whole of his fortune (£10 000) to his mistress, the Duchess of Marlborough, who saw to it that he was buried in Westminster Abbey.

JOHN GAY (1685-1732) The first dramatist to provoke a Court official, the Lord Chamberlain, to use his powers of censorship over the English stage. Gay's Newgate pastoral, *The Beggar's Opera* (1728) was instantly popular with its satirising of leading politicians as thieves, highwaymen and pimps. On the first night the smiling Prime Minister, Walpole, joined in the applause. But in December 1728, Gay submitted his next work, *Polly*, in which his highwayman-hero Macheath is transported to the West Indies, to the Lord Chamberlain. The work was 'banned without any reasons assigned' said Gay, 'or any charge against me of having given any particular offence'. Gay, buried in Westminster Abbey, died at the height of his fame.

OLIVER GOLDSMITH (1728-74) 'Here lies Nolly Goldsmith, for shortness called Noll, Who wrote like an angel but talk'd like poor Poll.' So wrote David Garrick after Goldsmith's death. But then Goldsmith had written of Garrick: 'On the stage he was natural, simple, affecting, 'Twas only when he was off he was acting'. Having endured a succession of misfortunes (he qualified as a doctor but attracted hardly any patients) the Irish-born Goldsmith established himself as a playwright with *The Good-Natured Man* (1768) but his finest achievement was *She Stoops To Conquer* (1773) in which a private house is mistaken for an inn. The author claimed

John Gay whose popular classic, 'The Beggar's Opera', led to 240 years of theatrical censorship.

The spectacular 'Corsican Brothers' (1880) by the prolific Irish playwright, plagiarist and pioneer, Dion Boucicault.

he had made just such a mistake on one occasion, himself.

JOHN O'KEEFFE (1747-1833) Author of over 70 dramas, pantomimes, comic operas and farces including the highly popular *Wild Oats* (1791) recently revived by the Royal Shakespeare Company. Hazlitt said of him: 'O'Keefe might well be called our English Molière. The scale of the modern writer was smaller but the spirit is the same.' His tragedy was that he was blind from his late twenties and so on first nights his son would take him to the pass-door so that he could listen to the audience's response. If hisses were heard, he put his hands to the side of his head. 'Thus would he remain without sight or hearing till some unexpected sally of humour in his drama once more put the house in good temper, and they would begin to laugh and applaud; on which his son would pull him by the elbow and cry out, "Now, father, listen again".'

RICHARD BRINSLEY SHERIDAN (1751-1816) Irish-born playwright, manager and politician. Lord Byron: 'Whatever Sheridan has done or chosen to do has been *par excellence* the *best* of its kind. He has written the best comedy *(The School for Scandal)*, the best opera *(The Duenna)*, the best farce *(The Critic)* and the best address (The Monologue on Garrick) and to crown all, delivered the best oration (the famous Begum speech) ever conceived or heard in this country.' As a dramatist, he certainly had a distinguished career, starting with *The Rivals* in 1775. As a manager, he became sole owner of Drury Lane in 1778 at the age of 27 and remained so until it was burned down in 1809. And as a member of Parliament from 1780 he was an eloquent orator, achieving particular fame for his 5½ hour speech in 1787 in the impeachment of Warren Hastings because of abuses by the East India Company. He was buried in Poets Corner next to David Garrick.

DION BOUCICAULT (1820-90) Popular Irish playwright and actor who wrote some 200 plays, pioneered the matinée performance, the box-set and fireproof scenery, coined the phrase 'plays are not written, they are rewritten', lobbied the US Congress to establish author's copyright (somewhat ironically in view of his own plagiarism) and established the phrase 'sensation drama'. Among the sensational scenes he put on stage were a ship blowing up, an avalanche, the Oxford and Cambridge boat race and the Derby. Born in Dublin as Dionysius Lardner Boursiquot, he was not only a great showman but also a fine dramatist whose best-known plays are *London Assurance* (1841), *The Octoroon* (1859) which daringly dealt with interracial marriage, *The Colleen Bawn* (1860) based on the murder of an Irish girl by a British officer 40 years earlier, and *The Shaughran* (1875) the most popular Irish play of the century. He was also a great magpie. Borrowing a French play called *Les Pauvres de Paris*, he changed its name to *The Streets of London, New York* or *Liverpool* depending on where it was playing at the time. A great influence on later Irish dramatists, he suggested as the inscription on his tombstone: 'His first holiday'.

OSCAR WILDE (1854-1900) Author of one of the most technically perfect and verbally witty comedies in the English language, *The Importance of Being Earnest* (1895). In the same year Wilde, looking according to a contemporary 'like a Roman Emperor carved out of suet' was found guilty at the Old Bailey of 'committing acts of gross indecency with other male persons' and confined for two years to Reading Gaol. Wilde's comedy, however, lives on as also, to a lesser extent, do his epigram-stuffed, society dramas *Lady Windermere's Fan* (1892), *A Woman of No*

Comic style at its greatest: Sir John Gielgud, Dame Edith Evans and Margaret Leighton in a scene from 'The Importance of Being Earnest', "a trivial comedy for serious people".

Oscar Wilde, playwright, poet, novelist and aesthete brought down by one of those English periodic fits of morality at the very height of his power.

Importance (1893), and *An Ideal Husband* (1895). His only other play, *Salome* (1891) was banned by the Lord Chamberlain but was given its première in Paris in 1896 when Wilde was still in prison. Wilde himself died wretched and penniless in Paris punished by English society not simply for sexual impropriety but for congress with working-class boys.

ARTHUR WING PINERO (1855-1934) Popular English Victorian dramatist who was an actor with Irving's Lyceum Company from 1876 to 1881 and who wrote his first play, *The Money Spinners* in 1880. Today he is best remembered for his farces, *The Magistrate* (1885) and *Dandy Dick* (1886) and for *Trelawny of the Wells* (1898), a warm and glowing tribute to the acting generation of the 1860s. But in his own day he was more applauded for serious society dramas such as *The Second Mrs Tanqueray* (1893) and *The Notorious Mrs Ebbsmith* (1895) in which Mrs Patrick Campbell famously rescued a Bible from the flames and hot-pressed it to her bosom.

GEORGE BERNARD SHAW (1856-1950) Prolific, unstoppable playwright of genius who only started as a dramatist at the age of 36 and who thereafter wrote some 57 plays nearly all accompanied by a weighty preface. Before establishing himself as a playwright he wrote five unsuc-

cessful novels and enjoyed dazzling careers as a critic of art, music and drama. Among his most durable plays are *Mrs Warren's Profession* (1893), *You Never Can Tell* (1896), *Man and Superman* (1901-3), *John Bull's Other Island* (1904), *Misalliance* (1910), *Pygmalion* (1912), *Heartbreak House* (1913-16), *Saint Joan* (1923), *Too True To Be Good* (1932). His last play, *Buoyant Billions*, was written in 1949 at the age of 93 making him **the oldest practising playwright ever.** Shaw proved that the opposition of ideas can be theatrically gripping; that wit and seriousness are allies rather than enemies; that prose can be as musical as any poetry. He has been praised and reviled in equal proportions. He has scarcely ever gone unperformed. When Frank Hauser was asked at the Oxford Playhouse in the early 1960s if he thought Shaw was coming back, he replied 'I

George Bernard Shaw who is still, after Shakespeare, the most vibrant and revivable playwright in the English language.

Mrs Patrick Campbell as Eliza, and Sir Herbert Beerbohm Tree as Professor Higgins in the original production of Shaw's 'Pygmalion' in 1914.

didn't know he'd ever been away'. But there have always been those like James Agate who said that Shaw's plays are the price we pay for Shaw's prefaces, and those like John Osborne who regard him as one of the most untheatrical dramatists who ever lived. Audiences, however, have the last word. Shaw's plays are always in the London repertory and there is an annual festival devoted to him at Niagara on the Lake, Ontario thus putting him on a par with Shakespeare (Stratford-upon-Avon) and Wagner (Bayreuth).

J. M. BARRIE (1860-1937) Vapid and Pinerotic said Shaw. 'Sugar without the diabetes', sneered George Jean Nathan. But this sentimental Scottish playwright wrote several durable works including *The Admirable Crichton* (1902), *What Every Woman Knows* (1908) and the everlasting *Peter Pan* (1904). First staged in London at the Duke of York's in 1904 by the son of Dion Boucicault and in New York a year later, it has since become a hardy Christmas annual. It was also turned into a silent film by Paramount in 1925 and into a coloured cartoon film by Walt Disney in 1925. In 1954, Leonard Bernstein and Jule Styne also wrote a musical version which enjoyed a long Broadway run, with Sandy Duncan, from 1979 to 1981.

JOHN MILLINGTON SYNGE (1871-1909) Born in an outer Dublin suburb, he wandered Europe as a young man and in Paris met W.B. Yeats who told him to go to the remote Aran Islands in the West of Ireland: 'Express a life that has never found expression. Live there as if you were one of the people'. He did and the results were *In The Shadow of the Glen* and *Riders to the Sea* (1902) and *The Playboy of the Western World* (1907). All were produced at the Abbey Theatre, Dublin with the last producing one of the most famous riots in theatre history. From opening night on Saturday, 26 January 1907 there were riots through the succeeding week by Irish nationalists. One of them condemned the play in *Sinn Fein* as 'a vile and inhuman story told in the foulest language we have ever listened to on a public platform'. The play was finally heard right through only because the police were there 'thick as blackberries in September'.

SOMERSET MAUGHAM (1874-1965) **Created a record in 1908 by having four plays running simultaneously in the West End:** *Lady Frederick* at the Court, *Mrs Dot* at the Comedy, *Jack Straw* at the Vaudeville, *The Explorer* at the Lyric. Between 1898 and 1933 he wrote 27 full-length plays including such durable comedies as *The Circle* (1921) and *The Constant Wife* (1926). 'He instilled into me', wrote Noel Coward, 'the tremendous importance of construction. He complimented me early in our friendship on my facility for dialogue but he warned me that this facility could be a danger as well as an asset. Good dialogue, he said, is like the most charming interior decoration of a house but it is of little use if the foundations are insecure and the drains don't work.'

SEAN O'CASEY (1880-1964) born a Protestant in a Dublin slum, he grew up in extreme poverty: unskilled, self-educated, often unemployed and militantly committed to the workers' cause. His fame today rests on three great plays all reflecting the chaos which the Easter Rising of 1916 and the Civil War inflicted on the ordinary people of Dublin: *The Shadow of a Gunman* (1923), *Juno and the Paycock* (1924) and *The Plough and the Stars* (1926). All three were produced by the Abbey Theatre, Dublin, though the last-named produced a riot at its première. 'You have disgraced yourselves again', shouted Yeats at the audience. However he rejected O'Casey's next play, *The Silver Tassie* (1928) and when it did finally have its Irish première in 1935 there were attacks from Church and press on play and author. O'Casey never wrote for the Abbey again.

BEN TRAVERS (1886-1980) The best British farce-writer after Pinero and the longest-surviving playwright after Shaw. He wrote his first farce, *The Dippers*, in 1922: his last, *After You With The Milk*, in 1979. But his most famous work was done for the Tom Walls/Ralph Lynn team at the Aldwych in the 1920s: *Rookery Nook* (1926) ran for 409 performances, *Thark* (1927) for 401, *Plunder* (1928) for 344. He lived long enough to have a new work, *The Bed Before Yesterday*, (1975) staged in the West End in his 90th year and to see *Plunder* in the opening repertory of the new National Theatre in 1976.

T. S. ELIOT (1888-1965) American-born poet, critic and playwright who attempted to re-establish verse as a natural medium of drama with *Murder in the Cathedral* (1935), *The Family Reunion* (1939), *The Cocktail Party* (1949), *The Confidential Clerk* (1953) and *The Elder Statesman* (1958). His attempt took modern drama up an interesting side-alley. But Eliot's most potent dramatic piece remains *Sweeney Agonistes: Fragments of an Aristophanic Melodrama.*

J. B. PRIESTLEY (1894-) Forthright English dramatist who has combined commercial success with more experimental pieces about the nature of time based on theories by J. W. Dunne and Ouspensky. *The Good Companions* (1931) ran for 331 performances; *Laburnum Grove* (1933) for 335; *When We Are Married* (1938) for 277, *The Linden Tree* (1947) for 422. Of the 'time' plays the most celebrated are *Time and the Conways* (1937) and *I Have Been Here Before* (1937). Priestley himself in 1938 played the role of the pickled photographer in *When We Are Married* for several nights when the original actor was injured.

NOEL COWARD (1899-1973) Prolific playwright, composer, librettist, actor, dancer, singer: known in theatrical circles as 'The Master'. Success came early: in 1925 he equalled Somerset Maugham's record by having his name outside four West End theatres at the same time with *Fallen Angels, On with the Dance, The Vortex* and *Hay Fever* ('Everyone but

Somerset Maugham said I was a second Somerset Maugham'). Of the 46 plays and musicals he wrote (some unproduced) the most durable are *Hay Fever* (1925), *Private Lives* (1930), *Design For Living* (1933), *Blithe Spirit* (1941), *Present Laughter* (1942). Coward took the fat off English comic dialogue, wrote great star parts, usually with himself in mind, and, under a seeming superficiality, waged a great campaign

Below top: Nina Boucicault as Peter and Hilda Trevelyan as Wendy in the first 1904 production of J.M. Barrie's 'Peter Pan' at the Duke of York's Theatre. Below bottom: The flying Lockwoods: Margaret as Peter and 16-year-old Julia as Wendy in 'Peter Pan' in 1957. This was the first time mother and daughter had appeared together in this play.

for individual fulfilment in the teeth of bourgeois conformity. After a lean post-war period, he lived to see his work rediscovered, commencing with revivals of *Private Lives* at Hampstead Theatre and *Hay Fever* by the National Theatre Company in 1963. 'I'm thrilled and flattered and frankly a little flabbergasted', he said at the time, 'that the National Theatre should have had the curious perceptiveness to choose a very early play of mine and to give it a cast that could play the Albanian telephone directory'.

SAMUEL BECKETT (1906-) Author of the most influential play in post-war drama, *Waiting For Godot* (1953); of **the shortest play in world drama,** the 30-second *Breath* (1969); the only Nobel Prize winner to appear in the cricketer's almanac, *Wisden;* and an endless source of critical analysis (a book about books about Beckett, published in 1970, runs to 383 pages). Beckett studied at Trinity College, Dublin; returned as a lecturer and there wrote his first dramatic work, *Le Kid* (a Corneille parody) in 1931; lived in Paris, worked for James Joyce, wrote a series of pessimistic novels and was stabbed by a pimp named Prudent in 1938. His fame, however, rests on his plays: *Waiting For Godot* (1953), *Endgame* (1957), *Krapp's Last Tape* (1958), *Happy Days* (1961), *Not I* (1973). He has relentlessly shown how much drama can do without while at the same time preserving an almost musical exactness of form. He himself denies this. 'If you insist on finding form', he once said to Harold Pinter, 'I'll describe it for you. I was in hospital once. There was a man in another ward, dying of throat cancer. In the silence, I could hear his screams continually. That's the only kind of form my work has.'

TERENCE RATTIGAN (1911-79) Like Coward, a dramatist who went through the cycle of extravagant acclaim, equally extravagant attack and belated restoration within his own lifetime. His longest-running plays were *French Without Tears* (1936) which ran for 1049 performances — still the greatest success ever enjoyed by a West End debutant — *Flare Path* (1942), which had 670 performances, *While The Sun Shines* (1943) which lasted for 1154 performances, *The Deep Blue Sea* (1952) which had 513 performances and *Ross* (1960) which had 763 performances. Rattigan not only wrote 18 well-crafted

Above: Noel Coward: the Master. Above left: A fastidious romp. Gertrude Lawrence and Noel Coward wrestle on the floor while Laurence Olivier and Adrienne Allen look on with astonishment in the 1930 production of 'Private Lives'. Below left and far left: Margaret Rutherford's happy medium, Madame Arcati, and sceptically surveyed by Kay Hammond and Fay Compton in the 1941 production of 'Blithe Spirit' at the Piccadilly.

The play that changed the course of modern drama. Hugh Burden, Paul Daneman, Peter Woodthorpe and Peter Bull in Peter Hall's 1955 production of 'Waiting for Godot' at the Arts Theatre.

plays between 1936 and 1977, he also bequeathed to us the figure of Aunt Edna, archetypal London theatregoer, 'a nice, respectable, middle-class, middle-aged maiden lady with time on her hands and money to help her pass it'.

BRENDAN BEHAN (1923-64) Ebullient Irish playwright of slender output, large intake and reckless talent. He wrote *The Quare Fellow* (1956) and *The Hostage* (1959) which, in Joan Littlewood's production, ran for 452 performances at the Theatre Royal, Stratford East and Wyndham's. Both plays showed Behan to be a lord of language. But he was also a life-loving lord of misrule who preferred the spendour of talk to the drudgery of writing.

ROBERT BOLT (1924-) English dramatist with a capacity for popularising history and for writing meaty star parts. His greatest successes have been *Flowering Cherry* (1957) with Ralph Richardson as a self-aggrandising salesman (435 performances), *A Man For All Seasons* (1961) with Paul Scofield as Sir Thomas More (315 performances) and *Vivat, Vivat Regina* (1970) with

Sarah Miles and Eileen Atkins as Mary, Queen of Scots and Elizabeth (442 performances). A National Theatre play about Russia in 1917, *State of Revolution* (1977) seemed to tame history rather than popularise it.

PETER SHAFFER (1926-) English dramatist profitably obsessed with the conflict between Apollo and Dionysus, rational and instinctual man. His first play, however, was a middle-class domestic drama, *Five Finger Exercise* (1958) that ran for 607 performances in the West End. Since then he has explored his recurrent theme in *The Royal Hunt of the Sun* (1964), *The Battle of Shrivings* (1970), *Equus* (1973), and *Amadeus* (1979). He has also written a brilliant farce, *Black Comedy* (1970) which adapts the Chinese classical theatre convention of miming darkness with the lights full on.

PETER NICHOLS (1927-) English dramatist who blends autobiographical exploration with exuberant comedy of pain. His major works are *A Day In the Death Of Joe Egg* (1967), *The National Health* (1969), *Forget-me-not-Lane* (1971),

Paul Scofield as the aged Salieri in Peter Shaffer's 'Amadeus' at the Olivier Theatre in 1979. "Tripe" said 'The Sunday Times'. "A near masterpiece" claimed 'The Times'.

Chez Nous (1974), *The Freeway* (1974), *Privates on Parade* (1977), *Born in the Gardens* (1980), *Passion Play* (1981). 'Nichols', wrote Roger Woddis, 'offers no easy answers. He disturbs us because he is honest. He is a worried man, and that is his strength.'

JOHN OSBORNE (1929-) English dramatist who helped change the face of his native theatre with his first play, *Look Back In Anger* (1956). It put social issues and youthful frustration onto the cosy post-war London stage; it made a lot of money for the newly-founded English Stage Company at the Royal Court; it liberated numberless other writers. Nothing of Osborne's since has had the same measurable impact but he has written many fine plays including *The Entertainer* (1957), *Luther* (1961), *Inadmissible Evidence* (1964), *A Patriot For Me* (1965), *Time Present* and *The Hotel In Amsterdam* (1968),

Richard O'Callaghan as Mozart and Frank Finlay as Salieri in 'Amadeus' when it transferred to Her Majesty's Theatre in 1981.

West of Suez (1971) and *Watch It Come Down* (1976). Osborne's plays are all full of rhetoric, feeling and sympathy for branded outsiders. He himself has written: 'We English are more violent than we allow ourselves to know. That is why we have the greatest body of dramatic literature in the world.'

JOHN ARDEN (1930-) Author of **the longest play on record:** *The Non-Stop Connolly Show* (1975) which took a full 26½ hours to perform in Dublin. Also wrote a series of complex moral fables that were a vital part of the new movement in British theatre: *Serjeant Musgrave's Dance* (1959), *The Workhouse Donkey* (1963) and *Armstrong's Last Goodnight* (1964). Since 1960 he has also written plays with his wife, Margaretta D'Arcy, and it was one of these, *The Island of the Mighty* (1972) that led to a bad-tempered dispute with the producing management, the Royal Shakespeare Company, and that unhappily led to the audience shouting Mr Arden off the stage so that his play might continue.

HAROLD PINTER (1930-) Supreme exponent of the loaded pause, of life as a constant battle for territory, of sinister outside forces taking over a room: all his plays are about space-invaders. As his income has soared so has that of his characters; but his obsessions remain as strong. His best plays are *The Birthday Party* (total week's takings during its first-ever run at the Lyric Hammersmith in 1958 was a pitiful £260 11s 8d); *The Caretaker* (1960), *The Homecoming* (1965), *Old Times* (1971), *No Man's Land* (1975), *Betrayal* (1978). He has also written numerous television plays and screenplays, is an associate director of the National Theatre and has spawned many imitators once dubbed 'the Pinteretti'.

EDWARD BOND (1935-) English playwright whose work has often produced hostile reactions from critics and censors. *Saved* (1965), presented by the Royal Court as a club production, led to 18 summonses being made against the English Stage Company by the Director of Public Prosecutions: the company was ordered to pay £50 costs. *Early Morning* (1968) was banned in *toto* by the Lord Chamberlain for its scenes of cannibalism and its portrayal of Queen Victoria as a gruff lesbian: it was **the last play ever banned** since the Lord Chamberlain's 231-year reign

over drama was ended by the Theatres Act of 1968. Bond has since achieved great eminence with works like *Lear* (1971), *The Sea* and *Bingo* (1973), *The Fool* (1975), *The Woman* (1978) which was the first new play to be given its première in the National's Olivier Theatre. Bond is still more honoured abroad than at home. By the end of the 1970s there had been 200 professional productions of his work abroad, 56 at home.

TOM STOPPARD (1937-) Born in Czechoslovakia, reared in Singapore, India and Yorkshire, he took root in Bristol in 1953 where he became a journalist. Achieved overnight fame when the National Theatre presented *Rosen-*

Left: Harold Pinter: the smiler with the knife under the cloak. Below: Michael Feast as Foster, Ralph Richardson as Hirst, John Gielgud as Spooner, Terence Rigby as Briggs in Harold Pinter's 'No Man's Land' at the Old Vic 1975 as seen through the eyes of 'Punch' cartoonist Bill Hewison.

NO MAN'S LAND

Susan Fleetwood and Paul Freeman in Edward Bond's 'The Woman' at the Olivier Theatre in 1978: the first new play to be given its première in the Olivier.

Diana Rigg and Peter Machin in Tom Stoppard's play about press freedom, 'Night and Day', at the Phoenix Theatre in 1979.

crantz and Guildenstern Are Dead (1967) which reflected Shakespeare's Elsinore through the eyes of two supernumeraries. Since then his works include Jumpers (1972), Travesties (1974), Dirty Linen (1976), Every Good Boy Deserves Favour (1977), which was **the first play ever to**

use a full-scale symphony orchestra as a vital feature of its cast, and Night and Day (1979). Stoppard has latterly turned from explorations of man's moral dilemmas into an unambiguous champion of political and press freedom; but he has retained his verbal wit, his high-jinks, his

eclipsed Maugham and Coward's record by having five plays running simultaneously in the West End: *The Norman Conquests* (a trilogy), *Absurd Person Singular*, and *Absent Friends*. His plays have been translated into 26 languages. He has also expanded the rules of playwriting. In *How The Other Half Loves* (1969) he interwove two dinner parties taking place on consecutive evenings. In *The Norman Conquests* (1973) he presented the events of a single weekend from three different vantage-points: dining-room, sitting-room and garden. In *Sisterly Feelings* (1979) he presented a play which had four possible versions depending on the toss of a coin at the end of the first scene and the decision of one of two actresses at the end of the second scene. Ayckbourn combines his prolific output with a job as unsalaried Director of Productions at the Stephen Joseph Theatre in Scarborough where his plays invariably receive their first production. 'How do we know you won't just disappear' a Scarborough councillor asked Ayckbourn when his company applied for a grant. 'I've been here since 1957', replied Ayckbourn, 'and that's longer than you'.

HOWARD BRENTON (1941-) Dramatist who caused the biggest furore in the National Theatre's history with *The Romans In Britain* (1980) which included a scene of simulated homosexual rape. It brought visits from Scotland Yard, threats of punitive action by the Greater London Council in terms of grant reduction, and a prosecution of the director, Michael Bogdanov, by Mrs Mary Whitehouse in 1982. It was Brenton's tenth full-length play. The others include *Magnificence* (1973), *The Churchill Play* (1974), *Weapons of Happiness* (1976), *Sore Throats* (1979). He has shown a constant fascination with epic themes at a time of preoccupation with psychological minutiae.

NOTABLE PLAYS BANNED BY THE LORD CHAMBERLAIN
Polly (1737) by John Gay.
Gustavus Vasa (1739) by Henry Brooke because the Vice-Regent of Denmark and Norway was thought to be a lampoon of the Prime Minister of England.

The Man of the World (1770) by Charles Macklin which was an attack on the Prime Minister, Lord Bute.
The Cenci (1819) by Percy Bysshe Shelley.

love of theatrical pyrotechnics and showbiz. He is now a moralist with a firecracker in each hand.

ALAN AYCKBOURN (1939-) The most popular English dramatist since Noel Coward. In 1975 he

Splendour in the grass. Andrew Cruickshank looks on in wry disgust as Selina Cadell and Greg Hicks wrestle on the ground in the picnic scene from Alan Ayckbourn's 'Sisterly Feelings' (a play with four possible permutations) at the Olivier Theatre in 1980.

The scene that caused Mrs Whitehouse to reach for her lawyer. The naked Druids about to be attacked by the Roman centurions, poised to draw their weapons, in Howard Brenton's 'The Romans in Britain' at the Olivier Theatre, 1980.

Charles 1 (1825) by Mary Russell Mitford.

Coningsby (1844) adapted by Shirley Brooks from Disraeli's novel.

La Dame aux Camélias (1852) by Alexandre Dumas *fils*.

Ghosts (1881) by Henrik Ibsen. 'I have studied Ibsen's plays pretty carefully', said the censor Mr Piggott, 'and all the characters in Ibsen's plays appear to me morally deranged'.

Mrs Warren's Profession (1893) by Bernard Shaw.

Salome (1893) by Oscar Wilde.

Damaged Goods (1902) because it dealt with venereal disease.

Bethlehem (1902) by Laurence Housman.

Waste (1907) by Harley Granville-Barker.

The Breaking Point (1907) by Edward Garnett which dealt with an unmarried girl's fear of pregnancy.

The Shewing Up of Blanco Posnet (1909) and *Press Cuttings* (1909) by Bernard Shaw.

Six Characters in Search of an Author (1921) by Luigi Pirandello.

Desire Under the Elms (1925) by Eugene O'Neill.

Vectia (1925) by Marie Stopes.

Green Pastures (1930) by Marc Connelly.

The Children's Hour (1934) by Lillian Hellman.

Pick-Up Girl (1946) by Elsa Shelley.

The Catalyst (1958) by Ronald Duncan which dealt with a Lesbian love-affair.

A Patriot For Me (1965) by John Osborne which contained a drag-ball scene.

Early Morning (1968) by Edward Bond not least because of its suggestion of a Lesbian relationship between Queen Victoria and Florence Nightingale.

PLAYS ABOUT THEATRE

The Knight of the Burning Pestle (1607) by Beaumont and Fletcher.

The Rehearsal (1671) by George Villiers, Duke of Buckingham.

The Critic (1779) by Sheridan.

Wild Oats (1791) by John O'Keeffe.

The Royal Family by Ferber and Kaufman (1927).

Red Peppers (1935) and *Present Laughter* (1942) by Noel Coward.

Harlequinade (1948) by Terence Rattigan.

On Monday Next (1949) by Philip King.

The Country Girl (1949) by Clifford Odets.

La Répétition (1950) by Jean Anouilh.

Kean (1954) by Jean-Paul Satre.

Privates on Parade (1979) by Peter Nichols.

The Dresser (1980) by Ronald Harwood.

Nicholas Nickleby (1981) by David Edgar.

Noises Off (1982) by Michael Frayn.

PLAYS FEATURING SPORT

Boxing *In The Jungle of the Cities* (1921-4) by Bertolt Brecht. *Golden Boy* (1937) by Clifford Odets. *A Sight of Glory* (1975) by Barrie Keeffe.

Cricket *Badgers Green* (1930) by R.C. Sherriff *A Bit of a Test* (1933) by Ben Travers *Time and Time Again* by Alan Ayckbourn (1971) *Outside Edge* (1979) by Richard Harris.

Soccer *Zigger-Zagger* (1967) by Peter Terson *Only a Game* (1973) by Barrie Keeffe *Into Europe* (1981) by Ron Hutchinson.

Tennis *Joking Apart* (1978) by Alan Ayckbourn.

Wrestling *Trafford Tanzi* (1981) by Claire Luckham.

SOME FAMOUS FLOPS

☐ Noel Coward's *Sirocco* (Daly's 1927) when everyone was booed at curtain-fall for 10 minutes, and the leading actress, Frances Doble, gave a curtain-speech saying that it was the happiest night of her life.

☐ William Douglas-Home's *Ambassador Extraordinary* (Aldwych 1948) about a young man who has landed from Mars by rocket. The gallery booed vociferously. The author, at the end, riposted: 'I hope some people have enjoyed the play. As for the others, it doesn't much matter whether they liked the play or not — because if they don't learn the lesson of compromise, taught tonight, in six month's time that gallery won't be here'. But it was.

☐ Charles Lincoln's *Storks Don't Talk* (Comedy 1951) featuring the Hollywood comedian, Mischa Auer. Greeted by a barrage of boos, shouts and catcalls, it contained (like all really bad plays) lines that seemed to invite derision: The hero's 'Don't tell me sir that I am the result of a *faux pas*' and the parlourmaid's 'I'm only working here to get atmosphere'.

☐ Steve Gooch's *The Women-Pirates: Ann Bonney and Mary Read* (Aldwych 1978) loudly booed on the first night, variously described as 'an awesome load of bilge' and 'Yo-ho-ho and a bottle of twaddle' and quickly withdrawn from the RSC repertoire after 19 performances.

☐ Philip Martin's *Thee and Me* (Lyttelton 1980) was an apocalyptic play set in the year 2040, stuffed with *Cold Comfort Farm* dialogue ('He came a-suitoring to me') and prematurely withdrawn, after much ridicule, from the National's repertory.

America

BRONSON HOWARD (1842-1908) The first US dramatist to rely solely on playwriting for a living; founder of the American Dramatists Club in 1891; one of the first US dramatists to draw on American characters and social conditions for his themes. His first success was *Saratoga* (1870 and enjoyably revived by the Royal Shakespeare Company in 1978) about a young hero 'who loved not wisely but four well'. He wrote 20 other plays anchored in American life of which the most popular were *Young Mrs Winthrop* (1882),

Estelle Mortimer, Edwin Stevens and Ethel Barrymore in Clyde Fitch's 'Captain Jinks of the Horse Marines' at New York's Garrick Theater, 1901.

The Henrietta (1887), a satire of financial life, and Shenandoah (1888), a drama of the war between the States.

WILLIAM CLYDE FITCH (1865-1909) One of America's most prolific dramatists: wrote 50 plays before his death at the age of 44. Also one of the first American playwrights to publish his plays. Began his career with Beau Brummell (1890) commissioned by Richard Mansfield. Had four plays on view simultaneously in the Broadway season of 1900-1901: The Climbers, Captain

Jinks of the Horse Marines, Barbara Frietchie and Lovers Lane. Often wrote plays tailor-made for a specific star, e.g. Her Own Way (1903) written for Maxine Elliott known as 'Venus de Milo with arms'. After his death, critic Walter Pritchard Eaton wrote that he raised the level of staging by his meticulous personal direction.

GEORGE KELLY (1887-1974) A one-time vaudeville actor and sketch-writer who wrote quite penetrative plays about the American character. His big hit was The Show-Off (1924) which ran for 575 performances and attacked the bluff and bragging of American business life. Craig's Wife (1925), a withering portrait of a coldly malevolent home, won the Pulitzer Prize and ran for 289 performances. He wrote another seven plays (the last in 1946) but none enjoyed anything like the same success.

MAXWELL ANDERSON (1888-1959) Prolific dramatist who tried to raise the tone of Broadway with historical plays, verse drama and pseudo-Shakespearean work. His greatest successes were *What Price Glory* (1924), *Elizabeth the Queen* (1930), *Mary of Scotland* (1933), *Winterset* (1935) dealing with the Sacco-Vanzetti case, *Key Largo* (1939) and *The Bad Seed* (1954). 'The quality of his work', wrote Brooks Atkinson, 'deteriorated in his last years although he never lost his commitment to freedom and to America'.

EUGENE O'NEILL (1888-1953) The first major American playwright; winner of the Nobel Peace Prize in 1936; four-time winner of the Pulitzer prize. His plays were hewn out of his own experience, often wordy but rarely devoid of formidable emotional power. The full list of them (several produced posthumously) is

1916 *Bound East For Cardiff*
1917 *The Long Voyage Home* and *Ile*
1919 *The Moon of the Caribbees*
1920 *The Emperor Jones* and *Beyond the Horizon*
1921 *Anna Christie*
1922 *The Hairy Ape*
1924 *All God's Chillun Got Wings*
1925 *Desire Under The Elms*
1926 *The Great God Brown*
1927 *Marco Millions*
1928 *Strange Interlude*
1931 *Mourning Becomes Electra*
1933 *Ah Wilderness*
1934 *Days Without End*
1938 *More Stately Mansions*
1939 *The Iceman Cometh*
1940 *A Touch of the Poet*

An island in the West Indies envisioned in Eugene O'Neill's 'The Emperor Jones' (1920). The staging is expressionist in style.

The Mayo farmhouse in Eugene O'Neill's first Broadway production, Pulitzer Prize-winning 'Beyond The Horizon' (1920). The staging is here in the naturalistic tradition.

1941 *Hughie* and *Long Day's Journey Into Night*
1943 *A Moon for the Misbegotten*
The onset of the Second World War and a tremor diagnosed as Parkinson's Disease put an end to O'Neill's most fertile period. In the end he couldn't even hold a pen to write. 'A man wills his own defeat when he pursues the unattainable', O'Neill said. 'But his *struggle* is his success. Such a figure is necessarily tragic. But to me he is not depressing, he is exhilarating.'

GEORGE S. KAUFMAN (1889-1961) Playwright, critic, director and producer. Known as 'The Great Collaborator' because almost all his writing was done with other authors including Marc Connelly (1890-1981), Moss Hart (1904-61) and Edna Ferber (1887-1968). He wrote only two full-length plays by himself: *The Cocoanuts* (1925) starring the Marx Brothers and *The Butter and Egg Man* (1925). His best known collaborations were: *The Royal Family* (1927), *Once in a Lifetime* (1930), *You Can't Take It With You* (1936) *The Man Who Came To Dinner* (1939). The first of these was with Edna Ferber the last three with Moss Hart. When asked by *Vanity Fair* magazine to write his own epitaph, Kaufman replied: 'Over my dead body'.

Top right: George S. Kaufman and Edna Ferber's 'The Royal Family' at the Selwyn Theater New York in 1927: a comedy about the theatre inspired by the exotic Drew-Barrymore clan.
Bottom right: Jo Mielziner's extraordinary set for Elmer Rice's 'Street Scene' (1929). An actual house at 25 West 65th Street was duplicated for this famous setting.

ELMER RICE (1892-1967) Dramatist, director and producer, pioneer of Expressionist drama in America; the first dramatist to use the flashback technique on stage which he did in his first play, *On Trial* (1914). Most famous plays: *The Adding Machine* (1923), a grim satire on automation; *Street Scene* (1929), a sketch of neighbourhood life on a frowzy New York block; *Dream Girl* (1945). Rice was a socialist, a rationalist, an advocate of good causes who professed not to like the theatre. When he accepted the Pulitzer Prize for *Street Scene* in 1929, he chilled the atmosphere by declaring 'I do not like playgoing'.

THORNTON WILDER (1897-1975) Dramatist and novelist famous for his use of anti-naturalist devices. Best-known plays: *The Long Christmas Dinner, The Happy Journey to Trenton and Camden, Pullman Car Hiawatha* (1931: all one-acters); *Our Town* (1938) which strips the stage of scenery to present a picture of American community life; *The Skin of Our Teeth* (1942); *The Matchmaker* (1954), a revised version of his own *The Merchant of Yonkers* (1938) which in turn was based on Nestroy's Viennese farce, *Einen Jux will er sich machen* (1842). Eventually this became the musical *Hello Dolly* (1964). 'It was ironic', wrote Brooks Atkinson, 'that Wilder's biggest hit had none of his personal quality'.

LILLIAN HELLMAN (1905-) America's most successful woman playwright. Wrote her first play, *The Children's Hour,* in 1934. It ran for 691 performances. Her most successful plays after that were *The Little Foxes* (1939: 410 performances) *Watch on the Rhine* (1941: 378 performances) and *Another Part of the Forest* (1946: 182 performances). Since then she has written *The Autumn Garden* (1951), the book for the musical *Candide* (1956) and *Toys in the Attic* (1960). *The Little Foxes* was revived in 1981 to great acclaim with Elizabeth Taylor playing her first speaking role in the theatre (she made her debut as a silent Helen of Troy in *Dr Faustus* at the Oxford Playhouse in 1966).

CLIFFORD ODETS (1906-63) Left-wing dramatist with great sympathy for the exploited. Co-founder (with Harold Clurman, Cheryl Crawford and Lee Strasberg) of the Group Theatre in 1931 and author of many potent plays: *Waiting for Lefty* (1935), about the cab-strike in New York: *Till the Day I Die* (1935), an anti-Nazi play; *Golden Boy* (1937) about a professional boxer; *The Big Knife* (1949) about the evil of Hollywood; and *Winter Journey* (1952) about a ruined alcoholic actor. At the peak of his career in the 1930s he said he wanted to discover how, in a materialistic world, a man could retain 'the conviction of innocence'. Some say he was his own best exhibit.

TENNESSEE WILLIAMS (1911-) Poetic, confessional, prolific playwright who has written some of the key works of modern drama as well as some sensationalist ephemera. His early works *(Cairo, Shanghai, Bombay* 1935, *Candles to the Sun* 1936, *The Fugitive Kind* 1937) were highly promising one-acters. But his reputation was established by *The Glass Menagerie* (1945), *A Streetcar Named Desire* (1947), *Summer and Smoke* (1947), *Cat on a Hot Tin Roof* (1955), *Suddenly Last Summer* (1958) and *Sweet Bird of Youth* (1959). 'There is no one in the English-speaking theatre today', wrote Eric Bentley, 'who can outdo Mr Williams's dialogue at its best' adding that his problem is ambiguity of aim. 'He seems to want to kick the world in the pants and yet be the world's sweetheart, to combine the glories of martyrdom with the comforts of success'.

ARTHUR MILLER (1915-) A major exponent of psychological realism fascinated by the relationship of two sons with their father, a theme he explored in his first three plays: *The Man Who Had All The Luck* (1944), *All My Sons* (1947), *Death of a Salesman* (1949). Other major work includes *The Crucible* (1953), *A View from the Bridge* (1955), *After the Fall* (1964), *The Price* (1968) which returns to the theme of two sons and a father. 'Miller's plays', wrote Kenneth Tynan, 'are hard, patrist, athletic, concerned mostly with men. Tennessee Williams's are soft, matrist, sickly, concerned mostly with women. What links them is their love for the bruised individual soul and its life of quiet desperation'.

Elizabeth Taylor in Lillian Hellman's 'The Little Foxes' which rode in triumph through Broadway in 1981 and London's West End in 1982.

David Schofield as Nick and Margaret Tyzack as Martha in Edward Albee's 'Who's Afraid of Virginia Woolf?' revived at the National's Lyttelton Theatre in 1981.

start on Broadway with *Come Blow Your Horn* (1961) and his numerous hits since then include *Barefoot in the Park* (1963), *The Odd Couple* (1965), *Plaza Suite* (1968), *The Last of the Red Hot Lovers* (1969), *The Gingerbread Lady* (1970), *The Sunshine Boys* (1972), *California Suite* (1976), *Chapter Two* (1978). Re-reading his plays in book form, Simon once said: 'When I was good, I was very, very good. . . when I was bad, we folded'. Rarely have his plays folded.

EDWARD ALBEE (1928-) Exploratory, experimental American dramatist who has never repeated the commercial success of his early plays. But he keeps plugging away on Broadway in the belief that someone has to try and keep the straight play alive. Major works: *Zoo Story* (1958), *The American Dream* (1960), *Who's Afraid of Virginia Woolf?* (1961), *Tiny Alice* (1964), *A Delicate Balance* (1966), *All Over* (1971), *Seascape* (1974), *Counting the Ways* (1976), *The Lady from Dubuque* (1977). His themes are basically isolation and despair but he is writing in a theatre hungry for comfort and optimism.

SAM SHEPARD (1943-) Leading avant-garde playwright who describes his plays as 'painting in space'. His dream-like work also contains a strange mix of characters: 'Hoboes, thieves, rock 'n rollers, Martians, cowboys, moguls, madmen — Shepard's heroes range as widely as his interests', according to critic John Lahr. Main works: *Chicago, Icarus's Mother, Red Cross* (1966), *La Turista* (1967), *Tooth of Crime* (1972), *Angel City* (1976), *Curse of the Starving Class (1978), Buried Child* (1979) which won the Pulitzer Prize and *True West* (1981).

DAVID MAMET (1947-) Highly promising new playwright with a talent for picking laughter out of the aggression and bullishness of everyday American speech. Has written: *Sexual Perversity in Chicago* and *Duck Variations* (1974), *American Buffalo* (1977), *The Water Engine* (1978), *A Life in the Theatre* (1978). Lately he has written for the movies *(The Postman Always Rings Twice,* 1981) but one hopes his future lies with the theatre.

NEIL SIMON (1927-) Reckoned to be the most financially successful playwright in the history of the theatre: his annual income from royalties has been estimated at over two million dollars. He arranges most of his own financing, owns his own theatre (the Eugene O'Neill) and often adapts the plays for the movies. Achieved his

Above and below: Sitting Bull presides over an Indian dance that recalls some of the pride and tragedy of the Sioux nation, from 'Annie Get Your Gun' (1947). (BBC Hulton Picture Library).

The Royal Shakespeare Company's production of 'Nicholas Nickleby', with David Threlfall (left) as Smike and Roger Rees (right) as Nicholas. (Chris Davies).

The National Theatre on the South Bank which opened in 1976. (National Theatre).

Above: Ellen Terry, Irving's partner, as Lady
Macbeth. Right: Coquelin (1841-1909) as Napoleon
in 'Plus Que Rien'. Below: Edmund Kean as Richard
III. (All Mary Evans Picture Library).

Above: 'Timour, the Tartar', an equestrian melodrama, produced at Covent Garden in 1811. (Victoria and Albert Museum). Below: Festival performance at the multi-tiered Grand Imperial Theatre, Moscow. (Mary Evans Picture Library).

A programme cover for the most popular American play, 'Uncle Tom's Cabin,' in one of its frequent revivals.

The first play written by an American was *Gustavus Vasa* by Benjamin Colman (1673-1747) acted by students of Harvard College, 1690.

The first American tragedy was *The Prince of Parthia* 1765, by Thomas Godfrey. A neo-classical work in the manner of Addison's *Cato* (1713). Produced in Philadelphia. Also **the first American play to be performed by professional actors.**

The first American comedy was *The Contrast* 1787, by Royall Tyler. Also presents the first important native stock-type, the rural Yankee. Although modelled on the comedies of Sheridan, Tyler's theme is the superiority of Americans to foreigners.

The first example of the Indian as hero was Augustus Stone's *Metamora* (1829), in which the noble savage resists the duplicity and cruelty of the white invaders.

The first anti-slavery play was *The Gladiator,* 1831, about an uprising of slaves in ancient Rome.

The first play by an American black was *Escape or A Leap for Freedom* 1858, by William Wells Brown.

The first serious treatment of the American black was *The Octoroon* or *Life in Louisiana* by Dion Boucicault, 1859.

The first long-run American production was *The Drunkard* or *The Fallen Saved*, 1844, which ran for 130 performances at the Boston Museum. Harry Watkins, the leading actor, almost killed himself imitating delirium tremens.

The most popular American play is *Uncle Tom's Cabin* which appeared in numerous dramatisations as soon as Mrs Harriet Beecher Stowe's

Gabriel with his horn in the 1930 Broadway production of Marc Connelly's 'The Green Pastures'. Because it put God on the stage the play was automatically banned in Britain by the Lord Chamberlain.

novel was published in 1852. The most popular version was adapted by George L. Aiken and first played at Troy (USA) in 1852. During the 1890s 400-500 troupes were playing it.

The longest American play title is *Oh Dad, Poor Dad Mama's Hung You In The Closet and I'm Feelin' So Sad* by Arthur Kopit, 1960.

The first American Hamlet was Lewis Hallam Jr., 1761.

The first successful play by a black American on Broadway was *Run, Little Chillun*, 1933, about folk religion.

The first black playwright to win the New York Critics Circle Award was Lorraine Hansberry with *Raisin in the Sun*, 1959.

The first American play to put God on the stage was Marc Connelly's *The Green Pastures*, 1930. It also provided the most famous entrance cue in modern drama. 'Gangway', called the Angel Gabriel, 'Gangway for de Lawd God Jehovah'. On stage walked 62-year-old Richard B. Harrison, grandson of fugitive slaves and a lecturer and teacher who had never acted before. He played the role for 1659 consecutive performances until his death in 1935 and he was treated as if a special divinity surrounded him. He was, for instance, constantly asked to baptise children in Harlem churches. He was also thought to have healing powers in his touch. After his death, it became impossible to keep *The Green Pastures* on stage.

American plays dealing with homosexuality are Edward Albee's *The Zoo Story* (1959), The

LONGEST RUNS IN NEW YORK OF NON-MUSICAL PLAYS

	Number of performances
Life With Father (1939)	3224
Tobacco Road (1933)	3182
Abie's Irish Rose (1922)	2327
Harvey (1944)	1775
Born Yesterday (1946)	1642
Mary, Mary (1961)	1572
Barefoot in the Park (1963)	1530
Arsenic and Old Lace (1941)	1444
Cactus Flower (1965)	1234
Sleuth (1970)	1222

American Dream (1961), *Tiny Alice* (1963); Robert Anderson's *Tea and Sympathy* (1953); Mart Crowley's *The Boys in the Band* (1968); Lillian Hellman's *The Children's Hour* (1934); Mordaunt Sharp's *The Green Bay Tree* (1934); Tennessee Williams's *Cat on a Hot Tin Roof* (1955) and *Suddenly Last Summer* (1958).

Most frequent winners of the Pulitzer Prize awarded annually since 1917 for the 'Best original American play performed in New York': Eugene O'Neill won it four times for *Beyond the Horizon* (1920) *Anna Christie* (1922), *Strange Interlude* (1928), and *Long Day's Journey Into Night* (1957). Robert Sherwood won it three times for *Idiot's Delight* (1936), *Abe Lincoln in Illinois* (1939), and *There Shall Be No Night* (1941). Thornton Wilder also won it three times for *The Bridge of San Luis Rey* 1928 (fiction prize), *Our Town* (1938), *The Skin of Our Teeth* (1943).

The only American play to take place in the human stomach is *Another Interior* by Edward Goodman, 1915. The leading character was called Gastric Juice.

Notable American plays about fiendish children were Lillian Hellman's *The Children's Hour*, 1934; Maxwell Anderson's *The Bad Seed*, 1954; Arthur Miller's *The Crucible*, 1953.

American plays about trials are *The Crucible*, 1953; *The Caine Mutiny Court Martial*, 1954; *Inherit The Wind*, 1955; *The Andersonville Trial*, 1960.

American plays about strikes are *Black Pit*, 1935, about a miners' strike; Clifford Odets's *Waiting For Lefty*, 1935, about a taxi-drivers' strike; *Days to Come*, 1936, about a labour strike.

American actors who have played the same role on stage and screen are Marlon Brando in *A Streetcar Named Desire*, Humphrey Bogart in *The Petrified Forest*, Rex Harrison in *My Fair Lady*, James Earl Jones in *The Great White Hope*, Jack Lemmon in *Tribute*, Paul Newman and Geraldine Page in *Sweet Bird of Youth*, Paul Robeson in *Show Boat*, Sidney Poitier in *A Raisin in the Sun*, Katharine Hepburn in *The Philadelphia Story*, Ben Gazzara in *End As A Man*, Walter Matthau in *The Odd Couple*.

BEST PLAYS
In 1940 leading critic George Jean Nathan com-

piled his own list of the best play written by each of the leading American playwrights. It was as follows:

Eugene O'Neill: *Strange Interlude* (although I can never without difficulty dismiss the short play, *The Moon of the Caribbees*)

S.N. Behrman: *Rain From Heaven*

Maxwell Anderson: *What Price Glory*

Lillian Hellman: *The Little Foxes*

Clifford Odets: *Awake and Sing*

Robert Sherwood: *Abe Lincoln in Illinois*

Elmer Rice: *Street Scene*

George Kelly: *Craig's Wife*

Sidney Howard: *Dodsworth* (with Sinclair Lewis)

George S. Kaufman: *The Royal Family* (with Edna Ferber). Musical: *Of Thee I Sing* (with Morrie Ryskind)

Moss Hart: *Once in a Lifetime* (with George S. Kaufman)

John Steinbeck: *Of Mice and Men*

William Saroyan: *The Time of Your Life*

Thornton Wilder: *Our Town*

Marc Connelly: *The Green Pastures*

Paul Green: *Johnny Johnson*

Philip Barry: *The Animal Kingdom*

Sidney Kingsley: *Dead End*

George M. Cohan: *Seven Keys to Baldpate*

George Abbott: *Broadway* (with Philip Dunning)

Sam and Bella Spewack: *Boy Meets Girl*

Zoe Atkins: *A Texas Nightingale*

Paul Osborn: *On Borrowed Time*

Robert Ardrey: *Star Spangled*

Irwin Shaw: *The Gentle People*

Mark Reed: *Yes, My Darling Daughter*

John Howard Lawson: *Processional*

The Heywards: *Porgy*

Hecht and MacArthur: *The Front Page*

Frank Craven: *The First Year*

Lula Vollmer: *Sun-Up*

Harry Wagstaff Gribble: *March Hares*

Albert Bein: *Little Ol' Boy*

The author's list of best American plays (in chronological order) since 1940 would be as follows:

Eugene O'Neill: *Long Days Journey Into Night*

Arthur Miller: *Death of a Salesman*

Tennessee Williams: *A Streetcar Named Desire*

Edward Albee: *Who's Afraid of Virginia Woolf?*

Neil Simon: *The Odd Couple*

'The Front Page' at the Times Square Theater Broadway in 1928. This comic classic by Ben Hecht and Charles MacArthur, set in the press room of the Criminal Courts Building Chicago, put more of America on to the stage than any play of its generation.

William Inge: *Picnic*
Jack Gelber: *The Connection*
Arthur Kopit: *Indians*
Lanford Wilson: *The Fifth of July*
Mike Weller: *Fishing*
Thomas Babe: *A Prayer for My Daughter*
David Mamet: *American Buffalo*
David Rabe: *Sticks and Bones*
Sam Shepard: *Buried Child*
Jean-Claude van Itallie: *America Hurrah*
Albert Innaurato: *Gemini*
Arthur Laurents: *The Time of the Cuckoo*
Robert Anderson: *I Never Sang For My Father*
Lorraine Hansberry: *A Raisin in the Sun*
George Axelrod: *The Seven Year Itch*
Ira Levin: *Deathtrap*
Jean Kerr: *Mary, Mary*
Bernard Pomerance: *The Elephant Man*

The wittiest author in American drama was undoubtedly George S. Kaufman who, between 1903 and 1961, wrote and co-wrote some 70 plays (as well as movie scripts for the Marx Brothers).

☐ He once deflated a very bad actor by the name of Guido Nadzo with the comment: 'Guido Nadzo is nadzo guido'.

☐ When Raymond Massey, after scoring a huge success playing Abraham Lincoln, became more and more Lincolnesque in his manner and speech off-stage, Kaufman observed: 'Massey won't be satisfied until someone assassinates him'.

☐ During a rehearsal of *Animal Crackers*, which he wrote with Morrie Ryskind for The Marx Brothers, he so despaired of the fraternal improvisations that he walked up on stage saying: 'Excuse me for interrupting but I thought for a minute I actually heard a line I wrote'.

☐ Of a monster American director, Jed Harris, a mutual acquaintance once remarked: 'Jed is his own worst enemy'. 'Not', said Kaufman, 'while I'm alive'.

☐ Asked by an interviewer if his boyhood had been rich or poor, he replied: 'When I was born, I owed twelve dollars'.

☐ After a particularly bad performance by Leonora Corbett in *Park Avenue* (1946) he said: 'You've heard of people living in a fool's paradise. Well, Leonora has a duplex there'.

☐ Once, in an apartment building, he ran into an old girlfriend proudly displaying a new con-

David Schofield in the National Theatre's 1980 production of Bernard Pomerance's 'The Elephant Man'.

sort. 'This', said the girl lording it over the playwright, 'is Mr Phillips and he's in cotton'. Kaufman regarded the couple calmly: 'And them as plants it is soon forgotten', he said as he got into the lift.

The USSR

The first known Russian plays appeared in the 16th century: morality plays of a very simple kind performed inside the churches.

The first attempt to catch up with western drama came in 1672. Johann Gregory, pastor of Moscow's German Lutheran Church, staged German religious plays at Moscow's newly-founded Imperial Theatre. The first of these plays was based on the Biblical story of Esther and called *Artaxerxes Play*.

The first important steps to widen the audience for Russian theatre came from Peter the Great. He imported from Germany a theatrical company headed by Johann Kunst. In 1702 he moved the Imperial Theatre from the palace grounds to Moscow's Red Square. In 1709 he established the St. Petersburg Imperial Theatre in his new capital. This enabled Russian audiences to see the work of western playwrights (such as Corneille). It also fostered native acting and playwriting.

The first major Russian playwright was DENIS FONVIZIN (1745-92). His first play, *The Brigadier* (1769) sprang out of an inspection tour of Catherine the Great's empire that he made with the empress herself: appalled by what he saw, he used his play to satirise the ignorance, brutality and primitive ways of the gentry.

The first important Russian play, however, and one that became the prototype of 'Russian realistic theatre' was Fonvizin's *The Minor* (1782). Again, it satirises the mores of the pig-raising and often pig-ignorant Russian gentry. A phrase much used by the oafish, 16 year-old hero, 'I don't want to study, I want to marry' has remained in common use to this day. And the realistic view of often absurd characters had a big influence on Russian dramatists from Gogol to Chekhov.

The natural successor to Fonvizin was ALEXANDER GRIBOYEDOV (1795-1829). His comedy, *Woe From Wit* (1823-24) dealt with all the topical themes of the day in a racy vernacular. In the author's own words, it contains 'twenty-five fools and one sensible man': the hero, Chtasky, who returns to Moscow after three years abroad and who meets a succession of ignorant blimps, vicious countesses, phony

Richard Pasco and Alan Howard as the strolling players who upset the bourgeois applecart in Adrian Noble's 1981 production of Ostrovsky's 'The Forest' for the RSC.

liberals. The play was not performed in its entirety until 1869 but it left an indelible imprint on the Russian language: in 1894 a scholar calculated that 61 phrases and aphorisms from the play had been accepted as Russian proverbs.

ALEXANDER PUSHKIN'S play *Motsart i Salieri (Mozart and Salieri,* 1832) was the forerunner of Peter Shaffer's *Amadeus* (1979). It was based on the rumour that Mozart had been poisoned by his less talented rival. It was turned into an opera by Rimsky-Korsakov in 1898.

The greatest early Russian comedy was Nikolai Gogol's *The Inspector General* (1836). Although the censors at first rejected the play, Tsar Nicholas I liked it so much that he overruled them and it was produced at the Alexandrinsky Theatre in St. Petersburg a few months after it was written. It is the story of a petty clerk who is mistaken by the officials of a small town for a government inspector: they indulge his every whim in order to prevent him exposing local bribery and corruption. Soviet critics today interpret the play as an attack on the Tsarist regime: the West tends to see it as a satire on perennial Russian bureaucracy. When the great Russian director, Vsevolod Meyerhold, tackled the play in 1926 he told his actors: 'What you must see is an aquarium where the water has not been changed for a long time, a greenish water where the fish move in circles and emit slow bubbles'.

Censorship blighted many theatrical careers. IVAN TURGENEV (1818-83) wrote his classic play, *A Month In the Country*, in Paris between 1848 and 1850. The original text was not printed until 1869 or performed until 1872. But for that Turgenev might have come down to posterity as a playwright rather than a novelist. Turgenev also fell foul of officialdom for his public praise of Gogol in the letter he wrote to the press on the latter's death in 1852. 'Only thoughtless and short-sighted people', he wrote 'do not feel the presence of a living flame in everything uttered by him'. Turgenev was sent to jail for a month and exiled to his estate where he remained under police supervision.

ALEXANDER OSTROVSKY (1823-86) was **the most prolific of Russian playwrights**. He wrote 48 full-length original plays as well as over 30 translations and collaborations and, at a time when the Russian theatre was dominated by foreign imports, created a national repertory. Tolstoy predicted his plays would become national classics, and by 1940 an average of 28 Ostrovsky plays were in production every day of the year in the Soviet Union. Today he is still the most widely produced playwright in the USSR. His play, *The Forest* (1871) also enjoyed a huge success when revived by the RSC in 1981.

ANTON CHEKHOV (1860-1904) is **the world's most widely performed Russian playwright.** He wrote 10 short plays of which the best-known are *The Bear* (1888), *The Proposal* (1888-89) and *The Wedding* (1889-90). He wrote seven full-length plays: *Platonov* 1880-81, *Ivanov* (1887-89), *The Wood Demon* (1889-90), *The Seagull* (1896), *Uncle Vanya* (1897), *Three Sisters* (1900-1), and *The Cherry Orchard* (1903-4). His plays are structured like music ('If a gun is hanging on the wall in the first act', he once said, 'it must fire in the last'), convey a tragic sense of human destiny, and yet are also suffused with moments of lyric gaiety. They also deal with universally recognisable experiences: solitude, unrequited

Anton Chekhov: the symphonic realist of Russian drama.

Claire Bloom and John Gielgud in Chekhov's 'Ivanov' at the Phoenix Theatre in 1965.

love, despair, drunkenness, parting from loved places and people, the consolation of work, the fading of youthful dreams and hopes. Chekhov always denied, however, that his plays were simply realistic. 'Realistic? But the stage is art. Kramskoy has a picture on which the faces are painted beautifully. What would happen if one cut out the nose of one of the faces and substituted a real one for it? The nose would be realistic. But the picture would be ruined'.

The first English productions of Chekhov's four greatest plays were *The Seagull*, Little Theatre, London, 31 March 1912; *Uncle Vanya*, Aldwych (Stage Society) 10 May 1914; *Three Sisters* Barnes, 16 February 1926; *The Cherry Orchard* Aldwych (Stage Society), 28 May 1911.

Above: The young Elsa Lanchester (with rifle) and James Mason (seated on the ground) in the Old Vic's 1933 revival of Chekhov's 'The Cherry Orchard' directed by Tyrone Guthrie.

Below: Mia Farrow and Paul Rogers in Gorky's 'The Zykovs' revived by David Jones at the Aldwych Theatre in 1976.

The longest straight runs enjoyed by Chekhov plays on the London stage were *The Cherry Orchard* at the Lyric Hammersmith in 1925 with 136 performances and *The Seagull* at the New Theatre in 1936 with 109 performances. But Laurence Olivier's production of *Uncle Vanya* (with a cast headed by Olivier himself, Redgrave, Joan Plowright and Max Adrian) played two seasons at the Chichester Festival Theatre in 1962 and 1963 before joining the repertory of the National Theatre at the Old Vic in 1963. It was described by Harold Hobson in *The Sunday Times* as 'the admitted master achievement in British twentieth century theatre'.

MAXIM GORKY (1868-1936) Playwright, novelist, essayist, short-story writer and poet. Most famous play: *The Lower Depths* presented by the Moscow Art Theatre in 1902. Set in a flophouse for derelicts, it presents one of the classic conflicts of modern drama: the battle between soothing lies and acceptance of truth. Chekhov wrote of it in 1903: 'Gorky is the first in Russia and in the world at large to have expressed contempt and loathing for the petty bourgeoisie and he has done it at the precise moment when society is ready for protest'. Gorky was also popular abroad: Max Reinhardt's production of *The Lower Depths* at his Kleines Theater in Berlin ran for over 500 performances. Between 1902 and 1915 he wrote 14 plays many of which have been revived by the RSC: *Summerfolk* (1904), *Enemies* (1905), *Children of the Sun* (1905), *The Zykovs* (1913). Living abroad during the 1920s, Gorky returned to Russia in 1931, completed his last three plays and died in 1936 in circumstances never clarified.

ALEKSEI ARBUZOV (1908-) **The most widely-performed of contemporary Russian dramatists.** Orphaned, he wandered the country homeless in the aftermath of the Revolution until taken in by his aunt. Wrote his first play, *Class*, in 1930. Since then has written 30 more. The most popular is *The Promise* (1965) which has had 1695 performances in 66 theatres throughout the Soviet Union. It was first staged in Britain at the Oxford Playhouse in 1966. His play *Old World*, about two old folk who meet at a sanitorium in Riga, had its world première in Lodz (Poland) in 1975 and has since been produced all around the world. At one stage in 1975, it was playing simultaneously in 50 theatres in the Soviet Union: which just goes to show there is a widespread hunger for geriatric sentiment.

France

The key figures in French drama were:

PIERRE CORNEILLE (1606-84) **The first great tragic French writer** and one of the founders of French classical drama. His first dramatic work was a comedy *Mélite* (1630). His first tragedy, *Médée* (1635). His most famous play, *Le Cid* (1637). This story of two lovers torn between passion and family honour caused uproar. Other writers accused Corneille of immorality, vulgarity and breaking the classical unities of time, place and action. On the orders of Cardinal Richelieu the Académie Française investigated the case. They upheld the criticisms but added that the play was first-rate entertainment. Corneille's later tragedies *(Horace, Cinna* both 1640, *Polyeucte* 1641, *La Mort de Pompée* 1643) stressed the parallels between Roman history and political conditions under Louis XIII and Louis XIV.

MOLIÈRE (real name: Jean-Baptiste Poquelin) (1622-73) Playwright and actor who raised comedy to equal rank with that of tragedy. Co-founded a troupe of actors (*L'Illustre Théâtre* in 1643), had his first full-length play (*L'Étourdi*) staged at Lyon in 1655, enjoyed his first triumph with *Les Précieuses Ridicules* in 1659. Subsequent masterpieces include *Tartuffe* (1664 but banned from public performance until 1669), *Dom Juan* (1665), *Le Misanthrope* (1666), *George Dandin* (1668), *Le Malade Imaginaire* (1673). Molière's own life was pocked with tragedy. In 1662 he married Armande Béjart, twenty years his junior and much of the anguish of that relationship was revealed in *Le Misanthrope*. In 1672 Louis XIV also withdrew his support from Molière and his death came a year later on the fourth night of *Le Malade Imaginaire* during which he suffered a convulsion.

JEAN RACINE (1639-99) Master of French tragedy. Lifelong enemy of Molière after he took his play *Alexandre et Porus* (1665) away from Molière's Palais Royal and handed it over to the rival Hôtel de Bourgogne. Most famous plays: *Britannicus* (1669), *Bérénice* (1670), *Bajazet* (1672), *Phèdre* (1677). 'Phèdre', wrote George Steiner, 'is the keystone in French tragic drama. The best that precedes it seems in the manner of preparation; nothing which comes after surpasses it.' Racine is said to have written the play (which deals with Phèdre's love for her husband's son) to prove what he argued in conversation, that 'a good poet could get the greatest crimes excused and even inspire compassion for the criminals'.

PIERRE-AUGUSTIN CARON DE BEAUMARCHAIS (1732-99) Inventor of a revolutionary watch-mechanism (the escapement which communicates the motive-power of the spring to the working parts of the clock) and author of a revolutionary play, *Le Mariage de Figaro* (1784), regarded as the most politically inflammatory work in western drama. Louis XVI called the text detestable and said: 'The Bastille would have to be torn down before the presentation of this play could be anything but a dangerous folly'. At its opening performance in Paris (27 April 1784) the privileged classes

Molière, France's greatest playwright, complete with chubby cherubs.

Molière's 'Le Malade Imaginaire' as performed at the Court of Versailles in 1674. It's a full house.

discovered just how widespread was the contempt for the social order to which they belonged. The play was first performed in London at the National Theatre on 9 July 1974 in a production by Jonathan Miller. No revolution followed.

ALEXANDRE DUMAS *fils* (1824-95) Author of **the most popular romantic drama of all time,** *La Dame aux Camélias*. He wrote it as a novel in 1848, turned it into a play in 1852. Later Verdi used it as the source of his opera, *La Traviata*, and under the title, *Camille* it was a cinematic magnet for great stars from Bernhardt in 1912 to Garbo in 1936. But although the plot is sentimental, Dumas *fils* was raising serious questions in this and other plays such as *Le Demi-Monde* (1855) and *Les Idées de Mme Aubray* (1867). 'He was alarmed by the increasing power of courtesans in French society and politics. At the same time he pleaded incessantly for women to be judged by the same standards as men.' (Harold Hobson).

GEORGES FEYDEAU (1862-1921) The greatest French comic dramatist after Molière and a supreme master of farce. His two greatest successes came in 1892: *Monsieur chasse* at the Palais Royal and *Champignole malgré lui* at the Théâtre des Nouveautés. Both ran for more than 1000 performances. Later hits included *Un Fil à la patte* (1894), *La Dame de chez Maxim* (1899) and *La Puce à l'oreille* (1907) which is the best-known modern production in the Comédie Française repertoire. Feydeau wrote prolifically to make up for the fortune he lost on the stockmarket. But he remained a man as witty in life as in the theatre. He was once present at a salon where a fellow-guest was a miserly industrialist. 'Whenever anyone accosts me on the street and asks me for charity', said the industrialist, 'I instantly put my hand in my pocket'. 'Only you don't take it out again', said Feydeau.

JEAN ANOUILH (1910-) 'The most deeply searing as well as the greatest of modern French dramatists' (Harold Hobson). 'He uses fairy-tale or mythical plots of bald simplicity to make his people disrobe their souls' (Kenneth Tynan). His especial themes are the corruption of innocence, the melancholy of old age, the impossibility of making contact. Most famous plays: *Antigone* (1943), *L'Invitation au Château* (1947), *La Valse des Toréadors* (1952), *Pauvre Bitos* (1956), *Becket* (1959).

JEAN GENET (1910-) Playwright, novelist and poet whose works are a strange mixture of sexual perversion, religious ritual (he sees the Mass as the most effective form of drama) and physical revenge. His best play, *Les Bonnes* (1949) is about two maids playing out a servant – mistress relationship in a ceremonial which ends in murder. *Le Balcon* (1956) is set in a brothel designed for the fulfilment of any fantasy however bizarre. 'For all its faults', wrote Tynan, 'it is a theatrical experience as startling as anything since Ibsen's revelation seventy-six years ago, that there was such a thing as syphilis'.

EUGÈNE IONESCO (1912-) Romanian-born prankster whose plays deal, in Absurdist terms, with a mechanical universe, the clichés of ordinary conversation, the unanswerable fact of death. His first play *The Bald Prima Donna* (1948) is a hilarious assault on suburbia in which a young couple find, after lengthy cross-examination, that they have been married for several years and in which a family is discussed all of whose members go under the name of Bobby Watson. Most famous plays since then: *La Leçon* (1951), *Les Chaises* (1952), *Rhinocéros* (1959), *Macbett* (1972).

Germany

The key figures in German drama are:

GOTTHOLD EPHRAIM LESSING (1729-81) **The first great German dramatist and drama critic.** His essays, *Hamburgische Dramaturgie* (1767-69) are an attack on the principles of Aristotle and the French classicists and an endorsement of Shakespeare as an example of true tragedy. But he was not against the Attic tradition of drama: what he wanted was an alliance of Sophocles *and* Shakespeare. As a dramatist, he also introduced to Germany the idea of bourgeois, domestic tragedy with *Miss Sara Sampson* (1755) written in prose. His greatest play, however, was *Minna von Barnhelm* (1767) about a discharged army officer, innocent of any offence, whose Prussian sense of honour prevents him from marrying his fiancée. On top of this, Lessing was also **the theatre's first dramaturg:** a post he took up at the Hamburg National Theatre in 1767.

JOHANN WOLFGANG VON GOETHE (1749-1832) Playwright, poet, novelist, scientist; embodiment of the ideal of German culture; a man 'who felt that in the drama of the future the Greek conception of tragic fate should be allied to the Shakespearean vision of tragic will'. His early plays experimented with pastoral drama, the romantic *Sturm und Drang* style (*Götz von Berlichingen,* 1773) and contemporary subjects (*Clavigo,* 1774 and *Egmont,* 1775). But his masterpiece was *Faust* (Part One: 1808, Part Two: 1830). This is the first attempt at the *Gesamtkunstwerk*, the total art-form that mixes different poetic styles, music and ballet. He was also a practical man of the theatre who, from 1791 to 1817, was director of the Weimar Court Theatre. As a scientist, he is also the only dramatist to have made a contribution to anatomical knowledge having discovered a small bone between the upper and lower jaw.

FRIEDRICH VON SCHILLER (1759-1805) Playwright and poet. 'In his dramas and heroic ballads, the romantic generation found its repertoire of emotion' (Steiner). Indeed his first play, *Die Rauber* (1781) unleashed great floods of passion at its Mannheim première. 'Complete strangers fell sobbing into one another's arms and fainting women tottered towards the exits. The effect was of universal release, as when a new creation bursts forth from out of the mists of Chaos.' Subsequent works included *Kabale und Liebe* (1783), *Don Carlos* (1787) a vast unwieldy poetic tragedy over 6000 lines long which makes it nearly double the length of *Hamlet, Maria Stuart* (1800) and *Wilhelm Tell* (1804). His plays became, after Shakespeare, the most popular in 19th century Germany and Eastern Europe.

HEINRICH VON KLEIST (1777-1811) Unrecognised and virtually unperformed in his lifetime; always writing about heroes poised between crucial choices; shot himself after first shooting an incurably sick woman who had begged him to kill her. His most famous plays are *Der Zerbrochene Krug* (1808), *Kätchen von Heilbronn* (1810), *Prinz Friedrich von Homburg* (published posthumously in 1821 and memorably revived by Manchester's Royal Exchange in 1976).

GEORG BUCHNER (1813-37) Highly influential as a forerunner of German naturalism and psychological realism. Wrote only three plays before dying of typhoid fever at age of 23: *Danton's Tod* (1835), *Leonce und Lena* (1836), *Woyzeck* (1836). 'His absurdly premature death is a symbol of waste more absolute than that of either of the two instances so often quoted in indictment of mortality, the deaths of Mozart and Keats' (Steiner). 'Antedating not only Zola but also Turgenev and Ostrovsky, he is an illustration of the fact that dramatic naturalism was not an invention of the 1880s' (Eric Bentley).

GERHART HAUPTMANN (1862-1946) Key figure in German naturalism. Also writer of the first great tragedy not of an individual but of a social mass: *Die Weber* (1893) in which the protagonist was a collective in revolt against capitalist society. His later plays range from comedy to bleak introspection to neo-pagan mysticism. He won the Nobel Prize in 1912 but later declined into a patron of Nazi Kultur. 'What Hauptmann lacks is the moral and intellectual stature of a great artist'. (Eric Bentley).

FRANK WEDEKIND (1864-1918) Playwright, actor, cabaret singer, satirical journalist, precursor of Expressionism and influence on Brecht. His greatest play, *Fruhlings Erwachen* (written in 1891 but not performed until 1906) was about the sexual awakening of three adolescents and the destructive nature of a repressive society. *Erdgeist* (1895) and *Die Büchse der Pandora* (1903) were conceived as a single monster tragedy known as *Lulu* (source of Alban Berg's opera). 'Like Tolstoy and Strindberg, Wedekind was one of the great educators of modern Europe. His greatest work was his own personality.' (Brecht).

BERTOLT BRECHT (1898-1956) **Most influential and universally performed dramatist of the century.** Also very important as director and theorist. His ideas that spectators should always be reminded that they are watching an unreal spectacle, that the actors should not encourage emotional identification, that the only props should be those essential to the action, that theatre should be a place of education rather than escape, that music is a key element in drama have had a big influence on all countries.

☐ First ever performance of a Brecht work in Britain: *Anna Anna (The Seven Deadly Sins)* at the Savoy Theatre, 1933.

☐ First visit to Britain of Brecht's company, the Berliner Ensemble, was to the Palace Theatre, London, 1956.

☐ First Brecht production by a major British subsidised company: *The Good Woman of Setzuan*, Royal Court Theatre, 1956.

☐ Most popular Brecht production in Britain: *The Life of Galileo* which played in Olivier Theatre repertory from August 1980 to October, 1981.

☐ Most popular play with amateur and student groups in Britain: *The Caucasian Chalk Circle* which between 1947 and 1976 had 443 productions (more than three times as many as its rival, *The Good Woman of Setzuan*).

Key Brecht dictum 'I do not like plays to contain pathetic overtones: they must be convincing like court pleas. The main thing is to teach the spectator to reach a verdict.'

Key Brecht plays

Baal (1918); *In the Jungle of the Cities* (1924); *Man is Man* (1926); *The Threepenny Opera* (1928); *The Rise and Fall of the City of Mahagonny* (1929); *St Joan of the Stockyards* (1931); *The Life of Galileo* (1938); *Mother Courage and Her Children* (1939); *The Resistible Rise of Arturo Ui* (1941); *The Good Woman of Sezuan* (1942); *Schweik in the Second World War* (1943); *The Caucasian Chalk Circle* (1945); *The Days of the Commune* (1949).

Opinions about Brecht

'Brecht was a very simple person. If you met him in the yard, he might be deep in conversation but he was never so wrapped up that he overlooked one of the workers. He said good morning to a cleaning woman from 20 yards away: the workers soon noted this.' Gerhard R., electrician.

'Brecht's epic theatre was designed as the theatre of the scientific age, a theatre that conveyed insight and knowledge in a sensual way, and in which understanding and enjoyment were one and the same for the audience.' Ernst Schumacher.

'He did not like things to be pre-chewed; this robbed him of the joy of eating. He interpreted the sentence "Truth is concrete" in a productive way; by long practice he has made himself in-

Ekkehard Schall making a triumphal entry in the Berliner Ensemble's production of 'Coriolanus' which visited the Old Vic, London in 1965.

capable of understanding dry abstractions. Manfred Wekwerth.

'Brecht. If it hadn't been for Adolf Hitler he'd still be selling Lipton's tea behind the bacon counter in Oberammergau'. Anonymous English actor.

Norway

The first recorded performance of a play was *Adam's Fald (The Fall of Adam)* in 1562 in the cathedral churchyard in Bergen and adapted from a European model by Absalon Pedersson Beyer.

Henrik Ibsen: a theatrical master-builder who resolved his own spiritual and intellectual conflicts in the greatest drama since Shakespeare.

BJØRNSTJERNE BJØRNSON (1832-1910) was a playwright, poet, novelist and critic and **the first Scandinavian to be awarded the Nobel Prize** (1903). He wrote chronicle plays, problem plays, comic plays, plays that often gave offence: *The Gauntlet* in 1883 argued the case for pre-marital chastity in the male and incurred the displeasure of the Bohemian community. The only play of his to be revived in Britain in recent time was *Mary Stuart in Scotland* (1863) given at the Gateway Theatre, Edinburgh in 1960. It led Kenneth Tynan to conclude: 'Apart from *Macbeth*, there are no great plays about Scotland'.

HENRIK IBSEN (1828-1906) After Shakespeare, the greatest of the world's dramatists: a poet, a heretic, an abjurer of all parties, an intellectual pioneer, a passionate believer in spiritual regeneration, a master builder whose plays are perfectly-structured pieces of architecture. 'You are like two people who cannot agree', says someone of the poet Falk in *Love's Comedy*. The same is true of Ibsen. 'The dialogue of his spirit', wrote Harold Clurman, 'would find its natural expression in drama, the art *par excellence* of conflict. The crosscurrents of his soul became eloquent in his stage characters. The inner fire which racked and might have destroyed him was checked by the icy discipline of his craft. Driven by inner necessity, he was a born dramatist.'

He wrote 24 plays in a variety of styles: chronicle plays, verse dramas, realistic problem plays, symbolist works. They are: 1850 *Catiline*, 1852 *Midsummer's Eve*, 1854 *Lady Inger of Ostraat*, 1855 *The Feast at Solhaug*, 1856 *Olaf Liljekrans*, 1857 *The Vikings at Helgeland*, 1862 *Love's Comedy*, 1863 *The Pretenders*, 1866 *Brand*, 1867 *Peer Gynt*, 1869 *League of Youth*, 1873 *Emperor and Galilean*, 1877 *Pillars of Society*, 1879 *A Doll's House*, 1881 *Ghosts*, 1882 *An Enemy of the People*, 1884 *The Wild Duck*, 1886 *Rosmersholm*, 1888 *The Lady From the Sea*, 1890 *Hedda Gabler*, 1892 *The Master Builder*, 1894 *Little Eyolf*, 1896 *John Gabriel Borkman*, 1899 *When We Dead Awaken*.

According to Ibsen's biographer, Michael Meyer, *A Doll's House* has been professionally performed more often in both England and the United States than any other of Ibsen's plays, followed in each country by *Ghosts*'. *A Doll's House*, in which Nora leaves her home and husband in order to achieve self-fulfilment, had its première at the Royal Theatre in Copenhagen on 21 December 1879. At the first German production in March 1880 at Flensburg, Frau Hedwig Niemann-Raabe who was to play Nora refused to perform the final scene as written on the grounds that 'I would never leave my children'. Ibsen was obliged to write a 'happy' ending in which Nora does not leave the house but is forced by Helmer to the doorway of the children's bedroom where she sinks to the floor as the curtain falls. This version was never a success and even Frau Niemann-Raabe reverted finally to the original text.

Ghosts, which dealt with the topic of venereal disease, aroused the greatest storm of all Ibsen's plays. When it was first performed in London in 1891 Clement Scott of *The Daily Telegraph* described it as 'an open drain, a loathsome sore, an abominable piece, a repulsive and degrading work'.

Ghosts was given its world première on 20 May, 1882 in Chicago before an audience of Scandinavian immigrants. This was the first record of any Ibsen play in America. In Europe it was published in book form before it was seen on the stage. Herman Bang, a celebrated Scandinavian novelist, described the impact it made when it first appeared in print in 1882: 'The play was distributed to the booksellers towards evening. The keenest buyers ran out in the dark to get it

Beatrix Lehmann in a 1943 revival of Ibsen's 'Ghosts'. Behind her the fjords glower.

. . . One or two restless people who had nothing to lose, having no good name to be smeared by association with *Ghosts*, gave public readings. People flocked to the obscure places where these readings took place, out by the bridges, far into the suburbs . . .

Hedda Gabler is Ibsen's most popular play after *A Doll's House* and *Ghosts*. London has seen no less than 22 productions since Elizabeth Robins first played it in 1891. The strangest was Charles Marowitz's free adaptation at the Round House in 1980 in which a sexually energetic Hedda (played by Jenny Agutter) was renamed by one critic, *Hedda Gobbler*.

When Ibsen died in 1906 his son and only child, Sigurd, decided to have the hammer of a *bergmann* — mountain-miner — engraved on his tombstone. This is taken to be a reference to Ibsen's penultimate play, *John Gabriel Borkman*, in which the miner's hammer not only hews away at the mountain but also makes the iron ore 'sing for joy'.

Sweden

The oldest preserved play is *Tobie Comedia (Comedy of Tobias)* which dates from 1550.
The most famous dramatist is August Strindberg (1849-1912). He was playwright, novelist and prolific polymath and the collected edition of his works runs to 55 volumes. Much of the material for his drama and fiction came from his three tempestuous marriages to professional women: Siri von Essen (1877-91), an aspiring actress, Frida Uhl (1893-94), an Austrian journalist, and Harriet Bosse (1901-4), a Norwegian actress.

He made his theatrical debut with *In Rome* (1870), a short play about the artist's life in the Italian capital. His best-known and most-performed plays are: *The Father* (1887) in which an army captain is driven first to madness and then a stroke by his wife's superior will; *Miss Julie* (1889), which Strindberg described as the first naturalistic play in Scandinavia and which deals with a midsummer sexual encounter between a slumming aristocrat and a rising footman; and *The Dance of Death* (1900), a play in two parts which describes a ruthless sexual duel between an army officer and a wife ten years his junior.

In answer to a questionnaire in May 1897 Strindberg gave the following replies:

What is the predominant trait in your character? — This strange mixture of the deepest pessimism and utter recklessness.

What quality do you rate highest in a man? — Lack of pettiness.

In a woman? — Motherliness.

Your motto? — 'Speravit infestis' (he hoped in adversity).

CHAPTER 5

Musicals

The musical is one of the few art forms to have been developed in America. It is a highly eclectic form combining the influences of the minstrel show, vaudeville, burlesque, English comic opera, European operetta, revue, musical comedy and ballad opera. The modern Broadway musical is a highly sophisticated machine drawing on many of these elements.

In England the musical dates back to Gilbert and Sullivan comic opera and George Edwardes musical comedy of the 1890s. It has enjoyed fitful bursts of popularity (*Chu Chin Chow*, (1916) the Novello and Coward musicals of the interwar years, *The Boy Friend* (1954)) and *Salad Days* (1954) but only recently, with *Evita* and *Jesus Christ Superstar*, has it shown it can match Broadway at its own game. To all intents and purposes, the modern musical is an American phenomenon.

The first known musical theatre production in America was *Flora or Hob in the Well* (18 February 1735), a ballad farce by the Englishman, Colley Cibber, performed at the Courthouse, Charleston, South Carolina.

The first American musical was *The Black Crook* (1866). It was originally intended to be a Faustian melodrama. But when the New York Academy of Music on 14th Street was burnt down shortly before a French ballet troupe was due to open there, William Wheatley, manager of Niblo's Garden Theatre, hired the 100 dancing girls and their scenery and incorporated them into his new melodrama, *The Black Crook*. The production, with tunes adapted and arranged by Giuseppi Operti, lasted 5½ hours and was

a huge success grossing a million dollars — the most popular and profitable American production of the 19th century. It ran for 474 performances and then toured and periodically returned to New York between 1866 and 1903. Its success may have been helped by the clergy's disapproval of so many barelegged dancers. The story of putting on *The Black Crook* was later told in another musical, *The Girl in Pink Tights* (1954) with music by Sigmund Romberg.

MINSTRELS
The Black Crook notwithstanding, the most popular musical entertainment in America from 1840 to the turn of the century was the minstrel show. White performers painted their faces with burnt cork and purported to imitate black songs and dances, using Afro-American dialect, grotesque gestures and movements. Many people, who had never seen blacks, believed these caricatures to represent what they were really like and when black minstrels took to the boards after 1855 they too distorted their faces with make-up.

The first popular blackface act was that of Thomas D. Rice (1808-60). In 1828, Rice had seen an old black crippled with rheumatism dancing and singing 'Ebery time I weel about, I jump Jim Crow'. Rice adapted the dance, added new verses to the song (an old Irish folk tune, in fact) and even wore the old man's clothes.

Paul Nicholas suffers in the cause of art in the landmark British musical 'Jesus Christ Superstar' at the Palace Theatre 1971.

The most famous minstrel composer was Stephen Foster (1826-64) who wrote over 200 songs for minstrels including 'O Susanna' (the theme song of pioneers of the California gold rush in 1849), 'Old Folks at Home', 'Camptown Races' and 'My Old Kentucky Home'.

The best-known minstrel song was 'Dixie'. Written for the banjo by Dan Emmett, who was **the first blackface performer to use original material,** 'Dixie' later acquired new lyrics and became the battle hymn of the Confederacy during the Civil War.

The first structured minstrel show was presented by Dan Emmett and the Virginia Minstrels in 1843. The format was developed by the Christy Minstrels into a three-act production. Act One began with the company seated in a semi-circle with Mr Tambo (on tambourine) and Mr Bones (playing on a jaw-bone or rib-bone) at either end. The end men exchanged repartee with Mr Interlocutor, the Master of Ceremonies, in the middle. Act Two, the fantasia, included speciality acts. Act Three was a burlesque often of a well-known play. *Macbeth,* for example, became *Bad Breath, the Crane of Chowder.*

The first minstrel show by black artists was *Mocking Bird Minstrels* (1855). Black minstrel shows became popular after the Civil War and specialised in presenting 'plantation life'. From minstrel shows it was a short step to **the first all-black musical** in New York which was the dubiously entitled *A Trip to Coontown* (1898). More sophisticated entertainment, happily, was to follow such as **the longest-running, all-black revue,** *Blackbirds of 1928* (518 performances), and a succession of great black musicals.

Through the minstrel shows the whites shamelessly purloined the black man's music. Since then the whirligig of time has brought its revenge with a large number of all-black versions of white-originated shows. They include *Carmen Jones* (1943) which was black, updated Bizet, *Hello Dolly* in which Pearl Bailey in 1967 became Mrs Dolly Gallagher Levi, *The Wiz* (1975) derived from *The Wizard of Oz, The Black Mikado* (1975) based on Gilbert and Sullivan, *Guys and Dolls* (1976) which was transmogrified Loesser and, in London, *I Gotta Shoe* (1976) which was a rewrite of an earlier Caryl Brahms/ Ned Sherrin black fairytale, *Cindy-Ella* (1962).

VAUDEVILLE

A blend of character songs, sketches and speciality acts, was another precursor of the modern musical. The term itself came from Val-de-Vire in Normandy where the 15th century French villagers were noted for composing and performing ballads and satirical songs. Vaudeville flourished in the States from 1878 to 1925 and has since been reconstructed in a hugely popular show on Broadway, *Sugar Babies* (1980), starring Mickey Rooney and Ann Miller.

BURLESQUE

A blend of bawdy comedy, hootchie-kootchie acts, shimmy-shakers and strippers. The form declined after the Great War but was kept partially alive by the celebrated stripper, Gypsy Rose Lee (1914-70) whose mother-dominated life was the subject of the 1959 musical, *Gypsy.*

REVUE

A non-book musical entertainment often built around star performers, was equally popular in America and England between the wars.

The first Broadway revue was *The Passing Show* (1894). **The longest-running annual revues** were *The Ziegfeld Follies* (1907-57) which went through 25 editions, *The Passing Show* (1912-24) with 12 editions, *George White's Scandals* (1919-31) with 11 editions, *Earl Carroll Vanities* (1923-32) with 11 editions, and *The Greenwich Village Follies* (1919-28) with 8 editions.

The greatest exponent of American revue was Florenz Ziegfeld (1867-1932) whose shows represented the epitome of glamour and extravagance. Half the cost of his productions went towards the costumes and over the years the Ziegfeld girls included Marion Davies, Mae Murray, Barbara Stanwyck, Paulette Goddard, Irene Dunne.

Ziegfeld's lucky number was 13. The first *Ziegfeld Follies* were called *Follies of 1907* because Ziegfeld wanted a title with no more than 13 letters in it. His fixation with 13 even led him to install his mistress, actress Lillian Lorraine, on the 13th floor of his hotel while he lived with his wife on the 10th floor.

Ziegfeld always carried a small red cornelian elephant for luck. He also collected elephant replicas of all sorts but only with their trunks held high. If he was given an elephant with a down-turned trunk, it had to be removed and destroyed immediately. He even bought his daughter a real baby elephant.

The first black entertainer to star in an otherwise white show was Bert Williams (1874-1922) in the *Follies of 1910*. Comedian and singer, he played the sort of person who 'if they get served soup always have a fork and not a spoon in sight'. A proud, sensitive man he suffered deeply because of the indignities he had to endure to please sophisticated New Yorkers.

The first English revue was *Under the Clock* (1893) produced by Seymour Hicks and Charles Brookfield. Spectacular revues followed but the emphasis, begun by C. B. Cochran with *Odds and Ends* at the Ambassadors in 1914, was more on wit than on dress and dancing. Cochran and fellow-impresario, André Charlot, fostered the talents of Noel Coward, Beatrice Lillie, Gertrude Lawrence and Jack Buchanan. Indeed these last three artists took Broadway by storm when they transferred *Charlot's Revue of 1924* from London to New York (even though an electrical fault on the neon sign often led the show to be billed as *Harlot's Revue of 1924*). Intimate revue flourished in London during and after the war at the Ambassadors with *Sweet and Low* (1943), *Sweeter and Lower* (1944) and *Sweetest and Lowest* (1946) and continued with *Pieces of Eight* (1959) featuring the inimitable Kenneth Williams. But both the girls-and-glamour, fishnet-tight revue and the more intimate, theatrically incestuous form were dealt a death-blow by the brilliant *Beyond the Fringe* (1961) from which they have never quite recovered.

BALLAD OPERA

A musical drama often using popular tunes or folk songs of the day. The most popular example was John Gay's *The Beggar's Opera* (1728) which satirised Italian opera, the aristocracy, the British government and Prime Minister Robert Walpole as Macheath. Bertolt Brecht and Kurt Weill in *Der Dreigroschenoper* (1928) gave the story a new twist, setting it in a fantasy London in which Soho is apparently a Thames-side village. Their song, 'Mack the Knife' went on to become a chart-topping hit. The rotund Zero Mostel and Alfred Drake also starred in a Broadway version, *Beggar's Holiday* (1946), written by Duke Ellington and John Latouche.

The longest-running Broadway revues	Number of performances
Hellzapoppin (1938)	1404
Oh, Calcutta (1969)	1314
Pins and Needles (1937)	1108
Don't Bother Me, I Can't Cope (1972)	1065
La Plume de ma Tante (1958)	835

Seymour Hicks in the first English revue, 'Under the Clock' (1893).

Der Dreigroschenoper (The Threepenny Opera) ran for 4000 performances in Berlin from 1928 on; was banned by Hitler in 1933; was a resounding flop in New York in the same year; and finally reached London in 1956 in a production at the Royal Court starring Bill Owen. A 1954 off-Broadway revival played for 2611 performances and is the second longest-running off-Broadway production after *The Fantasticks* (1960).

Gilbert and Sullivan between 1875 and 1896 produced 13 light operas that achieved instant popularity both in Britain and America (*HMS Pinafore* was so successful in 1878 that within a year there were 90 Pinafore companies touring the USA). The D'Oyly Carte Opera Company is dedicated to the performance of their work and

The "shark-song" from Brecht's 'The Threepenny Opera' in a 1958 production from the Meiningen Theatre staged in honour of Brecht's 60th birthday.

has continued in the teeth of much abuse ('*The Gondoliers* was sung by a large number of fat people most of them of determinate age': Kenneth Tynan 1946) and official criticism (Their performances are often 'tired and wooden': Arts Council report 1981). The Company gave its last performance at the Adelphi Theatre, London on 27 February, 1982.

MUSICAL COMEDY
A light-hearted entertainment with minimal plot, the emphasis being on singing and dancing and lavish sets.

The first musical comedy was *In Town* (1892)

produced by George Edwardes (1855-1915). It opened at London's Prince of Wales and later transferred to the Gaiety which, under Edwardes's management, became the home of musical comedy. The biggest Gaiety hit was *Our Miss Gibbs* (1909) which ran for 636 performances.

The most popular English musical comedy was *Chu Chin Chow* which opened at Her Majesty's in 1916 and ran for 2238 performances. This oriental fantasy began its life during a wet week in Manchester in 1915 when the actor, Oscar Asche, in a moment of profound boredom hired a typist, settled in a corner of his hotel and dictated half of the story-line, as well as lyrics and descriptions of sets and costumes. He completed the second half of the book alone three weeks later in Glasgow. Sir Herbert Beerbohm Tree, whose theatre *Chu Chin Chow* occupied for five years, returned home from America, saw the show and, gazing wanly at the diaphanous costumes, remarked: 'I see — more navel than military'. The production, which cost £5356 17s 9d to mount, made over £200 000 in profit for Asche alone.

The most classic musical comedy song (one still parodied by Ken Dodd) was 'Tell Me, Pretty Maiden' from *Floradora* which opened in London in 1899 and New York in 1900. The song was sung by six young men in silk hats to six young women, the Floradora Sextette, in ostrich plumes.

The most notorious of the *Floradora* females was Evelyn Nesbit who married Pittsburgh millionaire, Harry K. Thaw. On the opening night of *Mamzelle Champagne* in 1906 at the roof theatre of Madison Square Garden Thaw shot his wife's lover, architect Stanford White (who had designed Madison Square Garden) declaring 'You deserve this. You have ruined my wife.' He pleaded insanity, was committed to the state asylum at Matteawan, escaped in 1913 and was never recaptured.

OPERETTA
A European form combining a trivial book with an often beautiful score, was introduced to America by Victor Herbert, Sigmund Romberg and Rudolf Friml.

Victor Herbert (1859-1924) was **the first impor-**

scores included *Maytime* (1917), *The Student Prince of Heidelberg* (1924), *The Desert Song* (1926), *Up in Central Park* (1945).

Fred and Adele Astaire made their New York debut in Romberg's *Over the Top* (1917).

Critic George Jean Nathan described Romberg's *May Wine* (1935) as 'a musical mothball laid scenically in Vienna and critically in Cain's' (a theatrical warehouse where discarded shows went for destruction).

Rudolf Friml (1879-1972) was a Prague-born infant prodigy **who composed more than 30 operettas** including *You're in Love* (1917), which gave Oscar Hammerstein II his first job as Assistant Stage Manager, *Rose-Marie* (1924), *The Vagabond King* (1925) and *The Three Musketeers* (1928). 'A full-blooded libretto with luscious melody, rousing choruses and romantic passions', was Friml's recipe for success.

The musicmakers

The first great American theatre composer was JEROME KERN (1885-1945). His series of musicals produced for the 299-seat Princess Theatre in collaboration with Guy Bolton and P. G. Wodehouse introduced the intimate musical to Broadway. Their biggest successes were *Very Good Eddie* (1915) and *Oh, Boy* (1917) which ran for 475 performances in New York, which cost $29262.56 to produce and which made a profit of $181641.54. It left Bolton and Wodehouse, in the latter's words, 'sitting on top of the world and loving it'.

Kern's *Showboat* (1927), with book and lyrics by Oscar Hammerstein II and based on an Edna Ferber novel, was **the first musical to combine a serious plot with singing and dancing.** Produced by Florenz Ziegfeld, it ran for 572 performances.

The first performer to sing 'Ol' Man River' in *Showboat* was Jules Bledsoe. The song was written for Paul Robeson but because of delays in production Robeson didn't play the part of Joe on Broadway until the 1932 revival (he played it in London in 1928).

The first known showboat was *Noah's Ark* (1817) owned by Noah Ludlow who managed the American Theatrical Commonwealth Company.

Evie Greene as a robust Dolores in the 1899 London production of the classic musical 'Floradora'.

tant composer of the American musical stage. His first success, *The Wizard of the Nile* (1895), was set in Egypt and written for the popular comedian, Frank Daniels. Herbert was a great lover of food and wine and whilst composing simultaneously the scores of four operettas in 1899-1900 *(Cyrano de Bergerac, The Singing Girl, Ameer* and *The Viceroy)* drank a different wine with each score, keeping the bottles cool in a washtub of ice.

Herbert's *It Happened in Nordland* (1904) was a musical about a lady ambassador at the court of a mythical country. Irving Berlin's *Call Me Madam* (1950) had a distinctly similar theme.

The first moving electric sign on Broadway was at the Knickerbocker Theater (1906) where Herbert's biggest success, *The Red Mill,* was playing.

The most prolific composer of popular musicals was Sigmund Romberg (1887-1951). His 60

Eccentric dancing by one half of the Wallace Brothers from the 1951 London production of Cole Porter's 'Kiss Me Kate'.

IRVING BERLIN (1888-), despite his lack of a musical education, became America's greatest songwriter. He introduced ragtime into the theatre with *Watch Your Step* written for the dancers, Vernon and Irene Castle (1914). He caught the mood of the public with such songs as 'Oh, How I Hate To Get Up in the Morning' from *Yip, Yip, Yaphank* (1918) and 'Easter Parade' from *As Thousands Cheer* (1933). He wrote two long-running Broadway hits in *Annie Get Your Gun* (1946) which ran for 1147 performances and *Call Me Madam* (1950) which, with its song

'They Like Ike' opened Eisenhower's election campaign two years early. 'Irving Berlin has no place in American music', wrote Jerome Kern, 'he *is* American music'.

COLE PORTER (1891-1964) Composer and lyricist of immense style and sophistication who overcame the handicap of being born rich. First Broadway musical, *See America First* (1916), satirised the flamboyant jingoism of George M. Cohan and resoundingly flopped. But, after several years enjoying fashionable life in post-war Europe, a succession of hit shows followed: *The Gay Divorce* (1932), *Anything Goes* (1934), *Kiss Me Kate* (1948), and *Can-Can* (1953). He was a capricious rhymster, a tireless traveller and a

brilliant magpie. 'No one else', said Brooks Atkinson, 'could have written The Kling-Kling Bird on the Divi-Divi Tree based on music they had heard in Jamaica'.

GEORGE GERSHWIN (1898-1937) was a Brooklyn-born innovator who had a revitalising effect on the Broadway musical stage. He wrote his first Broadway show, *La La Lucille*, at the age of 21. He went on to write numbers (some of them classics such as 'Somebody Loves Me') for five editions of *George White's Scandals*. In 1927 he wrote the score for George S. Kaufman's stringent satire on American militarism, *Strike Up The Band*. He wrote **the first musical, *Of Thee I Sing* (1931), to receive the Pulitzer Prize for drama,** 1932. He also wrote **the first American folk opera**, *Porgy and Bess* (1935) which lost 70 000 dollars, the entire production cost, but went on to become a durable classic. A rather self-admiring figure ('Tell me, George', asked Oscar Levant, 'if you had to do it all over again, would you still fall in love with yourself?') he nonetheless widened the horizons of the musical stage.

RICHARD RODGERS (1902-79) and LORENZ HART (1895-1943) as composer and librettist were a remarkable combination of sweet-and-

Cecil Beaton's famous designs for the Ascot scene from 'My Fair Lady' with Rex Harrison and Julie Andrews centre stage.

sour. Their first published song was 'Any Old Place With You' in *A Lonely Romeo* (1919). Their first success was *The Garrick Gaieties* (1925). Their first book musical was *Dearest Enemy* (1925). They introduced **the first genuine ballet,** 'Slaughter on Tenth Avenue' into a Broadway musical, *On Your Toes* (1936): it was staged by George Balanchine and danced by Ray Bolger and Tamara Geva. They also, in *Pal Joey* (1940), wrote **the first Broadway musical with a louse for a hero.**

After Hart's death Rodgers formed a new partnership with Oscar Hammerstein II (1895-1960). Together they wrote **the first fully-integrated modern musical,** *Oklahoma!* (1943), which overcame massive preliminary troubles to enjoy a run of 2212 performances and to make a profit of five million dollars on an investment of 83 000 dollars. *Oklahoma!* was also **the first musical for which an original cast album was recorded.** They also wrote **the first musical ever about Chinese-Americans:** *Flower Drum Song* (1958). It starred two Japanese actresses and was dismissed by Kenneth Tynan as 'the world of woozy song'. The shortest run for a Rodgers and Hammerstein musical was *Pipe Dream* (1955) which had 246 performances.

ALAN JAY LERNER (1918-) and FREDERICK LOEWE (1904-), librettist-lyricist and composer produced the most elegant, frequently-revived modern musical, *My Fair Lady* (1956). It played for 2717 performances on its original Broadway run, 2281 performances on its first London run at Drury Lane and has since been revived both in America (with Rex Harrison playing his original role of Professor Higgins) and in Britain. All this despite the fact that, according to Brooks Atkinson, 'it may be the only musical play in which the hero and heroine never kiss or embrace'.
□ *My Fair Lady* was also the original title of an unsuccessful Gershwin musical later called *Tell Me More* (1925).
□ The first actor to 'speak' songs in the manner adopted by Rex Harrison as Professor Higgins was Joe Coyne, American light comedian, in *The Merry Widow* (1907) in London.
□ Other musical adaptations of Shaw plays: *The Chocolate Soldier* (1909) and *Her First Roman* (1968). The former was based on *Arms and the Man*, the latter on *Caesar and Cleopatra*.

STEPHEN SONDHEIM (1930-) composer-yricist of great innovative force whose own unaided shows are *A Funny Thing Happened on the Way to the Forum* (1962), *Anyone Can Whistle* (1964), *Company* (1970), *Follies* (1971), *A Little Night Music* (1973), *Pacific Overtures* (1976), *Sweeney Todd* (1979) and *Merrily We Roll Along* (1981).
□ Most intriguing Sondheim project that never saw the light: a musical version of Brecht's *The Exception and the Rule* in collaboration with Leonard Bernstein and playwright John Guare with Zero Mostel to star. Abandoned in 1969.
□ Most spectacular Sondheim flop: *Anyone Can Whistle* which ran on Broadway from 4-11 April 1964. Legend has it that those who caught the show have annual reunion dinners at which they discuss what went wrong.
□ Most surprising breakthroughs: *Pacific Overtures*, **the first-ever Broadway Kabuki musical for which the entire cast was Japanese;** *Sweeney Todd*, **the first-ever Broadway musical about cannibalism;** and *Merrily We Roll Along*, **the first-ever musical to tell its story in reverse chronological order.**

Behind the score

One-night musical flops were *The Yearling* (1964), *Home, Sweet Homer* (1976), a musical version of *The Odyssey* starring Yul Brynner.

The most bizarre musical ever was *Lieutenant* (1975). A rock opera about the massacre of civilian natives by American forces at My Lai during the Vietnam War. Featuring such songs as 'Kill' and 'Massacre', it lasted for 9 performances.

The first musical to feature murder as an essential ingredient was *Rose-Marie* (1924) in which a fur-trapper is falsely accused of killing. Other musicals featuring death: *Porgy and Bess* (1935), *Carmen Jones* (1943), *Oklahoma!* (1943), *Perchance to Dream* (1945), *Carousel* (1945), *Lost in the Stars* (1949), *The King and I* (1951), *West Side Story* (1957), *Irma La Douce* (1958), *Redhead* (1959), *Oliver!* (1960), *Belle or The Ballad of Dr Crippen* (1961), *Evita* (1979), *Sweeney Todd* (1979).

Untimely deaths: Jerome Kern (1885-1945) collapsed after auditioning singers for a revival of *Show Boat* and died six days later. Ivor Novello (1893-1951) died during the run of *King's Rhapsody* and Jack Buchanan took over the role of King Nikki. Gertrude Lawrence (1898-1952) died of cancer during the run of *The King and I*. Gower Champion (1920-80) died on the eve of the first night of his production of *42nd Street*. The producer, David Merrick, announced his death from the stage at the end of the first-night.

Musicals featuring Nazis were *Leave It to Me* (1938), a Cole Porter show; *The Dancing Years* (1939), though the Drury Lane management protested to Ivor Novello that the subject of Germany's treatment of the Jews was out of place in a musical; *The Sound of Music* (1959); *Cabaret* (1966).

Above right: Virginia McKenna teaches Yul Brynner's King of Siam a lesson in the London Palladium production of 'The King and I'.
Below right: American stars of 'West Side Story' at the Alhambra Theatre, Paris, rehearsing before the opening night.

Musicals featuring sport

Baseball in *Damn Yankees* (1955), *The First* (1981)

Boxing in *Hold Everything* (1928), *Golden Boy* (1964), *Buck White* (1969)

College Football in *All American* (1902), *Leave It to Jane* (1917), *Good News* (1927), *Too Many Girls* (1939), *Toplitzky of Notre Dame* (1946)

Golf in *Kid Boots* (1923) with Eddie Cantor, *Follow Thru* (1929)

Rugby Football in *Tom Brown's Schooldays* (1972).

Original titles of musicals

'Robin Hood' became *Maid Marion* (1892)

'My Fair Lady' became *Tell Me More* (1925)

'Mayfair', 'Miss Mayfair' and 'Cheerio' became *Oh, Kay* (1926)

'Lady Fair' *The Desert Song* (1926)

'Smarty' *Funny Face* (1927)

'Jenny Get Your Gun' *Something For the Boys* (1943)

'Oklahoma and Away We Go!' *Oklahoma!* (1943)

'My Lady Liza' and 'The Talk of London' *My Fair Lady* (1956)

'East Side Story' *West Side Story* (1957)

'Holly Golightly' *Breakfast at Tiffany's* (1966).

Musicals adapted from movies

Hazel Flagg (1955) from *Nothing Sacred*

Silk Stockings (1955) from *Ninotchka*

Shangri-La (1956) from *Lost Horizon*

New Girl in Town (1957) from *Anna Christie*

Here's Love (1963) from *Miracle on 34th Street*

Sweet Charity (1966) from *Nights of Cabiria*

Ilya Darling (1967) from *Never on Sunday*

Promises, Promises (1968) from *The Apartment*

Golden Rainbow (1968) from *A Hole in the Head*

Zorba (1968) from *Zorba the Greek*

Mr and Mrs (1968) from *Brief Encounter*

Roundelay (1969) from *La Ronde*

Georgy (1970) from *Georgy Girl*

Applause (1970) from *All About Eve*

Ari (1971) from *Exodus*

Gone With the Wind (1972) from *Gone with the Wind*

Sugar (1972) from *Some Like It Hot*

A Little Night Music (1973) from *Smiles of a Summer Night*

Chicago (1975) from *Roxie Hart*

Shenandoah (1975) from *Shenandoah*.

42nd Street (1981) from *42nd Street*

Nine (1982) from *8½*.

Musicals based on works by Charles Dickens

were *Oliver!* (1960); *Pickwick* (1963); *Two Cities* (1969); *Great Expectations* (1975 Guildford); *Coming Uptown* (1979) adapted from *A Christmas Carol*.

Musicals inspired by ancient Greece and Rome

were *By Jupiter* (1942); *Out of This World* (1950); *The Golden Apple* (1954); *The Happiest Girl in the World* (1961); *A Funny Thing Happened on the Way to the Forum* (1962); *The Wedding of Iphigenia* (1971); *Lysistrata* (1972); *Home Sweet Homer* (1975).

Musical adaptations of Shakespeare plays

'The Comedy of Errors': *The Boys From Syracuse* (1938); *The Comedy of Errors* (1977) presented by The Royal Shakespeare Company.

'Hamlet': *Rockaby Hamlet* (1976) staged by Gower Champion.

'The Merchant of Venice': *Fire Angel* (1977).

'A Midsummer Night's Dream': *Swingin' The Dream* (1939); *Babes in the Wood* (1964).

'Othello': *Catch My Soul* (1970).

'Romeo and Juliet': *Jumbo* (1935) used elements of the play in its story of two circus families brought together by the daughter and son of the feuding owners; *West Side Story* (1957).

'The Taming of the Shrew': *Kiss Me Kate* (1948).

'Twelfth Night': *Love and Let Love* (1968); *Your Own Thing* (1968); *Music Is . . .*(1976).

'Two Gentlemen of Verona': *Two Gentlemen of Soho* (1927); *Two Gentlemen of Verona* (1971).

Musicals based on poems (all by Longfellow)

Evangeline (1874); *Hiawatha* (1880); *Excelsior Jr* (1895); *Hiawatha* (1978) staged first by the Young Vic and then the National Theatre.

Other classics turned into musicals

Louisa May Alcott, 'Little Women': *A Girl Called Jo* (1955).

Daisy Ashford, 'The Young Visitors': *The Young Visitors* (1968).

Jane Austen, 'Pride and Prejudice': *First Impressions* (1959); *Pride and Prejudice* (1966 Birmingham).

J. M. Barrie, 'Peter Pan': *Peter Pan* (1954); 'The Admirable Crichton': *Our Man Crichton* (1964); 'What Every Woman Knows': *Maggie* (1977).

Boccaccio, 'Decameron': *Boccaccio* (1975).

Chaucer, 'The Canterbury Tales': *The Canterbury Tales* (1968).

Alexandre Dumas, 'The Three Musketeers':

Shakespeare transformed in Rodgers and Hart's 'The Boys from Syracuse' at the Alvin Theater New York, 1938.

Three Musketeers (1928); *Four Musketeers* (1967).

T. S. Eliot, 'Old Possum's Book of Practical Cats': *Cats* (1981).

Henry Fielding, 'Rape Upon Rape': *Lock Up Your Daughters* (1959).

Lillian Hellman, 'The Little Foxes': *Regina* (1949).

Thomas Hughes, 'Tom Brown's Schooldays': *Tom Brown's Schooldays* (1972).

Henry James, 'The Ambassadors': *Ambassador* (1971).

Sean O'Casey, 'Juno and The Paycock': *Juno* (1959).

Alan Paton, 'Cry The Beloved Country': *Lost in the Stars* (1949).

Arthur Wing Pinero, 'Trelawny of the Wells': *Trelawny* (1972).

Edmond Rostand, 'Cyrano de Bergerac': *Cyrano* (1973).

Harriet Beecher Stowe, 'Uncle Tom's Cabin': *Topsy and Eva* (1924).

Thackeray, 'Vanity Fair': *Vanity Fair* (1962).

Mark Twain, 'A Connecticut Yankee in King Arthur's Court': *A Connecticut Yankee* (1927).

Jules Verne, 'Around the World in 80 Days': *Around the World* (1946).

Voltaire, 'Candide': *Candide* (1956).

H. G. Wells, 'Kipps': *Half a Sixpence* (1963).

H. G. Wells, 'Ann Veronica': *Ann Veronica* (1969).

Oscar Wilde, 'The Importance of Being Earnest': *Half in Earnest* (1958); *Ernest in Love* (1960).

Oscar Wilde, 'Lady Windermere's Fan': *After the Ball* (1954).

P. G. Wodehouse: *Jeeves* (1975).

Thomas Wolfe, 'Look Homeward Angel': *Angel* (1978).

Writers depicted in musicals

Elizabeth Barrett and Robert Browning (played by June Bronhill and Keith Michell): *Robert and Elizabeth* (1964).

Cervantes (Richard Kiley): *Man of La Mancha* (1965).

Colette (Cleo Laine): *Colette* (1980).

Goethe (Dennis King): *Frederika* (1937).

Christopher Marlowe (Patrick Jude): *Marlowe* (1981).

Samuel Pepys (Frederick Ranalow): *Mr Pepys* (1926); (Leslie Henson) *And So To Bed* (1951).

Shakespeare (Daniel Ben-Zali): *Music Is...*(1976).

George Bernard Shaw (John Neville): *Boots With Strawberry Jam* (1968).

Mark Twain (Trevor Peacock): *White Suit Blues* (1977).

François Villon (Dennis King): *The Vagabond King* (1925).

Alexander Woollcott, renamed Sheridan Whiteside (Clive Revill): *Sherry* (1967).

Musicals based on comic-strip characters were

Above: Tony Kishman, James Poe, Louis Colucci, Mike Palaikis impersonate the famous four in 'Beatlemania' at the Astoria Theatre, London in 1979. Left: Three Elvises for the price of one: Shakin Stevens, P.J. Proby and 16 year old Timothy Whitnall who all played the central role in Jack Good's 1977 production of 'Elvis' at the Astoria.

'Joseph and the Amazing Technicolour Dreamcoat', first spun in 1973 and still going strong at Sadlers Wells in 1981.

Buster Brown (1905); Little Nemo (1908); Bringing Up Father (1925); Li'l Abner (1956); It's a Bird, It's a Plane, It's Superman (1966); You're a Good Man, Charlie Brown (1967); Annie (1977); Andy Capp (1982).

Musicals about God were Salvation (1969); Two by Two (1970); Gantry (1970); Godspell (1971); Jesus Christ Superstar (1971); The Survival of St. Joan (1971); Hard Job Being God (1972); Joseph and the Amazing Technicolour Dreamcoat (1973); Your Arm's Too Short to Box with God (1976).

Musicals about rock stars
The Beatles: John, Paul, George, Ringo and Bert (1974); Beatlemania (1978); Lennon (1981).
Elvis Presley: Bye Bye Birdie (1960); Elvis (1978).
The Rolling Stones: Let The Good Stones Roll (1978).

The classic composers most frequently plundered for musical scores are Chopin, Offenbach and the Strausses, Jr. and Sr. Musicals adapted from other men's work include:
Bizet: Carmen Jones (1943).
Borodin: Kismet (1953).
Chopin: White Lilacs (1928); The Damask Rose (1930); Waltz Without End (1942); Polonaise (1945).
Dvorak: Summer Song (1956).
Grieg: Song of Norway (1944).
Mozart: An Elephant in Arcady (1938).
Offenbach: The Love Song (1925); Can-Can (1946); Music at Midnight (1950); The Happiest Girl in the World (1961).
Rossini: Once Over Lightly (1942).
Scarlatti: An Elephant in Arcady (1938).
Schubert: Blossom Time (1921); Lilac Time (1922).
Johann Strauss Jr: Casanova (1932); Mr Strauss Goes to Boston (1945). With Strauss Sr: Waltzes from Vienna (1931); The Great Waltz (1937). With Oscar Strauss: Three Waltzes (1945).
Tchaikovsky: Catherine (1923); Music in my Heart (1947).
Verdi: My Darlin' Aida (1952).

Musicals have always been such stuff as dreams are made on. **The first notable dream sequence** was in A Connecticut Yankee (1927) in which Martin Barrett is hit on the head and dreams he is in the court of King Arthur. In Strike Up The Band (1927) a war with Switzerland over a 50 per cent tariff on Swiss cheese is part of an extended dream sequence. In DuBarry Was a

Lady, (1939) with Bert Lahr and Ethel Merman, a washroom attendant in a nightclub dreams he is Louis XV and the star of the club's show is Mme DuBarry. In *Lady in the Dark* (1941) all but one of the musical numbers are sung during dream sequences. Danny Kaye stopped the show singing 'Tchaikovsky' which included a chorus of 49 consecutive Russian composers' names which he belted out in 39 seconds. In *One Touch of Venus* (1943) the eponymous heroine (Mary Martin) dreams she is in love with barber Rodney Hatch but decides to turn back into a marble statue instead. In *Oklahoma* (1943) the heroine dreams of her abduction by the menacing Jud Fry and of her release at the hands of the handsome Curly. Musicals have also ventured into the workaday world. **The first to be set in a factory** was *The Sunshine Girl* (1912) where the cast manufactured soap. Since then *Strike Up the Band* (1927) was set in a cheese factory, *Carmen Jones* (1943) in a parachute factory, *The Pajama Game* (1954) in a pajama factory and *Strike a Light* (1966) and *The Matchgirls* (1966) both in a match factory.

The first American President to be featured in a musical was President Wilson in *The Ziegfeld Follies of 1919*. Since then President Adams has appeared in *1600 Pennsylvania Avenue* (1976), Coolidge in *The Garrick Gaieties* (1925), Hoover in *As Thousands Cheer* (1933), Jefferson in *1600 Pennsylvania Avenue* (1976), F.D. Roosevelt in *I'd Rather Be Right* (1937), *So Long 174th Street* (1976) and *Annie* (1977), Truman in *Call Me Madam* (1950).

Left: The programme cover for Buffalo Bill's show at Earl's Court, 1892.

George Grossmith and Connie Ediss in 'The Sunshine Girl' (1912), the first musical to be set in a factory.

The ten longest-running musicals on Broadway	Number of performances
Grease	3388
Fiddler on the Roof	3242
Hello Dolly	2844
My Fair Lady	2717
Man of La Mancha	2328
Oklahoma!	2212
Pippin	1928
South Pacific	1925
Hair	1750
Mame	1508

The ten longest-running musicals in London	Number of performances
Jesus Christ, Superstar	3351
Oliver!	2618
Salad Days	2283
Chu Chin Chow	2238
Charlie Girl	2202
The Boy Friend	2084
Canterbury Tales	2082
Me and My Girl	1646
The Maid of the Mountains	1352
Perchance to Dream	1022

The first musical show about the West was *Buffalo Bill's Wild West*. This extravaganza, starring Buffalo Bill Cody, Annie Oakley, Sitting Bull and a horde of real cowboys and Indians, toured America in the 1880s in a special 26-car train and in 1887 sailed to England to celebrate Queen Victoria's Golden Jubilee. It was almost single-handedly responsible for the romantic image of the West we still cherish. Musicals since then about the West: *Rainbow* (1928), *Whoopee* (1928), *Hold On To Your Hat* (1940), *Oklahoma!* (1943), *Annie Get Your Gun* (1946), *Texas L'il Darlin'* (1949), *Paint Your Wagon* (1951), *Little Mary Sunshine* (1959), *The Unsinkable Molly Brown* (1960), *Belle Star* (1969), *Shenandoah* (1975), *The Best Little Whorehouse in Texas* (1977).

Spectacular British musical failures of recent years
The World of Paul Slickey (1959) with a book by

'Hair': a musical milestone which brought pro-pot anti-draft protest on to Broadway and London stages and which in 1968 became the first theatrical production to benefit from the official demise of censorship.

John Osborne that attacked gossip columnists, popular newspaper proprietors, the aristocracy and three separate pairs of adulterers. The show ended with two of the leading characters changing their sex. *Twang* (1965) a Lionel Bart musical about Robin Hood. The director, Joan Littlewood, left before the first night of the provincial try-out, the book was endlessly re-written and the plot, according to *The Times*, was 'as clear as a tattered cobweb'.

The Good Old Bad Old Days (1972) by Anthony Newley and Leslie Bricusse which attempted to survey man's history from Roman times to the present day. The plot hinged on a conflict between God and the Devil, resistibly retitled 'Gramps and Bubba'. But at least the title song had a certain bounce.

Thomas and the King (1977). The story of Becket and Henry II blessed with such great numbers as 'Will No-One Rid Me?' and such memorable lines as Queen Eleanor's 'Seize that monk' as she espied a copulating religious functionary.

Barnardo (1980). **The first musical about a hero**

Tom Thumb and Beefeaters from the hit musical 'Barnum'. (Reg Wilson).

Above: The Black and White Minstrel Show which clocked up 4344 performances at the Victoria Palace. (BBC Hulton Picture Library). Below: 'The Mousetrap': 30 years on and still going strong. (Robert Clarke Studio).

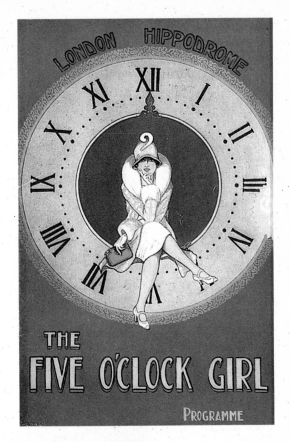

Above: Programme cover for the variety
programmes at the Palladium from 1927 to 1931.
Right: 'The Five O'clock Girl' first produced at the
London Hippodrome, 1929. (Both Victoria and
Albert Museum).

Programme cover for a performance of 'The Mikado' at the Savoy Theatre,
1885. (Victoria and Albert Museum).

The whirl of the gingham in a celebratory dance from 'Oklahoma' (1947). (BBC Hulton Picture Library).

Three gorgeous pussies from 'Cats' at the New London Theatre. (Dewynters).

Rachel Roberts as a friendly Liverpool scrubber in Lionel Bart's 1964 musical, 'Maggie May', at the Adelphi Theatre.

who was, in real-life, tone-deaf. The kind of musical that summarised the whole history of The Boer War by having a paper-boy run across the stage shouting 'Mafeking Besieged'.

Ivor Novello was the most popular provider of British musicals in the 1930s. *Glamorous Night* (1935), *Careless Rapture* (1936), *Crest of the Wave* (1937), *The Dancing Years* (1939) all won him an adoring public. But the critics were not always kind. After *Crest of the Wave*, *The Observer* wrote: 'One staggers out sated and a trifle stunned observing, with a bloated species of relief, as one does at the end of a long Christmas dinner with the family, that this occasion is over for another year'. Novello himself could also be pleasantly self-mocking about his shows inventing for them such distorted titles as *The Prancing Queers*, *Perchance to Scream*, *Careless Rupture*. Novello died in his flat above the Strand Theatre on 6 March 1951 four hours after playing the lead in his own production of *King's Rhapsody* at the Palace Theatre.

Outside the musical stage, Novello wrote **the best-known song of the First World War**, *Keep The Home Fires Burning* which earned him £15 000 during the first five years of its life. He was goaded into doing it by his Mother (Mam) who in 1914 wrote an execrable patriotic song herself and threatened to perform it in public if Ivor didn't do one of his own.

Noel Coward's most popular musical work for the stage was *Bitter Sweet: an Operette* which opened in 1929 at Her Majesty's and played there and at the Palace Theatre for 697 performances. Coward's subsequent musicals — *Conversation Piece* (1934), *Operette* (1938), *Pacific 1860* (1946), *Ace of Clubs* (1950) and *Sail Away* (1961) — never enjoyed comparable success though the scores of each contained splendid individual tunes.

Lionel Bart (with *Oliver*, *Blitz* and *Maggie May*), **Sandy Wilson** (with *The Boy Friend* and *Valmouth*) and **Julian Slade** (with *Salad Days*, *Free as Air* and *Follow that Girl*) dominated the British musical theatre of the 1950s and 60s. Bart's most successful show was *Oliver* (1960) which ran originally in the West End for 2618 performances and which has since been revived

Above: That certain thing called 'The Boy Friend' which began life at London's Players Theatre Club in April, 1953 and which wound up on Broadway a year later. Sandy Wilson's pastiche even survived a Ken Russell film. Left: Stephanie Lawrence as Eva and John Turner as Peron in the London production of 'Evita', the Andrew Lloyd-Webber and Tim Rice musical which Hal Prince directed with a dark, ferocious verve. Right: The poster for 'Sweeney Todd', one of the musicals with which Harold Prince and Stephen Sondheim changed the face of Broadway in the 1970s.

twice. Of *Blitz* (1962), a musical about London during the German air raids, Noel Coward commented: 'Half as long as the original and twice as loud'.

The first British musical to be based on an LP record was *Jesus Christ Superstar* by Andrew Lloyd-Webber and Tim Rice. As a double gramophone record, it sold over 7 million copies. The stage production opened at the Palace Theatre in August 1972 and closed there in August, 1980.

It was the most successful musical show of the 1970s and one of the most popular ever. It has been translated into 11 languages, performed in

RICHARD BARR   CHARLES WOODWARD
ROBERT FRYER   MARY LEA JOHNSON   MARTIN RICHARDS
IN ASSOCIATION WITH
DEAN & JUDY MANOS
PRESENT

ANGELA LANSBURY   LEN CARIOU

IN

Sweeney Todd
The Demon Barber of Fleet Street

A MUSICAL THRILLER

MUSIC AND LYRICS BY
STEPHEN SONDHEIM

BOOK BY
HUGH WHEELER

BASED ON A VERSION OF "SWEENEY TODD" BY CHRISTOPHER BOND

DIRECTED BY
HAROLD PRINCE

PRODUCED FOR RECORDS BY
THOMAS Z. SHEPARD

AWARDS FOR BEST MUSICALS

Year	Tony Awards sponsored first by American Theatre Wing, then by League of New York Theatres; named in honour of Antoinette Perry	London Evening Standard (now The Standard) Awards
1949	Kiss Me Kate	
1950	South Pacific	
1951	Guys and Dolls	
1952	The King and I	
1953	Wonderful Town	
1954	Kismet	
1955	The Pajama Game	The Pajama Game
1956	Damn Yankees	Cranks
1957	My Fair Lady	No award
1958	The Music Man	West Side Story
1959	Redhead	Make Me an Offer
1960	Fiorello	Fings Ain't Wot They Used T'Be
	The Sound of Music	
1961	Bye Bye Birdie	Beyond the Fringe
1962	How To Succeed in Business Without Really Trying	No award
1963	A Funny Thing Happened on the Way to the Forum	Oh What a Lovely War
1964	Hello, Dolly	Little Me
1965	Fiddler on the Roof	No award
1966	Man of La Mancha	Funny Girl
1967	Cabaret	Sweet Charity
1968	Hallelujah Baby	Cabaret
1969	1776	Promises, Promises
1970	Applause	No award
1971	Company	No award
1972	Two Gentlemen of Verona	Applause
1973	A Little Night Music	The Rocky Horror Show
1974	Raisin	John Paul George Ringo . . . and Bert
1975	The Wiz	A Little Night Music
1976	Chorus Line	A Chorus Line
1977	Annie	Elvis
1978	Ain't Misbehavin'	Annie
1979	Sweeney Todd	Songbook
1980	Evita	Sweeney Todd
1981	42nd Street	Cats
1982		

22 countries, has grossed £100 million worldwide. The London production alone was seen by two million people and made £7 million pounds at the box-office. It had its first empty seat after 15 weeks of the run (Evita, also by Lloyd-Webber and Rice, didn't record an empty seat until week 78). After its original Broadway opening, its producer, Robert Stigwood, announced: 'Jesus Christ could be the biggest thing in history'.

The most unlikely British musical hit of recent years was The Rocky Horror Show which opened at the minuscule Theatre Upstairs above the Royal Court Theatre in June 1973. It transferred to two other theatres in the King's Road and has since played all over the world and been filmed. The movie version has attracted its own cult following with members of the audience frequently dressing in the transvestite, Transylvanian garb of its hero, Frank-n-furter.

FOOTNOTE ON MUSICAL SHOWS

From *Encyclopaedia of the Theatre* by George Jean Nathan. 'Some fifteen or more years ago the late Arthur Bingham Walkley and William Archer, celebrated English dramatic critics, gave a dinner for me, on a visit to London, at the Garrick Club. A number of the younger British critics, along with a group of theatrical illuminati, were present and there were speeches. When it came to my turn I got up and proceeded at the behest of my hosts to expatiate on the American theatre. 'The recent tendency in American drama' I gravely began. 'The devil with the recent tendency in American drama', howled Walkley and Archer in unison. 'What we want to hear about is the *Ziegfeld Follies*'.

Another governess with a testy patriarch in another Rodgers and Hammerstein musical: Jean Bayless and Roger Dann in the 1961 London production of 'The Sound of Music' at the Palace.

CHAPTER 6

The Laughter Makers

Comedy is as old as theatre itself. At their Dionysian Festivals the Greeks enjoyed satyr-plays, burlesquing mythic heroes, after the tragic trilogy. From 486 BC comedy was also presented competitively at the Lenaea Festival in January. The comedies presented revelled in libel, obscenity, blasphemy, bawdy with actors wearing enlarged phalluses and grotesque padding.

The Romans also enjoyed the more sophisticated plays of Plautus (252-184 BC) and Terence (190-159 BC) as well as the coarser mime plays on such themes as drunkenness, greed and adultery. But the mime-plays also indulged the Roman appetite for physical cruelty. Emperor Heliogabalus (3rd century AD), if a mime play included an execution, ordered condemned criminals to be killed during the performance. For adultery plays (very popular) he ordained that 'those things which should be done in fiction were to be carried out in reality'.

The first recorded mime-artist was the Graeco-Roman poet, playwright and entertainer, Livius Andronicus (284-204 BC). When his voice failed during one of his *saturae* (popular variety shows) he got a slave to speak the words while he mimed the action.

Light entertainment was also a staple part of medieval life: from the 11th to the 14th centuries popular entertainers roamed Europe performing at feasts and fairs, at the nobleman's hall and in the market place. But a distinction must be made between *bufos* (specialists in tumbling, juggling and buffoonery), *jongleurs* (musicians and singers) and troubadours (composers of music and poetry). Plays like the Second Shepherd's Play in the English Wakefield Mystery Cycle (14th century) also imply the presence of a gifted comic actor in the role of Mak the sheep-stealer.

UK and Ireland

In England **the first professional clown** was *Richard Tarleton (d. 1588).* A short thick-set man with a squint and a distinctive flat nose, he was noted for his improvised doggerel verse, known as Tarletonising, and his Jig, a farce in rhyme, sung and danced to popular tunes of the day. He was Queen Elizabeth's favourite jester and allegedly the prototype of Yorick over whose skull Hamlet laments. By the mid 1570s he made the change from court to stage where he became a member of the Queen's Men who were chosen by the Master of Revels from among the best actors in London. Tarleton obviously died at his peak to judge by the obituary of one John Scottowe:

> The party now is gone
> And closely clad in clay
> Of all the jesters in the land
> He bare the praise away.

Thus began a long line of British clowns and comics stretching from Elizabethan ages to the present day. Their numbers include:

WILLIAM KEMPE (d.1603) Famous English comic actor who from 1596 was with Shakespeare's company, the Lord Chamberlain's Servants, playing at the Globe in summer and

Blackfriars in winter. He took such parts as Peter in *Romeo and Juliet* (1595-96), Dogberry in *Much Ado About Nothing* (1598-99), Justice Shallow in *Henry IV Part Two* (1598). But he was most famous for dancing a morris from London to Norwich in the spring of 1599. Nine days of dancing on the road were interspersed with fourteen days of rest. When he got to Norwich the Mayor entertained him and gave him a gift of £5. He made further money from his account of the stunt, *Kempe's Nine Days Wonder*, which was published in 1600 and which he said he wrote 'to satisfie his friends the truth against all lying ballad makers'.

ROBERT ARMIN (1568-1615) Successor to Tarleton and Kempe and supposedly a more subtle clown than his two predecessors. Joined the Lord Chamberlain's Men in 1599 and created the roles of Touchstone in *As You Like It* (1599), Feste in *Twelfth Night* (1601-2) and the First Gravedigger in *Hamlet* (1601-2). Was also an author. Wrote *Foole upon Foole* (1599), a book about jesters; *Quips upon Questions* (1600), and the play *Two Maids of More-clacke* (1609) in which he also appeared.

JOHN RICH (1692-1761) The father of English pantomime. As manager of Lincoln's Inn Fields Theatre, in 1716 he copied the Italo-French idea of short comic ballets with, 'performed for the first time', *A New Italian Mimic Scene between a Scaramouche, a Harlequin, a Country Farmer, his Wife and Others* with himself (under the name of Lun) as Harlequin and John Thurmond as Scaramouche. This, one month later, had become entitled *Harlequin Executed; or, The Farmer Disappointed* indicating that the action had become more English. **The word 'pantomime' in the sense of a balletic show on a traditional theme was first used on 2 March, 1717 at Drury Lane** when John Weaver, a dancing master, staged *The Loves of Mars and Venus*, 'A new Dramatic Entertainment of Dancing after the manner of the Ancient Pantomimes'. But it was Rich who, playing the trickster Harlequin, established pantomime in England presenting it every Christmas from 1717 to 1760.

CHARLES DIBDIN (1745-1814) Actor, composer, theatre manager and comedian who appeared on the stage for 45 years. An early precursor of the stand-up comic. He built the tiny

Richard Tarleton, ancestor of all British clowns.

theatre *Sans Souci* (1793) in Leicester Square where for 10 years he performed his one-man show, *The Whim of the Moment* (with frequent variations and for which he wrote nearly 1000 songs): a mix of comic dialogues, pathetic tales, anecdotes and songs all presented in a relaxed manner as if to a roomful of friends. Dibdin was also noted for his sea-songs: 'Tom Bowling' and 'The Lass That Loves a Sailor' were said to have 'brought more men into the Navy than all the press-gangs could'.

JOSEPH GRIMALDI (1778-1837) **Most famous of all English clowns.** He created the clown costume still recognised today: wide breeches, tufts of hair on a bald wig, white face with red triangle on each cheek. He revolutionised English pantomime by taking it away from its Italian *commedia dell'arte* roots, by making it verbal, earthy and comedy-centred. He also laid

Dan Leno, the inspiration for many modern music-hall performers and a man with, according to Marie Lloyd, "the saddest eyes in the whole world".

THE GREAT VANCE (1839-88) The original coster comedian best known for his comic Cockney songs (e.g. 'The Chickaleery Cove'). Later he developed his act as a 'lion comique': a parody of the city swell in flash fashionable gear. He and George Leybourne (1842-88) developed a friendly rivalry going through the wine list for song topics: Vance's 'Cliquot' versus Leybourne's 'Champagne Charlie' started the vinous competition.

GEORGE LEYBOURNE (1842-88) The original 'lion comique': a term invented by J. J. Poole, musical director of the Metropolitan, Edgware Road, who heard Leybourne at the Canterbury in 1867 and dubbed him 'a regular lion of a comic'. Born Joe Saunders, a midlands mechanic, Leybourne affected on stage a man-about-town appearance complete with monocle, whiskers and fur collar and hymning the delights of drink. He was encouraged to live the part off-stage as well by dressing extravagantly, driving a carriage-and-four and drinking only champagne (Moët). His best-known song, in fact, was 'Champagne Charlie' (1866). But others sought to copy his grand style: Harry Liston (1843-1929) once arrived at a theatre in a carriage drawn by four white donkeys.

the foundation for 19th-century panto by incorporating fairy tales and nursery rhymes into the shows he wrote: his first great success, in fact, was *Harlequin and Mother Goose or The Golden Egg* (Covent Garden 1806). An anonymous contemporary wrote: 'He was a master of grimace; and whether he was robbing a pieman, opening an oyster, affecting the polite, riding a giant cart-horse, imitating a sweep, grasping a red-hot poker, devouring a pudding, picking a pocket, beating a watchman, sneezing, snuffing, courting, or nursing a child, he was so extravagantly natural that the most saturnine looker-on acknowledged his sway; and neither the wise, the proud, the fair, the young, nor the old were ashamed to laugh till tears coursed down their cheeks at Joe and his comicalities'. He was forced to retire at Christmas 1823, too crippled to carry on. His last public appearance was at an 1828 Drury Lane benefit where he sang his most popular song, 'Hot Codlins', about an old woman who sold roasted apples and drank too much gin. Even today all clowns are called Joey after Grimaldi.

DAN LENO (1860-1904) Epitome of Cockney comedy born George Galvin. Made his debut at the age of 4 at the Cosmotheka Music Hall, Paddington, as 'Little George the Infant Wonder, contortionist and posturer'; at 18 was 'champion clog-dancer of the world'; made his Drury Lane debut in 1888 as the Baroness in *Babes in the Wood*. He played Dame there every year for 15 years. Five foot tall with the saddest eyes in the world, a squeaky voice and large down-turned mouth, Leno performed monologues rather than songs. He said he had 'mislaid his voice' when he became a comic singer. Always showed surprise when people laughed at his jokes but his long, rambling, slight surrealist anecdotes were told with great speed. His most popular sketch (a favourite with Edward VII) was one in which a Beefeater shows visitors round the Tower while extolling the dubious virtues of the Refreshment Room. In 1901 a comic paper was named after him. He died, overworked and insane, in 1904. 'So little and frail a lantern could not long harbour so big a flame', wrote Max Beerbohm in *The Saturday Review*.

ALBERT CHEVALIER (1861-1923) Originally an actor and even opera singer, he made his debut on the halls in 1891 at The London Pavilion singing 'The Coster's Serenade'. A great exponent of mawkish Cockney humour, his most famous songs were 'My Old Dutch', 'Knocked 'em in the Old Kent Road', and ''Appy 'Ampstead'.

GUS ELEN (1862-1940) Another in the line of Cockney coster comedians who flourished in Victorian and Edwardian music-hall. Began his career as a street busker, graduated to singing in pubs with a minstrel show. Made his debut as a coster comedian at the Middlesex Music Hall (1891). His best known songs were 'It's a Great Big Shame', 'Down the Road', and 'If It Wasn't For The Houses in Between'.

VESTA TILLEY (1864-1952) **The best-known male impersonator of the music-hall.** Made her debut at 3½ as the Great Little Tilley at St. George's Hall, Nottingham. First appeared in male attire in Birmingham aged 5 as the Pocket Slim Reeves (Reeves was a famous tenor). 'Male dress' was considered to be tights, spangles and fringe worn with a man's top-hat and cane. Later she wore full male attire designed by Savile Row. Noted for her immaculate costumes, attention to detail and particularly the walk of the character she was impersonating. Her most popular songs were 'Burlington Bertie', 'Following in Father's Footsteps', and 'Good luck to the girl who loves a soldier'. She retired from the stage in 1920.

HARRY CHAMPION (1866-1942) First appeared as a black-face comedian called Will Conray. As white-face comedian Harry Champion specialised in songs of a culinary bent sung at terrific speed: 'Boiled beef and carrots', 'Hot tripe and onions', 'Hot meat pies', 'Savaloys and trotters', 'Baked sheep's heart, stuffed with sage and onions'.

LITTLE TICH (1868-1928) Comedian, dancer, acrobat and mime, Little Tich appeared in music-hall and pantomime (1891-93 played with Marie Lloyd, Herbert Campbell and Dan Leno in Christmas panto at Drury Lane). Equally popular in Britain and the USA, he portrayed odd characters: a miniature Sergeant Major, a female Spanish dancer, a seasick sailor. Only 4ft 6in high (and with an extra finger on each hand) his *tour de force* was the Big Boot dance in which

Vesta Tilley: the epitome of bowler-hatted manhood.

he balanced on the tips of his giant-sized boots which were half as long (28 inches) as he was high.

GEORGE ROBEY (1869-1954) The self-styled 'Prime Minister of Mirth'. Made his first appearance at the Aquarium Music Hall in 1891. Played in pantomime, revue, musicals and even straight plays. His stock-in-trade was a black bowler, two enormous arched black eyebrows, clerical collar and a cane. His speciality was a tone of dignified, mock-reproof: 'Desist. And I am surprised at *you*, Agerness'. He was, said Nevile Cardus, a comic actor: he absorbed himself into a character and a scene. Apart from topping the bill in every major music-hall, he appeared in revue (starting with *The Bing Boys Are Here* in 1916), played Sancho Panza in Chaliapin's film of *Don Quixote* (1933), Falstaff in a stage production of *Henry IV Part One* (1935) and made his television debut in 1938. 'He saw the comedy of life', wrote Henry Raynor in *The Times* in 1969, 'maintaining an essential innocence and sharing it among us all'.

MARIE LLOYD (1870-1922) The Queen of the Halls and the most important music-hall entertainer Britain ever produced. Born in Hoxton, she made her debut in 1885 at the Royal Eagle Music Hall. By the age of 18 she had established a reputation for her saucy renditions of slightly off-colour songs such as 'She'd Never Had Her Ticket Punched Before' (another favourite was

George Robey, complete with the bowler, the eyebrows, the clerical collar and the cane that were all part of his dignified persona.

'She Sits Amongst the Cabbages and Peas'). Noted for her famous wink, her energy and her sense of joy, her extravagant costumes were a legend. But when she dressed for 'character' songs like 'My Old Man' and 'One of the Ruins That Cromwell Knocked About a Bit' the details were correct down to the battered birdcage or shabby handbag she held in her hand. T. S. Eliot said of her 'I have called her the expressive figure of the lower classes; there is no such expressive figure for any other class'. James Agate wrote of her that 'She had a heart as big as Waterloo Station'. Despite her popularity she was never invited to take part in a Royal Command Performance largely because of her so-called scandalous private life (she was married three times, twice divorced on grounds of adultery). But on the evening of the first Royal Command in 1912, she performed at the Pavilion. Pasted on the bills was the notice that 'Every performance given by Marie Lloyd is a Command Performance by order of the British Public'.

NELLIE WALLACE (1870-1948) 'The Essence of Eccentricity'. Born in Glasgow, she was the mistress of broad humour and of the grotesque. Her wispy spinster character was dressed in a bizarre attempt at elegance: tartan skirt, red flannel, hat with balding feather and ragged fur piece which she called 'me little bit of vermin'. She appeared on the opening bill of the Palladium (1910) and was one of the few successful female Panto Dames. When music-hall faded, she appeared with great success in revue: *Whirl of the World* (1923) and *Sky High* (1925), both at the Palladium. Her most famous songs: 'I Lost Georgie in Trafalgar Square', 'My Mother always said look under the bed', 'Half Past Nine'.

HARRY LAUDER (1870-1950) **The first music-hall artist to be knighted** (1919) for his contribution to the war effort. Called 'The Laird of the Halls', he was born in Portobello, Scotland.

The Crazy Gang in 'These Foolish Things' at the Victoria Palace 1956.

Made his first appearance in England in 1896 at Birkenhead as an Irish comedian singing 'Calligan Call Again'. Was the most popular British music-hall star in the USA making his debut in New York in 1907. Most famous songs: 'I love a lassie' (his first big hit), 'Roamin' in the Gloamin', 'Keep right on to the end of the road', 'Stop yer tickling, Jock'. Most of the songs were overly sentimental but the comic ones include 'That's the reason noo I wear a kilt'.

WILL FYFFE (1885-1947) Scottish comedian and character actor. Born in Dundee he toured Scotland as a boy in a stock company run by his father even playing Polonius in *Hamlet* at 15. Made his London debut in 1916 at the Middlesex. In 1921 became an overnight hit at the Palladium followed by the Royal Command Performance in 1922. Performed character sketches as gamekeeper, Highland railway guard, old shepherd, etc. Best known sketches were of Glasgow working-man singing 'I belong to Glasgow' and tale of the death of Jim McGregor in which the villiage idiot, after giving his life savings of £17 to McGregor's widow was not permitted to go to the funeral in case he made the mourners laugh.

WILL HAY (1888-1949) The Schoolmaster Comedian. Created the schoolmaster of the 4th form at St. Michael's, Dr. Benjamin Twist, tyrannical master of misinformation with wild hair and a chalky voice. Played the halls and first appeared on film in *Boys Will Be Boys* (1935) as Dr Alec Smart and dubbed Smart Alec.

MAX MILLER (1895-1963) The highest paid comedian of his time earning, at his peak, £1500 a week. Drove a glass-topped Rolls Royce and owned a cabin cruiser. First billed as The Cheeky Chappie in 1924 and was at the height of his fame during the Second World War. He was the banjo-strumming master of the *double entendre* with loud clothes (white trilby, plus fours and kipper tie) and two gag-books, white and blue, containing jokes graded clean or dirty. 'He was', wrote John Osborne, 'the type of flashiness. He was flashiness perfected and present in all things visible and invisible. The common, cheap and mean parodied and seized on as a style of life in face of the world's dullards'. Often played the Holborn Empire, the Finsbury Park Empire and the Palladium. His signature tune was 'Mary from the Dairy' and his best-known catchphrase 'There'll never be another'. Not strictly true since John Bardon does a full-dress impersonation of Miller in his one-man show, *Here's A Funny Thing* first seen at the Edinburgh Festival in 1980 and at London's Fortune Theatre in 1982.

BUD FLANAGAN (1896-1968) and CHESNEY ALLEN (1894-) were the most famous English double-act. They teamed up for the first time in Florrie Forde's *Flo and Co* (1924) with their songs and cross-talk comedy routines. They worked together until Allen's retirement because of crippling rheumatism in 1945. Their famous 'Underneath the Arches' act was first introduced in Birkenhead in 1931. Their many hit songs included 'We're going to hang out the washing on the Siegfried line', 'Run Rabbit Run', and 'Umbrella Man'. They were also an integral part of the Crazy Gang though not, curiously, founder-members. The Crazy Gang originated in 1932 at the Palladium in a show called *Crazy Week* comprising three double-acts and one eccentric: Nervo and Knox, Naughton and Gold, Caryll and Mundy and Monsewer Eddie Gray. Flanagan and Allen joined the troupe in their third production *Crazy Month* (1932) followed by seven more shows. *London Rhapsody* (1937) was the first show to use the name Crazy Gang. The Blitz ended the Gang's occupation of the Palladium. They re-formed in 1947, minus Chesney Allen, at the Victoria Palace opening with *Together Again* (1566 performances) and finally retired in 1962. Their careers were reconstructed in *Underneath the Arches* first seen at Chichester in 1981 and then at the Prince of Wales in 1982.

ARTHUR ASKEY (1900-) Product of Liverpool and eternally popular as Big-Hearted Arthur with the large-horn-rimmed glasses, the perky manner and the dapper suit. Turned professional at 24 and graduated from touring concert party to big summer-shows and music-hall. Became a household name with a radio show, *Band Wagon*, in 1938 in partnership with Richard 'Stinker' Murdoch which led to a stage version at the Palladium. Has played every pantomime Dame and continued to appear in panto at Richmond Theatre even in his 82nd year; has appeared in nine Command Performances; and is famous worldwide for tongue-twisting songs like 'The Busy Bee'.

GEORGE FORMBY (1904-61) The youngest professional jockey ever (at the age of 10) he was the son of music-hall comic George Formby Sr. The young Formby made his debut in 1921 in Earlstown and for the rest of his career successfully played his ukelele and sang his 'daft little songs'. Once he had developed his act, by 1923, it never varied: the monotonous fast-speed strumming accompaniment to comic songs like 'When I'm cleaning windows', 'Leaning on a lamp-post', 'Mr Wu', and 'With me little ukulele in me hand'.

MAX WALL (1908-) Early recognition as eccentric dancer in cabaret. Made his West End debut as a speciality dancer in *The London Revue* (1925) and American debut in *Earl Carroll's Vanities* (1932) where he included comedy in his

Sid Field prepares for his first role on the legitimate stage in 'Harvey' in 1949. In fact, the rabbit was a figment of the hero's imagination.

Arthur Askey as Buttons with Erica Yorke as Cinderella in a Golders Green 'Cinderella' at Christmas 1961.

SID FIELD (1904-50) Made his stage debut in 1916 but didn't appear in the West End until 1943 in *Strike a New Note* at the Prince of Wales. Other successes followed: *Strike It Again* (1944), the musical *Piccadilly Hayride* (1946) and the play *Harvey* (1949). His forté was the comic character study in partnership with his straight man Jerry Desmonde. There was Slasher Greene from the Elephant and Castle in vastly-beshouldered overcoat and pencilled moustache, his impetuous cavorting velvet-coated, blond-wigged photographer and his famous golfing-sketch in which he was belaboured by a serious pro ('I could have been having my music lesson with Miss Bollinger' he used to explain with careful scorn). With his elephantine bulk, he epitomised a roguish camp long before the word was in use.

George Formby, with his little ukulele in his hand.

Above: Max Wall on ice: in 'White Horse Inn on Ice' at the Empress Hall London, 1954, Belita is keeping him at foot's length.

act for the first time. In 1946 in *Make It A Date* he introduced his most famous character, the grotesque pianist, Professor Walloffski in shoulder-length black wig, tails, black tights and large boots. His career has had its ups and downs but he was hailed by a new generation in a revue *Cockie* (1973) and hasn't looked back since. He was acclaimed a genius for his lunatic dancing, his desperate jokes ('If they sawed a woman in half, I'd get the half that eats'), his weary lugubriousness, his ability to spin an act out of the air. His own one-man show *Aspects of Max Wall* (1975) was an oft-repeated success and he has appeared in plays by Beckett, Osborne, Pinter, and Wesker. Watching Wall you feel you are seeing the last surviving link with the great era of grotesque physical clowning.

TOMMY TRINDER (1909-) Made his variety debut in 1922 at Collins Music Hall, Islington as

Tommy Trinder combining his two interests: comedy and football. It was Trinder who, when asked in pantomime "What is the mystery of Orient?" cried: "They won two-nil at home on Saturday."

O naughty Francis: Mr Howerd casting mock-lecherous glances at Anne Aston's busty substances.

Below: Ken Dodd, clutching his tickling-stick, with four Bluebell Girls at Blackpool, 1966.

Red Nirt (Trinder spelt backwards). Height of success came in the 1940s at the Palladium starting with *Gangway* (1941) with Bebe Daniels and Ben Lyon. In the 1950s he returned there to compère the televised Sunday Night at the London Palladium variety shows. With his jutting chin and trilby, he is the fast-talking master of the ad lib always dealing with hecklers enthusiastically, encouraging them on when they weren't demonstrative enough. Possessed of a large but endearing ego, he once advertised himself on billboards all over London, including one opposite Aldgate Station printed in Hebrew.

FRANKIE HOWERD (1921-) Bulky, spinsterish, rumpled comic as much a part of English comic life as Dickens's Sairey Gamp. Made his professional stage debut in Sheffield in 1946. By 1950 he was appearing at the Palladium in *Out of This World* and on radio in Variety Bandbox. His career slumped for a while but revived in 1963 with an invitation to appear on the *TW3* television show and at the Establishment Club. Is famous for his calculated inarticulacy, his abuse of his employers and his pianist ('Camp? She doesn't know the meaning of the word — she thinks Richard Dimbleby is camp') and his long lugubrious features which are the kind you might see in a spoon. Made his debut in opera in 1981 in *Die Fledermaus* at the London Coliseum.

TOMMY COOPER (1922-) Comic magician with fez, a bulky top-heavy body, a set of seemingly unrehearsed conjuring tricks and a string of inane jokes all greeted with his own high-pitched maniacal laugh. Made his debut in 1947 in Windermere Floor Show followed by long-running successes in revue: *Encore de Folies* (1951), *Paris by Night* (1955) and *Blue Magic* (1959). Probably the most imitated comic in Britain today whose phrase 'Just like that' is on every other comedian's lips.

KEN DODD (1929-) Performer of **the longest stand-up comedy routine ever:** a non-stop *Marathon Mirthquake* at the Royal Court, Liverpool in 1974 in which he told jokes unceasingly for three hours, six minutes and thirty seconds. He is, even in normal circumstances, a one-man anthology of comedy whose gargantuan act combines verbal jokes, physical jokes, songs, musical instruments, ventriloquism and a group of slightly alarming children called the Diddymen. Born in Knotty Ash, Liverpool in 1929, he has managed to turn it into part of English comic mythology: his surrealist humour has also proved popular with figures as diverse as Harold Wilson and John Osborne. Dodd says: 'When you come out of a laughter show, you should feel as if you've been through a wringer'. His act leaves one well-wrung.

America

WEBER AND FIELDS (Joe Weber (1867-1942) and Lew Fields (1867-1941) were the first successful American Vaudeville team. They joined forces at age 9 in minstrel shows around New York. Developed a slapstick Dutch act with dialogue in broken English with Weber as Mike, short and innocent, and Fields as Myer, tall, thin and devious.

From 1895 to 1904 they operated their own music-hall, the Weber and Fields Theatre, in New York on 29th Street. After 1904 they occasionally appeared together (Hokey-Pokey and Roly Poly both 1912). Fields opened his own theatre (1918-30) and appeared on stage until 1929. Weber retired from performing in 1918, but continued to direct until 1928.

BERT WILLIAMS (1874-1922) Born in Nassau, began his career as a double act with George Walker with whom he appeared until Walker's death in 1911. In 1893 they joined Martin and Seig's Mastodon Minstrels; in 1896 they made their New York debut in The Gold Bug, with music by Victor Herbert. Appeared in eight editions of the Ziegfeld Follies (1910-19). Unlike most black performers of the time Williams did not resort to any eye-rolling exaggeration; he underplayed, as in the poker game sketch where a small spotlight illuminated head and shoulders as he mimed a poker play: holding cards close to his face, studying his hand, betting and bidding, looking suspiciously at his imaginary opponents, calling, and the disgust of losing.

His trademark song was 'Nobody' which he sang in the character of the shiftless loafer he made famous, in top-hat, shabby dress suit and big shoes. Other songs: 'You Got the Right Church but the Wrong Pew'; 'My Castle on the Nile'; and the anti-prohibitionist 'You Can't Make Your Shimmy Shake on Tea'.

WILL ROGERS (1879-1935) America's Poet Lariat was born in Indian Territory, Oklahoma. 'The World's Number One Wisecracker' was political satirist extraordinaire and droll raconteur. But he began his career in wild west shows, graduated to a horse and rope act in vaudeville (1905), and eventually added a commentary as he twirled his lariat ('There's no such thing as a big rope trick, rope tricks is all little'). In a lazy drawl he commented dryly on current affairs, politicians (he was particularly averse to Republicans), the rich, bankers, lawyers, missionaries, etc. He took part in five editions of the Ziegfeld Follies (1916-24), and after 1925 he appeared in movies. He was a newspaper columnist, radio commentator and lecturer.

W.C. FIELDS (1880-1946) Born William Claude Dukinfield in Philadelphia, his unhappy childhood there no doubt suggested to him that his epitaph should read 'on the whole, I'd rather be in Philadelphia'.

Debut at age 14 as an amusement park juggling act; 1897 debut as tramp juggler, later billing himself in vaudeville as 'the world's greatest juggler'. His silent act was an enormous success in the US and abroad, including Paris, where he was **the first American headliner of the** Folies-Bergère.

He spoke for the first time on stage in Ziegfeld Follies (1916) and from then comic monologues were included in the act. He appeared in seven editions of the Follies (1915-25).

In vaudeville Fields, an anarchic monster with his grandiloquent vocabulary, bogus grand manner and decidedly jaundiced view of humanity gained sympathy by surrounding himself with even more appalling foils. One of his best silent routines included a pool table. He would enter, meticulously take off coat, hat, chalk cue, etc., pocket all 15 balls with a single shot and depart.

With his bulbous nose (permanently swollen from too many boyhood fights), and his rasping voice (due to neglect of health from an early age) he was epitomised in the musical comedy Poppy (1923) which introduced that irascible carnival swindler, Professor Eustace McGargle, a character he played for the rest of his life. The film version (Sally of the Sawdust, 1925) was directed by the great D.W. Griffith. In 1931 he abandoned the stage for Hollywood.

W.C. Fields: different he certainly was with, according to Tynan, "a nose like a doughnut pickled in vinegar or an eroded squash ball" and a voice like a cement-mixer.

AL JOLSON (1886-1950) **'The World's Greatest Entertainer'**, born Asa Yoelson, son of a Russian-Jewish rabbi. Jolson's stage career began at age 12. By 18 he had joined his brother Hirsh and Joe Palmer (Jolson, Palmer and Jolson) to form an act called 'A Little of Everything' (1904) when Jolson wore blackface for the first time. It wasn't until 1931 (in the musical comedy *Wonder Bar*) that he appeared without blackface again. He was **the inventor of the Mammy song** and sang his first in San Francisco, 1909, in blackface and down on one knee, a posi-

N.º 11.

Mʳ GRIMALDI ᴀꜱ CLOWN.

Price Halfpenny.

ILLUMINATING THE ENTRANCE TO OLD GUTTER LANE.

London, Pub.Feb 16, 1833, by J.K.Green, 3, George Street, Walworth new Town.

Joseph Grimaldi, the most famous of all English clowns. (Victoria and Albert Museum).

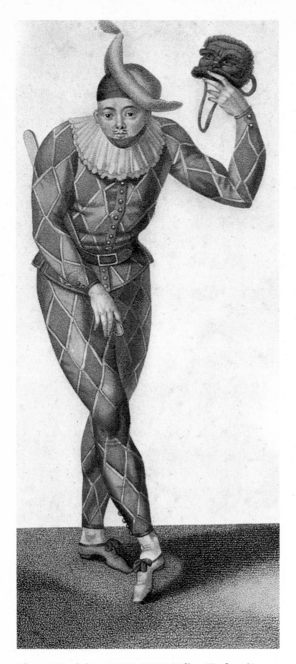

Above: Dominique (1640-1688): Italian Harlequin. (Victoria and Albert Museum).

Above right: William Gillette, American actor and playwright, with gun and pipe in 'Sherlock Holmes' (1901). (Victoria and Albert Museum).

Below right: Rachel (1820-1858), great French actress, as Roxane in Racine's 'Bajazet'. (Victoria and Albert Museum).

tion he was liable to take at the slightest provocation. Noted for his dynamic and energetic personality, he was known to dismiss the cast of a show and carry on single-handed for hours. Great on gestures, high emotion and often real tears. Appeared in a number of lavish Shubert productions between 1911 and 1931, usually playing the part of someone called Gus: he was Gus in *The Whirl of Society* (1912), *The Honeymoon Express* (1913), *Dancing Around* (1914), *Robinson Crusoe Jr.* (1916), *Sinbad* (1921), *Big Boy* (1925). His biggest hits were *Sinbad* (1918) and *Bombo* (1921), the latter opening the Jolson Theatre on 59th Street. Hit songs associated with Jolson: 'Rockabye your baby with a Dixie melody', 'Swanee', 'April Showers', 'California, here I come', 'Toot, toot, tootsie! Goo'bye'.

FANNY BRICE (1891-1951) Star of nine editions of the *Ziegfeld Follies* (1910-36); debut at an amateur night at Keeney's Theatre, Brooklyn; toured Pennsylvania at age 15 playing an alligator in a show called *A Royal Slave* (1906).

Noted for comic dialect songs (an early one was Sadie Salome, composed by Irving Berlin and sung in a Yiddish accent), her mimicry and burlesques of ballet and modern dance (including the dying swan and Martha Graham), one of her most popular routines was the 4½ year-old baby-talking brat 'Baby Snooks' who became the star of a radio show (1938-49). Popular songs: 'Second Hand Rose' and 'My Man', her biggest hit, first sung 1921 with lyrics by Channing Pollock.

First straight role, *Fanny* (1926). Biggest stage hit *Ziegfeld Follies* (1934) sponsored by the Shuberts after Ziegfeld's death. The *Follies* of 1936 was her last Broadway appearance, though 28 years later Fanny Brice was on Broadway again, in *Funny Girl*, played by Barbra Streisand.

MARX BROTHERS Chico (Leonard) (1891-1961); Harpo (Adolph) (1893-1964); Groucho (Julius) (1895-1977); Gummo (Milton) (1897-1977); Zeppo (Herbert) (1901-) One of the most unwanted acts in vaudeville, it was 15 years before the brothers Marx made it on Broadway in *I'll Say She Is* (1924). Their first small success came in Nacogdoches, Texas, in 1914 as 'The Six Mascots' (featuring Gummo, Chico, Groucho, Harpo, mother Minnie and her sister Hannah). The audience abandoned the theatre for the more amusing spectacle of a mule demolishing a cart in the street. As a result, the brothers proceeded to make fun of their own performances, themselves and everyone else. The audience returned to their seats and the Marx Bros were on their way.

In 1914, Minnie's brother Al Shean (of Gallagher and Shean) wrote a 40 minute skit 'Home Again' for Harpo, Chico and Groucho. Harpo played the silent clown — and never spoke again on stage, and, because Chico played the piano, Harpo took up the harp, and thereby got his nickname. By 1922 the act was fully developed. Groucho the leader and master of madness, the moustache, cigar, bushy eyebrows and leering innuendos. Chico with the Italian accent and art of misunderstanding. Silent Harpo with the wild, curly hair who communicated by honks, whistles, blowing bubbles and wild pantomime. In 1931, after Broadway successes including *The Cocoanuts* (1925) by George S. Kaufman, music by Irving Berlin, and *Animal Crackers* (1928) by Kaufman and Morrie Ryskind, the Marx Brothers moved to Hollywood.

EDDIE CANTOR (1892-1964) 'Banjo-Eyes' born Edward Iskavitz in New York City. Had great success in vaudeville as a blackface comedian and in the *Ziegfeld Follies* (1917-19) with his staccato style delivery (he moved around a lot on stage, too, a habit developed in the days when he was dodging rotten tomatoes).

Broadway successes include *Whoopee* (1928) and *Banjo Eyes* (1941). Songs: 'If You Knew Susie', 'Dinah', 'Ma, He's Making Eyes at Me', 'Ain't She Sweet?', and 'Toot-Toot-Tootsie'.

JIMMY DURANTE (1893-1980) 'The Schnozzle'. The man with the nose — once insured by Lloyd's of London for $1 million, the heavy New York accent abounding with mispronunciations and malapropisms. Career began as a ragtime pianist at age 17 in Diamond Tony's saloon on Coney Island. Comedy came later, teaming up with Lou Clayton and Eddie Jackson in their own nightclub, Club Durant (1923). In 1931 the team broke up after a phenomenal success in vaudeville, Ziegfeld's *Show Girl* (1929) and Cole Porter's *The New Yorkers* (1930).

Durante's act consisted of exuberant talk-singing, interrupting himself with asides, comments and stories. Wrote many songs including 'Inka Dinka Do', 'Did you ever have the feelin'' that you wanted to go, still you have the feelin' that you wanted to stay?', and 'I know darn well I can do without Broadway, but can Broadway do without me?'.

Appearances on Broadway include successes in *Strike Me Pink* (1933), *Jumbo* (1935), *Red, Hot and Blue* (1936) with Ethel Merman, and *Stars in Your Eyes* (1939), also with Merman. Hollywood wasn't so kind. His best solo movie was the first, *Get-Rich-Quick Wallingford* (1932), written by Ben Hecht and Charles MacArthur.

MAE WEST (1893-1980) Debut at age 7 at Royal Theatre, Brooklyn. Early career in vaudeville and burlesque. Broadway debut in revue *A La Broadway and Hello, Paris* (1911). Wrote her first play *Sex* (1926) about a Montreal prostitute called Margie La Mont, and thereafter she wrote all her own material. In 1927 a reform group called the Society for the Suppression of Vice got the police to raid three Broadway shows, including *Sex*. Mae served 8 days of a 10-day sentence in prison, claiming afterwards that it was the only time she got anything for good behaviour.

Biggest success, which she also wrote, was the comic melodrama *Diamond Lil* (1928). The role epitomised the character she played for the rest of her life: with slow, nasal drawl, those famous gestures of hand to hip or hair, hourglass figure in clinging dress and train which she kick-

Mae West who once said she liked to wake up every morning feeling a new man.

Jack Benny with his greatest comic prop.

ed aside, blond, glamorous and wise-cracking, she made fun of sex as no one had ever dared to before. The most famous line of the show, spoken to a Salvation Army captain, was 'Come up and see me sometime'. The 1933 movie version, renamed *She Done Him Wrong* also starred Cary Grant. Another big success was *The Constant Sinner* (1931).

Mae West was immortalised by the RAF in the Second World War when they named an inflatable life-jacket after her. In 1932 she went to Hollywood. In 1954 she made her debut in Las Vegas with a bevy of musclemen in loin cloths.

JACK BENNY (1894-1974) Born Benjamin Kubelsky. American monologist who created an instantly recognisable character for himself, renowned for his stinginess about money, his violin, which he always carried on stage, like a 'security blanket' (though in later years rarely played), his vanity and for the fact that he claimed to be eternally 39 years old.

Vaudeville debut 1912 with Cora Salisbury in straight musical act 'Salisbury and Kubelsky — From Grand Opera to Ragtime'. Best remembered for his radio show *The Jack Benny Show*, with wife Mary Livingstone, Phil Harris and Eddie 'Rochester' Anderson, which ran for 22 years (1932-54).

One of the classic Benny routines was about the hold-up man who confronted him: 'Your money or your life'. Long pause. 'Well?'. Benny: 'I'm thinking it over'.

BERT LAHR (1895-1967) The Cowardly Lion of the film *The Wizard of Oz* (1939) with the mournful face radiated, according to Brooks Atkinson, 'a kind of genial lunatic good nature'. He was also renowned for his leering, bellowing and grimacing. He perfected his act as a vulgar buffoon, and Dutch dialect character in burlesque and vaudeville; made his Broadway debut in *Harry Delmar's Revels* (1927), and became a star in *Hold Everything* (1928) as a punch-drunk fighter. *The Show is On* (1936) included one of his most famous routines, the comic baritone singing of 'The Song of the Woodman', which he later repeated in *Make Mine Manhattan* (1949). Played straight roles as well as comic ones, notably *Waiting for Godot* (1956) with Kurt Kasznar and E.G. Marshall. *Foxy* (1964) for which he won a Tony, was a musical adaptation of Jonson's *Volpone*, set in the Klondike during the Gold Rush.

BURNS AND ALLEN George Burns (1896-) and Gracie Allen (1907-64). Both began their careers in vaudeville as children. Teamed up together in 1923, and married in 1926.

Originally Burns delivered the comic lines, but Grace got all the laughs anyway, so they reversed roles. Burns, the cigar-smoking (the cigar was really a prop to give him something to do with his hands) straightman, and Grace the scatter-brain who told her surreal tales about relatives with total conviction. They continued their act on radio for 17 years, from 1932, and later on television. George Burns won an Oscar for Best Supporting Actor for *The Sunshine Boys* (1973).

GEORGE JESSEL (1898-1981) Comedian, song writer, producer and Toastmaster General of the US (appointed by President Truman). Will Rogers said of him 'Every time Jessel sees half a grapefruit he automatically rises and says: 'Ladies and gentlemen, we have here tonight...'".

Master of the ad lib and raconteur in Broadway revues, Jessel made his vaudeville debut in 1907. His most famous act was 'Hello, Momma', originating in 1917, in which he carried on a one-sided telephone conversation with his mother. Starred in the stage version of *The Jazz Singer* (1925) which played for over 1000 performances, though Al Jolson got the part in the movie (1930). Claimed to have invented the Bloody Mary cocktail.

Victor Borge once described as "the Danny Kaye of comedy".

HENRY YOUNGMAN (1906-) 'King of the One-Liners', born in Liverpool and grew up in Brooklyn. First success in 1930s on Kate Smith's radio show. Combining old jokes with new, and a deadpan delivery, he bombards his audience with a stream of jokes ('The reason the postal authorities haven't issued a Nixon stamp is that everyone would spit on the wrong side').

MILTON BERLE (1908-) Born Milton Berlinger in New York, television's Uncle Miltie of the 1950s at the height of his career. Made his screen debut aged 6 in the silent movie serial, *The Perils of Pauline* (1914), Broadway debut in *Floradora* (1920). Successes in *Ziegfeld Follies* (1936) and *Life Begins at 8:40* among others, and as a night-club act (1939-48).

As the master of ceremonies at Loew's State Theatre in 1925 he developed his comedy style, handling hecklers with expertise, and developing a reputation for 'stealing' other comedians' material. By 1949 he was said to have collected 50 000 jokes.

VICTOR BORGE (1909-) 'The unmelancholy Dane', born Borge Rosenbaum in Copenhagen.

Debut at age 13 (1922) as a concert pianist, his musical career continuing until 1934. 1932 comedy debut: with his droll, deadpan delivery he plays snatches of classics on the piano interspersed with comic remarks 'To be honest with you, I only know two numbers. One is 'Clair de Lune', and the other one isn't': or 'This concerto is written in four flats, because Rachmaninov had to move four times while he wrote it'.

Lily Tomlin, America's most successful modern comedienne.

Famous routines include renditions of 'Happy Birthday' as it might have been composed by Bach, Brahms, etc: phonetic punctuation, with punctuation marks represented by various descriptive sounds; and 'inflated language' (e.g. 'the second lieutenant ate the tenderloin' would become 'the third lieulevenant nined the elevenderloin').

LENNY BRUCE (c.1924-66) Born Leonard Alfred Schneider in New York. Social satirist considered by many obscene, and by others radically to the point. In his improvised act he would confront the audience with his unvarnished view of life's sacred monsters: religion, race, motherhood, police, law, etc. He said he approved the trend of 'people leaving the church and going back to God'. And 'Anytime some schmuck tells me he wouldn't want his daughter to marry one of *them*, I ask him, 'Which one do you mean? Suppose she had to choose between Hitler and, say Harry Belafonte. Would you make your decision along racial lines?'

Arrested and convicted of obscenity in 1961 and 1964 (in 1964, 100 leading scholars and representatives of the arts came to his defence, declaring he was 'in the tradition of Swift, Rabelais and Twain'). Deported from Britain in 1963; banned in Sydney after one performance and denounced for obscenity because of a blasphemous account of the Crucifixion; convicted in 1963 for illegal possession of drugs; declared bankrupt in 1965; Bruce died of an overdose in 1966.

LILY TOMLIN (1939-) Born in Detroit. One of the very few successful contemporary comediennes, famous for her character sketches (nearly 24 of them), particularly Ernestine, the frustrated, overbearing telephone operator with the nasal voice ('Is this the party to whom I am speaking?') and Tess, the bag woman, who lives on the street and carries all she owns in a carrier-bag.

First big success on television in Rowan and Martin's *Laugh-In* (1969). One-woman shows on Broadway. Has appeared in several films starting with *Nashville* (1975).

Masters of Mime

JEAN-GASPARD DEBURAU (1796-1846) Born of a family of acrobats, greatest Pierrot of the French stage. Until then Harlequin was usually the main character in pantomime. Created a costume of black skull-cap and white face, loose white trousers and blouse with large buttons but no ruffles at the neck. For 35 years until his death he appeared at the tiny Funambules theatre on the boulevard du Temple to enormous popular acclaim, an innocent, child-like poetic figure.

ÉTIENNE DECROUX (1898-) The father of modern mime, was **the first to develop a systematic language of mime,** which is the basis of modern technique. Studied at the Vieux-Colombier under Charles Dullin from 1923, and subsequently influenced Barrault and Marceau. Best remembered now for his role as Barrault's father in *Les Enfants du Paradis* (1944).

JEAN-LOUIS BARRAULT (1910-) Foremost French actor, director, producer and mime. Joined the Vieux-Colombier 1931-35 where he performed a number of mimes, beginning with *La Vie Primitive* with Decroux, who also wrote it. *Autour d'une Mère* (1935) was the first of a number of studio performances which combined spoken drama and mime. Has incorporated mime into many of his productions: *Baptiste* (1946)

Jean-Gaspard Deburau, the most famous Pierrot of the French stage.

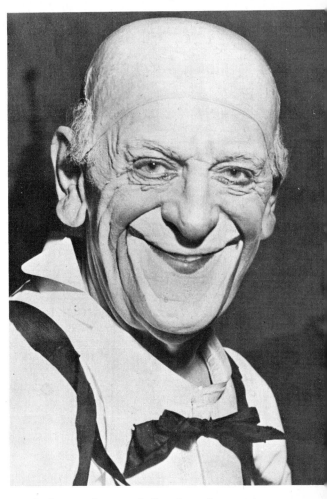

Grock, the most famous of all modern clowns.

written by Jacques Prévert for the film *Les Enfants du Paradis* was produced as a mime play, in which Barrault played the great mime Deburau.

MARCEL MARCEAU (1923-) **Greatest modern mime.** Created the character of Bip (after Pip, in *Great Expectations*), a whiteface clown dressed in white with striped dicky, stove-pipe hat and red flower. Bip made his debut at the Théâtre de Poche in Paris, 1946.

Marceau studied under Charles Dullin and Étienne Decroux, and in 1946 abandoned acting for mime, developing the mimodrama: drama of silence, the best known of which is *The Overcoat*, adapted from Gogol. In Mel Brooks' film *Silent Movie* Marceau had the distinction of being the only performer to speak.

Circus Clowns

COCO (1900-74) Born Nikolai Poliakoff in Latvia; clown apprenticeship in Russian circuses before finally settling in England where for 30 years he was star of Bertram Mills circus. He played the auguste — the clown who is always in the wrong. Noted for his water tricks — some including as many as 26 buckets full. It all started when a bucket accidentally fell on his head, bringing him to the ground. The audience loved it, and the 'accident' became part of the act.

GROCK (1880-1959) 'King of the Clowns' born Karl Adrian Wettach, son of a Swiss watch maker. One of the few clowns to be successful in the circus and on stage. A mainly mute clown whose act often involved musical instruments (he could play as many as 17 of them): falling through the seat of a chair while attempting to play a concertina; moving a piano nearer to the stool rather than the stool to the piano, in order to play; playing the piano with his feet.

EMMETT KELLY (1898-1979) American-born circus clown who created the hobo, Weary Willie, with mournful face, who never spoke, or laughed, or ever changed expression. Kelly would sometimes sit in the audience, without uttering a word, or pick out a woman in the crowd, and while eating a cabbage or a loaf of bread, watch her steadfastly with mournful eyes. As he said of himself, 'I am the hobo who found out the hard way that the deck is stacked... but there is always present that one, tiny, forlorn spark of hope still glimmering in his soul which makes him keep on trying. . . '.

Appeared with the Ringling Brothers and Barnum and Bailey Circus from 1942 until his semi-retirement in 1956. **The only circus clown to appear on Broadway**, in *Keep Off the Grass* (1940) with Jimmy Durante. Appeared in several movies, the most notable being C.B. DeMille's circus extravaganza, *The Greatest Show on Earth* (1952).

OLEG POPOV (1930-) **The most famous Soviet clown.** Clown of the Moscow Circus, born in Vyrubovo, near Moscow, who brought simple humanity to the art of clowning. Noted for his slack wire solo act, his black-and-white checked cap and red hair and lack of heavy clown make-up, he represents ordinary man, or, as Popov says of himself 'My hero is a simple fellow, in love with life. His most obvious quality is his modesty'. Making use of familiar objects, one of his sketches includes a washing machine which works perfectly until the guarantee has expired. Popov sneezes and it collapses in a thousand pieces — a satire on Russian workmanship, though its appeal is of course universal.

Oleg Popov, the leading Soviet clown communing with a chicken.

DAN RICE (1828-1900) The original Uncle Sam, King of clowns. Born Daniel McLaren in New York; early career as a jockey, circus strongman and half-owner of a trained pig called Lord Byron. As a clown he never wore make-up, but grew side whiskers and wore a red, white and blue suit and top hat: the original 'Uncle Sam'.

His extraordinary career ranged from press agent to Mormon prophet Joseph Smith (1841-44), to presidential candidate of the USA (1868), to imprisonment for slandering circus owner Dr Spaulding: He lost all he owned, but wrote a song 'Blue Eagle Jail', which made him out to be a martyr.

Free again he started up the first One Horse Show (1850), financed with his wife's jewels. He set out with a horse called Excelsior, two performers and a brass band. Temperamental, egotistical and often drunk he was noted for his quick-fire repartee. Popular with the people, managements grew to dread him for his unreliability, until in the end, no one would hire him.

DEATH
Comedians are not noted for longevity. Some survived into their 90s such as Fred Russell (95), Charles Coburn (93), Ada Reeve (92), Stanley Holloway (91) and Jay Laurier (90) but a high proportion die prematurely often from over-work and the demands of their profession. Many entertainers have collapsed on stage and died soon afterwards: Carl Hertz (1859-1924) an American illusionist; Harry Houdini (1876-1924) the escapologist; Marie Lloyd (1870-1922), the Cockney seamstress; Arthur Lucan (1887-1954) who was Old Mother Riley; Ella Shields (1879-1952), the music-hall performer; Nellie Wallace (1870-1948), the popular comedienne; Bert Williams (1874-1922), the black revue performer.

The most dramatic death on stage was that of Chung Ling Soo (William Elsworth Robinson), an American conjuror. He was shot on stage at the Wood Green Empire in 1913 during his act which included catching bullets, fired by his assistant, in a plate. It was never clear whether it was suicide or an accident.

Other bizarre deaths. Harry Fragson (1896-1913), an Anglo-French comedian, was shot dead by his own father in a fit of jealousy over his son's successful career. George Gorin,

known as Letine and the leader of an acrobatic bicycle act, was stabbed to death outside the stage door of the Canterbury Music Hall in 1889 by Nathaniel Curragh. Curragh who believed Letine was responsible for his daughter's death (in fact, she died of TB) was declared insane. Scottish comedian Will Fyffe (1885-1947) died during a dizzy spell, induced by an ear operation, and fell out of a hotel window at St. Andrews. Bert Savoy (1888-1923), an American drag artist, was struck by lightning at a famous homosexual resort, Fire Island in New York.

STRANGE ACTS
Multiple acts of seven have often occurred. *The Seven Ashtons* were Australian tumbling acrobats popular in the 1940s. *The Elliotts, The World's Cycling Wonders* were a family of seven with a bicycle-mounted band in the 1880s. Being a versatile group, they had a second act called *The Seven Musical Savonas*. Eddie Foy (1854-1928), a solo comedian of vaudeville, burlesque and Broadway, introduced a family act in 1913, *Eddie Foy and the Seven Little Foys*. Bob Hope appeared in a film of that title in 1954.

The strangest ventriloquial acts were around the turn of the century when quantity and originality were the prime requisites. 'Lieutenant' Cole used eight dummies; Frank Travis (1854-1931) used as many as 13; Frederic Neiman (1860-1910) had a minstrel group of seven dolls and a ventriloquial parliament peopled (or dummied) with contemporary politicians. Other leading ventriloquists and their dolls: Edgar Bergen (1903-78) and Charlie McCarthy; Peter Brough (1916-) and Archie Andrews; Johnson Clark (1886-), and Hodge the Yokel; Coram (1883-1937), the military ventriloquist, and Jerry Fisher; Arthur Prince (1881-1948) and Able Seaman Jim; Fred Russell, father of Val Parnell, and Able Seaman Jim. The cinema has also shown a fascination with ventriloquists dominated by their dolls: *Dead of Night* (1945) and *Magic* (1978) both dealt with this subject.

Eccentric acts in the late nineteenth century included Bertha Mills, an American whose claim to fame was 19-inch feet; Laloo who had a twin brother consisting of arms and legs growing out of his stomach; Waxman who presented a pastoral play complete with farmyard animals; Lockhart's Elephants in which Captain Joe

Taylor toured the halls with four elephants called Salt, Vinegar, Mustard and Saucy. In the English variety theatres of the 1940s and 50s the more unusual acts included Kardomah who filled every inch of the stage with flags and Wilson, Keppel and Betty who did a sand-dance while attired in Egyptian costume and often against a background of the Pyramids.

DRAG

The spectacle of men in women's clothing has always been a popular part of entertainment.

The greatest American drag artist was Julian Eltinge (1882-1941) who had a theatre built and named after himself (1910). He appeared in plays which were specially written for him and always about a man who has to disguise himself as a woman (*The Fascinating Widow, Countess Charming, Her Grace the Vampire*). **The most popular English transvestite performer is Danny La Rue (1928-).** He has taken drag out of the clubs and into the West End in shows like *Come Spy With Me* (1966) and *Passionella* (1968) and achieved huge popularity in the English provinces, in Australia and the USA.

MALE IMPERSONATORS

The first Principal Boy was Madame Vestris (1797-1856). As well as being a highly successful theatre manager of the Olympic from 1830, she also played Ralph in *Puss in Boots* and The Prince in *The White Cat*. **The most famous English principal boy of this century was Dorothy Ward** who first appeared in Pantomime in 1907 and who continued to play Boy to her husband, Shaun Glenville's Dame, until 1957. **The first member of a classical company to play Principal Boy was Judy Buxton** who donned white tights to play Kit in the Royal Shakespeare Company's pantomime, *The Swan Down Gloves*, in Stratford and London in 1981.

Leading male impersonators in the music-hall were Millie Hylton (1868-1920), Hetty King (1883-1972), Nelly Power (1853-1887), Fanny Robina (1862-1927), Vesta Tilley (1864-1962).

COMEDIANS IN STRAIGHT PLAYS

Many comedians have established a new reputation for themselves appearing in classic and contemporary plays.

They include: Bobby Clark in *Le Bourgeois Gentilhomme* (1946); Ken Dodd in *Twelfth Night* (1971); Joseph Grimaldi in *Hamlet* (1800, 1805); Frankie Howerd in *Charley's Aunt* (1955) and *A Midsummer Night's Dream* (1957); Jimmy Jewel in *Comedians* (1975) and *The Sunshine Boys* (1975); Dave King in *Teeth 'n Smiles* (1975) and *American Buffalo* (1979); Bert Lahr in *Waiting For Godot* (1956), *Hotel Paradiso* (1957) and *A Midsummer Night's Dream* (1960); Jay Laurier in *Pygmalion* (1936) and *Candida* (1941) as well as 13 of Shakespeare's plays between 1938 and 1942; George Robey in *Henry IV Part One* (1935); and Max Wall in *Ubu Roi* (1966), *The Old Ones* (1972), *The Entertainer* (1974) and *Waiting for Godot* (1981).

MISCELLANEOUS

The first purpose-built music-hall was Canterbury Hall, Lambeth (1852) built by Charles Morton (1819-1904) who also built another famous music-hall, the Oxford.

The first artist to have a signature-tune was Albert Whelan (1876-1961) who whistled 'The Jolly Brothers' while taking off his top hat and gloves at the beginning of his act.

The first non-command performance attended by a reigning monarch was on February 26, 1948 when George VI together with Queen Elizabeth, Princess Elizabeth, the Duke of Edinburgh and Princess Margaret saw Danny Kaye at the London Palladium.

The most spectacular accident in popular theatre came at Sir Oswald Stoll's newly-opened Coliseum in 1904. The Derby was re-enacted on stage complete with crowds, pickpockets, bookmakers, mounted police and six horses ridden by professional jockeys on a revolving platform. Two horses collided. Fred Dent's horse momentarily found itself with its forelegs on the permanent stage and its hindlegs still on the moving stage travelling at 15 m.p.h. The horse rolled over the footlights. The jockey, Dent, was hurled across the stage head-first against the side of the auditorium. There were cries of alarm, the curtain was rung down and Dent was taken to Charing Cross Hospital where he died a quarter of an hour after arrival. But the Derby was run again at the next performance with a safety rope put across the footlights.

CHAPTER 7

Makers of Theatre COMPANIES AND DIRECTORS

Every major theatrical country has its institutions that possess a strong individual personality and its individual personalities who become as famous as institutions. These are some of the key names in the making of modern theatre:

UK

THE OLD VIC
Built in 1818 as a house of melodrama called the Royal Coburg Theatre. Its opening presentation was a spectacle, *Trial by Battle or Heaven Defend The Right* by William Barrymore preceded by a Harlequinade and followed by a grand Asiatic ballet. **Its first presentation of Shakespeare** was *Julius Caesar* in 1819 with Junius Brutus Booth, performed in defiance of the monopoly of the Patent Theatres.

It reopened in 1833 under the name of the Royal Victoria Theatre with *Black Ey'd Susan*. **Its first woman manager** was Eliza Vincent who took over the running of it in 1852. She had appeared on its stage at the age of 8 as the Infant Roscius reciting The Seven Ages of Woman. In 1880 Emma Cons, a social reformer, took over as manager and lessee and renamed it the Royal Victoria Coffee and Music-Hall. From 1898 she was assisted by her niece, Lilian Baylis, who acquired full management of the theatre in 1912.

Lilian Baylis (1874-1937) was a forceful personality and cultural missionary who combined a love of theatre and religion. She made the Old Vic internationally famous by initiating in 1914 a policy of Shakespeare at popular prices. All the plays of Shakespeare in the First Folio were pro-duced, for the first time ever, between October 1914 and November 1923 when *Troilus and Cressida* completed the cycle. In 1931 she founded the Vic-Wells Ballet and Opera companies under Ninette de Valois and Charles Corri, respectively. She was also a legend for what she did and said. She used to cook sausages on a gas-ring in the wings with the smell often floating into the auditorium. She once sent up a prayer: 'Dear God, please send me good actors — and cheap'. She said of critics: 'Why should we give the bounders free seats and let them earn their wretched livings by saying scurrilous things about us'. She once turned on an actress and said 'Well dear you've had your chance — and failed'.

The Old Vic company ceased its existence in 1963 with a performance of *Measure for Measure*. The National Theatre Company then occupied the building from October 1963 to March 1976. The Prospect Theatre Company (later granted the title of the Old Vic company) took over the running of the building later that year but were driven out of business in May 1981 when the Arts Council formally cut off their grant of £300 000. Since then the Old Vic company has ceased to exist and the building has awaited a new tenant.

THEATRE WORKSHOP
The first genuine ensemble group in England. It was founded in 1945 by Joan Littlewood. It was based successively in Kendal, Ormesby Hall, Manchester and Glasgow. It performed mainly one-night stands all over the country taking

Richard Burton's Old Vic Henry V (1955) with Zena Walker as the Princess of France.

theatre to the people. It operated as a collective in which members shared income equally. Its key figures, apart from Joan Littlewood herself, were Ewan MacColl (writer), John Bury (designer), Gerry Raffles (administrator) and Howard Goorney (actor).

It gave its first performance in its permanent home, the Theatre Royal, Stratford East, in February 1953. The vintage years at Stratford were from 1954 to 1956 when the repertory included Shakespeare, Jonson, Molière, Ibsen, Shaw, O'Neill and O'Casey and the players included Harry H. Corbett, Avis Bunnage, Maxwell Shaw, Glynn Edwards.

The first Theatre Workshop production transferred to the West End was *The Good Soldier Schweik* (1956). Subsequent successes — and transfers — included Brendan Behan's *The Quare Fella* (1956) and *The Hostage* (1958), Shelagh Delaney's *A Taste of Honey* (1958), Frank Norman's *Fings Aint What They Used To Be* (1959), *Oh What a Lovely War* (1963). Success helped to destroy Theatre Workshop: frequent transfers of productions to the West End (combined with meagre Arts Council subsidy) undermined the ensemble work of the Company.

The company's most popular productions were *Fings Aint What They Used To Be* (1959) which ran at the Garrick for 897 performances and *Oh What a Lovely War* (1963) which ran at Wyndhams for 507 performances. The title Theatre Workshop was dropped in 1978.

Agnes Lauchlan, Alan Bates and Rachel Kempson in Angus Wilson's 'The Mulberry Bush'.

ENGLISH STAGE COMPANY
Founded in 1955 by George Devine (1910-66). The original intention was to take over the Kingsway Theatre, blitzed and derelict though it was, to stage new, non-commercial plays with a permanent company and a permanent setting. Eventually it took over the Royal Court. The ESC's first production there was *The Mulberry Bush* by Angus Wilson on 2 April 1956. But Devine and his assistant Tony Richardson (1928-) had launched an appeal for new plays that attracted 750 entries. Out of that batch came the ESC's first and most durable success, John Osborne's *Look Back In Anger* which opened at the Royal Court on 8 May 1956.

George Devine had the vision of the true

pioneer. He had worked as an actor with the Old Vic and John Gielgud's company at the Queen's (1937) and played Tesman to Peggy Ashcroft's Hedda Gabler (1954). He was a teacher and producer with the London Theatre Studio (1936-39). He worked with Michel St. Denis as a director of the Old Vic School in 1945. He expressed his philosophy in a letter to a godson: 'For me the theatre is a temple of ideas and ideas so well expressed that it may be called art. So always look for the quality in the writing above what is being said. This is how to choose a theatre to work in and, if you can't find one you like, start your own. A Theatre must have a recognisable attitude. It will have one, whether you like it or not.'

In the first 25 years of its existence the Royal

The Memorial Theatre, Stratford-upon-Avon opened in 1879, and was destroyed by fire in 1926.

MEMORIAL THEATRE

Court staged 450 plays, played a decisive role in the abolition of censorship, launched a whole new generation of writers including John Osborne, Arnold Wesker, John Arden, Edward Bond, N.F. Simpson, David Storey, and, more recently, Caryl Churchill, Stephen Lowe, Nigel Williams, Paul Kember. It has also opened its own studio theatre, the Theatre Upstairs (1968), sent its plays round the world and fostered its own Young People's Theatre Scheme.

The ESC always enjoyed a hostile relationship with the official censor, the Lord Chamberlain. **The first play to be banned** in *toto* at the Court was *The Catalyst* (1957) by Ronald Duncan. **The last play to be banned** by the Lord Chamberlain before the official disbandment of censorship was *Early Morning* by Edward Bond. It featured cannibalism and a lesbian relationship between Queen Victoria and Florence Nightingale. It was given a Sunday Night performance on 31 May 1968. Under threat of prosecution the second performance was called 'a critics' dress rehearsal': invited guests were admitted through a side door and admission was free.

Directors of the ESC at the Royal Court:

George Devine, assisted by Tony Richardson (1955-65); William Gaskill (1965-69); William Gaskill, Lindsay Anderson, Anthony Page (1969-72); Oscar Lewenstein (1972-75); Robert Kidd, Nicholas Wright (1975-80); Max Stafford-Clark (1980-).

ROYAL SHAKESPEARE COMPANY

Created in 1960 by Peter Hall to take over what was then the Shakespeare Memorial Theatre in Stratford-upon-Avon and (in December 1960) the Aldwych Theatre in London.

The first Shakespeare Memorial Theatre opened in Stratford-upon-Avon on 23 April 1879 with a performance of *Much Ado About Nothing* starring Barry Sullivan and Helen Faucit. The building itself was a mixture of Gothic and Tudor with a narrow Elizabethan-style auditorium. It was granted a Royal Charter in 1925 but destroyed by fire in 1926. Bernard Shaw sent a telegram to the theatre's governor, Sir Archibald Flower, saying: 'Congratulations. It will be a tremendous advantage to have a proper modern building. There are a number of other theatres I should like to see burned down.'

The new Shakespeare Memorial Theatre, designed by Elizabeth Scott, opened on 23 April 1932 in the presence of the Duke of Windsor with a performance of *Henry IV Part One and Two* given on the same day. Over 100 000 people came to Stratford for the festivities but the occasion was not a success artistically. Many critics attacked the refridgerative effect of the new theatre and W.A. Darlington wrote in *The Daily Telegraph* that the production was 'a dull and spiritless affair . . . The fact was that the players were tired out'. Under the direction of Sir Barry Jackson from 1948 to 1951, Anthony Quayle from 1951 to 1956 and Glen Byam Shaw from 1953 (when he was co-director) to 1959 the theatre acquired a legendary reputation.

Peter Hall (1930-), a successful young director of Beckett and Anouilh, took over a prosperous, thriving theatre, in 1960 and established the pattern of the Royal Shakespeare Company as we know it today. He introduced flexible long-term contracts for the actors, acquired the lease of a London theatre (the Aldwych), introduced modern plays into the London repertoire and in 1962 appointed Peter Brook (1925-) and Michel St. Denis (1897-1971) to run the company with him. His own many triumphant productions included *The Wars of the Roses* (1963), *Hamlet* (1965) and Pinter's *The Homecoming* at the Aldwych (1965). He also introduced a new approach to verse-speaking with the emphasis on the sense as much as the sound.

Peter Hall was succeeded as director of the RSC in 1968 by *Trevor Nunn* (1940-). At first he was obviously following in Hall's footsteps but he has left his own indelible imprint on the company with thematic seasons (such as one devoted to Shakespeare's Roman plays in 1972), with the expansion of the company into small theatres such as Stratford's Other Place in 1974 and London's The Warehouse in 1977 and not least through his own brilliant and meticulous productions of *The Comedy of Errors* and *Macbeth* (1976), *The Three Sisters* (1978) and (with John Caird) *Nicholas Nickleby* (1980) which conquered London and Broadway.

Today the RSC can legitimately claim to be **the largest company in the world.** It now operates in two theatres in London (the Barbican and The Pit), two in Stratford-upon-Avon (the Royal Shakespeare Theatre and the Other Place) as well as playing regular seasons in Newcastle

and transferring its productions to the West End and Broadway. In the year 1980-81 its work was seen by 1.2 million people in the UK. Its subsidy was also a much smaller proportion of its costs (38.35 per cent) than that of any other national company anywhere. When the RSC opened *Nicholas Nickleby* at the Aldwych in June 1980 the company itself was rightly described by one critic as 'a national treasure'.

The RSC has also **won more awards than any other British theatre company.** In the first 21 years of its history from 1960 to 1981 it picked up 140 major awards.

THE NATIONAL THEATRE

The first person to propose a National Theatre was Effingham Wilson (1783-1868), a London publisher and bookseller.

The first site of the proposed theatre was in Bloomsbury. Land was bought in 1913 for the Shakespeare Memorial National Theatre (as it was to be called), to be built on the corner of Gower and Keppel Streets. **The first SMNT committee** included such notables as Sir Herbert Beerbohm Tree, Sir Johnston Forbes-Robertson, Bernard Shaw, Sir Arthur Wing Pinero, Harley Granville-Barker, William Archer, Mrs Edmund Gosse, and Mrs Alfred Lyttelton. In 1938 a second site was proposed and purchased in South Kensington, opposite the Victoria and Albert Museum.

The first foundation stone for the National Theatre was laid in Gower Street, then in South Kensington (1938) and then on the South Bank by the Princess Elizabeth (13 June 1951) deputising for George VI. Made of Portland stone and measuring 4ft by 3ft 1in thick, it was shifted to various sites on the South Bank. When it was decided the building was not to be constructed of Portland stone after all, a Ceremonial Cement Pouring was held on 3 November 1969.

The first home of the National Theatre was the Old Vic (1963-76). The first director of the company was Laurence Olivier (1963-73) after whom the largest, 1160 seat auditorium of the new building was named.

The first production of the National Theatre at the Old Vic was *Hamlet* with Peter O'Toole, directed by Laurence Olivier. *Hamlet* with Albert Finney directed by Peter Hall was also the last NT production at the Old Vic in December 1975.

The first words to be spoken on any of the stages in the new National Theatre on the South Bank were 'Who's there?' — the first lines of *Hamlet*. They were uttered by actor Daniel Thorndike on the stage of the Lyttelton (the first of the three theatres to be completed) during a rehearsal on 17 November 1975.

The longest rehearsed play at the National Theatre was *Tamburlaine the Great*. Rehearsals began on 20 April 1976 and were intended to last 10 weeks. Due to building delays, the play opened in the Olivier on 4 October 1976 after almost 6 months of rehearsals.

Of the National Theatre's income, 58.8 per cent comes from subsidies, 24.8 per cent from box office, 16.4 per cent from catering, programmes, bookstalls, etc.

Just before the lights go down and the first lines of the play are spoken on every first night, 'Ralph's Rocket' is fired from the roof: an idea started by Sir Ralph Richardson when the National Theatre itself opened.

Sir Peter Hall has been director of the National Theatre since 1973. His productions for the company (to the end of 1981) are: *The Tempest, No Man's Land, John Gabriel Borkman, Happy Days, Hamlet, Judgement, Tamburlaine the Great, Bedroom Farce* (with Alan Ayckbourn), *Volpone, The Country Wife, The Cherry Orchard, Macbeth, Betrayal, Amadeus, Othello, The Oresteia*.

EDWARD GORDON CRAIG (1872-1966)
The son of Ellen Terry and E.W. Godwin. Stage designer and visionary. His actual achievements were few but his effect was vast. He influenced, for example, Max Reinhardt, Jean-Louis Barrault, designers Norman Bel Geddes and Robert Edmond Jones. Craig saw the director as, in effect, a dictator: the supreme and unrestricted artist of the theatre and, with his anti-realist theories, he re-invented stage design. He gave new importance to scenery which became as three-dimensional as the actors. His sets consisted of abstract geometric shapes: moveable steps, screens, rostra and stairways. Dramatic lighting and shadow created movement. But the actor he saw essentially as a puppet or *uber-marionette*.

The first production designed by Craig was *Dido and Aeneas* (1900) for the Purcell Operatic Society at the Hampstead Conservatoire of Music. He also designed Otway's *Venice Preserv'd* (Berlin, 1905), Ibsen's *Rosmersholm* for Eleonora Duse (Florence, 1906), *Hamlet* (Moscow, 1912). His theories are incorporated in his two books: *The Art of the Theatre* (1905) and *On the Art of the Theatre* (1911). Said Kenneth Tynan: 'If today we call stage-managers directors and scene-painters designers, it is largely Craig's doing'. From 1929 on he lived in France. He was made a Companion of Honour in 1955 but was unable to come to London to accept the honour because he couldn't afford the fare.

TYRONE GUTHRIE (1900-71)
Director, author and occasional actor who relentlessly pioneered the concept of the open stage at a time when the proscenium-arch held sway. Also a great director whose own productions handled crowds as majestically as the Royal Tournament and burst at the seams with a sense of fun. He directed Shakespeare at the Old Vic from 1933 to 1936 and from 1939 to 1945 was Administrator of the Old Vic and Sadler's Wells Theatres. In 1948 he revived David Lindsay's *Ane Pleasant Satyre of the Thrie Estaitis* proving that the Assembly Hall of the Church of Scotland could make a magnificent open stage theatre. From 1953 to 1957 he ran the Shakespeare Festival Theatre at Stratford, Ontario once again establishing the open stage principle (first in a tent, then in a permanent theatre). On 7 May 1963 a theatre named after him opened in Minneapolis where he directed many productions. He also directed the opening production at the new Nottingham Playhouse (*Coriolanus* in November 1963) and advised on the open-stage Crucible Theatre in Sheffield which opened in 1971. He was restless, experimental, unorthodox, brilliant and a huge influence on the shape and style of modern theatres.

PETER BROOK (1925-)
A guru of modern theatre. A small, curious, gnome-like, intensely alive man who has directed Shakespeare, musicals, comedies, opera and who has devoted the last decade to exploration and research as well as to production. His genius is to question everything about the modern theatre asking whether everything we take to be necessary really is so. He is the great stripper away of superfluity.

Peter Brook's first production was Marlowe's *Dr Faustus* (1943) at the Torch Theatre, London.

Above: Tyrone Guthrie's Old Vic production of 'The Country Wife' with Freda Jackson, Ursula Jeans and Ernest Thesiger.

Below: The Crucible Theatre, Sheffield strongly influenced by Guthrie's open-stage theories.

He was 18 at the time. His **first Stratford production** was *Love's Labour's Lost* (1946). Sir Barry Jackson who brought Brook to Stratford described him as 'the youngest earthquake I have known'. His first production at Covent Garden was *Salome* (1949) by Richard Strauss with designs by Salvador Dali. Other notable productions include *Venice Preserv'd* (1953) at the Lyric Hammersmith and at Stratford *Measure for Measure* (1950), *The Winter's Tale* (1951), *Titus Andronicus* (1955 — the first time the play had been presented at Stratford), *King Lear* (1962). His most famous Stratford production, however, was *A Midsummer Night's Dream* (1970). Set in a stark white box with coils of wire representing the forest, it used elements of Meyerhold, circus and *commedia dell'arte*. The play launched the longest-ever RSC tour in 1972-73 visiting 31 cities and 13 countries in 12 months.

But Brook has always been interested in experiment. He launched a famous Artaud-influenced Theatre of Cruelty season at LAMDA Theatre London in 1964 which inspired a much-acclaimed production of the *Marat-Sade* by Peter Weiss later in 1964. In 1970 he established in Paris the International Centre of Theatre Research to explore the question 'Is there another language, just as exacting for the author as the language of words? Is there a language of actions, a language of sounds?' He sought to find the answer in *Orghast* (1971) at the Shiraz-Persepolis Festival in Iran: a production written in a language invented by Ted Hughes. In 1972 he took the centre on tour of Africa to discover if they could communicate to audiences unfamiliar with theatre. He also staged with the group at the Théâtre Bouffes du Nord in Paris: *Timon of Athens* (1974), *The Ik* (1975), *Ubu Roi* (1977), *The Conference of the Birds* (1978). His most recent productions in Paris are *The Cherry Orchard* and *Carmen* (1981).

Ireland

THE ABBEY THEATRE
The first state-subsidised theatre in the English-speaking world. It was founded in Dublin in 1904 by W.B. Yeats (1865-1939), and Lady Gregory (1852-1932) with the help of Annie Horniman (1860-1937) as a permanent repertory company devoted to the performing of plays on Irish themes by native dramatists. In the early days, poetic drama dominated but when Lennox Robinson took over the management from 1910 to 1958 realistic drama held the stage. Leading dramatists associated with the Abbey include J.M. Synge, Sean O'Casey and G.B. Shaw. Leading actors include Sara Allgood (1883-1950) who created the role of Juno; Arthur Sinclair (1883-1951), Barry Fitzgerald (1888-1961), Cyril Cusack (1910-) and Siobhan McKenna (1923-).

The first performance at the Abbey was on 27 December 1904. The plays were *On Baile's Strand* by W.B. Yeats and a one-act dialect play by Lady Gregory, *Spreading the News*.

The most famous riot at the Abbey was during the first performance of Synge's *The Playboy of the Western World* on 26 January 1907. There were objections to the bad language (Lady Gregory herself was upset that 'there were too many violent oaths'.) Nationalist critics also claimed to be upset by the offensive and unreal portrayal of peasant life in the west of Ireland. As a result, on the second performance on Monday, 28 January the play was greeted with hisses, boos and stamping feet. The last act ended with cries of 'Sinn Fein' and 'Kill the author' from the audience. There were fights in the theatre every night and by the end of the week (the play closed on 2 February) 500 police were needed to keep order. There were also protests when the company toured the play to America. In New York in November 1911 there were stink bombs in the auditorium and 'potatoes, an old watch, a tin box with a cigar in it and a cigarette box' were hurled at the stage. In Philadelphia in January 1912 the whole company was arrested (and released) for presenting a play likely to corrupt the morals of the citizens of Philadelphia. Bernard Shaw interviewed in London said: 'All decent people are arrested in the United States'.

The Abbey's most performed play was O'Casey's *The Plough and the Stars*. It first played there, to pandemonium and the arrival of the police, in 1926. It was also playing there on the night of 17 July 1951 when, after the performance, the theatre was totally destroyed by fire. Ironically, the play closes with soldiers singing 'Keep the home fires burning . . .'. The new Abbey Theatre opened in July 1966. It was intended that *The Plough and the Stars* be the first play on the new stage. In the event it was the second.

The first was *Recall The Years* by Walter Macken re-enacting the history of the Abbey. The first new play to be performed in the re-built Abbey Theatre was *One for the Grave* by Louis McNeice (1966).

America

American theatre is traditionally based on profit, Broadway acclaim and getting the best bounce out of the buck. But it has also had its share of pioneers and throughout the century there has been a continuing idealistic opposition to the Broadway ethos.

WASHINGTON SQUARE PLAYERS (1914-18)
Started out as an amateur theatre group doing summer seasons at Provincetown, Cape Cod, then in an old stable in Macdougal Street in Greenwich Village and then at the 40-seat Band Box Theater in East 57th Street. But in 1916 they moved to the 600-seat Comedy Theater just east of Broadway with a season of plays by Ibsen, Andreyev and Eugene O'Neill: in fact, they gave the first Broadway production of this pioneering dramatist with his sea play, *In the Zone* (1916). 'Of a very high order both as a thriller and as a document in human character and emotion', said *The New York Times*. They also launched the careers of some distinguished players including Katharine Cornell (1898-), who made her theatrical debut in *Bushido* (1916), and of the pioneering set designer Robert Edmond Jones (1887-). They disbanded on 13 May 1918, partly because of the war and partly because they were broke, but then evolved into the Theater Guild.

THE THEATER GUILD (1919-50)
'The most enlightened and influential theater organisation New York has ever had', wrote Brooks Atkinson. It was founded by ex-members of the Washington Square Players as a cooperative, professional acting company to present both American and foreign non-commercial plays. For all that, it staged many profitable productions.

The first Theater Guild production was *The Bonds of Interest* (1919) by Jacinto Benavente at the Garrick Theater. The actors were paid 25 dollars plus a share of the profits — if there were any. To economise, they used scenery left behind by the previous tenant, French director Jacques Copeau. During American Actors Equity's first strike (1919) the Guild's second production, *John Ferguson* by St. John Ervine, was the only play on Broadway not blacked out.

In 1925 the company opened its own theatre: the Guild Theater on 52nd Street. It opened on 13 April with Shaw's *Caesar and Cleopatra* starring Helen Hayes and Lionel Atwill. It was a beautiful 1000-seat theatre whose walls were covered with expensive Gobelin tapestries. Wisecracked critic Alexander Woollcott, 'The Gobelins will get you if you don't watch out'. Ever ambitious the Guild also established the repertory principle and, for example, between 1926 and 1928 produced an outstanding roster of plays including O'Neill's *Strange Interlude* and *Marco Millions*, Shaw's *Pygmalion* and *The Doctor's Dilemma*, Jonson's *Volpone*, Pirandello's *Right You Are If You Think You Are*.

In terms of popular success, the Guild's greatest decades were the 1930s and 40s. They gave the world première of O'Neill's *Mourning Becomes Electra* (1931), George Gershwin's *Porgy and Bess* (1935), Philip Barry's *The Philadelphia Story* (1938), Rodgers and Hammerstein's *Oklahoma* (1943) and *Carousel* (1945), O'Neill's *The Iceman Cometh* (1946). But by 1950, when the Guild Theater was renamed the ANTA, the company's original ideals had been taken over by the growing number of off-Broadway theatres.

Glenn Anders, Charles Walters and Lynn Fontanne in Eugene O'Neill's 'Strange Interlude' (1928).

GROUP THEATER (1929-41)

Founded by Harold Clurman (1901-81), Cheryl Crawford (1902-) and Lee Strasberg (1901-82), it was based on hostility to Broadway commercialism and on a passionate belief in ensemble acting, social realism and the need for theatre to grow out of a shared vision. It lasted little over a decade but it produced some remarkable actors and directors including John Garfield (1913-52), Franchot Tone (1905-68), Elia Kazan (1909-) and Stella Adler (1904-).

Group Theater's first independent production (originally it was an off-shoot of the Theater Guild) was Maxwell Anderson's *Night Over Taos* (1932). Its biggest success was Sidney Kingsley's *Men in White* (1933) which ran for 351 performances. Subsequent productions included Clifford Odet's *Waiting for Lefty* and *Awake and Sing* (1935) and *Golden Boy* (1937). Robert Ardrey's *Thunder Rock* (1939). Odet's *Golden Boy* ran for 250 performances. The Group Theater eventually disbanded because of internal dissensions and the steady seepage of its talent. But it fertilised Hollywood and Broadway and Harold Clurman left behind an eloquent account of its struggles in *The Fervent Years* (1945). In that book he writes: 'The basic defect in our activity was that while we tried to maintain a true theater policy artistically, we proceeded economically on a show business basis'.

FEDERAL THEATER PROJECT (1935-39)

The first nationwide federally-financed theatre in the USA and created specifically to give employment to theatre people during the Depression. It encouraged writers, actors, directors and designers to carry out experimental projects and at its peak it employed 10 000 people (half in New York, half outside) and operated theatres in 40 states. The Project eventually collapsed because of political pressure. Mrs Hallie Flanagan (1890-1969), its national director, was accused of being a Communist and a number of the Project's productions were banned.

Federal Theater Project's most widely-seen play was *It Can't Happen Here* by Sinclair Lewis and John C. Moffitt which opened simultaneously in 21 cities on 21 October 1936. The most popular production of its Negro Theater wing was an all-black voodoo *Macbeth* (1936) set in Haiti, directed by Orson Welles and starring Jack Carter, Edna Thomas and Canada Lee.

The first FTP production to be banned was *Ethiopia* (1936) written by Elmer Rice and presented by Living Newspaper which used cinematic techniques to present important living issues. The production was based on Mussolini's invasion of Ethiopia but, since the government didn't want to offend Mussolini at that time, the work was stopped and the author resigned.

The most spectacular event involving an FTP production was the effective banning of the musical satire, *The Cradle Will Rock* (1937). The Washington administration of the FTP closed all Federal theatres across the country on the night of the dress rehearsal, 15 June 1937. The Venice Theater in New York was then booked at the last moment and all the cast and audience made their way there. Because of Equity regulations, the cast had to buy their tickets too and sat in the audience together with the orchestra. Director Orson Welles acted as master of ceremonies; composer Marc Blitzstein played his score on a piano on stage. There were no costumes and in later performances the show was presented as an impromptu rehearsal.

MERCURY THEATER (1937-39)

Adventurous, short-lived theatre founded by Orson Welles (1915-) and John Houseman (1902-) in the Comedy Theater on 41st Street. Its first production was of *Julius Caesar* on 11 November 1937. It was done in modern dress with Caesar shown as Mussolini, with Welles himself playing Brutus and George Coulouris Mark Antony. The production ran for 157 performances and made considerable impact. Subsequent Mercury Theater productions: *The Shoemaker's Holiday* (1938), *Heartbreak House* (1939) and *Danton's Death* (1939). The Mercury Theater also took to the air and produced a famous radio production of H.G. Wells's *The War of the Worlds* (1938) which convinced large numbers of listeners that an invasion from Mars had actually taken place. Suits of over ¾ million dollars were filed against the CBS radio company for damages, injuries and miscarriages by outraged listeners.

THE LIVING THEATER (1950-70)

Founded by Julian Beck and his wife Judith Malina as an off-Broadway repertory company and commune presenting a varied programme including Cocteau, Pirandello, Gertrude Stein and Strindberg. the company's peak achievements were Jack Gelber's *The Connec-*

Above: Clifford Odet's 'Awake and Sing' at the Belasco Theater New York, 1935 one of the Group Theater's greatest triumphs.

Below: The futuristic sets for O'Neill's 'Dynamo' which dealt with "the death of an old god and the failure of science and materialism".

tion (1959) which was a poetic piece about drug addiction and Kenneth H. Brown's *The Brig* (1963) which was ferociously anti-military. In the 1960s the company achieved fame with a series of nomadic productions, including *Paradise Now* (1968) which attempted to shock and outrage a bourgeois audience. But in the end the group's commitment to anarchy and confrontation declined into a rather generalised sloppiness.

LA MAMA (1962-)

Leading avant-garde theatre founded in Greenwich Village in 1962 by Ellen Stewart, a black fashion designer. Principally devoted to experimental productions of classics and new works by such writers as Jean-Claude van Itallie, Sam Shepard, Leonard Melfi, Rochelle Owens and Megan Terry. Made great impact on London in 1968 when they visited the Mercury Theatre in Notting Hill not least with Rochelle Owens' *Futz* which is about a young man who enjoys sex with pigs. Visiting companies have also played at La Mama including Peter Brook's International Centre for Theatre Research which in 1980 presented *The Conference of the Birds*, *Ubu Roi* and *The Ik*. La Mama has thrown up many writers but one of their traits, according to Harold Clurman, 'is a difficulty or an incapacity to write full-length plays'. The company's best known director is Tom O'Horgan who staged *Futz* (1967) and *Tom Paine* (1968) and who later moved to Broadway as director of *Hair* (1968) and *Jesus Christ Superstar* (1971).

OPEN THEATER (1963-)

Disciplined and impressive company founded by Peter Feldmann and Joseph Chaikin both former members of the Living Theater. Their best work was *The Serpent* (1968), a brilliant exploration of the Book of Genesis using sound and gesture as much as language to convey meaning. The company visited the Royal Court Theatre in London in 1967 where their production of Jean-Claude van Itallie's *America Hurrah* was banned by the Lord Chamberlain largely because of 'unflattering references to a head of state' (President Johnson). It was therefore staged as a club production.

STEELE MACKAYE (1842-94)

Actor, manager, playwright, innovator. Acquired the Madison Square Theater (1879) where, with the help of Thomas A. Edison, he in-

stalled overhead lighting to replace footlights for the first time in America. Other original devices included two elevator stages so that entire sets, complete with actors, could be raised or lowered in 40 seconds; a modern ventilation system in the auditorium; folding theatre chairs with a hat and coat rack attached. His most successful play was *Hazel Kirke* (1880) which ran for 486 performances at the Madison Square Theater.

ROBERT EDMOND JONES (1887-1954)

Set designer and director. Studied in Germany at the Deutsches Theater Berlin. First design was for Granville-Barker's production of *The Man Who Married a Dumb Wife* (1915) in New York. His credo as a designer was 'Keep in your soul some images of magnificence'. Influenced by the ideas of Gordon Craig, his Expressionist designs included those for *Macbeth* (1921) with lopsided archways seemingly as unbalanced as Macbeth himself and for John Barrymore's *Hamlet* (1922) centred on a huge and controversial staircase. Also designed almost all of O'Neill's plays. By 1940 he came to believe that well-equipped stages with realistic sets were killing the promise of American drama. He wanted to go back to a bare stage stripped of all scenic accessories. In that sense his ideas pre-empt those of Peter Brook. But American theatre has always remained wedded to realism.

LEE STRASBERG (1901-82)

Polish-born US director and teacher who adapted Stanislavsky's ideas to American theatre and formulated a technique known as the Method. In its American version it emphasised improvisation as much as skill and placed great stress on 'effective memory': using past experiences to produce the necessary emotion on stage. It has led to some great acting on stage and screen: at its worst it has also produced what Harold Clurman called 'a kind of constipation of the soul'.

The Stanislavsky system was first taught in America in 1923 at the Neighbourhood Playhouse. The managers of the Playhouse arranged for Richard Boleslavsky, a former Stanislavsky student who had appeared in the first Broadway season of the Moscow Art Theatre, (1923) to lecture to their students and produce two plays. Boleslavsky founded the American Laboratory Theater (1924-29) and was joined by Maria Ouspenskaya, another

Stanislavsky student. Early members included Lee Strasberg, Stella Adler and Harold Clurman, all members of the Group Theater.

Lee Strasberg became director of the New York Actors Studio (founded in 1947) in 1951. This became the home of the Method: its aim was to give professional actors the chance to widen their experience through individual exploration and team criticism. Past members include Marlon Brando, James Dean, Julie Harris, Maureen Stapleton, Kim Stanley, Marilyn Monroe, Shelley Winters, Patricia Neal, Robert De Niro and Al Pacino. Its teaching is probably better than its own occasional productions: Lee Strasberg's version of Chekhov's *Three Sisters* (1965) was roundly condemned when it visited London for the World Theatre Season.

HAROLD PRINCE (1928-)

Producer and director who has given Broadway musicals a new style. First show as producer: *The Pajama Game* (1954) about an industrial dispute. First show he also directed: *She Loves Me* (1963). Has also directed *Cabaret* (1968) setting the tone through the epicene seediness of the Emcee; *Company* (1970) with a plexiglass, vertically-moving set; *Follies* (1971), an opulent evocation of Ziegfeld; *Candide* (1974), an environmental, multi-stage show inspired by the fairground displays of Prince's youth; *Pacific Overtures* (1976) which owed a debt to Japanese Kabuki theatre; *Evita* (1978), a political carnival; *Sweeney Todd* (1979) which showed London in turmoil under a glass-roofed sweatshop. Prince is a musical pioneer who brings bits of Brecht, Meyerhold and Reinhardt into his shows.

France

THE COMÉDIE FRANÇAISE
The oldest National Theatre in the world. It was founded in 1680 by Louis XIV. During the Revolution (1789) the company split: the conservatives went to the Théâtre de la Nation, the more revolutionary actors under Talma became the Théâtre de la République at the Palais Royal. In

The auditorium and stage of the Comédie Française in 1892 when the theatre was named Théâtre de la République.

1803 the Comédie Française was re-formed and has remained in being ever since. It is a cooperative in which each actor holds a share: a new member is admitted on probation and called a *pensionnaire* and then, after the death or resignation of a full member, he may become a *sociétaire*. It has acquired its continuity at the expense of a certain conservatism; and in 1927 a union of French theatres (under the direction of Gaston Baty, Charles Dullin, Louis Jouvet, Georges Pitoëff) called the Cartel was formed in opposition to its academic style of performance. After 1940, however, several members of the Cartel worked at the Comédie. In recent years it has acquired a renewed vitality often by importing outside directors such as the Englishman Terry Hands who since 1972 has staged there *Richard III, Pericles, Twelfth Night, Le Cid* and *Murder in the Cathedral*.

THE THÉÂTRE LIBRE (1887-94)

Founded in opposition to the triviality of boulevard theatre and the rigorous classicism of the Comédie Française. It was the inspiration of *André Antoine* (1858-1943) who was actor, producer, manager and one of the pioneers of modern theatre. He introduced the new naturalistic drama to France and revolutionised acting and set design. Most of his actors were amateurs. They were told to act naturally on stage and ignore the audience. Naturalistic acting complemented realistic set designs. Furniture painted on canvas was replaced by real furniture. In *The Butchers* (1888) Antoine took realism to the extreme of hanging real carcasses of beef on stage.

Antoine introduced to Paris audiences Tolstoy's *The Power of Darkness* (1888), Ibsen's *Ghosts* (1890) with himself as Oswald, Goncourt's *La Fille Élisa* (1890) about the pensionnaire of a brothel who kills her lover; and plays by Strindberg, Verga and Hauptmann. From 1906 to 1913 Antoine became director of France's second national theatre, the Odéon. Though his productions were successful, he created a financial disaster because he would not allow long-run productions of even the most popular plays *The School for Scandal* (1913), for example, ran only one night, Goldoni's *La Locandière* for two performances, *Sylla* by Alfred Mortier for another two performances. Wrote Harold Hobson: 'Antoine, like the fashionable ladies who in 1913 at Deauville launched the topless bathing dress, had a passion for taking everything off as quickly as possible . . . But with Antoine a new spirit was coming into the theatre. The affairs of ordinary life were being brought into the drama. Lords and ladies gave way to seamstresses, prostitutes and coal-miners.'

THE THÉÂTRE DU GRAND GUIGNOL

Opened by Max Maurey in Paris in 1899. It catered to sensation-hungry tastes with short plays of violence, murder, rape, ghosts, torture, insanity and suicide. Its authors included Edgar Allen Poe, Georges Courteline and Oscar Méténier. The term Grand Guignol also became a generic name for this kind of theatre.

THE THÉÂTRE DU VIEUX COLOMBIER

Founded in 1913 by Jacques Copeau (1879-1949). It opened with Thomas Heywood's *A Woman Killed With Kindness*. His productions were characterised by their simplicity: minimal scenery, ensemble acting, a scrupulous regard for text. He attributed the failure of Antoine to his hunger for revolutionary plays and himself preferred Shakespeare and Molière. 'He revolutionised the avant-garde. He gave it an austere and scrupulously disciplined beauty. He was the Jansenist of the French theatre.' (Harold Hobson). Copeau's most famous production was of *Twelfth Night* which between 1913 and 1924 had 187 performances.

Copeau worked in New York between 1917 and 1919. In 1924 he retired to Burgundy taking with him a young troupe of actors known as Les Copiaux. They toured the country playing in barns and market-places. They improvised or wrote their own texts; used no scenery; studied mime and commedia dell'arte. When Copeau finally retired in 1929 his nephew Michel St Denis (1897-1971) turned Les Copiaux into the Compagnie des Quinze. They made their debut at the Vieux-Colombier in 1931 with André Obey's *Le Viol de Lucrèce, Noë* and *La Bataille de la Marne*. Their productions were highly successful in Paris and London but the group disbanded in 1934.

THE COMPAGNIE RENAUD-BARRAULT

Founded in 1946 and is still going strong. It was the creation of the famous husband-and-wife team of Jean-Louis Barrault (1910-) and Madeleine Renaud (1903-). Barrault is actor, director, producer and an unquenchably youthful theatrical missionary. He studied drama under Charles Dullin and mime under Étienne Ducroux. His first independent production was *Autour d'une mère* (1935), a mime-play based on William Faulkner's *As I Lay Dying*. He has long been a champion of the plays of Paul Claudel (1868-1955) and of total theatre combining drama, music, spectacle, dance and mime. Barrault's ideals were epitomised in his productions of Claudel's *Le Soulier de Satin* (1943), *Christophe Colomb* (1953) and *Rabelais* (1969) which he described as 'a dramatic game for actors and audience'.

Breaking away from the Comédie Française, he and his wife formed their own company in 1946. Over a period of 35 years they have had nine 'permanent' homes starting at the Théâtre Marigny and winding up at the Théâtre du Rond Point only a few yards away: in every sense they have come full circle. They have worked in a former boxing arena (Élysée Montmartre), in a former railway station (Gare d'Orsay) and a former ice-rink (Théâtre du Rond Point). They are also the most travelled French company having made several world tours and visited everywhere from Vietnam and Haiti and from the USSR and Japan to the Americas. Even today M. Barrault is full of plans for the future and hopes to turn his current theatre into a centre of world theatre.

THEATRE OF CRUELTY
A theory developed by the French director, actor and poet Antonin Artaud (1896-1948). Artaud (greatly influenced by the troupe of Balinese dancers who performed in Paris in 1931) rejected the traditional Western approach to theatre with its emphasis on 'the text' for a theatre of gesture, mime and dance. He believed that music, chanting and movement could express more than words. He also rejected the traditional theatre building for a more flexible space: a hangar or barn where the spectators would be seated in the centre on mobile chairs and the action would unfold around them. 'Cruelty' refers to the belief that the spectator must suffer *with* the actors and that the theatre would act as a catalyst in releasing his repressions.

Artaud thought the Marx Brothers came closest to carrying out his theories in *Animal Crackers* (1930) and *Monkey Business* (1931).

Those directly influenced by Artaud include Jean-Louis Barrault, Peter Brook, Jerzy Grotowski and The Living Theatre. The closest Artaud came to realising his theories was a production in Paris of *Les Cencis* (1935). It was a failure and ran for only 17 performances. 'Tragedy on the stage is not enough for me. I'm going to bring it into my life', Artaud once said to Barrault.

Artaud was certified insane on 9 September 1937. He spent nine years in asylums: at Quatremarre, Scotteville-les-Rouen, Sainte Anne, Chazel-Benoit, Ville-Evrard and Rodez. Between 1944 and 1946 he was given 50 electric shock treatments which, among other things, resulted in his losing his teeth. To facilitate his release from Rodez, Jean Paulhan organised a benefit to which Picasso and Dubuffet contributed paintings. In all they raised over one million francs and Artaud was removed to a private hospital in Ivry, Paris. After his release he survived for two years, dying of cancer. On 4 March 1948 he was found dead, sitting upright at the foot of his bed, determined not to surrender, even at the end.

THEATRE OF THE ABSURD
A term invented by critic Martin Esslin in 1961 to denote an anti-literary movement in drama in which absurd (meaning out of harmony) objects and images were employed and language was often contradicted by the action on stage. *The Chairs* (1952) by Ionesco featured a stage full of empty chairs and a deaf and dumb orator; *Rhinoceros* (1959) also by Ionesco showed a whole town transformed into rhinos; *Paolo Paoli* (1957) by Adamov relates butterflies and ostrich feathers to the causes of the First World War; *Le Ping Pong* (1955) by Adamov is about a pinball machine; and in N.F. Simpson's *A Resounding Tinkle* (1957) a suburban couple buy an elephant. The first 'absurdist' play was the *Myth of Sisyphus* (1942) by Albert Camus. The most successful absurdist play was Samuel Beckett's *Waiting for Godot* first performed in Paris in 1953 at the Théâtre de Babylone where it ran for 400 performances before being transferred to another theatre. It has since become the most widely-performed play in the avant-garde repertory.

Germany

GEORGE, DUKE OF SAXE-MEININGEN (1826-1914)

Introduced the ensemble principle into German theatre and was the country's first director. Along with his actress wife, Ellen Franz, he formed a private theatrical company that from 1874 to 1890 made theatre history. Although the stage manager, Ludwig Kronek, put the plays on, the Duke set the tone for the company: the emphasis on ensemble, the way leading actors often played minor roles, the handling of crowd scenes, the devotion to historical accuracy in costumes and scenery. The company first appeared outside its own town when it took *Julius Caesar* to Berlin in 1894. It also toured Europe and influenced the ideas of André Antoine in Paris and Stanislavsky in Moscow.

MAX REINHARDT (1873-1943)

The first director to acquire an international reputation. He successfully adapted Gordon Craig's theories on lighting and design; overcame the limitations of the proscenium arch by projecting the stage into the arena; and set his productions in large non-theatrical spaces: a Vienna circus for *Oedipus Rex* (1910), the Olympia Exhibition Hall, London for *The Miracle* (1911), a cathedral square in Salzburg for *Everyman* (1920), and a riding school in Salzburg for *Faust* (1921).

As well as being a master at moving large numbers of people on stage, he also excelled at intimate theatre production. He founded the Kammerspiele (chamber theatre) in Berlin in 1906 and the avant-garde Das Junge Deutschland in 1917 where the first Expressionist play (*Der Bettler* by Reinhard Soroc) was performed. When Hitler came to power in 1933, he left Germany for America where he worked in theatre and in cinema making a film of *A Midsummer Night's Dream* (1934).

The longest Reinhardt production was *The Eternal Road,* a biblical pageant by Franz Werfel with music by Kurt Weill staged at the Manhattan Opera House. It opened at 8.0 p.m. on 7 January 1937 and the first night performance finished at 3.0 a.m. the next morning. In later performances the last two acts were cut. The play ran to full houses for 153 nights but production costs were so high that the house lost 5000 dollars a week.

GEORG KAISER (1878-1945) and ERNST TOLLER (1893-1939)

Playwrights who pioneered the Expressionist movement in the theatre. In drama, Expressionism was characterised by inner struggle, violent emotion, a revolt against realism, a concern with psychological essences rather than detail. Characters often had no names and were impersonally known as Man, Girl, Mother, Doctor, Captain, etc. A common theme was the search for spiritual renewal. Kaiser wrote over 60 plays of which the most important were *Gas I* and *II* (1918-20) which gave a symbolic picture of industrialism crashing to destruction and taking with it the civilisation which it has ruined. Toller began writing while serving a five-year prison sentence for his part as one of the leaders of the abortive Bavarian Soviet Republic. He wrote four plays in prison, the first being *Die Wandlung* (*Transfiguration*) staged in Berlin in 1919. His other key work was *Die Maschinensturmer* (*The Machine Wreckers*) staged in 1922 and dealing with the Luddite Riots in England in 1815.

The first Expressionist play staged in England was *The Rumour* (1922) by C.K. Munro. The most important American Expressionist playwright was Elmer Rice (1892-1967) whose play *The Adding Machine* (1923) about an elderly bookkeeper Mr Zero satirised the dilemma of man in the machine age. Expressionism also had great influence on set-design in both theatre and cinema: the most famous example was the German silent film classic, *The Cabinet of Dr Caligari* (1920).

ERWIN PISCATOR (1893-1966)

A German director and disciple of Max Reinhardt who pioneered the notion of 'Epic' theatre: (i.e.) something episodic, large-scale, political, and using all possible mechanical devices to drive home the argument. He worked in Berlin from 1919 to 1930 and his most famous production was his adaptation of the classic Czech novel, *Die Abenteuer des braven Soldaten Schweik* (1927). Piscator also used stylised settings and documentary devices such as the use of film.

BERTOLT BRECHT (1878-1956)

As both dramatist and director was a follower of Piscator. But he also developed his own ideas:

Above: Max Reinhardt's opulent production of 'The Miracle' which reached Broadway in 1924 with sets and costumes by Norman Bel Geddes.
Right: Angelika Hurwiez as Grusche in Bertolt Brecht's original 1954 production 'The Caucasian Chalk Circle'.

the Alienation Effect which seeks to distance the spectator from the action rather than demand his emotional involvement; the use of slides, narration, a white traverse curtain to turn each scene into a separate event; the interruption of a scene by song to break the mood. Brecht's ideas about a cool acting style, a flat, white, non-atmospheric light, the employment of used materials in costume and an aesthetic spareness of presentation have had enormous influence on European directors and designers such as Roger Planchon, Peter Stein and William Gaskill.

Brecht developed his theories with his company the Berliner Ensemble which he founded in 1949 in East Berlin at the Deutsches Theater, later moving to the Theater am Schiffbauerdam. The company made landmark visits to London in 1956 and 1965 and have left their imprint on large sections of European theatre.

USSR

KONSTANTIN STANISLAVSKY (1863-1938)

The most influential Russian director, actor and teacher. He founded the Moscow Art Theatre in 1898 with Vladimir Nemirovich-Danchenko (1859-1943) as a cooperative. Its aims were simplicity, truth, the complete illusion of reality, a totally naturalistic style of acting. The first Moscow Art Theatre production was of Alexei Tolstoy's *Tsar Feodor Ivanovich* on 14 October 1898. It was about Ivan the Terrible's son and was produced with totally authentic sets and costumes. The playwright most associated with Stanislavsky was Anton Chekhov whose masterpieces of symphonic naturalism, *The Seagull* (1898), *Uncle Vanya* (1899), *The Three Sisters* (1901) and *The Cherry Orchard* (1904), were all premièred by the Moscow Art Theatre.

The Moscow Art Theatre's longest rehearsed production was *Hamlet* (1912). It was rehearsed for two years and had a set by Gordon Craig consisting of hinged screens which were to be moved in full view of the audience. On opening night they collapsed just before the curtain was due to go up.

Stanislavsky produced the most codified and complete view of acting on record in his books *My Life in Art* (1924), *An Actor Prepares* (1926), *Stanislavsky Rehearses Othello* (1948) and *Building a Character* (1950). It is a myth that he placed little emphasis on external technique. His books were designed to help an actor improve and sustain his performance through observation, intense work and a state of psychological preparedness.

The first actors commune was established in Russia in 1913 by L.A. Sulerjitsky, formerly Stanislavsky's assistant, who had spent time in a lunatic asylum for refusing to do military service and who had been exiled to Siberia. On his return he established a commune called the First Studio on a plot of land overlooking the Black Sea. The actors built communal buildings, shared domestic tasks and worked as a group. The same principle was carried out by Jacques Copeau with Les Copaize; by Michel St. Denis and the Compagnie des Quinze; by the Group Theater and the Living Theater in the USA.

VSEVOLOD MEYERHOLD (1874-1943)

Actor, director, theoretician and teacher. Worked with Stanislavsky at the MAT from 1898 to 1902. In 1918 became the first worker in theatre to offer his services to the new Soviet Government. In 1920 became the first director to put on a Soviet play *Mystery Bouffe,* at his own newly-formed theatre which became known as the Theatre of Meyerhold. Here in his own Theatre Workshop he developed his theory of bio-mechanics. It trained actors as combined athletes, acrobats, dancers and gymnasts. They worked without make-up, wore an all-purpose blue overall, trained on gymnastic and circus apparatus. The idea was that the actor should function as a machine, devoid of human feeling. The first play produced in this style was *The Magnificent Cuckold* (1922) by Ferdinand Crommelynck. Meyerhold's most controversial production was of *The Government Inspector* (1926) by Gogol in which the actors were replaced by dummies in the final scene. In 1938 the Meyerhold Theatre was closed because it did not conform to Stalin's doctrine of socialist realism. Meyerhold disappeared in 1939. His name was expunged from Soviet records, his death shrouded in mystery, though he has since been reinstated.

The first use of film in a play was in *Earth Rampant* by Sergei Tretyakov (4 March 1923) directed by Meyerhold. Two screens projected titles and slogans. It was closely followed by Berthold Viertel's Berlin production of *Nebeneinander* by Georg Kaiser (3 November 1923) although Erwin Piscator made the greatest use of film in his productions starting with the historical revue, *Trotz Alledem* (1925). In Germany before the First World War film had already been used in opera and in a revue in Hamburg *Rund um den Alster* (1911).

Poland

JERZY GROTOWSKI (1933-)

Polish director. Major figure in contemporary theatre who took over the Polish Theatre Laboratory (1959) in Wroclaw where he established an experimental laboratory theatre where actors undergo physical and psychological training and perform mostly in plays adapted by Grotowski: Byron's *Cain* (1960), Marlowe's *Dr Faustus* (1963), Calderon's *The Constant Prince* (1965). Grotowski outlined his theories in his book *Towards a Poor Theatre* (1969). In the 'rich' theatre the actor is aided by make-up, lighting, scenery. In the Poor Theatre, theatre is reduced to its minimal requirements. There are no props, no make-up, no music. The emphasis is on the actor and on theatre as ritual.

Through intensive training, Grotowski would like the actor to achieve a state of trance, thereby giving a more open performance. His theories have had a direct influence on Peter Brook, the Living Theatre and Joseph Chaikin of the Open Theatre.

Charles Laughton, Flora Robson and Ursula Jeans in the Old Vic production of 'The Cherry Orchard', October 1933.

CHAPTER 8

Critics and Criticism

The first critic — in the sense of someone who tries to formulate the rules of theatre — was Aristotle (384-322 BC). His treatise, *Peri Poietikes* (commonly known as *The Poetics*) is an attempt to analyse the nature of tragic drama using Sophocles and Euripides as his key models.

In England, journalistic criticism of particular theatrical events got under way in the 18th century. Sir Richard Steele wrote in *The Tatler* of 7 June 1710: 'It is a very good office one man does another when he tells him the manner of his being pleased; and I have often thought that a comment upon the capacities of the players would very much improve the delight that way, and impart it to those who otherwise have no sense of it'. In *The London Chronicle* from 1757 to 1823 one finds just such accounts of plays and players at Covent Garden and Drury Lane.

But the first English writers to reveal the capacities of dramatic criticism as an art in itself were Leigh Hunt (1784-1859) and William Hazlitt (1778-1830). From 1805 to 1807 Leigh Hunt was critic for the *News* and from 1808 to 1813 for *The Examiner* where Hazlitt followed him. Hazlitt's tenure coincided with the finest performances of Edmund Kean which he immortalised in print.

In America the first drama critic of real stature was James Huneker. Born in Philadelphia in 1860, he became a drama critic on *The Sun* in New York in 1902 and established a reputation for cosmopolitanism, sanity and taste. He championed Ibsen ('In his bones he is a moralist, in practice an artist') and Shaw ('jester to the

cosmos and the most serious man on the planet') long before it was fashionable to do so. He travelled widely and lived vigorously.

The most virulent American critic was William Winter, drama critic of the *New York Tribune* from 1865 to 1909. He was paid 50 dollars a week: the smallest salary paid to the head of a drama department in any New York newspaper. His speciality was sanctimonious abuse. Duse, Réjane and Bernhardt he dismissed as 'foreign strumpets', and he described Ibsen as 'a reformer who calls you to crawl with him into a sewer, merely to see and breathe its feculence'.

There is a long history in New York and London of managements seeking to exclude critics whom they regarded as unhelpful. Notable instances:
1915
The powerful Shubert management in New York sought to bar Alexander Woollcott of *The New York Times* from their theatres after his negative review of a French farce, *Taking Chances*. The *Times* brought an injunction against the Shuberts and refused to publish their advertising. Eventually the Shuberts capitulated sending Woollcott a conciliatory box of cigars. 'The whole thing', said Woollcott, 'went up in smoke'
1957
Donald Wolfit unsuccessfully tried to prevent *Observer* critic, Kenneth Tynan, from reviewing his production of *The Master of Santiago* at the Lyric Hammersmith.
1969
Lindsay Anderson, Royal Court director, an-

Marie Lloyd: Agate said "she had a heart as big as Waterloo Station".

nounced it would no longer send free tickets to Hilary Spurling of the *Spectator* because it didn't find her 'attitude to our work illuminating and we do not believe it furthers our relationship with the public'. Three critics refused in consequence to review Court productions. Six months later the Court conceded after the Arts Council had threatened to withdraw its grant from the theatre. (A comparable instance occurred in the cinema when, after failing to respond to MGM's *Gone With the Wind*, Dilys Powell was banned for six months from MGM productions. She described it as 'the happiest six months of her life'.)

On various occasions critics have also been personally assaulted:

- Laurence Olivier hit James Agate (drama critic of *The Sunday Times* a glancing blow across the shoulder on the first night of *The Skin of Our Teeth* (18 May 1945).
- Richard Burton once took a swing at Kenneth Tynan for some unflattering remarks he had made about the actress playing opposite him.
- David Storey cuffed Michael Billington about the head in the Royal Court bar for his notice of *Mother's Day* at the Royal Court in September, 1976.
- Actress Sylvia Miles poured a plate of spaghetti over the head of New York critic John Simon for one of his less chivalrous reviews.

The only critic to have been judicially executed was Robert Brasillach who was shot at the fort of Montrogue, France on 6 February 1945. He was 35 years old. Throughout the Occupation by the Germans he had edited a magazine, *Je suis partout*, in which he eagerly supported their cause, in which he demanded the execution of resistance actors like Georges Mandel and in which he expressed a virulent hatred of Jews. But alone of the staff of *Je suis partout* he refused to seek refuge in Germany after the Liberation of Paris. After his arrest, a petition was organised to save his life but it failed. Since his death, however, a society has been formed called *The Friends of Robert Brasillach* and he served as the model for the drama critic in François Truffaut's film, *the Last Metro* (1980).

The only English theatre critic to have played on Broadway is Sheridan Morley, *Punch* drama critic, who on 1 March 1982 appeared at the Booth Theater, New York hosting his own compilatory show, *Noel and Gertie.*

Critics (and indeed professional theatre-workers) are nothing, if not fallible. These were some of the verdicts on the ten longest-running hits in Broadway history from critics and people in the theatre:

1 *Grease* (3388 performance) which dealt with late-50s rock-and-roll and which was variously retitled *Vaselino* (Mexico City), *Brilliantine* (Paris) and *Glease* (Tokyo). 'The show', wrote Clive Barnes in *The New York Times* in 1972 'is a thin joke' adding that '1959 was a great year for Burgundy'.

2 *Fiddler On The Roof* (3242 performances) which opened in 1964 in Detroit during a newspaper strike and which was greeted by a *Variety* stringer with the verdict 'No smash hit, no blockbuster'.

3 *Life With Father* (3224 performances) was, according to the *Daily Worker* in 1939, 'good propaganda, bad art. There is not a moment of honest joy or passion in its daguerreotype tableau.'

4 *Tobacco Road* (3182 performances) was dismissed in 1933 by Burns Mantle as 'ugly, wallowing sort of drama' about life among redneck rustics. 'It isn't the sort of entertainment folks buy in the theatre', he added.

5 *Hello Dolly* (2844 performances) was booed,

panned and nearly abandoned altogether during its out-of-town tour. Then three songs were dropped, three added, half the first act cut and a hit born in 1964.

6 *My Fair Lady* (2717 performances). 'Those dear boys have lost their talent', grieved Broadway star Mary Martin in 1955 after hearing five songs from what was then called *Lady Liza* by Lerner and Loewe.

7 *A Chorus Line* (still running). 'The paltriness of the music was hideously apparent' wrote one critic on the show's opening in 1975.

8 *Man of La Mancha* (2328 performances). When it was revived in New York in 1977 Richard Eder of the *New York Times* described it as 'a work that fights itself and loses'.

9 *Abie's Irish Rose* (2327 performances). 'So cheap and offensive that it might serve to unite all the races of the world in a common hymn of hate', wrote Heywood Broun in 1922 when this

Sarah Bernhardt as Shakespeare's Hamlet. When she played the role in London in 1899, Max Beerbohm wrote that "The customs-house officials at Charing Cross ought to have confiscated her sable doublet and hose".

sentimental comedy first opened. 'Of course it's terrible', said Walter Kerr in the *Herald-Tribune* in 1954 when it was revived 'but apart from that it isn't so bad'.

10 *Oklahoma* (2248 performances). 'No legs, no jokes, no chance' was the legendary dismissal out of town in New Haven before the show achieved its Broadway triumph in 1943.

Below is an anthology of some of the most memorable things critics have written both in praise and withering denunciations.

JAMES AGATE (1877-1947) Drama critic of *The Sunday Times* from 1923 to 1970.

On Sarah Bernhardt:
'You would know a scene of Sarah Bernhardt's if you met it in your dreams. To say of the very greatest actress of this type that she is always herself is obviously to mean that whatever quality she expresses will be expressed in its highest power.'

On Marie Lloyd:
'She knew, though she could not have put her knowledge into words, that her art was one with the tradition of English letters which has always envisaged the seamy side of life with gusto rather than deprecation.'

On the first production of Shaw's *Saint Joan* (1924)
'The dresses made a kind of music in the air and at the end Joan was allowed to stand for a moment in all that ecstasy of tinsel and blue in which French image-makers enshrine her memory.'

On Maurice Evans:
'A great actor must include the forbidding in his facial range: when last I saw Maurice he could do no better in this line than stave off with impudence.'

On Marie Tempest:
'Her technique was flawless and her comedy had everything comedy should have, except the gift of tears.'

On Robert Helpmann's Hamlet:
'This was acting on the androgynous plane of pure poetry, as indeed one expected from an artist in the school of Nijinsky.'

On Donald Wolfit:
'Will not Mr Wolfit try to realise that an actor is known by the company he keeps?'

On Ralph Richardson:
'Like all great Falstaffs his heart warms to Feeble, for though the old rapscallion may not practise valour, he knows what it is.'

On Eleonora Duse:
'Her features have the placidity of long grief; so many storms have broken over them that nothing can disturb again this sea of calm distress.'

On Gertrude Lawrence:
'She has extraordinary variety of expression and the supreme gift of the artist in comedy, that of thinking with her features so that you know exactly the significance of every sentence.'

On *Cyrano de Bergerac*:
'*Cyrano* is the Crystal Palace of poetry. In this play, Rostand says nothing with unexampled virtuosity.'

On the purpose of drama:
'The theatre is not a night-school. Its drama illumines philosophy, sociology, politics and the rest by reflection in that it lights up the philosopher, the sociologist and the politician.'

MAX BEERBOHM (1872-1956) Shaw's successor as drama critic of *The Saturday Review*.

At the Tivoli:
'The aim of the music-hall is, in fact, to cheer the lower classes up by showing them a life uglier and more sordid than their own.'

On critics:
'I do not much care about good criticism. I like better the opinions of strong, narrow, creative personalities.'

On W. S. Gilbert's *Pygmalion* (1900):
'No fantasy is good unless it be founded in solid reality.'

On the heroines of Shaw's early plays:
'They were just dowdy and ill-conditioned shrews — wasps without waists. I am glad to think that I have seen the last of them.'

On the public:
'Go to any little picture gallery where some new kind of work is being exhibited or to any theatre lent for the production of a play written by an unknown or foreign dramatist and you will always find the same public — the same wan and dishevelled men and women.'

On Duse as Ibsen's Hedda:
'However it was not the only performance of Hedda Gabler. There was another and, in some ways, a better. While Signora Duse walked through her part, the prompter threw himself into it with a will. A more raucous whisper I never heard than that which preceded the Signora's every sentence. It was like the continous tearing of very thick silk.'

On Dan Leno:
'The technique for acting in a music-hall is of a harder, perhaps finer, kind than is needed for acting in a theatre; inasmuch as the artist must make his effects so much more quickly and without the aid of any but the slightest 'properties' and scenery and without the aid of anyone else on the stage.'

On Oscar Asche's *As You Like It* (1907):
'Perhaps if they (the players) were not munching apples quite so assiduously the verse and the prose would stand a better chance.'

On the report of the Shakespeare Memorial Executive Committee (1909):
'What is needed of course "to further the development of the modern drama" is a quite small theatre decently endowed with one enlightened despot to govern it. The Court theatre, for example; and, for example, Mr Granville Barker.'

ERIC BENTLEY (1916-) Drama critic of *The New Republic* from 1952 to 1956.

On musicals:
'The last scene of *Carousel* is an impertinence. I refuse to be lectured by a musical comedy scriptwriter on the education of children, the nature of the good life and the contribution of the American small town to the salvation of souls.'

On Tennessee Williams:
'Mr William's problem is not lack of talent. It is, perhaps, an ambiguity of aim: he seems to want to kick the world in the pants and yet be the world's sweetheart, to combine the glories of martyrdom with the comforts of success.'

On the Comédie Française:
'Whatever theorists say in favour of ensembles, the old playwrights wrote for stars. Molière went even further: he wrote for himself.'

On *The Boy Friend* (1954):
'The joke against the generation immediately preceding one's own is vulgar, provincial, second-rate. First-rate jokes are against one's own generation.'

JOHN MASON BROWN (1900-) Drama critic of *The Saturday Review of Literature.*

On adaptations:
'Dramatisations as a rule prove more like sieves than containers for the virtues of a book.'

PENELOPE GILLIATT Drama critic of *The Observer*, 1964-68.

On Beckett:
'Beckett's *Waiting For Godot*, revived in a production as fine and keen as its own prose, arrived in London ten years ago like a sword burying itself in an over-upholstered sofa.'

On Congreve:
'Congreve's comedies aren't about people who see sex as a pleasure; they are really about sex used as form of currency to purchase something else. In Noel Coward, sex sometimes seems to be a coin to pay for the company of wit at breakfast. In Congreve's *Love for Love* it is used to buy money, with every courtship in the plot wooing an estate: love for loot.'

On Feydeau:
'Seventy-five per cent of the action of farce springs from huffiness. The rest comes from panic and architecture . . .

William Hazlitt: the first great English critic of acting. Kean's performances live again through him.

It isn't really lechery that gets the characters into trouble because they never feel any emotion so conscious as lechery is of someone else. Their undoing is their disastrous mixture of rock-hard vanity and jelly fluster.'

WILLIAM HAZLITT (1778-1830) Critic of *The Examiner, The Morning Chronicle*, etc.

On Mrs Siddons:
'She was tragedy personified. She was the stateliest ornament of the public mind. She was not only the idol of the people, she not only hushed the tumultuous shouts of the pit in breathless expectation, and quenched the blaze of surrounding beauty in silent tears but to the retired and lonely student, through long years of solitude, her face has shone as if an eye had appeared from heaven.'

HAROLD HOBSON (1904-) Drama critic of *The Sunday Times*, 1947-76.

On the sense of threat in Pinter's *The Birthday Party*:
'It breathes in the air. It cannot be seen, but it enters the room every time the door is opened. There is something in your past — it does not matter what — which will catch up with you. Though you go to the uttermost parts of the earth, and hide yourself in the most obscure lodgings in the least popular of towns, one day there is a possibility that two men will appear. They will be looking for you and you cannot get away. And someone will be looking for *them* too. There is terror everywhere.'

GEORGE HENRY LEWES (1817-78) Critic of *The Leader.*

On Rachel:
'Her range, like Kean's was very limited but her expression was perfect within that range.'

On Frédéric Lemaître:
'There was always something offensive to good taste in Frédéric's acting — a note of vulgarity, partly owing to his daring animal spirits but mainly owing, I suspect to an innate vulgarity of nature.'

DESMOND McCARTHY (1878-1952) Drama critic of *The New Stateman.*

On Chekhov's *Uncle Vanya* (1914):
'During the last act we live in poor Vanya's heart, feeling his exhaustion and shame, and that dreariest of all sensations: beginning life

Above left: Peter Hall, founder of the Royal
Shakespeare Company in 1960 and director
of the National Theatre since 1973.

Above right: Mrs. Patrick Campbell
(1865-1940), legendary English actress for
whom Bernard Shaw created the role of Eliza
Doolittle. (Mary Evans Picture Library).

Below left: The sweeping, curved auditorium
of the National's Olivier Theatre.
(Brecht-Einzig, courtesy of National Theatre).

A Gaiety Theatre programme for 'The Orchard' starring Gertie Millar.
(Halcyon Cards Limited).

G.H. Lewes dramatist and critic for whom "the actor was greatest who was greatest in the highest reaches of his art".

again on the flat when, a few hours before, it has run shrieking up the scale of pain till it seemed the very skies might split.'

GEORGE JEAN NATHAN (1882-1958) Drama critic of *The American Mercury, Vanity Fair, Newsweek, Theatre Arts,* etc.

On criticism:
'Do not confound an aphrodisiacal actress with a talented one . . .'
'The better and more honest a critic you are, the fewer friends will eventually send flowers up the funeral parlour . . .'
'Don't be afraid of being labelled a destructive critic. You will be in good company. Where would you rather be: in Hell with Swift, Voltaire and Nietzsche or in the American Academy of Arts and Letters with Richard Burton, Clayton Hamilton and Hermann Hagedorn?'
'The only way for a critic to get on in the world is to roast the living tar out of everything that calls for such roasting and never stop for a minute and to praise the living roses back into everything that calls for such praise and likewise never stop for a minute.'

On English comedy:
'Much of the contemporary English polite comedy writing suggests a highly polished and very smooth billiard table with all the necessary brightly polished cues, but without balls.'

On musicals:
'It seems that the moment anyone gets hold of an exclamation point these days, he promptly sits down and writes a musical show around it.'
'These shows are to the theatres what wines are to a substantial dinner.'

On modern Hamlets:
'In Leslie Howard's he was the Duke of Windsor out to get Stanley Baldwin and wife with Winston Churchill playing both Rosencrantz and Guildenstern. In John Giegud's he was Lord Alfred Douglas having an exciting melodramatic cup of tea with Beverly Nichols.'

On some of the ways one may spot a bad play within ten minutes of curtain-rise:
'The moment anyone puts anything into a drawer with a furtive look.'
'In four cases out of five, when at the rise of the curtain the wife is writing a letter and the husband, in an easy chair, is reading a newspaper.'
'When, as the curtain goes up, you hear newsboys shouting "Extra. Extra".'
'Any mystery play in which, at the very start, someone remarks that the nearest house is two miles away.'
'As soon as you hear the line: "If a man kills a man, that's murder. Why isn't it then also murder if a man in uniform does the same thing. War is murder".'
'Any translation from the Hungarian in which the heroine is called the Countess Katinka.'
'The one about the timid little man who has a yen to be a hero.'

On Charles Morgan's *The Flashing Stream* (1938):
'Margaret Rawlings, ordinarily an actress of distinction, further succumbed to the fault of confusing intonation with lyricism, in which confusion Godfrey Tearle handsomely backed her up with the inference that he must have had a Wurlitzer for dinner.'

On Cornelia Otis Skinner's one-woman show:
'A woman talking steadily for two hours is hardly my idea of entertainment whether in the theatre or in private.'

On improvisation:
'An actor without a playwright is like a hole without a doughnut.'
On critics:
'No chronically happy man is a trustworthy critic.'

GEORGE BERNARD SHAW (1856-1950) Drama critic of *The Saturday Review* from 1895 to 1898.

On *Romeo and Juliet* (1895) at the Lyceum:
'Mrs Patrick Campbell's dresses, says the programme, carried out by Mrs Mason of New Burlington Street. I can only say that I wish they had been carried out and buried .... Mr Forbes Robertson has evidently no sympathy with Shakespeare's love of a shindy: you see his love of law and order coming out in his stage management of the fighting scenes .... Romeo has lines that tighten the heart or catch you up into the heights alternately with heartless fustian and silly ingenuities that make your curse Shakepeare's stagestruckness and his youthful inability to keep his brains quiet.'

On Shakespeare:
'With the single exception of Homer there is no eminent writer, not even Sir Walter Scott, whom I despise as entirely as I despise Shakespeare when I measure my mind against his.'

On *The Sorrows of Satan* (1897):
'Mr Yorke Stephens fulfils his obligations to Miss Corelli and the audience most scrupulously but with the air of a man who has resolved to shoot himself the moment the curtain is down.'

On Oscar Wilde:
'I cannot say that I cared greatly for *The Importance of Being Earnest*. It amused me, of course, but unless comedy touches me as well as amuses me, it leaves me with a sense of having wasted my evening. I go to the theatre to be moved to laughter, not to be tickled or bustled into it.'

On theatres:
'It is clear to me that we shall never become a playgoing people until we discard our fixed idea that it is the business of the people to come to the theatre and substitute for it the idea that it is the business of the theatre to come to the people.'

On *A Doll's House* (1897):
'Nora's revolt is the end of a chapter of human history. The slam of the door behind her is more momentous than the cannon of Waterloo or Sedan because when she comes back it will not be to the old home; for when the patriarch no longer rules, and the breadwinner acknowledges his dependence, there is an end of the old order.'

On Duse and Bernhardt:
'No physical charm is noble as well as beautiful unless it is the expression of a moral charm; and it is because Duse's range includes these high moral notes that her compass, extending from the depths of a mere predatory creature like Claude's wife up to Marguerite Gautier at her kindest or Magda at her bravest, so immeasurably dwarfs the poor little octave and a half on which Sarah Bernhardt plays such pretty canzonets and stirring marches.'

J. C. TREWIN (1908-) Drama critic and theatre historian.

On Olivier's *Richard III* (1944):
'It is the marriage of intellect and dramatic force, of bravura and cold reason that so distinguishes Mr Laurence Olivier's study at the New Theatre. Here indeed we have the true double Gloucester, thinker and doer, mind and mask. Blessedly the actor never counterfeits the deep tragedian, the top-heavy villain weighted by his ponderous and marble jaws. His Richard gives to every speech a fire-new glint. His diction, flexible and swift — often mill-race swift — is bred of a racing brain.'

KENNETH TYNAN (1927-80) Drama critic of *The Observer* from 1954 to 1958 and 1960 to 1963.

On *The Glorious Days* (1953):
'There was a heated division of opinion in the lobbies during the interval but a small conservative majority took the view that it might be as well to remain in the theatre.'

On Olivier:
'Sir Laurence Olivier's Titus, even with one hand gone, is a five-finger exercise transformed into an unforgettable concerto of grief. This is a performance which ushers us into the presence of one who is, pound for pound, the greatest actor alive.'

On John Osborne:
'I doubt if I could love anyone who did not wish to see *Look Back In Anger*. It is the best young play of its decade.'

On actors:
'Between good and great acting is fixed an inex-

A round-table chat about 'Saint Joan' with Lewis Casson, Sybil Thorndike and Bernard Shaw.

orable gulf which may be crossed only by the elect whose visas are in order. Gielgud, seizing a parasol, crosses by tightrope; Redgrave, with lunatic obstinacy, plunges into the torrent usually sinking within yards of the opposite shore; Laurence Olivier polevaults over, hair-raisingly, in a single animal leap.'

On Noel Willman's Claudius:
'At his first entrance Mr Willman strikes a note of decent banality from which he never afterwards departs. To establish that he is a crafty fellow, he keeps his eyes roving from side to side, like air-pockets in a pair of spirit-levels; and he clinches the case against Claudius by eating grapes. It is a rule of Shakespearean production that men who eat grapes are definitely voluptuaries and probably murderers.'

STARK YOUNG (1881-1963) Drama critic of *The New Republic* from 1921 to 1947.

On Lee Strasberg's direction of James Barrie:
'To obscure the essential nature of a thing in art is a stupid resolution, false and flat . . . There is nothing very distinguished in these improving confusions and these misleading aspirations — they are mostly the result of greedy encroachments.'

On *The Glass Menagerie* (1945):
'What we need in the theatre is a sense of language, a sense of texture in speech, vibration and impulse in speech. Behind the Southern speech in the mother's part is the echo of great literature or at least a respect for it. There is the sense in it of her having been born out of a tradition, not out of a box. It has the echo and the music of it.'

CHAPTER 9

Final Curtain

TENNIS COURT THEATRES

Noting the flamboyant theatrical style of some tennis players today, e.g. Jimmy Connors, Ilie Nastase and John McEnroe, it isn't surprising to learn that tennis courts were once considered ideal facilities for converting into theatres.

In the 16th century there was only one permanent theatre in Paris, the Hôtel de Bourgogne. But by then, in Paris and London, many tennis courts were being enclosed and roofed over, and with the simple addition of a platform, converted into temporary theatres. In Paris alone there were between 250 and 1800 tennis courts (estimates vary widely!). An early home of the Comédie Française was in a tennis court in St. Germain-des-Près. **Molière first appeared on stage** at the Illustre Théâtre (1644), a tennis court; and the former Lisle's Tennis Court in London became, in 1661, Lincoln's Inn Fields Theatre, **first theatre to have a proscenium arch.**

PLAYS PERFORMED WITHOUT THEIR LEADING CHARACTERS

☐ George Frederick Cooke (1756-1812) was too drunk to play the lead in Charles Macklin's *Love à la Mode* at a performance at Covent Garden Theatre. Nevertheless, the show went on without him, and without an understudy in his place.

☐ *Hamlet* was performed without Hamlet at the Richmond Theatre (1787) when an inexperienced actor named Cubit was too overcome to go on on the second night of the run. Sir Walter Scott, who was in the audience,

considered that his fellow spectators thought the play much improved without its namesake.

THEY WOULDN'T LIE DOWN

☐ Robert 'Romeo' Coates (1772-1842) bejewelled, wealthy American amateur actor famous for his long drawn out, and often repeated, death scenes. On the opening night of *The Fair Penitent* (1811) he was so reluctant to die that he cancelled the final act (having himself died in the previous act) and recited a monologue to the audience instead.

☐ A young actor appeared with Donald Wolfit in *Macbeth* for several seasons. As the messenger he came on crying 'My lord, the Queen is dead'. After repeatedly asking Wolfit for a more demanding role, in disgust one evening, instead of his usual line, he rushed on stage and said 'My lord, the Queen is much better and is even now at dinner'.

TRANSVESTITES/SEX CHANGE

Drag (1926) by Mae West in which a high-kicking chorus line of 40 transvestites appeared. Played for two weeks in Paterson, New Jersey and never opened in New York as originally planned — Mae West was advised not to.

The World of Paul Slickey (1959) by John Osborne, and music by Christopher Whelan featured two sex changes.

SUPERSTITIONS

Macbeth

An unlucky play because it is said to include a black magic incantation. Innumerable deaths, disasters, injuries and misfortunes associated with productions have reinforced this belief. The most disaster-struck production was probably that of John Gielgud (1942) during which four actors died, and the designer, John Minton, later committed suicide.

never say Macbeth

Never mention the name of the play directly in the theatre (or indeed anywhere else according to some). It is always referred to as The Scottish Play or some such euphemism.

never quote from Macbeth *in the dressing-room.*

Considered extremely unlucky. The antidote is to go outside, turn around three times, spit, knock on the door three times and beg admittance. Another is to quote 'angels and ministers of grace defend us'.

never whistle in the dressing-room

Indicates a short run. Antidote: go outside, turn around three times, knock and wait to be invited back in again.

never knit in the wings

never use real flowers on stage

Unlucky, particularly where dancers are concerned, for the practical reason that someone might slip on falling petals which can be very slippery.

never leave a bar of soap behind in the dressing-room

Means you will never come back to that theatre.

unlucky to wear green in a play

Probably originates in 18th to 19th century when the green spotlight (the 'lime' light) was used to pick out the leading actor. If he was wearing green it effectively made him nearly invisible. Tony Hancock was so superstitious that he wouldn't allow it to be worn at rehearsals either.

never speak the last line of a play during rehearsal

Because anything which is finished and complete is inviting some sort of disaster.

putting clothes on inside out

If you do this by accident you must wear them like that all day — to change is bad luck.

thread

If a thread sticks to your clothes backstage or on stage (but not in the dressing-room) someone else must pick it off. Wind it around your finger. Each turn corresponds to the length of time (days, weeks or months) you will have to wait for your next contract to come up. Alternatively each wind around the finger indicates a letter of the alphabet (1-A; 2-B, etc), the letters being the initials of the producer who will employ you.

unlucky to wish an actor good luck on opening night

The usual alternative is 'break a leg'.

unlucky for a visitor to enter dressing-room with the left foot first

He must exit, and re-enter right foot foremost.

good luck to fall flat on your face making an entrance

On the theory that nothing worse could happen on the first night.

unlucky to have a smooth dress rehearsal

It will be the prelude to a disastrous opening night.

peacocks

Peacock feathers or designs are considered unlucky, as is the name Peacock in the title of a play. (*Cry of a Peacock* by Anouilh and *Juno and the Paycock* by O'Casey have never had long runs).

GHOSTS

Haymarket Theatre

John Buckstone, actor, playwright and manager of the Haymarket (1853-78) so loved the theatre that when he died he returned to haunt it. Has been heard rehearsing in one of the dressing-rooms, has been seen by several people, among them Margaret Rutherford. Said to appear only when productions are doing well.

Theatre Royal, Drury Lane

The Man in Grey is said to be the ghost of a man stabbed to death on stage in a fight in the late 18th century. Has only been seen in daylight, e.g. on stage during a matinée of *At the Drop of Another Hat* and in the upper circle. Considered a good-luck omen. May be the ghost of a man found bricked up in a hollow wall, a knife in his ribs, when the old theatre was rebuilt.

Adelphi Theatre

Ghost of William Terris, the actor who was murdered outside the stage door, dressed in frock coat and top hat.

The Adelphi Theatre in the days when it was managed by A. and S. Gatti.

Bristol Old Vic

Sarah Siddons, the famous 18th century actress, is resident theatre ghost at the Bristol Old Vic. She has haunted it ever since her lover hanged himself there. Actor Frank Barrie recalls: 'One night I was standing alone on the edge of the stage after a dress rehearsal when I was tapped on the shoulder. I turned and saw her sitting in one of the boxes at the edge of the stage. Later I told Professor G. Wilson Knight, the Shakespearean scholar about it and he said 'She's come to help you if you have any problems in your career'.

In 1980 Barrie did a one-man show, *Macready*, based on the actor who was Sarah's protégé, in New York and his wife gave him a poster of Sarah which he tacked onto his dressing-room mirror. Barrie recalls: 'Some time later I arrived at the theatre for a performance wondering whether I could go on. I felt ill and tired. I keep some bottles of booze for guests though I never drink during a performance. That night I was reaching for the bottle when suddenly Sarah's picture fell off the mirror. I know she was telling me not to have a drink. Now she is my idol.'

MURDERS OF ACTORS

☐ Walter Clun was fatally stabbed on his way home from the theatre, 1664.

☐ William Knell (1583-1603), member of the Queen's Men, was stabbed in the throat at Thame.

☐ Charles Macklin (1699-1797) who was the first actor to play Shylock as a non-comic role (1741) and manager of Drury Lane (1734-43) murdered actor Hallam in the Green Room of the Drury Lane (1735). In an argument over a wig, Macklin stabbed Hallam through the eye with a stick. He was found guilty of manslaughter but was never imprisoned. He paid a fine to the dead man's family instead.

☐ William Terris (1847-97), star of nautical melodrama at the Adelphi, was stabbed to

Peter O'Toole as Macbeth: a modern tragedy as depicted in 'Punch'.

death (1897) by a fellow actor, Richard Prince, in a fit of jealous rage in Maiden Lane, near the stage door of the Adelphi. Prince was declared insane and spent the rest of his life in Broadmoor asylum for the criminally insane.

DEATH AT SEA

☐ Charles Frohman, Broadway impresario, died in the sinking of the *Lusitania*, 1915.

☐ Tyrone Power (1795–1841) great-grandfather of the film star went down with the *President*.

☐ Frank Vosper (1899–1937) English actor and dramatist drowned at sea.

FLOPS

The longest-running flop in theatre history was *The Ladder* (1926). Backed by Texas oil tycoon, Edgar. B. Davis and author J. Frank Davis, the play ran for 17 months in New York at a loss of 750 000 dollars. By the end of 1927 seats were free at every performance and the show ran to near empty houses. Davis later opened it again in Boston. It was a drama of reincarnation, presenting the same characters in four different periods: 1360, 1670, 1844 and 1926. *The New York Times* Theatre critic Brooks Atkinson said 'Life came in for very earnest consideration with a great deal of scenery, many lavish costumes and considerable dialogue.'

The most expensive flop in theatre history is *Can-Can* (1981) which, starring Zizi Jeanmaire,

closed on Broadway after five performances and lost over 2 million dollars. Both *Bring Back Birdie* (1981) and *Frankenstein* (1981) also lost close to 2 million dollars during their brief Broadway runs. *Frankenstein* only ran for one night.

The most popular fiasco in theatre history was Walter Reynold's *Young England* which opened at the Victoria Palace on 10 September 1934 and ran for 278 performances (one spectator was said to have gone 150 times). The play was a rickety melodrama full of Virtue and Vice, astounding coincidences and ending with a patriotic transformation scene in which Britannia stood on high among massed Guides, Scouts and policemen with an electric sign, YOUNG ENGLAND, overhead and the cast sang 'Land of Hope and Glory' and the National Anthem.

The play was treated by its audiences with jocular derision. When the wicked Scoutmaster stole the money from the Scouts' safe the house would shout out 'Don't forget to wipe the handle' and collapse in mirth when he did wipe it. The Boy Scout song 'Away we go, a cheery jolly Scout band' received rude accompaniments from the stalls and at the last performance in May 1935 (by now the play had transferred to the Kingsway) a man was found to be asleep in the stalls. 'Stop acting while we wake him', cried the audience and the cast obligingly agreed. Walter Reynolds, a veteran actor of 82, said at the end of it all: 'My next play will be something different'.

The most popular flop of recent times was the Old Vic *Macbeth* (opening night: 3 September 1980) starring Peter O'Toole and directed by Bryan Forbes. On the opening night audiences hooted with laughter as Lady Macbeth fainted and was tossed by Banquo to a passing thane as in a game of pass-the-parcel: as Brian Blessed's Banquo turned up at the banquet dripping from head-to-toe with a substance known as Kensington Gore (allegedly recommended by Princess Margaret); and as Lady Macbeth cried, after her husband had careered around the stage deliriously, 'Think of this good peers but as a thing of custom'. The production played to packed houses for the whole of its run but the Old Vic lost its Arts Council grant of £300 000 at the end of the season.

Many plays have played to small houses. One of the smallest came in 1980 when a show called

Dig For Victory (billed as 'a wonderfully funny and irreverent look at the experience of a particularly eccentric family during the Second World War') was staged by Barnet's Old Bull Arts Centre to raise money for a theatre in the area. But it had to be called off when Joy Pitts, her husband and 16-year-old son were the only people to turn up — apart from the local paper's critic.

HITS

When the musical *Barnum* opened at the London Palladium on 11 June 1981 it became **the highest-insured show in British theatre history**. Producers put the total cover at £5 million with £3 million of that going on Michael Crawford who walked the high wire and slid down a rope extending from the topmost box to the stage . . . . For the first time in the Palladium's 70 year history the boxes were out of commission as they were used for the performance of the show . . . . Before the show opened police were on the lookout for a 12 foot tall thief who stole stiltwalker Sue Barbour's stilts while she went to a costume fitting . . . .

Britain's longest-running Alternative Theatre production ever is *Accidental Death of an Anarchist* which opened at Wyndhams Theatre on 5 March 1980 and which closed there on 24 October 1981. During that time it was given 622 performances and seen by over 400 000 people. The play was written by Dario Fo and presented by the Belt and Braces company.

The most consistently high attendance for a straight play in the West End was achieved by *Rose* in 1980. Starring Glenda Jackson, it opened on 20 February and closed on 30 August having given 200 totally sold-out performances. The show grossed £¾ million and allowed investors to double their money.

Agatha Christie's *The Mousetrap* has broken every record for a long-running play. On 14 May 1981 it also became **the first West End play to be given to an audience of entirely deaf people**. Interpreters at the side of the stage translated the play into sign language.

The highest advance-money taken at the box-office for any British production was 2 million dollars for *The Sound of Music* at the Apollo Victoria in 1981.

The highest amount of money taken in a single week for a production is 409 884 dollars which the revival of *My Fair Lady* with Rex Harrison raked up at the 2699-seat Pentagess Theater in Los Angeles in January 1981.

The longest-running one-man show in West End history is *An Evening with Tommy Steele*. It opened at the Prince of Wales on 11 October 1979 and closed on 29 November 1980.

The Smallest Theatre in the World (called precisely that) seats an audience of two with one squatting on the other's lap. It was begun in 1972, designed by Marcel Steiner and built on a 650cc Russian-made Neval motor-bike. It has so far visited 12 countries, including America and Canada, with a repertoire including *Ben Hur*, *The Guns of Navarone* and *The Rise and Fall of the Third Reich*. It has also offered *The Tempest* in the car-park of the Royal Shakespeare Theatre, Stratford-upon-Avon while the RSC were performing the same play inside the main building.

The second smallest theatre in the world was seen on the Fringe of the Edinburgh Festival in 1981. The Bogdan Club performed *2001* in the back of a Hillman Avenger (UPV 779K) to maximum audiences of 4 at venues around the city.

The Edinburgh Festival Fringe is **the largest festival in the world**. It began at the same time as the first International Festival in 1947 when eight theatre companies turned up to offer their shows in addition to the official programme. The following year Robert Kemp in the *Edinburgh Evening News* previewed events happening 'round the Fringe' and the name stuck. In 1959 the Festival Fringe Society was formed to co-ordinate events. By 1981 more than 450 companies turned up putting on 844 shows and giving a record figure of 10 128 performances.

Britain's oldest theatrical trade-paper is *The Stage* which celebrated 100 years of continuous existence on 31 January 1980. **America's oldest trade-paper** is *Variety* which celebrated its 75th birthday in December 1980. *Variety* achieved fame for its own particular, specialised vocabulary. An 'aisle-sitter' is a theatre critic, 'heavy mitting' means loud applause, prostitutes and hookers are variously 'B-girls, prosties, femmes du pavé and joy girls'. When Maria Callas created a hubbub at the New York Metropolitan Opera it was 'Callasthenics'. And when air-conditioning collapsed in Pittsburgh theatres, the headline was 'Pitt Caught With its Plants Down'.

Brigid Larmour became **the first woman ever to direct** for Cambridge's Marlowe Society with a production of *Love's Labour Lost* in 1981. Women were first admitted to the Marlowe Society as actresses in a 1934 production of *Antony and Cleopatra*. The Marlowe Society was founded in 1907.

The first toilet to appear on stage was in André Antoine's production of Goncourt's *La Fille Élisa* in Paris on 24 December 1890. The play's heroine is the pensionnaire of a brothel who kills her lover rather than allow him to have sex in a cemetery; and the first act is set in a hotel room complete with toilet and washbasin. Mme Alfred Vallette (called Rachilde), wife of a famous editor, described the plays Antoine produced as 'kitchen sink (*la cuvette*), confinements and public miscarriages'. She thereby gave the word 'kitchen-sink' to the critical vocabulary. It was revived in England in the 1950s to describe the social realist paintings of Bratby and others and the plays of dramatists such as Wesker and Livings. Other plays to feature a toilet: *Spring Awakening* (1891), *Ubu Roi* (1896), *Stop It Whoever You Are* (1962), *Rites* (1969) by Maureen Duffy. But although you can now show a toilet with impunity, as recently as 1953 the Lord Chamberlain banned the sound of a lavatory being flushed off-stage in Graham Greene's *The Living-Room*.

The most assiduous royal patron of the British stage was Queen Victoria. Between the ages of 12 and 42 she attended the theatre as much as three times a week: drama, ballet, opera and circus all included. For the last 40 years of her life — after the death of Prince Albert — she never entered a theatre again. But, towards the end of her reign, the theatre came to her. Between 1881 and 1901, 28 Command Performances took place at various royal residences, including Irving and Terry in *The Bells* and in *The Merchant of Venice* Trial scene at Sandringham (1889), Eleanora Duse in *La Locandiera* at Windsor (1894) and Sarah Bernhardt in *Jean Marie* at Cimiez (1897).

Drama contains much thought for food as well as

Rex Harrison as Professor Higgins: the quintessence of elegant, short-tempered Englishness.

food for thought. Some famous theatrical meals:

Titus Andronicus (1594) Tamora, Queen of the Goths, ends up eating her two sons baked in a pie ('tête de fils en pâté pour deux personnes' as one critic pointed out).

Timon of Athens (1607-8) Timon, the host, presents his guests with dishes which, when

Dinsdale Landen in ferocious mood in Tom Stoppard's 'On the Razzle' at the Lyttleton Theatre.

uncovered, turn out to be full of warm water. He then proceeds to hurl the dishes at them and drives them out.

The Revenger's Tragedy (1607) Ends with a banquet in which masqued revengers kill the four chief guests as they sit at table.

You Never Can Tell (1898) Eight Shavian characters in the second act sit down to a multi-course meal served impeccably by William, the perfect servant.

Old Flames (1975) A Ted Whitehead play in which four women, between the first and second acts, deliriously consume their male guest ('That was delicious', begins the second act).

The Norman Conquests (1974) One third of Ayckbourn's comic trilogy is set in the dining-room where a disastrous comic meal involves one guest sitting on a low stool with his head just protruding above the table.

Sweeney Todd (1979) Cannibalism again. At Mrs Lovett's pie-shop the diners noisily bang their tankards on the table demanding 'More hot pies'. The pies are, of course, made up of barber Sweeney Todd's former clients.

Can't Pay, Won't Pay (1974) Madcap Dario Fo farce in which a Milanese husband is served a meal consisting of millet-soup, dog-food and frozen rabbit's heads.

The first British production to visit the USSR after the October Revolution was *Hamlet* in 1956 directed by Peter Brook and starring Paul Scofield. The first British director to work with a Russian company since the Revolution was Peter James who in 1975 directed *Twelfth Night* at the Sevriomennik Theatre in Moscow. The first Russian director to work in Britain in 20 years was Oleg Tabakov who directed *The Government In-*

spector at the Crucible Theatre, Sheffield in 1976.

The most frequently-adapted play is John Oxenford's *A Day Well Spent* (1835). This one-act farce has been adapted as follows:

1842 *Einen Jux will er sich machen* by Johann Nestroy
1938 *The Merchant of Yonkers* by Thornton Wilder
1954 *The Matchmaker* by Thornton Wilder
1963 *Hello Dolly* by Jerry Herman and Michael Stewart
1981 *On The Razzle* by Tom Stoppard

Georgina Hale and Sheila Ruskin in 'Steaming' by Nell Dunn at the Comedy Theatre.

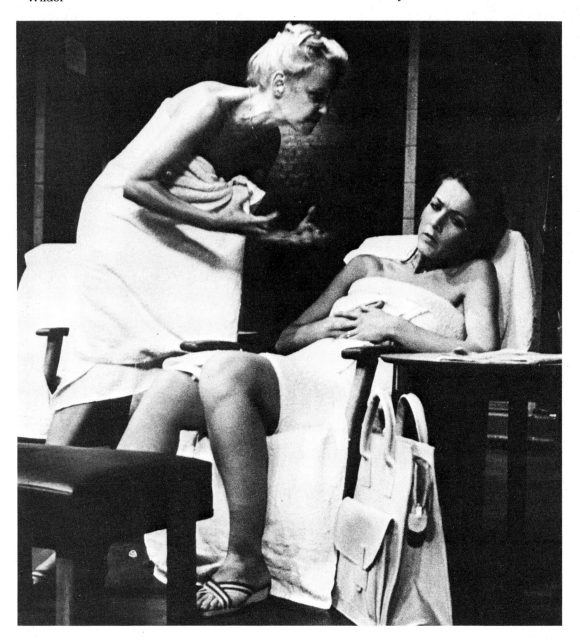

Trevor Eve and Elizabeth Quinn in 'Children of a Lesser God': a play that made a powerful case for the alternative world of the non-hearing.

The highest attendance figure for a single week of any British musical production was achieved by *The Sound of Music* at the Apollo Victoria from 26-31 October 1981. The 2600-seat theatre played to 101 per cent of seating capacity. The record was previously held by *The King and I* at the 2400-seat Palladium in 1979.

The only modern play to have been written around 2000 gallons of water is Nell Dunn's *Steaming* which opened at the Theatre Royal, Stratford East in June, 1981 and later transferred to the Comedy Theatre. Set in a Ladies Turkish Bath, it features a pool, filtered and heated by a motorised unit, that runs continuously for 21½ hours a day and that is only turned off because of noise when the play is in progress.

The only totally deaf actress to have starred in a West End play is the American Elizabeth Quinn who played the leading female role in the London production of Mark Medoff's *Children of a Lesser God* (1981). Ms Quinn won a Society of West End Theatres Award for her performance as Best Actress in a Straight Play.

The longest-established theatrical agent in the world was Nat Day (1886-1982). Having begun his stage career in variety in 1898, he went into the agency business in 1904 and stayed in it for the next 77 years. At one time he shared an office floor at Albion House, Oxford Street with Dr Crippen and booked is wife, Belle Elmore, for a number of engagements.

The record for opening and closing a door in a West End show belongs to Julie Rutherford. As stage manager of John Well's *Anyone For Denis* at the Whitehall Theatre, she had to open and close a sliding door 54 times during each performance. The show opened on 7 May, 1981 and closed on 22 May, 1982. So during 9 previews and 381 performances, Ms Rutherford opened and closed the door 20592 times. This proves that working backstage in a West End show does open doors in the theatrical profession.

The only play by a reigning Pope to have been seen on the London stage is *The Jeweller's Shop* which opened at the Westminster Theatre on May 25, 1982 three days before its author, John Paul II, arrived on a pastoral visit to Britain. Written in 1960 when he was auxiliary Bishop of Krakow, the play was written under his birth-name of Karol Wojtyla and consisted of a series of interwoven monologues about marriage. At its opening, there was much speculation about whether the play would get an audience.

Yul Brynner as the King of Siam, in 'The King and I' which played to packed houses at the Palladium.

Vanessa Redgrave as The Shrew, in 'The Taming of
The Shrew' at the Royal Shakespeare Theatre 1962.

A complete list of productions staged by the National Theatre, the Royal Shakespeare Company and the English Stage Company until the end of 1981. The directors' names are in brackets.

Royal Shakespeare Company

THE ROYAL SHAKESPEARE THEATRE, Stratford-upon-Avon

1960
The Two Gentlemen of Verona: Shakespeare (Peter Hall)
The Merchant of Venice: Shakespeare (Michael Langham)
Twelfth Night: Shakespeare (Peter Hall)
The Taming of the Shrew: Shakespeare (John Barton)
Troilus and Cressida: Shakespeare (Peter Hall and John Barton)
The Winter's Tale: Shakespeare (Peter Wood)

1961
Much Ado About Nothing: Shakespeare (Michael Langham)
Hamlet: Shakespeare (Peter Wood)
Richard III: Shakespeare (William Gaskill)
As You Like It: Shakespeare (Michael Elliott)
Romeo and Juliet: Shakespeare (Peter Hall)
Othello: Shakespeare (Franco Zeffirelli)

1962
Measure for Measure: Shakespeare (John Blatchley)
A Midsummer Night's Dream: Shakespeare (Peter Hall)
The Taming of the Shrew (revival): Shakespeare (Maurice Daniels)
Macbeth: Shakespeare (Donald McWhinnie)
Cymbeline: Shakespeare (William Gaskill)
The Comedy of Errors: Shakespeare (Clifford Williams)
King Lear: Shakespeare (Peter Brook)

1963
The Tempest: Shakespeare (Clifford Williams and Peter Brook)
Julius Caesar: Shakespeare (John Blatchley)
The Comedy of Errors (revival): Shakespeare (Clifford Williams)
Henry VI: Shakespeare (Peter Hall, John Barton and Frank Evans)
Edward IV: Shakespeare (Peter Hall, John Barton and Frank Evans)
Richard III: Shakespeare (Peter Hall, John Barton and Frank Evans)

1964
Richard II: Shakespeare (Peter Hall, John Barton and Clifford Williams)
Henry IV Parts 1 and 2: Shakespeare (Peter Hall, John Barton and Clifford Williams)
Henry V: Shakespeare (Peter Hall and John Barton)
Henry VI: Shakespeare (Peter Hall and John Barton)
Edward IV: Shakespeare (Peter Hall and John Barton)
Richard III: Shakespeare (Peter Hall and John Barton)

1965
Love's Labour's Lost: Shakespeare (John Barton)
The Jew of Malta: Marlowe (Clifford Williams)
The Merchant of Venice: Shakespeare (Clifford Williams)
The Comedy of Errors: Shakespeare (Clifford Williams)
Timon of Athens: Shakespeare (John Schlesinger)
Hamlet: Shakespeare (Peter Hall)

1966
Henry IV Parts 1 and 2: Shakespeare (John Barton, Trevor Nunn and Clifford Williams)
Hamlet: Shakespeare (Peter Hall)
Twelfth Night: Shakespeare (Clifford Williams)
Henry V: Shakespeare (John Barton and Trevor Nunn)
The Revenger's Tragedy: Cyril Tourneur (Trevor Nunn)

1967
The Taming of the Shrew: Shakespeare (Trevor Nunn)
Coriolanus: Shakespeare (John Barton)
The Revenger's Tragedy: Cyril Tourneur (Trevor Nunn)
All's Well That Ends Well: Shakespeare (John Barton)
As You Like It: Shakespeare (David Jones)

Macbeth: Shakespeare (Peter Hall)
Romeo and Juliet: Shakespeare (Karolos Koun)

1968
Julius Caesar: Shakespeare (John Barton)
King Lear: Shakespeare (Trevor Nunn)
The Merry Wives of Windsor: Shakespeare (Terry Hands)
As You Like It: Shakespeare (David Jones)
Dr Faustus: Marlowe (Clifford Williams)
Troilus and Cressida: Shakespeare (John Barton)
Much Ado About Nothing: Shakespeare (Trevor Nunn)

1969
Pericles: Shakespeare (Terry Hands)
The Merry Wives of Windsor: Shakespeare (Terry Hands)
The Winter's Tale: Shakespeare (Trevor Nunn)
Women Beware Women: Thomas Middleton (Terry Hands)
Twelfth Night: Shakespeare (John Barton)
Henry VIII: Shakespeare (Trevor Nunn)

1970
Measure for Measure: Shakespeare (John Barton)
Richard III: Shakespeare (Terry Hands)
Dr Faustus (TGR): Marlowe (Gareth Morgan)
Hamlet: Shakespeare (Trevor Nunn)
King John (TGR): Shakespeare (Buzz Goodbody)
The Two Gentlemen of Verona: Shakespeare (Robin Phillips)
A Midsummer Night's Dream: Shakespeare (Peter Brook)
The Tempest: Shakespeare (John Barton)

1971
The Merchant of Venice: Shakespeare (Terry Hands)
Twelfth Night: Shakespeare (John Barton)
Richard II (TGR): Shakespeare (John Barton)
Henry V (TGR): Shakespeare (John Barton)
Much Ado About Nothing: Shakespeare (Ronald Eyre)
The Duchess of Malfi: John Webster (Clifford Williams)
Othello: Shakespeare (John Barton)

1972
Coriolanus: Shakespeare (Trevor Nunn)
Julius Caesar: Shakespeare (Trevor Nunn)
The Comedy of Errors: Shakespeare (Clifford Williams)
Antony and Cleopatra: Shakespeare (Trevor Nunn)
Titus Andronicus: Shakespeare (Trevor Nunn)

1973
Romeo and Juliet: Shakespeare (Terry Hands)
Richard II: Shakespeare (John Barton)
As You Like It: Shakespeare (Buzz Goodbody)
Love's Labour's Lost: Shakespeare (David Jones)
The Taming of the Shrew: Shakespeare (Clifford Williams)

1974
King John: Shakespeare (John Barton)
Richard II: Shakespeare (John Barton)
Cymbeline: Shakespeare (John Barton)
Twelfth Night: Shakespeare (Peter Gill)
Measure For Measure: Shakespeare (Keith Hack)
Macbeth: Shakespeare (Trevor Nunn)

1975
Henry V: Shakespeare (Terry Hands)
Henry IV Part 1: Shakespeare (Terry Hands)
Henry IV Part 2: Shakespeare (Terry Hands)
The Merry Wives of Windsor: Shakespeare (Terry Hands)

1976
Romeo and Juliet: Shakespeare (Trevor Nunn)
Much Ado About Nothing: Shakespeare (John Barton)
The Winter's Tale: Shakespeare (John Barton and Trevor Nunn)
Troilus and Cressida: Shakespeare (John Barton and Barry Kyle)
The Comedy of Errors: Shakespeare (Trevor Nunn)
King Lear: Shakespeare (John Barton, Barry Kyle and Trevor Nunn)

1977
Macbeth: Shakespeare (Trevor Nunn)
A Midsummer Night's Dream: Shakespeare (John Barton and Gillian Lynne)
Henry VI Part 1: Shakespeare (Terry Hands)
Henry VI Part 2: Shakespeare (Terry Hands)
Henry VI Part 3: Shakespeare (Terry Hands)
Henry V: Shakespeare (Terry Hands)
As You Like It: Shakespeare (Trevor Nunn)
Coriolanus: Shakespeare (Terry Hands)

1978
The Tempest: Shakespeare (Clifford Williams)
The Taming of the Shrew: Shakespeare (Michael Bogdanov)
Measure For Measure: Shakespeare (Barry Kyle)
Love's Labour's Lost: Shakespeare (John Barton)
Antony and Cleopatra: Shakespeare (Peter Brook)

1979
The Merry Wives of Windsor: Shakespeare (Trevor Nunn and John Caird)
Cymbeline: Shakespeare (David Jones)
Twelfth Night: Shakespeare (Terry Hands)
Othello: Shakespeare (Ronald Eyre)
Julius Caesar: Shakespeare (Barry Kyle)

1980
As You Like It: Shakespeare (Terry Hands)
Romeo and Juliet: Shakespeare (Ron Daniels)
Hamlet: Shakespeare (John Barton)

Richard II: Shakespeare (Terry Hands)
Richard III: Shakespeare (Terry Hands)
The Swan Down Gloves: Bille Brown and Nigel Hess (Ian Judge)

1981
The Winter's Tale: Shakespeare (Ronald Eyre)
A Midsummer Night's Dream: Shakespeare (Ron Daniels)
Titus Andronicus with The Two Gentlemen of Verona: Shakespeare (John Barton)
All's Well That Ends Well: Shakespeare (Trevor Nunn)

THE ALDWYCH THEATRE
London

1960
The Duchess of Malfi: John Webster (Donald McWhinnie)
Twelfth Night: Shakespeare (Peter Hall)

1961
Ondine: Jean Giraudoux (Peter Hall)
The Devils: John Whiting (Peter Wood)
The Hollow Crown: (John Barton)
Becket: Jean Anouilh (Peter Hall)
The Taming of the Shrew (revival): Shakespeare (M. Daniels)
The Cherry Orchard: Anton Chekhov (Michel St-Denis)

1962
As You Like It: Shakespeare (Michael Elliott)
The Art of Seduction: De Laclos (John Barton)
The Caucasian Chalk Circle: Bertolt Brecht (William Gaskill)
The Collection: Harold Pinter (Peter Hall and Harold Pinter)
Playing With Fire: August Strindberg (John Blatchley)
A Penny for a Song: John Whiting (Colin Graham)
Curtmantle: Christopher Fry (Stuart Burge)
Troilus and Cressida: Shakespeare (Peter Hall)
The Devils: John Whiting (Peter Wood)
King Lear: Shakespeare (Peter Brook)
The Comedy of Errors: Shakespeare (Clifford Williams)

Arts Theatre Season
Everything in the Garden: Giles Cooper (Donald McWhinnie)
Nil Carborundum: Henry Livings (Anthony Page)
The Lower Depths: Maxim Gorki (Toby Robertson)
Afore Night Come: David Rudkin (Clifford Williams)
Women Beware Women: Thomas Middleton (Anthony Page)
Empire Builders: Boris Vian (David Jones)
Infanticide . . .: Fred Watson (William Gaskill)

1963
The Physicists: Friedrich Durrenmatt (Peter Brook)
King Lear (revival): Shakespeare (Peter Brook)
A Midsummer Night's Dream: Shakespeare (Peter Hall)
The Beggar's Opera: John Gay (Peter Wood)
The Representative: Rolf Hochhuth (Clifford Williams)
The Comedy of Errors: Shakespeare (Clifford Williams)

1964
The Wars of the Roses
Henry VI: Shakespeare (Peter Hall)
Edward IV: Shakespeare (Peter Hall)
Richard III: Shakespeare (Peter Hall)

The Rebel: Patrick Garland (Patrick Garland)
The Birthday Party: Harold Pinter (Harold Pinter)
Afore Night Come: David Rudkin (Clifford Williams)

Expeditions One
The Pedagogue: James Saunders (Robin Midgley)
The Keyhole: Jean Tardieu (Garry O'Connor)
Act Without Words: Samuel Beckett (Elsa Bolam)
Picnic on the Battlefield: Fernando Arrabal (Robin Midgley)
No Why: John Whiting (John Schlesinger)

Endgame: Samuel Beckett (Donald McWhinnie)
Victor: Roger Vitrac (Robin Midgley)
Marat/Sade: Peter Weiss (Peter Brook)
The Jew of Malta: Christopher Marlowe (Clifford Williams)
Eh?: Henry Livings (Peter Hall)
The Merry Wives of Windsor: Shakespeare (John Blatchley)

1965
The Comedy of Errors: Shakespeare (Clifford Williams)

Expeditions Two (Trevor Nunn and David Jones)
Don't Make Me Laugh: Charles Wood
If There Weren't Any Blacks They'd Have to Invent Them: Johnny Speight
The Wideawakes: Irene Coates
The Governor's Lady: David Mercer

Henry V: Shakespeare (John Barton and Trevor Nunn)
The Homecoming: Harold Pinter (Peter Hall)
Puntila: Bertolt Brecht (Michel St-Denis)
Marat/Sade (revival): Peter Weiss (Peter Brook)
The Thwarting of Baron Bolligrew: Robert Bolt (Trevor Nunn)
Hamlet: Shakespeare (Peter Hall)

1966
The Government Inspector: Nikolai Gogol (Peter Hall)
The Investigation: Peter Weiss (Peter Brook and David Jones)

Tango: Slawomir Mrozek (Trevor Nunn)
Days in the Trees: Marguerite Duras (John Schlesinger)
The Meteor: Friedrich Durrenmatt (Clifford Williams)
US: (Peter Brook)
Staircase: Charles Dyer (Peter Hall)
Belcher's Luck: David Mercer (David Jones)
The Homecoming: Harold Pinter (Peter Hall)
The Thwarting of Baron Bolligrew: Robert Bolt (Trevor Nunn)

1967
Ghosts: Henrik Ibsen (Alan Bridges)
Little Murders: Jules Feiffer (Christopher Morahan)
As You Like It: Shakespeare (David Jones)
The Taming of the Shrew: Shakespeare (Trevor Nunn)
The Relapse: John Vanbrugh (Trevor Nunn)
The Criminals: Jose Triana (Terry Hands)

1968
Macbeth: Shakespeare (Peter Hall)
All's Well That Ends Well: Shakespeare (John Barton)
Under Milk Wood (TGR): Dylan Thomas (Terry Hands)
Indians: Arthur Kopit (Jack Gelber)
The Merry Wives of Windsor: Shakespeare (Terry Hands)
The Relapse: Sir John Vanbrugh (Trevor Nunn)
The Latent Heterosexual: Paddy Chayevsky (Terry Hands)
God Bless: Jules Feiffer (Geoffrey Reeves)
Julius Caesar: Shakespeare (John Barton)

1969
A Delicate Balance: Edward Albee (Peter Hall)
Dutch Uncle: Simon Gray (Peter Hall)
Troilus and Cressida: Shakespeare (John Barton)
Landscape and Silence: Harold Pinter (Peter Hall)
Much Ado About Nothing: Shakespeare (Trevor Nunn)
The Silver Tassie: Sean O'Casey (David Jones)
Bartholomew Fair: Ben Jonson (Terry Hands)
The Revenger's Tragedy: Cyril Tourneur (Trevor Nunn)

1970
Tiny Alice: Edward Albee (Robin Phillips)
After Haggerty: David Mercer (David Jones)
London Assurance: Dion Boucicault (Ronald Eyre)
The Winter's Tale: Shakespeare (Trevor Nunn)
The Plebeians: Gunter Grass (David Jones)
Twelfth Night: Shakespeare (John Barton)
Major Barbara: Bernard Shaw (Clifford Williams)
Henry VIII: Shakespeare (Trevor Nunn)
Two Gentlemen of Verona: Shakespeare (Robin Phillips)

The Round House Season
When Thou Art King: (John Barton)
Arden of Faversham: Anon. (Buzz Goodbody)
King John: Shakespeare (Buzz Goodbody)
Dr. Faustus: Marlowe (Gareth Morgan)

1971
Old Times: Harold Pinter (Peter Hall)
A Midsummer Night's Dream: Shakespeare (Peter Brook)
Enemies: Maxim Gorky (David Jones)
The Man of Mode: George Etherege (Terry Hands)
Exiles: James Joyce (Harold Pinter)
The Balcony: Jean Genet (Terry Hands)
Much Ado About Nothing: Shakespeare (Ronald Eyre)

The Place Season
Occupations: Trevor Griffiths (Buzz Goodbody)
Subject to Fits: Robert Montgomery (A. J. Antoon)
Miss Julie: August Strindberg (Robin Phillips)

1972
All Over: Edward Albee (Peter Hall)
The Merchant of Venice: Shakespeare (Terry Hands)
The Lower Depths: Maxim Gorky (David Jones)
Othello: Shakespeare (John Barton)
Murder in the Cathedral: T. S. Eliot (Terry Hands)
The Island of the Mighty: John Arden/Margaretta D'Arcy (David Jones)

1973
The Romans
Antony and Cleopatra: Shakespeare (Trevor Nunn)
Julius Caesar: Shakespeare (Trevor Nunn)
Titus Andronicus: Shakespeare (Trevor Nunn)
Coriolanus: Shakespeare (Trevor Nunn)

Landscape/A Slight Ache: Harold Pinter (Peter Hall and Peter James)

The Place Season
Cries from Casement: David Rudkin (Terry Hands)
Section Nine: Philip Magdalany (Charles Marowitz)
Hello and Goodbye: Athol Fugard (Peter Stevenson)
Sylvia Plath: (Barry Kyle)
A Lesson In Blood and Roses: John Wiles (Clifford Williams)

1974
Sherlock Holmes: Arthur Conan Doyle/Gillette (Frank Dunlop)
Section Nine: Philip Magdalany (Charles Marowitz)
Duck Song: David Mercer (David Jones)
The Bewitched: Peter Barnes (Terry Hands)
Travesties: Tom Stoppard (Peter Wood)
Summerfolk: Maxim Gorky (David Jones)
Dr. Faustus: Marlowe (John Barton)
Richard II: Shakespeare (John Barton)
The Marquis of Keith: Frank Wedekind (Ronald Eyre)
Cymbeline: Shakespeare (Barry Kyle, John Barton, and Clifford Williams)

Above: Royal Shakespeare Company production of 'As You like It' 1961 starring Vanessa Redgrave as Rosalind.

Below: Peter Brookes' 'The Dream' at the Royal Shakespeare Theatre, Stratford-upon-Avon, 1970.

The Place Season
Comrades: August Strindberg (Barry Kyle)
The Can Opener: Victor Lanoux (Walter Donohue)
Lear: Shakespeare (Buzz Goodbody)
The Beast: Snoo Wilson (Howard Davies)

1975
King John: Shakespeare (John Barton)
Twelfth Night: Shakespeare (Peter Gill)
Macbeth: Shakespeare (Trevor Nunn)
Midwinter Spring: Nicol Williamson one-man show
Love's Labour's Lost: Shakespeare (David Jones)
Travesties: Tom Stoppard (Peter Wood)
Hedda Gabler: Henrik Ibsen (Trevor Nunn)
Dingo: Charles Wood (Richard Eyre)
The Marrying of Ann Leete: Granville Barker (David
    Jones)
Too True to be Good: Bernard Shaw (Clifford Williams)
Return of A. J. Raffles: Graham Greene (David Jones)

1976
Henry V: Shakespeare (Terry Hands)
Henry IV Part 1: Shakespeare (Terry Hands)
Henry IV Part 2: Shakespeare (Terry Hands)
The Merry Wives of Windsor: Shakespeare (Terry
    Hands)
The Zykovs: Maxim Gorky (David Jones)
The Iceman Cometh: Eugene O'Neill (Howard Davies)
The Devil's Disciple: Bernard Shaw (Jack Gold)
Ivanov: Anton Chekhov (David Jones)
Old World: Aleksei Arbuzov (Terry Hands)
Wild Oats: John O'Keeffe (Clifford Williams)

1977
Privates on Parade: Peter Nichols (Michael Blakemore)
King Lear: Shakespeare (Trevor Nunn)
Destiny: David Edgar (Ron Daniels)
The Comedy of Errors: Shakespeare (Trevor Nunn)
A Midsummer Night's Dream: Shakespeare (John
    Barton)
Much Ado About Nothing: Shakespeare (John Barton)
Romeo and Juliet: Shakespeare (Trevor Nunn)
Pillars of the Community: Henrik Ibsen (John Barton)
Troilus and Cressida: Shakespeare (Barry Kyle)
The Days of the Commune: Bertolt Brecht (Howard
    Davies)
The Alchemist: Ben Jonson (Trevor Nunn)

1978
The Way of the World: William Congreve (John Barton)
Henry V: Shakespeare (Terry Hands)
Henry VI Part 1: Shakespeare (Terry Hands)
Henry VI Part 2: Shakespeare (Terry Hands)
Henry VI Part 3: Shakespeare (Terry Hands)
Coriolanus: Shakespeare (Terry Hands)
The Dance of Death: August Strindberg (John Caird)

Women Pirates: Steve Gooch (Ron Daniels)
As You Like It: Shakespeare (Trevor Nunn and John
    Caird)
Cousin Vladimir: David Mercer (Jane Howell)
The Changeling: Thomas Middleton (Terry Hands)
Saratoga: Bronson Howard (Ronald Eyre)

1979
Love's Labour's Lost: Shakespeare (John Barton)
The Taming of the Shrew: Shakespeare (Michael
    Bogdanov)
The White Guard: Mikhail Bulgakov (Barry Kyle)
Wild Oats (revival): John O'Keeffe (Clifford Williams)
Antony and Cleopatra: Shakespeare (Peter Brook)
Once in a Lifetime: Kaufman and Hart (Trevor Nunn)
Children of the Sun: Maxim Gorki (Terry Hands)
Measure for Measure: Shakespeare (Barry Kyle)
Piaf: Pam Gems (Howard Davies)

1980
The Greeks: Euripides etc (John Barton)
Twelfth Night: Shakespeare (Terry Hands)
The Merry Wives of Windsor: Shakespeare (Trevor
    Nunn and John Caird)
Nicholas Nickleby: Dickens/Edgar (Trevor Nunn and
    John Caird)
Othello: Shakespeare (Ronald Eyre)
Juno and the Paycock: Sean O'Casey (Trevor Nunn)
Nicholas Nickleby (revival): Dickens/Edgar (Trevor
    Nunn and John Caird)

1981
Passion Play: Peter Nichols (Mike Ockrent)
The Suicide: Nikolai Erdman (Ron Daniels)
The Knight of the Burning Pestle: Beaumont and
    Fletcher (Michael Bogdanov)
Nicholas Nickleby: Dickens/Edgar (Trevor Nunn and
    John Caird)
Troilus and Cressida: Shakespeare (Terry Hands)
The Merchant of Venice: Shakespeare (John Barton)
As You Like It: Shakespeare (Terry Hands)
Love Girl and the Innocent: Alexander Solzhenitsyn
    (Clifford Williams)
Hamlet: Shakespeare (John Barton)
Romeo and Juliet: Shakespeare (Ron Daniels)
Richard II: Shakespeare (Terry Hands)
Richard III: Shakespeare (Terry Hands)
The Swan Down Gloves: Bille Brown and Nigel Hess
    (Ian Judge)

THE OTHER PLACE, Stratford-upon-Avon

1974
King Lear: Shakespeare (Buzz Goodbody)
I Was Shakespeare's Double: John Downie (Howard
    Davies)

Babies Grow Old: Mike Leigh (Mike Leigh)

The Tempest: Shakespeare (Keith Hack)

Afore Night Come: David Rudkin (Ron Daniels)

Uncle Vanya: Anton Chekhov (Nicol Williamson)

1975

Hamlet: Shakespeare (Buzz Goodbody)

The Mouth Organ: Ralph Koltai and Clifford Williams

Perkin Warbeck: John Ford (Barry Kyle and John Barton)

Man Is Man: Bertolt Brecht (Howard Davies)

Richard III: Shakespeare (Barry Kyle)

1976

Schweyk in the Second World War: Bertolt Brecht (Howard Davies)

Dingo: Charles Wood (Barry Kyle)

Macbeth: Shakespeare (Trevor Nunn)

Destiny: David Edgar (Ron Daniels)

Bingo: Edward Bond (Howard Davies)

1977

The Alchemist: Ben Jonson (Trevor Nunn)

'Tis Pity She's a Whore: John Ford (Ron Daniels)

The Lorenzaccio Story: Paul Thompson (Ron Daniels)

Queen Christina: Pam Gems (Penny Cherns)

The Sons of Light: David Rudkin (Ron Daniels)

1978

Dance of Death: August Strindberg (John Caird)

The Merchant of Venice: Shakespeare (John Barton)

Captain Swing: Peter Whelan (Bill Alexander)

The Churchill Play: Howard Brenton (Barry Kyle)

Piaf: Pam Gems (Howard Davies)

The Judgement on Hippolytus: David Rudkin/Euripides (Ron Daniels)

The Shepherds' Play: Compiled and arranged by John Barton

1979

Pericles: Shakespeare (Ron Daniels)

The Jail Diary of Albie Sachs: David Edgar (Howard Davies)

The Suicide: Nikolai Erdman (Ron Daniels)

Baal: Bertolt Brecht (David Jones)

Anna Christie: Eugene O'Neill (Jonathan Lynn)

Three Sisters: Anton Chekhov (Trevor Nunn)

1980

The Shadow of a Gunman: Sean O'Casey (Michael Bogdanov)

The Maid's Tragedy: Beaumont and Fletcher (Barry Kyle)

The Fool: Edward Bond (Howard Davies)

Timon of Athens: Shakespeare (Ron Daniels)

Hansel and Gretel: David Rudkin (Ron Daniels)

1981

The Twin Rivals: George Farquhar (John Caird)

A Doll's House: Henrik Ibsen (Adrian Noble)

The Witch of Edmonton: Dekker, Ford and Rowley (Barry Kyle)

Money: Edward Bulwer-Lytton (Bill Alexander)

Our Friends in the North: Peter Flannery (John Caird)

THE WAREHOUSE, London

1977

Schweyk in the Second World War: Bertolt Brecht (Howard Davies)

Macbeth: Shakespeare (Trevor Nunn)

That Good Between Us: Howard Barker (Barry Kyle)

Bandits: C. P. Taylor (Howard Davies)

Bingo: Edward Bond (Howard Davies)

Factory Birds: James Robson (Bill Alexander)

The Bundle: Edward Bond (Howard Davies)

Frozen Assets: Barrie Keeffe (Barry Kyle)

1978

Dingo: Charles Wood (Barry Kyle)

The Lorenzaccio Story: Paul Thompson (Ron Daniels)

The Dance of Death: August Strindberg (John Caird)

'Tis Pity She's a Whore: John Ford (Ron Daniels)

The Sons of Light: David Rudkin (Ron Daniels)

The Jail Diary of Albie Sachs: David Edgar (Howard Davies)

Savage Amusement: Peter Flannery (John Caird)

A and R: Pete Atkin (Walter Donohue)

Shout Across the River: Stephen Poliakoff (Bill Alexander)

Look Out . . . Here Comes Trouble!: Mary O'Malley (John Caird)

The Hang of the Gaol: Howard Barker (Bill Alexander)

Kids' Christmas Show: Peter Flannery and John Ford (Howard Davies and John Caird)

1979

The Churchill Play: Howard Brenton (Barry Kyle)

The Merchant of Venice: Shakespeare (John Barton)

The Innocent: Tom McGrath (Howard Davies)

Piaf: Pam Gems (Howard Davies)

The Judgement on Hippolytus: David Rudkin (Ron Daniels)

Sore Throats: Howard Brenton (Barry Kyle)

Men's Beano: Nigel Baldwin (Bill Alexander)

Captain Swing: Peter Whelan (Bill Alexander)

1980

Much Ado About Nothing: Shakespeare (Howard Davies)

Bastard Angel: Barrie Keeffe (Bill Alexander)

The Caucasian Chalk Circle: Bertolt Brecht (John Caird)

The Loud Boy's Life: Howard Barker (Howard Davies)

Above: The National Theatre production of Bernard Pomerance's 'The Elephant Man' starring from left to right, Karina Knight, Heather Tobias and David Schofield.

Below: Edward Bonds' 'The Woman' at the National Theatre 1981. From left to right: Yvonne Bryceland, Paul Freeman and Nicky Henson.

The Three Sisters: Anton Chekhov (Trevor Nunn)
Pericles: Shakespeare (Ron Daniels)
Anna Christie: Eugene O'Neill (Jonathan Lynn)
Educating Rita: Willy Russell (Mike Ockrent)
The Suicide: Nikolai Erdman (Ron Daniels)
Baal: Bertolt Brecht (David Jones)
No Limits to Love: David Mercer (Howard Davies)
The Irish Play: Ron Hutchinson (Barry Kyle)
Television Times: Peter Prince (Stephen Frears)

1981
Naked Robots: Jonathan Gems (John Caird)

The Accrington Pals: Peter Whelan (Bill Alexander)
Outskirts: Hanif Kureishi (Howard Davies)
Thirteenth Night: Howard Brenton (Barry Kyle)
The Forest: Alexander Ostrovsky (Adrian Noble)
The Shadow of a Gunman: Sean O'Casey (Michael Bogdanov)
Good: C. P. Taylor (Howard Davies)
The Fool: Edward Bond (Howard Davies)
The Maid's Tragedy: Beaumont and Fletcher (Barry Kyle)
Timon of Athens: Shakespeare (Ron Daniels)
Hansel and Gretel: David Rudkin (Ron Daniels)

The National Theatre

THE OLD VIC

1963
Hamlet: Shakespeare (Laurence Olivier)
Saint Joan: Bernard Shaw (John Dexter)
Uncle Vanya: Anton Chekhov (Laurence Olivier)
The Recruiting Officer: George Farquhar (William Gaskill)

1964
Hobson's Choice: Harold Brighouse (John Dexter)
Andorra: Max Frisch (Lindsay Anderson)
Play: Samuel Beckett (George Devine)
Philoctetes: Sophocles (William Gaskill)
Othello: Shakespeare (John Dexter)
The Master Builder: Henrik Ibsen (Peter Wood)
The Dutch Courtesan: John Marston (William Gaskill)
Hay Fever: Noel Coward (Noel Coward)
The Royal Hunt of the Sun: Peter Shaffer (John Dexter)

1965
The Crucible: Arthur Miller (Laurence Olivier)
Much Ado About Nothing: Shakespeare (Zeffirelli)
Mother Courage: Bertolt Brecht (William Gaskill)
Armstrong's Last Goodnight: John Arden (Gaskill and Dexter)
Trelawny of the Wells: Arthur Pinero (Desmond O'Donovan)
Love For Love: William Congreve (Peter Wood)

1966
A Flea in Her Ear: Georges Feydeau (Jacques Charon)
Miss Julie: August Strindberg (Michael Elliott)
Black Comedy: Peter Shaffer (John Dexter)
Juno and the Paycock: Sean O'Casey (Laurence Olivier)
A Bond Honoured: Lope de Vega (John Dexter)
The Storm: Alexander Ostrovsky (John Dexter)

1967
The Dance of Death: August Strindberg (Glen Byam Shaw)
Rosencrantz and Guildenstern Are Dead: Tom Stoppard (Derek Goldby)
The Three Sisters: Anton Chekhov (Laurence Olivier)
As You Like It: Shakespeare (Clifford Williams)
Tartuffe: Molière (Tyrone Guthrie)

1968
Volpone: Ben Jonson (Tyrone Guthrie)
Edward II: Bertolt Brecht (Frank Dunlop)
Oedipus: Seneca (Peter Brook)
The Advertisement: Natalia Ginzburg (Donald McKechnie)
Home and Beauty: Somerset Maugham (Frank Dunlop)
Love's Labour's Lost: Shakespeare (Laurence Olivier)

1969
H: Charles Wood (Geoffrey Reeves)
The Way of the World: William Congreve (Peter Wood)
Macrune's Guevara: John Spurling (Frank Dunlop)
Rites: Maureen Duffy (Joan Plowright)
Back to Methuselah: Bernard Shaw (Clifford Williams)
The National Health: Peter Nichols (Michael Blakemore)
The White Devil: John Webster (Frank Dunlop)
The Travails of Sancho Panza: James Saunders (Joan Plowright)

1970
The Beaux' Stratagem: George Farquhar (William Gaskill)
The Merchant of Venice: Shakespeare (Jonathan Miller)
Hedda Gabler: Henrik Ibsen (Ingmar Bergman)
The Idiot: Simon Gray (Anthony Quayle)

Cyrano de Bergerac: Edmond Rostand (Patrick Garland)

Mrs Warren's Profession: Bernard Shaw (Ronald Eyre)

1971

The Architect and the Emperor of Assyria: Fernando Arrabal — translated by Jean Benedetti (Victor Garcia)

The Captain of Kopenick: Carl Zuckmayer — adapted by John Mortimer (Frank Dunlop)

A Woman Killed with Kindness: Thomas Heywood (John Dexter)

Coriolanus: Shakespeare (Manfred Wekwerth and Joachim Tenschert)

The Good-Natured Man: Oliver Goldsmith (John Dexter

NEW THEATRE

The Rules of the Game — Luigi Pirandello — version by David Hare and Robert Rietty (Anthony Page)

Amphitryon 38: Jean Giraudoux (Laurence Olivier)

Tyger: Adrian Mitchell (Michael Blakemore and John Dexter)

Danton's Death: George Buchner — adapted by Jonathan Wells (Jonathan Miller)

Long Day's Journey Into Night: Eugene O'Neill (Michael Blakemore)

1972

Jumpers: Tom Stoppard (Peter Wood)

Richard II: Shakespeare (David William)

The School for Scandal: Richard Brinsley Sheridan (Jonathan Miller)

The Front Page: Ben Hecht and Charles MacArthur (Michael Blakemore)

Macbeth: Shakespeare (Michael Blakemore)

1973

The Misanthrope: Molière — version by Tony Harrison (John Dexter)

The Cherry Orchard: Anton Chekhov — translated by Ronald Hingley (Michael Blakemore)

Equus: Peter Shaffer (John Dexter)

The Bacchae: Euripides — adapted by Wole Soyinka (Roland Joffe)

Saturday Sunday Monday: Eduardo De Filippo — adapted by Keith Waterhouse and Willis Hall (Franco Zeffirelli)

The Party: Trevor Griffiths (John Dexter)

1974

The Tempest: Shakespeare (Peter Hall)

Eden End: J. B. Priestley (Laurence Olivier)

Next of Kin: John Hopkins (Harold Pinter)

Spring Awakening: Frank Wedekind — translated by Edward Bond (Bill Bryden)

The Marriage of Figaro: Pierre-Augustin de Beaumarchais — translated by John Wells (Jonathan Miller)

The Freeway: Peter Nichols (Jonathan Miller)

The Party: Trevor Griffiths (David Hare)

Grand Manoeuvres: A. E. Ellis (Michael Blakemore)

1975

Happy Days: Samuel Beckett (Peter Hall)

John Gabriel Borkman: Henrik Ibsen — translated by Inga-Stina Ewbank (Peter Hall)

Heartbreak House: Bernard Shaw (John Schlesinger)

No Man's Land: Harold Pinter (Peter Hall)

The Misanthrope: Molière — translated by Tony Harrison (John Dexter)

Engaged: W. S. Gilbert (Michael Blakemore)

Phaedra Britannica: Tony Harrison — after Jean Racine (John Dexter)

Comedians: Trevor Griffiths (Richard Eyre)

The Playboy of the Western World: J. M. Synge (Bill Bryden)

Hamlet: Shakespeare (Peter Hall)

Judgement: Barry Collins (Peter Hall)

1976

Plunder: Ben Travers (Michael Blakemore)

Watch It Come Down: John Osborne (Bill Bryden)

Move from Old Vic to new NATIONAL THEATRE on the South Bank

1976

Hamlet: Shakespeare (Peter Hall)

John Gabriel Borkman: Henrik Ibsen — version by Inga-Stina Ewbank and Peter Hall (Peter Hall)

Plunder: Ben Travers (Michael Blakemore)

Happy Days: Samuel Beckett (Peter Hall)

Watch It Come Down: John Osborne (Bill Bryden)

No Man's Land: Harold Pinter (Peter Hall)

Equus: Peter Shaffer (John Dexter)

Playboy of the Western World: J. M. Synge (Bill Bryden)

Blithe Spirit: Noel Coward (Harold Pinter)

Weapons of Happiness: Howard Brenton (David Hare)

Jumpers: Tom Stoppard (Peter Wood)

Tamburlaine the Great: Christopher Marlowe (Peter Hall)

Playboy of the Western World: J. M. Synge (Bill Bryden)

Il Campiello: Carlo Goldoni — version by Susanna Graham-Jones and Bill Bryden (Bill Bryden)

Royal opening of National Theatre 25 October 1976

The Force of Habit: Thomas Bernhard — translated by Neville and Stephen Plaice (Elijah Moshinsky)

Counting the Ways: Edward Albee (Bill Bryden)

1977

No Man's Land: Harold Pinter (Peter Hall)

Counting the Ways: Edward Albee (Bill Bryden)

Tales from the Vienna Woods: Odön von Horvath — translated by Christopher Hampton (Maximilian Schell)

Blithe Spirit: Noel Coward (Harold Pinter)

Bedroom Farce: Alan Ayckbourn (Alan Ayckbourn and Peter Hall)

Julius Caesar: Shakespeare (John Schlesinger)

Strawberry Fields: Stephen Poliakoff (Michael Apted)

The Passion: from York Mystery Plays — version by the company and Tony Harrison (Bill Bryden and Sebastian Graham-Jones)

Volpone: Ben Jonson (Peter Hall)

State of Revolution: Robert Bolt (Christopher Morahan)

Four to One: Gawn Grainger (Sebastian Graham-Jones)

To Those Born Later: Bertolt Brecht (Michael Kustow)

Old Movies: Bill Bryden (Bill Bryden)

The Madras House: Harley Granville-Barker (William Gaskill)

Bow Down: Tony Harrison — writer Harrison Birtwistle — music (Walter Donohue)

The Camilla Ringbinder Show: Trevor Ray/Richard Mangan (Sebastian Graham-Jones)

Judgement: Barry Collins (John Russell Brown)

Sir Is Winning: Shane Connaughton (Christopher Morahan)

The Plough and the Stars: Sean O'Casey (Bill Bryden)

The Passion: from the York Mystery Plays — version by the company and Tony Harrison (Bill Bryden and Sebastian Graham-Jones)

The Lady from Maxim's: Georges Feydeau — translated by John Mortimer (Christopher Morahan)

Lavender Blue: John Mackendrick (Sebastian Graham-Jones)

Half-Life: Julian Mitchell (Waris Hussein)

The Country Wife: William Wycherley (Peter Hall with Stewart Trotter)

Sir Gawain and the Green Knight: adapted by Peter Stevens — translated by Brian Stone (Michael Bogdanov)

The Hunchback of Notre Dame: Victor Hugo — adapted by Ken Hill (Michael Bogdanov)

1978

The Guardsman: Ferenc Molnar — version by Frank Marcus (Peter Wood)

The Cherry Orchard: Anton Chekhov — translated by Michael Frayn (Peter Hall)

Love Letters on Blue Paper: Arnold Wesker (Arnold Wesker)

Lark Rise: Keith Dewhurst — from Flora Thompson's book (Bill Bryden and Sebastian Graham-Jones)

Plenty: David Hare (David Hare)

Don Juan Comes Back From the War: Odön von Horvath — translated by Christopher Hampton (Stewart Trotter)

Brand: Henrik Ibsen — translated by Geoffrey Hill (Christopher Morahan)

Lost Worlds: Wilson John Haire (Robert Kidd)

Plunder: Ben Travers (Michael Blakemore)

Macbeth: Shakespeare (Peter Hall with John Russell Brown)

American Buffalo: David Mamet (Bill Bryden)

The Woman: Edward Bond (Edward Bond)

The Passion: York Mystery Plays — version by the company with Tom Harrison (Bill Bryden and Sebastian Graham-Jones)

Lark Rise: Keith Dewhurst — from Flora Thompson's book (Bill Bryden and Sebastian Graham Jones)

The Philanderer: Bernard Shaw (Christopher Morahan)

The Double Dealer: William Congreve (Peter Wood)

American Buffalo: David Mamet (Bill Bryden)

The World Turned Upside Down: Keith Dewhurst — from Christopher Hill's book (Bill Bryden and Sebastian Graham-Jones)

Betrayal: Harold Pinter (Peter Hall)

Has 'Washington' Legs?: Charles Wood (Geoffrey Reeves)

Strife: John Galsworthy (Christopher Morahan)

Herod: Paul Mills (Sebastian Graham-Jones)

A Fair Quarrel: Thomas Middleton and William Rowley (William Gaskill)

The Long Voyage Home: Eugene O'Neill (Bill Bryden)

The Fruits of Enlightenment: Leo Tolstoy — translated by Michael Frayn (Christopher Morahan)

1979

For Services Rendered: Somerset Maugham (Michael Rudman)

Lark Rise: Keith Dewhurst — from Flora Thompson's book (Bill Bryden and Sebastian Graham-Jones)

Close of Play: Simon Gray (Harold Pinter)

Dispatches: from Michael Herr's book — adapted by Bill Bryden and the company (Bill Bryden)

Undiscovered Country: Arthur Schnitzler — version by Tom Stoppard (Peter Wood)

As You Like It: Shakespeare (John Dexter)

Wings: Arthur Kopit (John Madden)

Death of a Salesman: Arthur Miller (Michael Rudman)

Richard III: Shakespeare (Christopher Morahan)

Amadeus: Peter Shaffer (Peter Hall)

Lark Rise Candleford: Keith Dewhurst — from Flora Thompson's book (Bill Bryden and Sebastian Graham-Jones)

When We Are Married: J. B. Priestley (Robin Lefevre)

The Wild Duck: Henrik Ibsen (Christopher Morahan)

1980

The Long Voyage Home: Eugene O'Neill (Bill Bryden)

Hughie: Eugene O'Neill (Bill Bryden)

Thee and Me: Philip Martin (Michael Rudman)

The Iceman Cometh: Eugene O'Neill (Bill Bryden)

Othello: Shakespeare (Peter Hall)

Early Days: David Storey (Lindsay Anderson)

The Browning Version and *Harlequinade:* Terence Rattigan (Michael Rudman)

Sisterly Feelings: Alan Ayckbourn (Alan Ayckbourn and Christopher Morahan)

The Elephant Man: Bernard Pomerance (Roland Rees)

The Life of Galileo: Bertolt Brecht — translated by Howard Brenton (John Dexter)

Line 'Em: Nigel Williams (Christopher Morahan)

Watch on the Rhine: Lillian Hellman (Mike Ockrent)

The Passion Part One *Creation to Nativity:* (Bill Bryden)

The Passion Part Two *Baptism to Judgement:* Bill Bryden and Sebastian Graham-Jones)

The Romans in Britain: Howard Brenton (Michael Bogdanov

The Provok'd Wife: Sir John Vanbrugh (Peter Wood)

The Crucible: Arthur Miller (Bill Bryden)

The Caretaker: Harold Pinter (Kenneth Ives)

Hiawatha: Longfellow — adapted by Michael Bogdanov (Michael Bogdanov)

Early Days: David Storey (Lindsay Anderson)

The Nativity Part One of *The Passion:* (Bill Bryden)

1981

Man and Superman: Bernard Shaw (Christopher Morahan)

The Ticket-of-Leave Man: Tom Taylor (Piers Haggard)

A Month in the Country: Ivan Turgenev T: Isaiah Berlin (Peter Gill)

The Crucible: Arthur Miller (Bill Bryden)

Don Juan: Molière — translated by John Fowles (Peter Gill)

Measure for Measure: Shakespeare (Michael Rudman)

Serjeant Musgrave's Dance: John Arden (John Burgess)

The Shoemakers' Holiday: Thomas Dekker (John Dexter)

One Woman Plays: Dario Fo and Franca Rame — version by Olwen Wymark (Michael Bogdanov)

Who's Afraid of Virginia Woolf?: Edward Albee (Nancy Meckler)

The Mayor of Zalamea: Pedro Calderon de la Barca (Michael Bogdanov)

Translations: Brian Friel (Donald McWhinnie)

Much Ado About Nothing: Shakespeare (Peter Gill)

On The Razzle: Tom Stoppard — adapted by Johann Nestroy (Peter Wood)

English Stage Company

THE ROYAL COURT THEATRE

This is a list of all dramatic productions presented by the English Stage Company at the Royal Court and Theatre Upstairs between April 1956 and December 1981. It does not include concerts, recitals, opera, ballet, music-hall, poetry readings or charity performances.

1956

The Mulberry Bush: Angus Wilson (George Devine)

The Crucible: Arthur Miller (George Devine)

Look Back in Anger — transferred to Lyric Hammersmith 5 Nov 1956: John Osborne (Tony Richardson)

Don Juan: Ronald Duncan (George Devine)

The Death of Satan: Ronald Duncan (George Devine)

Cards of Identity: Nigel Dennis (Tony Richardson)

The Good Woman of Setzuan: Bertolt Brecht — translated by Eric Bentley (George Devine)

The Country Wife — transferred to Adelphi 4 Feb 1957: William Wycherley (George Devine)

1957

The Member of the Wedding: Carson McCullers (Tony Richardson)

Look Back in Anger: John Osborne (Tony Richardson)

Fin de Partie: Samuel Beckett (Roger Blin)

Acte Sans Paroles: Samuel Beckett (Deryk Mendel)

The Entertainer — transferred to Palace 10 Sept 1957: John Osborne (Tony Richardson)

The Apollo de Bellac: Jean Giraudoux — translated by Ronald Duncan (Tony Richardson)

The Chairs: Eugene Ionesco — translated by Donald Watson (Tony Richardson)

The Correspondence Course: Charles Robinson (Peter Coe)

Yes — and After: Michael Hastings (John Dexter)

The Making of Moo: Nigel Dennis (Tony Richardson)

Purgatory — Devon Festival: W. B. Yeats (John Dexter)

The Waiting of Lester Abbs: Kathleen Sully (Lindsay Anderson)

How Can We Save Father?: Oliver Marlow Wilkinson (Peter Wood)

The Chairs: Eugene Ionesco — translated by Donald Watson (Tony Richardson)

Look Back in Anger: John Osborne (Tony Richardson)
Nekrassov: Jean-Paul Sartre — translated by Sylvia and George Leeson (George Devine)
The Waters of Babylon: John Arden (Graham Evans)
Look Back in Anger: John Osborne (John Dexter)
Requiem for a Nun: William Faulkner (Tony Richardson)
A Resounding Tinkle: N. F. Simpson (William Gaskill)
Lysistrata — transferred to Duke of York's 18 Feb 1958: Aristophanes — version by Dudley Fitts (Minos Volanakis)

1958

Epitaph for George Dillon — transferred to Comedy 29 May 1958 as *George Dillon*: John Osborne and Anthony Creighton (William Gaskill)
Love from Margaret: Evelyn Ford (John Wood)
The Sport of My Mad Mother: Ann Jellicoe (George Devine and Ann Jellicoe)
The Tenth Chance: Stuart Holroyd (Anthony Creighton)
Each His Own Wilderness: Doris Lessing (John Dexter)
The Catalyst — at the Arts Theatre Club: Ronald Duncan (Phil Brown)
A Resounding Tinkle: N. F. Simpson (William Gaskill)
The Hole: N. F. Simpson (William Gaskill)
Flesh to a Tiger: Barry Reckord (Tony Richardson)
The Lesson: Eugene Ionesco — translated by Donald Watson (Tony Richardson)
The Chairs: Eugene Ionesco — translated by Donald Watson (Tony Richardson)
Brixham Regatta: Keith Johnstone (William Gaskill)
For Children — at the Aldeburgh Festival: Keith Johnstone (Ann Jellicoe)
Gay Landscape — Glasgow Citizens: George Munro (Peter Duguid)
Chicken Soup With Barley — Belgrade Coventry: Arnold Wesker (John Dexter)
The Private Prosecutor — Salisbury Arts Theatre: Thomas Wiseman (Derek Benfield)
Dear Augustine — Leatherhead Repertory: Alison Macleod (Jordan Lawrence)
The Lesson: Eugene Ionesco (Tony Richardson)
The Chairs: Eugene Ionesco (Tony Richardson)
Major Barbara: Bernard Shaw (George Devine)
Lady on the Barometer: Donald Howarth (Miriam Brickman and Donald Howarth)
Live Like Pigs: John Arden (George Devine and Anthony Page)
Krapp's Last Tape: Samuel Beckett (Donald McWhinnie and George Devine)
Endgame: Samuel Beckett (Donald McWhinnie and George Devine)
More Like Strangers: George Hulme (Phil Brown)
Moon on a Rainbow Shawl: Errol John (Frith Banbury)

1959

The Long and the Short and the Tall — transferred to New Theatre 8 Apr 1959: Willis Hall (Lindsay Anderson)
Progress to the Park: Alun Owen (Lindsay Anderson)
A Resounding Tinkle — Cambridge ADC: N. F. Simpson (John Bird)
Sugar in the Morning — produced as *Lady on the Barometer* 14 Sept 1958: Donald Howarth (William Gaskill)
Leonce and Lena: Georg Büchner (Michael Geliot)
The Trial of Cob and Leach: Christopher Logue (Lindsay Anderson)
Jazzetry: Christopher Logue (Lindsay Anderson)
Orpheus Descending: Tennessee Williams (Tony Richardson)
The Shameless Professor: Luigi Pirandello (Victor Rietti)
Roots — Belgrade Coventry, transferred to Duke of York's 30 Jul 1959: Arnold Wesker (John Dexter)
Eleven Men Dead at Hola Camp: Keith Johnstone and William Gaskill (Keith Johnstone and William Gaskill)
Look After Lulu — transferred to New Theatre 8 Sept 1959: Noel Coward based on Georges Feydeau (Tony Richardson)
The Kitchen: Arnold Wesker (John Dexter)
Cock-a-Doodle Dandy: Sean O'Casey (George Devine)
Serjeant Musgrave's Dance: John Arden (Lindsay Anderson)
The Invention: Wole Soyinka (Wole Soyinka)
Rosmersholm — transferred to Comedy 5 Jan 1960: Henrik Ibsen — translated by Ann Jellicoe (George Devine)
The Naming of Murderer's Rock: Frederick Bland (John Bird)
One Way Pendulum — transferred to Criterion 23 Feb 1960: N. F. Simpson (William Gaskill)

1960

Christopher Sly: Opera: Thomas Eastwood, Libretto: Ronald Duncan (Colin Graham)
The Lily White Boys: Harry Cookson and Christopher Logue — Lyrics (Lindsay Anderson)
The Dumb Waiter: Harold Pinter (James Roose Evans)
The Room: Harold Pinter (Anthony Page)
One Leg Over the Wrong Wall: Albert Bermel (John Blatchley)
The Naming of Murderer's Rock: Frederick Bland (John Bird)
Eleven Plus: Kon Fraser (Keith Johnstone)
Rhinoceros — transferred to Strand 8 June 1960: Eugene Ionesco translated by Derek Prouse (Orson Welles)
The Sport of My Mad Mother — Bristol Old Vic Theatre School: Ann Jellicoe (Jane Howell)
Chicken Soup with Barley: Arnold Wesker (John Dexter)

Roots: Arnold Wesker (John Dexter)

Sea at Dauphin — New Way Theatre Co: Derek Walcott (Lloyd Reckord)

Six in the Rain — New Way Theatre Co: Derek Walcott (Lloyd Reckord)

I'm Talking About Jerusalem: Arnold Wesker (John Dexter)

The Keep: Gwyn Thomas (Graham Crowden)

The Happy Haven: John Arden (William Gaskill)

Platonov: Anton Chekhov — English version by Dimitri Makaroff (George Devine and John Blatchley)

You in Your Small Corner — Cheltenham Theatre Co: Barry Reckord (John Bird)

Trials by Logue

Antigone: Christopher Logue (Lindsay Anderson)

Cob and Leach: Christopher Logue (Lindsay Anderson)

The Maimed: Bartho Smit (Keith Johnstone)

On the Wall: Henry Chapman (Peter Duguid)

The Lion in Love: Shelagh Delaney (Clive Barker)

1961

The Changeling: Thomas Middleton and William Rowley (Tony Richardson)

Jacques: Eugene Ionesco — translated by Donald Watson (R. D. Smith)

Altona — transferred to Saville 5 June 1961: Jean-Paul Sartre — adapted by Justin O'Brien (John Berry)

The Departures: Jacques Languirand — translated by Albert Bermel (John Blatchley)

The Triple Alliance: J. A. Cuddon (Keith Johnstone)

The Blacks: Jean Genet — translated by Bernard Frechtman (Roger Blin)

Empress With Teapot: R. B. Whiting (Nicholas Garland)

The Kitchen: Arnold Wesker (John Dexter)

Luther — transferred to Phoenix 5 Sept 1961: John Osborne (Tony Richardson)

Humphrey, Armand and the Artichoke: G. Roy Levin (Piers Haggard)

The Kitchen: Arnold Wesker (John Dexter)

August for the People: Nigel Dennis (George Devine)

The Kitchen: Arnold Wesker (John Dexter)

The Death of Bessie Smith: Edward Albee (Peter Yates)

The American Dream: Edward Albee (Peter Yates)

That's Us — Cambridge Arts: Henry Chapman (William Gaskill)

The Keep: Gwyn Thomas (John Dexter)

Orison: Fernando Arrabal — translated by Barbara Wright (Nicholas Garland)

Fando and Lis: Fernando Arrabal — translated by Barbara Wright (Nicholas Garland)

The Scarecrow: Derek Marlowe (Corin Redgrave)

Box and Cox: John Maddison Morton (Lindsay Anderson)

The Fire Raisers: Max Frisch — translated by Michael Bullock (Lindsay Anderson)

1962

A Midsummer Night's Dream: Shakespeare (Tony Richardson)

Sacred Cow: Kon Fraser (Keith Johnstone)

Twelfth Night: Shakespeare (George Devine)

The Keep — transferred to Piccadilly 27 Mar 1962 Gwyn Thomas (John Dexter)

The Knack Ann Jellicoe (Ann Jellicoe and Keith Johnstone)

Chips with Everything — transferred to Vaudeville 13 Jun 1962 Arnold Wesker (John Dexter)

Period of Adjustment — transferred to Wyndham's 10 Jul 1962 Tennessee Williams (Roger Graef)

The Captain's Hero: Claus Hubalek — translated by Derek Goldby (Derek Goldby)

Plays for England

The Blood of the Bambergs: John Osborne (John Dexter)

Under Plain Cover: John Osborne (Jonathan Miller)

Brecht on Brecht: George Tabori (arranged by John Bird)

Day of the Prince: Frank Hilton (Keith Johnstone)

Happy Days: Samuel Beckett (George Devine)

The Pope's Wedding: Edward Bond (Keith Johnstone)

The Sponge Room: Keith Waterhouse and Willis Hall (John Dexter)

Squat Betty: Keith Waterhouse and Willis Hall (John Dexter)

1963

Misalliance — Oxford Playhouse: transferred to Criterion 29 Jan 1963: Bernard Shaw (Frank Hauser)

Jackie the Jumper: Gwyn Thomas (John Dexter)

The Diary of a Madman: Richard Harris and Lindsay Anderson — from Nikolai Gogol (Lindsay Anderson)

Naked: Luigi Pirandello — translated by Diane Cilento (David William)

Skyvers: Barry Reckord (Ann Jellicoe)

Spring Awakening: Frank Wedekind — translated by Thomas Osborn (Desmond O'Donovan)

Day of the Prince: Frank Hilton (Keith Johnstone)

Kelly's Eye: Henry Livings (David Scase)

Skyvers: Barry Reckord (Ann Jellicoe)

Wiley: Mary McCormick (Elaine Pransky)

Chips with Everything: Arnold Wesker (John Dexter)

Exit the King: Eugene Ionesco — translated by Donald Watson (George Devine)

Edgware Road Blues — transferred as *Travelling Light* to Prince of Wales 8 Apr 1964: Leonard Kingston (Keith Johnstone)

1964

ESC at the Queen's:

The Seagull: Anton Chekhov — translated by Ann Jellicoe (Tony Richardson)

Saint Joan of the Stockyards: Bertolt Brecht — translated by Charlotte and A. L. Lloyd (Tony Richardson)

Inadmissible Evidence — transferred to Wyndham's 17 Mar 1965 (John Osborne) (Anthony Page)
Cuckoo in the Nest: Ben Travers (Anthony Page)
Julius Caesar: Shakespeare (Lindsay Anderson)
Waiting for Godot: Samuel Beckett (Anthony Page)

1965

The Sleeper's Den: Peter Gill (Desmond O'Donovan)
Happy End: Dorothy Lane and Bertolt Brecht — translated by Monica Shelley, adapted by Michael Geliot (Michael Geliot)
Spring Awakening: Frank Wedekind — translated by Thomas Osborn (Desmond O'Donovan)
Miniatures: David Cregan (Donald Howarth)
Meals on Wheels: Charles Wood (John Osborne)
A Patriot for Me: John Osborne (Anthony Page)
A Collier's Friday Night: D. H. Lawrence (Peter Gill)
The Professor: Hal Porter (Robin Midgley)
The World's Baby — at the Embassy Theatre: Michael Hastings (Patrick Dromgoole)
Shelley: Ann Jellicoe (Ann Jellicoe)
The Cresta Run: N. F. Simpson (Keith Johnstone)
Saved: Edward Bond (William Gaskill)
Sergeant Musgrave's Dance: John Arden (Jane Howell)
Clowning: The Group (Keith Johnstone)

1966

A Chaste Maid in Cheapside: Thomas Middleton (William Gaskill)
The Dancers: David Cregan (Jane Howell)
The Knack: Ann Jellicoe (Desmond O'Donovan)
The Performing Giant: Keith Johnstone (William Gaskill and Keith Johnstone)
Transcending: David Cregan (Jane Howell)
Little Guy, Napoleon: Leonard Pluta (Tom Osborn)
The Local Stigmatic: Heathcote Williams (Peter Gill)
The Voysey Inheritance: Harley Granville Barker (Jane Howell)
Their Very Own and Golden City: Arnold Wesker (William Gaskill)
When Did You Last See My Mother? — transferred to Comedy 4 Jul 1966: Christopher Hampton (Robert Kidd)
Bartleby: Massimo Manuelli — after Herman Melville (Massimo Manuelli)
The Local Stigmatic: Heathcote Williams (Peter Gill)
Ubu Roi: Alfred Jarry — translated and adapted by Iain Cuthbertson (Iain Cuthbertson)
The Ruffian on the Stair: Joe Orton (Peter Gill)
It's My Criminal: Howard Brenton (Ian Watt-Smith)
Bartholomew Fair — National Youth Theatre: Ben Jonson (Paul Hill)

Little Malcolm and His Struggle Against the Eunuchs — National Youth Theatre: David Halliwell (Michael Croft)
Three Men for Colverton: David Cregan (Desmond O'Donovan)
Macbeth: Shakespeare (William Gaskill)
A Provincial Life: Peter Gill — after Chekhov (Peter Gill)
The Lion and the Jewel: Wole Soyinka (Desmond O'Donovan)

1967

The Soldier's Fortune: Thomas Otway (Peter Gill)
Roots: Arnold Wesker (Jane Howell)
A Touch of Brightness: Partap Sharma (Ian Watt-Smith)
The Daughter-in-Law: D. H. Lawrence (Peter Gill)
A View to the Common: James Casey (Desmond O'Donovan)
The Three Sisters: Anton Chekhov — translated by Edward Bond (William Gaskill)
The Ruffian on the Stair: Joe Orton (Peter Gill)
The Erpingham Camp: Joe Orton (Peter Gill)
A View to the Common: James Casey (Desmond O'Donovan)
The Restoration of Arnold Middleton —transferred to Criterion 31 Aug 1967: David Storey (Robert Kidd)
Dance of the Teletape — YPTS: Charles Hayward (Charles Hayward)
The Rising Generation — YPTS: Ann Jellicoe (Jane Howell)
OGODIVELEFTTHEGASON: Donald Howarth (Donald Howarth)
America Hurrah: Jean-Claude van Itallie
Interview: (Joseph Chaikin)
TV: (Jacques Levy)
Motel: — Open Theatre (Jacques Levy)
Fill the Stage With Happy Hours: — at the Vaudeville Theatre Charles Wood (William Gaskill)
The Journey of the Fifth Horse: Ronald Ribman (Bill Bryden)
Marya: Isaac Babel — version Christopher Hampton (Robert Kidd)
Dingo: Charles Wood (Geoffrey Reeves)
The Dragon: Yevgeny Schwartz — translated by Max Hayward and Harold Shukman (Jane Howell)
The Paperbag Players: (Judith Martin)

1968

Twelfth Night: Shakespeare (Jane Howell)
Backbone: Michael Rosen (Bill Bryden)
A Collier's Friday Night: D. H. Lawrence (Peter Gill)
The Daughter-in-Law: D. H. Lawrence (Peter Gill)
The Widowing of Mrs Holroyd: D. H. Lawrence (Peter Gill)
Early Morning: Edward Bond (William Gaskill)

A Lesson in a Dead Language: Adrienne Kennedy (Rob Knights)

Funnyhouse of a Negro: Adrienne Kennedy (Rob Knights)

Backbone: Michael Rosen (Bill Bryden)

Time Present — transferred to Duke of York's 11 Jul 1968: John Osborne (Anthony Page)

The Hotel in Amsterdam — transferred to New 5 Sept 1968: John Osborne (Anthony Page)

Captain Oates' Left Sock: John Antrobus (Barry Hanson)

Changing Lines: Nicholas Wright (Nicholas Wright)

Trixie and Baba: John Antrobus (Jane Howell)

Total Eclipse: Christopher Hampton (Robert Kidd)

The Houses by the Green: David Cregan (Jane Howell)

The Tutor: Jacob Lenz — adapted by Bertolt Brecht, translated by Richard Grunberger (Barry Hanson)

Look Back in Anger — transferred to Criterion 10 Dec 1968: John Osborne (Anthony Page)

The Beard: Michael McClure (Rip Torn)

This Story of Yours: John Hopkins (Christopher Morahan)

1969

Life Price: Michael O'Neill and Jeremy Seabrook (Peter Gill)

Saved: Edward Bond (William Gaskill)

Narrow Road to the Deep North: Edward Bond (Jane Howell)

A Comedy of the Changing Years: David Cregan (Michael Bogdanov)

Dandelion — Paperbag Players: Judith Martin (Judith Martin)

Early Morning: Edward Bond (William Gaskill)

La Turista: Sam Shepard (Roger Hendricks-Simon)

Erogenous Zones: Mike Stott (Geoffrey Reeves)

In Celebration: David Storey (Lindsay Anderson)

The Enoch Show: Peter Gill, Christopher Hampton, Edward Bond, Dilip Hiro, Shirley Matthews, Michael O'Neill, Jeremy Seabrook, Mike Stott, Heathcote Williams (Barry Hanson)

The Cry of the People for Meat: The Bread and Puppet Theatre (Peter Schumann)

Blim at School: Peter Tegel (Nicholas Wright)

Poet of the Anemones: Peter Tegel (Nicholas Wright)

The Double Dealer: William Congreve (William Gaskill)

Over Gardens Out: Peter Gill (Peter Gill)

The Beach Ball Show: The People Show

Saved: Edward Bond (William Gaskill)

Revenge: Howard Brenton (Chris Parr)

Narrow Road to the Deep North: Edward Bond (Jane Howell)

Dear Janet Rosenberg, Dear Mr Kooning — Traverse: Stanley Eveling (Max Stafford-Clark)

Oh! Les beaux jours — Compagnie Renaud-Barrault: Samuel Beckett (Roger Blin)

L'amante anglaise — Compagnie Renaud-Barrault: Marguerite Duras (Claude Regy)

The Contractor — transferred to Fortune 6 Apr 1970: David Storey (Lindsay Anderson)

Famine: Thomas Murphy (Clifford Williams)

The Sleepers' Den: Peter Gill (Peter Gill)

Insideout: Frank Norman (Ken Campbell)·

Over Gardens Out: Peter Gill (Peter Gill)

Pit: Peter Dockley

The Three Musketeers Ride Again: The Alberts and Bruce Lacey (Eleanor Fazan)

1970

Three Months Gone — Transferred to Duchess 4 Mar 1970: Donald Howarth (Ronald Eyre)

The Big Romance: Robert Thornton (Roger Williams)

Uncle Vanya: Anton Chekhov — translated by Nina Froud, version by Christopher Hampton (Anthony Page)

Christie in Love: Howard Brenton (David Hare)

A Who's Who of Flapland: David Halliwell (Michael Wearing)

Beckett/3

Come and Go: Samuel Beckett (William Gaskill)

Cascando: Samuel Beckett (Roger Croucher)

Play: Samuel Beckett (William Gaskill)

Widowers' Houses — Nottingham Playhouse: Bernard Shaw (Michael Blakemore)

An Account of the Marriage of August Strindberg and Harriet Bosse: John Abulafia (Shell Abulafia)

Brain — Incubus Theatre: John Abulafia and the cast (John Abulafia)

Strip Jack Naked — Sheffield Playhouse: Christopher Wilkinson (Colin George)

AC/DC: Heathcote Williams (Nicholas Wright)

Café La Mama Season

Ubu: Alfred Jarry (Andrei Serban)

Arden of Faversham: Anon (Andrei Serban)

Cinque: Leonard Melfi (Ching Yeh)

Rats Mass: Adrienne Kennedy (Ching Yeh)

The Sport of My Mad Mother — YPTS: Ann Jellicoe (Pam Brighton)

Home — transferred to Apollo 29 Jul 1970: David Storey (Lindsay Anderson)

Billy's Last Stand: Barry Hines (Michael Wearing)

Theatre Machine: (Keith Johnstone)

The Philanthropist — transferred to Mayfair 7 Sep 1970: Christopher Hampton (Robert Kidd)

When Did You Last See My Mother?: Christopher Hampton (Roger Williams)

Inédits Ionesco: Eugene Ionesco (Jean Rougerie)

Cheek: Howard Barker (William Gaskill)

Cancer: Michael Weller (Peter Gill)

Fruit — Portable Theatre: Howard Brenton (David Hare)

What Happened to Blake — Portable Theatre: David Hare (Tony Bicat)

Research — Teheran Theatre Workshop: Arby Ovanessian (Abbas Naalbandjan)

No One Was Saved — YPTS: Howard Barker (Pam Brighton)

Lulu — Nottingham Playhouse: Frank Wedekind — translated by Charlotte Beck, adapted by Peter Barnes (Peter Barnes and Stuart Burge)

Pirates: Keith Dewhurst (Bill Bryden)

The Hunchback and the Barber: (Keith Johnstone)

Professor Pleasant's Guest — Theatre Machine (Keith Johnstone)

1971

The Duchess of Malfi: John Webster (Peter Gill)

Captain Jack's Revenge: Michael Smith (Nicholas Wright)

Morality: Michael O'Neill and Jeremy Seabrook (Roger Croucher)

The Baby Elephant: Bertolt Brecht — translated by Steve Gooch (Bill Bryden)

A Game Called Arthur — Traverse: David Snodin (Michael Rudman)

Man is Man: Bertolt Brecht — translated by Steve Gooch (William Gaskill)

The Foursome — transferred to Fortune 4 May 1971: E. A. Whitehead (Jonathan Hales)

Stone Age Capers: Ken Campbell and Bob Hoskins

One at Night: Denis Cannan (Roger Williams)

Anarchist: Michael Almaz (Chris Parr)

Corunna!: Keith Dewhurst (Bill Bryden)

Slag: David Hare (Max Stafford-Clark)

Our Sunday Times — Traverse Workshop: Stanley Eveling (Max Stafford-Clark)

Amaryllis: David McNiven and Traverse Workshop (Max Stafford-Clark)

Skyvers — YPTS — transferred to Roundhouse 8 Sep 1971: Barry Reckord (Pam Brighton)

Sweet Alice — Traverse Workshop: Stanley Eveling (Max Stafford-Clark)

The Lovers of Viorne: Marguerite Duras (Jonathan Hales)

Boesman and Lena — transferred to Young Vic 16 Aug 1971: Athol Fugard (Athol Fugard)

West of Suez — transferred to Cambridge 6 Oct 1971: John Osborne (Anthony Page)

Do It: Pip Simmons (Pip Simmons)

As Time Goes By — Traverse: Mustapha Matura (Roland Rees)

Lay By — Portable Theatre/Traverse: Howard Brenton, Brian Clark, Trevor Griffiths, David Hare, Stephen Poliakoff, Hugh Stoddart, Snoo Wilson, (Snoo Wilson)

Lear: Edward Bond (William Gaskill)

The Front Room Boys: Alexander Buzo (Clive Donner)

AC/DC: Heathcote Williams (Nicholas Wright)

The Changing Room — transferred to Globe 15 Dec 1971: David Storey (Lindsay Anderson)

Friday: Hugo Claus — translated by Christopher Logue (Roger Croucher)

Sylveste: Ken Campbell Road Show

1972

Alpha Beta — transferred to Apollo 16 Mar 1972: E. A. Whitehead (Anthony Page)

Live Like Pigs — YPTS: John Arden (Pam Brighton)

Mary Mary — Freehold: Roy Kift (Nancy Meckler)

Veterans: Charles Wood (Ronald Eyre)

The Centaur: Jonathan Hales (Jonathan Hales)

Within Two Shadows: Wilson John Haire (Alfred Lynch)

Big Wolf: Harald Mueller — translated by Steve Gooch (William Gaskill and Pam Brighton)

Show Me the Way to Go Home: Phil Woods and the company (Pam Brighton)

Crete and Sergeant Pepper: John Antrobus (Peter Gill)

The Moon is East, the Sun is West: Tokyo Kid Brothers

Pretty Boy: Stephen Poliakoff (Colin Cook)

Hitler Dances — Traverse Workshop: Howard Brenton (Max Stafford-Clark)

Hedda Gabler: Henrik Ibsen — adapted by John Osborne (Anthony Page)

Was He Anyone?: N. F. Simpson (Nicholas Wright)

Dreams of Mrs Fraser: Gabriel Josipovici (Roger Croucher)

The Old Ones: Arnold Wesker (John Dexter)

Brussels — YPTS: Jonathan Hales (Jonathan Hales)

Richard's Cork Leg: Brendan Behan and Alan Simpson (Alan Simpson)

England's Ireland: Tony Bicat, Howard Brenton, Brian Clark, David Edgar, Francis Fuchs, David Hare, Snoo Wilson (David Hare and Snoo Wilson)

Eye Winker, Tom Tinker: Tom MacIntyre (Robert Kidd)

A Pagan Place: Edna O'Brien (Ronald Eyre)

State of Emergency: David Edgar (David Edgar)

Owners: Caryl Churchill (Nicholas Wright)

A Sense of Detachment: John Osborne (Frank Dunlop)

State of Emergency: David Edgar (David Edgar)

Pilk's Madhouse: Ken Campbell Road Show

1973

A Fart for Europe: Howard Brenton and David Edgar (Chris Parr)

Krapp's Last Tape: Samuel Beckett (Anthony Page)

Not I: Samuel Beckett (Anthony Page)

José Pigs/Cattle Show — The People Show 48

The George Jackson Black and White Minstrel Show — Pip Simmons Theatre Group

Wimbo the Wonder Dog — Hull Truck: Mike Bradwell (Mike Bradwell)

The Weekend After Next — Hull Truck: Mike Bradwell (Mike Bradwell)

Wholesome Glory: Mike Leigh (Mike Leigh)

Mothers and Others: Anne Raitt (Anne Raitt)
The Freedom of the City: Brian Friel (Albert Finney)
The Fourth World: David Caute (Buzz Goodbody)
The Unseen Hand: Sam Shepard (Jim Sharman)
Beowulf — Freehold — dramatised by Liane Aukin (Nancy Meckler)
Savages — transferred to Comedy 20 Jun 1973: Christopher Hampton (Robert Kidd)
Captain Oates' Left Sock: John Antrobus (Nicholas Wright)
Coming Attractions: Lizette Kocur, Neil Johnston and O Lan Shepard
The Orange Balloon: Andy Phillips (Robert Fox)
Give the Gaffers Time to Love You: Barry Reckord (Pam Brighton)
The Sea: Edward Bond (William Gaskill)
Millennium: Jeremy Seabrook and Michael O'Neill (Roger Croucher)
The Rocky Horror Show — transferred to Chelsea Classic 14 Aug 1973: Richard O'Brien (Jim Sharman)
Magnificence: Howard Brenton (Max Stafford-Clark)
The Removalists: David Williamson (Jim Sharman)
Sweet Talk: Michael Abbensetts (Stephen Frears)
Cromwell: David Storey (Anthony Page)
Bright Scene Fading: Tom Gallacher (Nicholas Wright)
Sizwe Bansi is Dead: Athol Fugard, John Kani and Winston Ntshona (Athol Fugard)
The Farm — transferred to Mayfair 1 Nov 1973: David Storey (Lindsay Anderson)
The Porter's Play: Anton Gill (Anton Gill)
Elizabeth I: Paul Foster (Walter Donohue)
The Merry Go Round: D. H. Lawrence (Peter Gill)
The Pleasure Principle: Snoo Wilson (David Hare)
Dick Whittington: Mike Leigh (Mike Leigh)

1974

The Island — transferred to Ambassadors 10 Apr 1974: Athol Fugard, John Kani and Winston Ntshona (Athol Fugard)
Sizwe Bansi is Dead — transferred to Ambassadors 10 Apr 1974: Athol Fugard, John Kani and Winston Ntshona (Athol Fugard)
Statements After an Arrest Under the Immorality Act: Athol Fugard (Athol Fugard)

Two Jelliplays: YPTS
Clever Elsie, Smiling John, Silent Peter: Ann Jellicoe (Ann Jellicoe)
A Good Thing or a Bad Thing: Ann Jellicoe (Ann Jellicoe)

Geography of a Horse Dreamer: Sam Shepard (Sam Shepard)
Runaway: Peter Ransley (Alfred Lynch)

Six of the Best — YPTS
Liberation City: Michael Belbin (Joan Mills)

Errand: Jim Irvin (John Barlow)
Big Business: Mark Edwards (Joan Mills)
Maggie's Fortune: Sheila Wright (Ann Jellicoe)
Fireman's Ball: Stephen Frost (Ann Jellicoe)
Event: James Clarke (John Barlow)
Zoological Palace: Conrad Mullineaux (Joan Mills)

Life Class: David Storey (Lindsay Anderson)
Bird Child: David Lan (Nicholas Wright)
Johnny: Robert Thornton (John Tydeman)
Shivvers — Joint Stock: Stanley Eveling (Max Stafford-Clark)
Tooth of Crime: Sam Shepard (Jim Sharman)
A Worthy Guest: Paul Bailey (Ann Jellicoe)
The Watergate Tapes: Sam Wanamaker — editor
The Sea Anchor: E. A. Whitehead (Jonathan Hales)
Play Mas — transferred to Phoenix 21 Aug 1974: Mustapha Matura (Donald Howarth)
Bingo: Edward Bond (Jane Howell and John Dove)
X — Joint Stock: Barry Reckord (Max Stafford-Clark)
Taking Stock: Robert Holman (Chris Parr)
Action: Sam Shepard (Nancy Meckler)
The Great Caper: Ken Campbell (Nicholas Wright)
In Celebration: David Storey (Lindsay Anderson)
Lord Nelson Lives in Liverpool 8: Philip Martin (Joan Mills)
Fourth Day Like Four Long Months of Absence — Joint Stock: Colin Bennett (Max Stafford-Clark)
The City — Tokyo Kid Brothers: Yutaka Higashi (Yutaka Higashi)
Remember the Truth Dentist: Heathcote Williams (Ken Campbell)

1975

Objections to Sex and Violence: Caryl Churchill (John Tydeman)
Innocent Bystanders: Gordon Graham (Denise Coffey)

Moments on Jaffa Beach: Michael Almaz (Peter Stevenson)
The Port Said Performance: Michael Almaz (Peter Stevenson)
Statements After an Arrest Under the Immorality Act: Athol Fugard (Athol Fugard)
Not I: Samuel Beckett (Anthony Page)
Mrs Grabowski's Academy: John Antrobus (Jonathan Hales)
Number One Rooster: David Throsby (William Alexander)
Don's Party: David Williamson (Michael Blakemore)
Loud Reports: John Burrows, John Harding and Peter Skellern (Mark Wing-Davey)
The Doomducker's Ball — Joint Stock: Carole Hayman, Neil Johnston, Mary Maddox, Dinah Stabb and Jeff Teare
Entertaining Mr Sloane — transferred to Duke of York's 2 June 1975: Joe Orton (Roger Croucher)

Paradise: David Lan (Tessa Marwick and Nicholas Wright)

Echoes from a Concrete Canyon: Wilson John Haire (Roger Croucher)

Loot: Joe Orton (Albert Finney)

Homage to Bean Soup: David Lan (Tessa Marwick)

Moving Clocks Go Slow: Caryl Churchill (John Ford)

Heroes: Stephen Poliakoff (Tim Fywell)

Black Slaves, White Chains: Mustapha Matura (Rufus Collins)

A 'Nevolent Society: Mary O'Malley (Henry Woolf)

What the Butler Saw — transferred to Whitehall 19 Aug 1975: Joe Orton (Lindsay Anderson)

Sex and Kinship in a Savage Society: Jeremy Seabrook and Michael O'Neill (William Alexander)

Mean Time: Richard Crane (Richard Crane)

Soul of the Nation: Sebastian Clarke (Donald Howarth)

Teeth 'n' Smiles — transferred to Wyndham's 24 May 1976: David Hare (David Hare)

Asleep at the Wheel: David Coulter (John Ford)

Stripwell: Howard Barker (Chris Parr)

Young Writers' Festival

Travel Sickness: Matilda Hartwell (John Ford)

Stepping Stone: James Bradley (Joan Mills)

Watercress Sandwiches: Zoe Tamsyn and Sophia Everest-Phillips (Joan Mills)

St George and his Dragon: Tanya Meadows (John Ford)

Interval: Jim Irvin and Tim Whelan (Joan Mills)

How do You Clean a Sunflower? — West Indian Drama Group (John Ford)

Under the Clock: Gordon Porterfield (William Alexander)

The Fool: Edward Bond (Peter Gill)

A Tale of Three Cities: Gebre Yohanse Asefaw (Nicholas Wright)

1976

Judgement — National Theatre: Barry Collins (Peter Hall)

Treats — transferred to Mayfair 6 Mar 1975: Christopher Hampton (Robert Kidd)

Parcel Post: Yemi Ajibade (Donald Howarth)

Waiting for Godot (in German) — Schiller Theatre, Berlin: Samuel Beckett (Samuel Beckett)

Endgame: Samuel Beckett (Donald McWhinnie)

Yesterday's News — Joint Stock: the actors and Jeremy Seabrook (William Gaskill and Max Stafford-Clark)

Play: Samuel Beckett (Donald McWhinnie)

That Time: Samuel Beckett (Donald McWhinnie)

Footfalls: Samuel Beckett (Samuel Beckett)

Amy and the Price of Cotton: Michael McGrath (William Alexander)

Small Change: Peter Gill (Peter Gill)

The Only Way Out: George Thatcher (David Halliwell)

T-Zee: Richard O'Brien (Nicholas Wright)

Just a Little Bit Less than Normal: Nigel Baldwin (John Ashford)

Mother's Day: David Storey (Robert Kidd)

Light Shining in Buckinghamshire — Joint Stock: Caryl Churchill (Max Stafford-Clark)

An' Me Wi' a Bad Leg Tae — Borderline Company: Billy Connolly (Stuart Mungall)

Rum an' Coca-Cola: Mustapha Matura (Donald Howarth)

Dracula — Pip Simmons Group: Pip Simmons

1977

Uhlanga: Mshengu and James Mthoba (James Mthoba)

Sizwe Bansi is Dead: Athol Fugard, John Kani and Winston Ntshona (Athol Fugard)

Traps: Caryl Churchill (John Ashford)

Short Sleeves in Summer: Tunde Ikoli (Michael Joyce)

Devil's Island — Joint Stock: Tony Bicat (David Hare)

Young Writers' Festival

Walking: Lenka Janiurek (Tim Fywell)

To Err is Human: Liz Bellamy (Gerald Chapman)

West Side Bovver: Shirley McKay and Christina Martin (Gerald Chapman)

Fishing: Alexander Matthews (Gerald Chapman)

Gimme Shelter — The Network, Soho Poly: Barrie Keeffe (Keith Washington)

For All Those Who Get Despondent — cabaret: Bertolt Brecht and Frank Wedekind (Peter Barnes)

Out of Our Heads: 7:84 Scotland — John McGrath (Dave Anderson)

I Made it Ma Top of the World: devised by John Chapman and Tim Fywell (John Chapman and Tim Fywell)

Curse of the Starving Class: Sam Shepard (Nancy Meckler)

For the West — transferred to Cottesloe 14 Aug 1977: Michael Hastings (Nicholas Wright)

Fair Slaughter: Howard Barker (Stuart Burge)

The Winter Dancers: David Lan (Ian Kellgren)

Sleak!: C. P. Lee (Charles Hanson)

Once a Catholic — transferred to Wyndham's 4 Oct 1977: Mary O'Malley (Mike Ockrent)

Sudlow's Dawn: Nigel Baldwin (Tim Fywell)

'tufff': Bille Brown (Diane Cilento)

The Good Woman of Setzuan — Newcastle Theatre Tyneside Co: Bertolt Brecht (Keith Hack)

No Pasaran — YPTS Free Form Roadshow '77: David Holman (Sean Cunningham)

Skoolplay: Alan Brown (Ian Kellgren)

Return to My Native Land: Aimé Cesaire — translated by John Berger and Anna Bostock (John Russell Brown)

Playpen: Heathcote Williams (Gerald Chapman)

Talbot's Box — Abbey Theatre: Thomas Kilroy (Patrick Mason)

The Trembling Giant — 7:84 Scotland: John McGrath (John McGrath)

1978

The Kreutzer Sonata — Birmingham Rep: Leo Tolstoy — adapted by Peter Farago (Peter Farago)

Our Own People — Pirate Jenny: David Edgar (Walter Donohue)

Prayer for My Daughter: Thomas Babe (Max Stafford-Clark)

Masada — Keskedee Workshop: Edgar White (Rufus Collins)

Wheelchair Willie: Alan Brown (Max Stafford-Clark)

1979

Anchorman — CVI Theatre Co: Ron Hutchinson (John Dove)

Mary Barnes — Birmingham Rep: David Edgar (Peter Farago)

On Top: Liane Aukin (Ann Pennington)

Full Frontal: Michael Hastings (Rufus Collins)

The Archangel Michael — rehearsed reading: Georgi Markov (Roger Michell)

The London Cuckolds: Edward Ravenscroft (Stuart Burge)

A Question of Habit — rehearsed reading: Jacki Holborough (Rio Fanning)

The Irish Soldier — rehearsed reading: David Stevens (Antonia Bird)

Old Ed'll Fix It — rehearsed reading: David Stevens (Antonia Bird)

The Dentist — rehearsed reading: Jonathan Gems (Ian Kellgren)

Young Writers' Festival

Miracles Do Happen: Douglas Parkin (Philip Hedley)

Island: Paul Lister (Mervyn Willis)

Me, I'd Like to Catch Miss Kerry: Julia James (Mervyn Willis)

I'm Just Trying to Convince Myself that Vampires Don't Exist: Mark Power (Mervyn Willis)

Humbug: A group of 13 children (Philip Hedley)

Cloud Nine — Joint Stock: Caryl Churchill (Max Stafford-Clark)

Psy-Warriors: David Leland (David Leland)

Bent — transferred to Criterion 4 Jul 1979: Martin Sherman (Robert Chetwyn)

An Empty Desk: Alan Drury (Keith Washington)

Happy Days: Samuel Beckett (Samuel Beckett)

The Smell of Fantasy — rehearsed reading: K. W. Ross (Antonia Bird)

Through the Kaleidoscope — rehearsed reading: John Stevenson (Roger Michell)

Reggae Britannia: Leigh Jackson (Keith Washington)

Marie and Bruce: Wallace Shawn (Les Waters)

Carnival War a Go Hot: Michael Hastings (Antonia Bird)

The Gorky Brigade: Nicholas Wright (William Gaskill)

Gogol: Richard Crane (Faynia Williams)

Sus — Soho Poly: Barrie Keeffe (Ann Michell)

Says I, Says He — Sheffield Crucible: Ron Hutchinson (David Leland)

Laughter: Peter Barnes (Charles Marowitz)

In the Blood: Lenka Janiurek (Tim Fywell)

Procreation: Anthony Trent (David Halliwell)

The Bear: Anton Chekhov — adapted by N. F. Simpson (Stuart Burge)

The Kreutzer Sonata: Leo Tolstoy — adapted by Peter Farago (Peter Farago)

Bad Dream in an Old Hotel: James Pettifer (Jonathan Holloway)

Class Enemy: Nigel Williams (William Alexander)

Black Slaves, White Chains: Mustapha Matura (Charles Hanson)

More, More: Mustapha Matura (Charles Hanson)

A Bed of Roses — Hull Truck: Mike Bradwell (Mike Bradwell)

Bleak House — Shared Experience: Charles Dickens (Mike Alfreds)

The Glad Hand: Snoo Wilson (Max Stafford-Clark)

Young Writers' Festival

From Cockneys to Toffs: Joanne Caffell (John Dale)

Artificial Living: Stephen Rowe (Gerald Chapman and Tim Fywell)

The School Leaver: Michael McMillan (Gerald Chapman)

Covehithe: Anna Wheatley (Tim Fywell)

I was Sitting on My Patio This Guy Appeared I Thought I was Hallucinating: Robert Wilson (Robert Wilson)

Flying Blind: Bill Morrison (Alan Dossor)

Irish Eyes and English Tears: Nigel Baldwin (Ian Kellgren)

Eclipse: Leigh Jackson (Stuart Burge)

Bukharin — rehearsed reading: Andy McSmith (Les Waters)

The Guise — rehearsed reading: David Mowat (Les Waters)

Prayer for My Daughter: Thomas Babe (Max Stafford-Clark)

Inadmissible Evidence: John Osborne (John Osborne)

Emigrants — Pirate Jenny: Peter Sheridan (Jim Sheridan)

Nightfall — Lumiere and Son: David Gale (Hilary Westlake)

The Slab Boys — Traverse Theatre: John Byrne (David Hayman)

Sergeant Ola and His Followers: David Lan (Max Stafford-Clark)

The Key Tag — rehearsed reading: Michael McGrath (Roger Michell)

The Guise — Foco Novo: David Mowat (Roland Rees)

Touch and Go — Oxford Playhouse: D. H. Lawrence (Gordon McDougall)

The Worlds — YPTS: Edward Bond (Edward Bond)

1980

Love of a Good Man — Oxford Playhouse: Howard Barker (Nicolas Kent)

Trees in the Wind — 7:84 England: John McGrath (Penny Cherns)

People Show No. 84

The Key Tag: Michael McGrath (Roger Michell)

The Liberty Suit — Project Arts Dublin: Peter Sheridan and Gerard Mannix Flynn (Jim Sheridan)

Young Writers' Festival

The Arbor: Andrea Dunbar (Max Stafford-Clark)

The Morning Show: Daniel Goldberg (Roger Michell)

The Personal Effects: Lucy Anderson Jones (Nicholas Wright)

Waking Dreams — rehearsed reading: Richard Boswell (Alby James)

Hamlet: Shakespeare (Richard Eyre)

Seduced: Sam Shepard (Les Waters)

Rutherford and Son — Mrs Worthington's Daughters: Githa Sowerby (Julie Holledge)

The Arbor: Andrea Dunbar (Max Stafford-Clark)

In and Out the Union Jacks — rehearsed reading: Ginnie Hole (Antonia Bird)

Wednesday Night Action — RSC rehearsed reading: Johnny Quarrell (John Chapman)

A Short Sharp Shock: Howard Brenton and Tony Howard (Rob Walker)

Fear of the Dark — RSC rehearsed reading: Doug Lucie (Walter Donohue)

Not Quite Jerusalem — rehearsed reading: Paul Kember (Les Waters)

Three More Sleepless Nights — Soho Poly: Caryl Churchill (Les Waters)

Cloud Nine: Caryl Churchill (Max Stafford-Clark and Les Waters)

Glasshouses — rehearsed reading: Stephen Lowe (Richard Wilson)

Submariners: Tom McClenaghan (Antonia Bird)

Sugar and Spice: Nigel Williams (Bill Alexander)

1981

Touched: Stephen Lowe (William Gaskill)

Faith Healer: Brian Friel (Christopher Fettes)

The Seagull adaptation: Thomas Kilroy (Max Stafford-Clark)

No End of Blame: Howard Barker (Nicolas Kent)

Restoration: Edward Bond (Edward Bond)

Heaven and Hell — Traverse Theatre Production: Dusty Hughes (Richard Wilson)

Tibetan Inroads: Stephen Lowe (William Gaskill)

Borderline — a Joint Stock/Royal Court production: Hanif Kureishi (Max Stafford-Clark)

People Show Cabaret People Show production.

INDEX OF NAMES, TITLES and SUBJECTS

Page numbers in bold indicate pictures

NAMES

SUBJECTS